W9-CZR-405

LIMITED ADVERSARIES
POST-COLD WAR SINO-AMERICAN MUTUAL IMAGES

LIMITED ADVERSARIES

POST-COLD WAR
SINO-AMERICAN MUTUAL IMAGES

Jianwei Wang

OXFORD
UNIVERSITY PRESS

OXFORD
UNIVERSITY PRESS

Oxford University Press is a department of the University of Oxford.
It furthers the University's objective of excellence in research, scholarship,
and education by publishing worldwide in

Oxford New York

Athens Auckland Bangkok Bogotá Buenos Aires Calcutta
Cape Town Chennai Dar es Salaam Delhi Florence Hong Kong Istanbul
Karachi Kuala Lumpur Madrid Melbourne Mexico City Mumbai
Nairobi Paris São Paulo Singapore Taipei Tokyo Toronto Warsaw

with associated companies in Berlin Ibadan

Oxford is a registered trade mark of Oxford University Press

Published in the United States by Oxford University Press Inc., New York

© Oxford University Press 2000

First published 2000
This impression (lowest digit)
1 3 5 7 9 10 8 6 4 2

British Library Cataloguing in Publication Data
available

Library of Congress Cataloging-in-Publication Data
available

ISBN 019-590609-8

Printed in Hong Kong
Published by Oxford University Press (China) Ltd
18th Floor, Warwick House East, Taikoo Place, 979 King's Road, Quarry Bay
Hong Kong

TO MY PARENTS

ACKNOWLEDEGMENTS

This book is based on the dissertation research I conducted when I was a PhD student at the University of Michigan. It finally has seen the light of day as a book after a long and sometimes agonizing journey. At this moment of joy and relief, my heart is filled with gratitude for all the individuals and institutions that have helped me reach this destination.

My most enduring intellectual debts are owed to Michel Oksenberg and Kenneth Lieberthal, who served as my academic mentors for seven years at Michigan. Michel Oksenberg's powerful vision, his stimulating ideas, and his strong desire for academic excellence guided me through my entire study at Michigan and through various stages of my dissertation. Kenneth Lieberthal's tireless attention to detail, his sharp eye for deficiencies and his patient step-by-step instruction initiated me into the craft of scholarship. Particularly in the final stage of writing, he provided constant, timely, and thoughtful advice.

I am also very much indebted to other members of my dissertation committee. Kent Jennings persistently pushed me toward methodological rigour by providing wise guidance in data collection and analysis. Harold Jacobson systematically introduced me to the discipline of world politics and contributed to the theoretical perspective of my dissertation in and outside the classroom. Eugene Burnstein offered useful advice concerning a psychological dynamic of national images and perceptions. I learned an enormous amount from all of them.

This study would have been impossible without financial support from the American educational establishment. A SSRC–MacArthur Foundation fellowship in International Peace and Security enabled me to turn an idea in my mind into the reality of a doctoral dissertation. In addition, the Rackham School of Graduate Studies at the University of Michigan granted me a one-term fellowship to complete my writing of the dissertation. I started the revision of my manuscript in the East-West Center, which generously provided me with a post-doctoral fellowship. Albert Kundstadter Family Foundation also provided timely financial support to facilitate further improvement of the manuscript. I would like to express thanks to these organizations and their staff for all they did during the various stages of research and writing.

I have been assisted and advised by many other institutions and individuals during my research. I would like to express special appreciation to the following institutions for providing me with training sites, office, space; and library facilities: the Center for Chinese Studies at the University of Michigan; the Psychology Department of Stanford University; the Institute for Sino-Soviet Studies at George Washington University; the Woodrow Wilson International Center for Scholars, the National Committee on US-China Relations (NCUSCR); the Committee on Scholarly Communication with the PRC; and the US-China Business Council. Professor Lee Ross in the Psychology Department at Stanford University merits special mention for his tutorial role on social psychology. I have also benefited from my enlightening conversations with many scholars, including Alexander George, Harry Harding, David Lampton, Merry Bullock, Robert Oxam, Doak Barnett, Warren Cohen, John Watt, James Anderson, David Shambaugh, and Irv Drasnin. Deep thanks also go to Lawrence Robinson of the State Department, Jan Berris of NCUSCR, Christine Kelley of China Forum, and Harry Thayer, for their efforts in facilitating my interviews. During the process of revision, I was particularly indebted to Professor Steven Lavine, who carefully read my manuscript and offered his systematic and meticulous comments. Dr. Yaacov Vertzberger also shared with me his insightful critique of the manuscript when I was at the East-West Center.

Furthermore, I must convey my sincere thanks to all the American and Chinese respondents who donated their precious time and thoughts in interviews. Indeed, talking to them was the most enjoyable part of this study. Without their cooperation, this book would not have been possible.

These acknowledgements would be incomplete without mentioning my friends and family members who gave me selfless and unfailing support during this long ordeal. Many friends in both the US and China contributed to this book in innumerable ways. I can only mention a few of them here. Dr Xian Liu lent valuable technical assistance to the data analysis and table and figure preparation. Katherine Dieterich, Liz Economy, and Flex Meredith read and edited some of the original chapters. Naturally my parents have been an inexhaustible source of love and care for my mental and physical well-being during the whole process. Although my mother passed away in 1988, she never really leaves me. Her spirit blessed my endeavour and will continue to light my road ahead.

Finally, my deep thanks go to Oxford University Press. Dr Samuel Kim has been instrumental and inspiring in my effort to turn my manuscript into a publishable book. It was a pleasant experience to work with Mary Child and David Youtz, the first commissioning editors, who offered their professional advice for the revision. Their successor, Anastasia Edwards, and assistant editor Rebecca Chau oversaw this project through to publication. The manuscript benefited greatly from their fine editing and polishing. Needless to say, I am solely responsible for all the views, analyses, and possible errors in this book.

CONTENTS

LIST OF TABLES

Tables

LIST OF FIGURES

Figures

LIST OF APPENDICES

Appendices

PREFACE

This book is a comparative study of Sino-American mutual images in the post-Tiananmen and post-Cold War context. The fundamental premise underlying this study is that national perceptions and images are instrumental to understanding the nature, potentials, and limitations of relations among nation-states. As in any bilateral interstate relationship, the longevity of Sino-American relations depends on the existence of common interests in strategic, political, and economic spheres. Interests, after all, become crucial to relations only when they are realistically perceived. History has witnessed numerous cases in which misperceptions on both sides either obliterated or exaggerated the interests on which the relationship was based. One of the greatest diplomatic tragedies since World War II, as many scholars have well recorded, was the twenty-year mutual isolation and confrontation between China and the United States, due in part to the mutual misunderstandings of each other's goals, motivation, characteristics, power, and interests.

With the long overdue rapprochement in Sino-US relations in the early 1970s, the Chinese and Americans' perceptions of each other underwent dramatic changes. Each side apparently no longer perceived the other as a menace to its security, but rather as a strategic ally offsetting the military threat from the Soviet Union, which was then seen as expanding its sphere of influence worldwide. With the normalization of the relationship and China's strategic decision to embark on modernization and to open its door to the West, the two countries experienced a new era characterized by unprecedented interactions in both bilateral and multilateral settings. This dynamic process provided motivation, mechanisms, and material for new image formation and increased sophistication by directly exposing millions of Americans and Chinese to the people, society, and culture of the other side. Each side ceased to see the other as an ideological untouchable. To Chinese eyes, instead of being a 'rotten capitalist country', the United States was seen as a valuable source of capital, technology, and managerial expertise for China's modernization. To American eyes, contrary to the traditional image of a 'ruthless and monolithic communist tyranny', China was perceived as a potential market for business opportunities and a fertile land to cultivate values cherished by Americans.

Since 1989, however, a wave of unpredicted structural dislocations undermined the taken-for-granted foundations for US-China relations, putting those seemingly well-shaped mutual images under serious strain. Among other things, the 1989 Tiananmen crackdown drastically changed the point of reference for Sino-American mutual images, from external-orientated to internal-oriented. Immediately after the Tiananmen tragedy, the bitter and emotional verbal exchanges between the two countries were reminiscent of the ideological labelling in the Cold War era. While China once again routinely accused 'American imperialism' of using the subversive strategy of 'peaceful evolution', the United States redefined China as the 'most repressive nation on earth', and one extremely hostile to the Western values of democracy and human rights.[1] The formerly positive mutual perceptions between China and the United States seemed to have reversed themselves overnight. The episode remained a major irritation in the relationship in the following years. To what extent is this apparent reversal real? How deep and lasting were the positive mutual images that manifested themselves before the Tiananmen crackdown and to what extent have they been lost or survived in the aftermath of this event? This study attempts to provide some clues in answering these questions.

The impact of this dramatic event on US-China mutual images should, nevertheless, be viewed from a broader landscape of world politics. The collapse of the Soviet empire and world communism took away the underpinning of the 'strategic triangle' perceived as a pillar to sustain Sino-American collaborations during the 1970s and 1980s. Americans and Chinese were propelled to search for a new foundation for the relationship. The old assumptions based on bipolarity can no longer be applied to the new reality of the 'structural uncertainty' of world politics. The boundaries between 'allies' and 'adversaries' or between 'friends' and 'enemies' have increasingly blurred, due to the more complicated and interdependent interactions among nations. As a result, the Americans and Chinese apparently have difficulties finding a sustainable overall rationale that can overcome other conflicting interests and values. It is therefore interesting to enquire systematically how American and Chinese elites perceive the dynamics and nature of Sino-American relations under the post-Cold War circumstances.

With a post-Cold War world and post-Tiananmen US-China relationships as backdrops, this book empirically identifies and articulates the mutual images held by selected Chinese and American elites during the early 1990s. Three broad research questions will be investigated. First, what are the cognitive structure and ingredients of Sino-American mutual images, and how do they converge or conflict with each other? Second, with the current mutual images of the American and Chinese elites as a base line, how have these images evolved in the last two decades, and what patterns of perceptual change have emerged? Third, how are the articulation and evolution of mutual images related to some important source variables such as personal interaction, 'reorganizing' events, and profession, and what are the intellectual and policy implications of these linkages for the sophistication of mutual images and hence for the state of Sino-American relations? In answering these questions, this research distinguishes itself from other similar studies in several respects. First, previous studies of Sino-American mutual perceptions have seldom been put into a broad theoretical framework of international relations. This study draws upon theories of both international relations and social psychology to conceptualize and test hypotheses concerning image structure, formation, evolution, and sources. Second, in contrast to other studies that focus on either the Chinese images of the United States or the American images of China, this research is a cross-national comparative study of mutual images under the same conceptual framework and applying similar research methodology. As a result, the perceptual convergence and divergence between the two sides can be more readily located, making the findings both more interesting and illuminating. Third, this study pays more attention to the 'structure' of mutual images, namely, the connections among various dimensions of national images. By revealing the degree of inner consistency or dissonance, we can better appreciate the structural complexity of mutual images. Fourth, methodologically, compared with other studies heavily based on documentary surveys and written material, this research is primarily an analysis of structured and in-depth interviews with more than 250 members of American and Chinese elites, thus providing a unique system of reference of Sino-American mutual images. A combination of qualitative contextual analysis of the richness and nuances of mutual images and quantitative analysis of general image patterns and trends makes the entire study both richer and more rigorous, thus alleviating the problems of 'over-interpretation' and 'under-interpretation'.[2]

In sum, this is a study of the cognitive dimension of Sino-American relations, serving as a supplement rather than a substitute for other more behaviour-oriented inquiries in the field. It also adds another case study for the existing scholarship in the study of national images in international relations. Although US-China mutual images have experienced many fluctuations since this study was done, the main findings remain useful and relevant to our better understanding of the relationship.

The book consists of eight chapters. Chapter 1 provides some intellectual and historical background against which this study stands, including theoretical and empirical literature pertinent to the perceptual-psychological approach in international relations studies, the evolution of Sino-American mutual images in general, and the existing scholarship recording the development. Chapter 2 endeavours to establish a conceptual framework for the ensuing empirical analysis. Theoretical constructs and models for image structure, image evolution, and image sources are developed and operationalized. Chapters 3 to 6 contain the bulk of the empirical analysis of this book. Guided by the conceptual framework set forth in Chapter 2 and using both qualitative in-depth and quantitative aggregate analyses, these four chapters portray Sino-American mutual images of people, society, culture and international behaviour in terms of cognitive, affective, evaluative, and evolutionary orientations. Bivariate analysis of image sources is also carried out in each of these chapters. Based on these empirical findings, Chapter 7 delineates structure and patterns of mutual perceptions at both micro and macro levels. A more rigorous multivariate regression analysis is applied to further explore the validity of various image sources. In the conclusion (Chapter 8), a summary of the principle findings of this study is presented. The theoretical and practical implications for the study of Sino-American relations in particular and for the study of international relations in general are also elaborated.

Notes to Preface

1   See Liu Liqun, 'The Image of the United States in Present-Day China', in Everette E. Dennis, George Gerbner, and Yassen N. Zassoursky (eds.), *Beyond the Cold War: Soviet and American Media Images*, Newbury Park: Sage Publications, 1991, pp. 116–125; Harry Harding, *A Fragile Relationship, The United States and China Since 1972*, Washington, DC: The Brookings Institution, 1992, p. 291.

2   Christer Jonsson (ed.), *Cognitive Dynamics and International Politics*, London: Frances Pinter, 1982, p. 9.

CHAPTER 1 ·
NATIONAL IMAGE STUDIES AND SINO-US RELATIONS

The Perceptual Approach in International Relations

The importance of cognitive variables has long been recognized in the analysis of politics in general and of international relations in particular. Since the late 1950s, following the behavioural revolution in the study of world politics, the perceptual-psychological approach has become pervasive in various research areas such as foreign policy decision-making, arms control, crisis management, conflict resolution, diplomatic negotiations, and cross-national interactions.[1] Two basic categories can be delineated in this large body of literature: studies of perceptions and images directly related to foreign policy decision-making processes, and studies of perceptions and images that may not have a direct bearing on foreign policy decision-making, but nevertheless are relevant to interstate relations in a broader sense.[2]

Increased attention to the problems of perceptions and images among nations was closely related to the emergence of the decision-making approach in the study of foreign policy. This approach was advocated as an alternative to the traditional realist school of international politics, which emphasizes structural constraints in the international system and the role of the unitary rational actor in decision-making.[3] In other words, the application of cognitive analysis has been used to expose important cognitive limits on the possibility of rational decision-making.

Harold and Margaret Sprout were among the first scholars to regard perceptions of foreign policy decision-makers as important for students of international relations. They pointed out that 'what matters is how the policy-maker imagines the milieu to be, not how it actually is'.[4] They distinguished the 'psychological environment' from the 'operational environment' and concluded that in most cases the two were not identical.[5] David Singer further distinguished two levels of analysis in foreign policy: the international level and the national level. The former focuses on the structural or systemic constraints on nation-states' foreign policy, whereas the latter analyses the goals, values, and perceptions of foreign policy decision-makers. Singer warned that in the analysis of foreign policy, 'the omission of the cognitive and the perceptual linkage would be disastrous'.[6]

Robert Jervis was perhaps the first scholar in international relations to systematically conceptualize the cognitive variables in foreign policy decision-making by applying theories and experimental findings from diverse areas of psychology. His *Perception and Misperception in International Politics* was regarded as a landmark in the study of psychological factors affecting foreign policy-making.[7] His major contributions lie in the following three areas. First, Jervis advanced the proposition that at the level of decision-making, 'it is often impossible to explain crucial decisions and policies without reference to the decision-makers' beliefs about the world and their images of others.'[8] Second, he applied diverse psychological concepts and theories, such as cognitive consistency and dissonance, evoked set, and learning process to a wide range of historical cases of decision-making. Third, drawing on both psychological theories and historical studies, he generalized a set of common misperceptions which are likely to prevent decision-makers from making rational choices. These misperceptions include the tendency of decision-makers to see other states as more hostile and centralized, and to fit incoming information into their existing perceptions and images.

Although Jervis's book provides numerous insights into the sources and manifestation of misperceptions in foreign policy-making, he did not offer a coherent theoretical framework to empirically investigate the structure of perceptions of decision-makers. Since the 1960s, however, under the rubric of the cognitive-psychological approach, various theoretical models have been applied to the study of the perceptions of foreign policy decision-makers.[9]

The 'operational code' (OC) approach is one of the most widely used frameworks for exploring the relationship between decision-makers' belief systems and their policy orientations and behaviours. The 'operational code' was originally introduced by Nathan Leites in his study of the 'Bolshevik doctrine' of the Soviet politburo.[10] In the late 1960s, Alexander George redefined the term and tried to develop it into a general approach to tap decision-makers' belief systems. The operational code, in George's interpretation, points to a political leader's belief system about the nature of politics and political conflict. More specifically, the operational code can be classified into philosophical and instrumental components. The former deals with political leaders' views about the 'essential' nature of political life, the fundamental character of one's political opponents, the future for the realization of one's fundamental political goals, and the sense of historical controllability. The latter refers to strategies to fulfil political goals. These strategies include the best approach to selecting political objectives, how to effectively pursue these goals, risk-taking, timing, and utility of different means.[11]

A considerable number of empirical studies have utilized George's framework.[12] Most of these studies are limited to ascertaining the OCs of one or two particular political leaders.[13] These studies usually elicit 'philosophical' and 'instrumental' OCs from individual policy decision-makers' public statements or documents using either quantitative or qualitative content analysis. Authors often make efforts to establish 'congruence' between decision-makers' OCs and their policy decisions.[14]

Two main advocates of the OC approach, George and Ole Holsti, admit that on the whole, results of these empirical inquiries have been uneven and not entirely satisfactory.[15] Along with the problems related to various authors' analytic techniques, the approach itself has some important limitations.[16]

First, as George himself realized at the outset, a decision-maker's belief system 'influences, but does not unilaterally determine, decision-making; it is an important, but not the only, variable that shapes decision-making behaviour.'[17] Therefore, the OC approach, like other cognitive methods in the field, is inherently limited in its capacity for establishing a direct causal relationship between the operational code and foreign policy decision-making. Second, most OC research has made individual policy-makers the basic unit of analysis, although the extent to which a country's foreign policy is determined by a single leader's OC, even if the policy is favoured by that leader, is questionable.[18] On most occasions, decision-making is a collective action that could be heavily influenced by group OCs. Third, most authors have used individual decision-makers' public statements to infer their belief systems. The often-raised question is the extent to which these public statements reflect their actual OCs.[19] Fourth, the ten fixed items in George's original list of questions to determine leaders' OCs are too abstract to guide empirical research. Furthermore, these items are not necessarily mutually exclusive.[20] Analysts who apply the same OC approach often operationalize the ten OC items differently. This has led to problems of inter-coder reliability and validity, and has severely limited the cumulative nature of findings.[21] Fifth, George's ten questions were derived primarily from the Soviet OC, which is based on a unique ideology. They may not apply to decision-makers in different political culture contexts. Most OC studies, however, have dealt with American foreign policy-makers rather than Soviet or other Marxist foreign policy-makers. Clearly, a typology that encompasses different OC belief systems has to be developed before a meaningful comparative study can be carried out.[22] To various degrees, these limitations are applicable to other studies of perceptions and images in international relations.

While decision-making is definitely one of the important topics in the study of international relations, it is by no means the only area to which the perceptual-psychological approach can and should be applied. Moreover, decision-making itself should be viewed in a broader context of national perceptions and images. Many scholars have devoted themselves to the study of the perceptions and images that nation-states hold of each other and of important international issues. These national perceptions, held either by leaders, elites, or the public, may not have direct correlations with foreign policy outcomes, yet they do influence the long-term direction or environment of a country's foreign policy. Comprehending the formation of and changes in these national images aids our assessment of the deep roots of international conflict and cooperation.

In his pioneering work on the relationship between national image and international politics, Kenneth Boulding defines an image as 'subjective knowledge of the world which governs people's behaviour'.[23] He stresses the importance of value systems in the formation of images and points out that people do not process information freely but rather through the filter of a value system. It is this value system that gives rise to the possibility of misperception or distortion. He argues that one of the main purposes of national education is to distort the image of other countries in the interests of the nation. Through constant reiteration these acquired values become internalized and thus form a semi-permanent 'transcript', handed down from generation to generation. He further maintains that symbolic national images are of great importance in international relations. The symbolic images that nations hold of each other lead to the disastrous phenomenon of the arms race. For this reason, he calls for more studies of symbolic national images.[24]

The national image approach has been most intensively applied to the study of American-Soviet relations during the Cold War.[25] Uri Bronfenbrenner coined the term 'mirror image' to describe the perceptions the United States and the Soviet Union held of one another. On his visit to the Soviet Union in the summer of 1960, Bronfenbrenner was dismayed to find that 'the Russians' distorted picture of us was curiously similar to our view of them—a mirror image.'[26] Each side perceived the other as the aggressor; each side thought that the other government exploited its people; each side believed that people in the other country did not support their government; each side found the other untrustworthy and its policies irrational. As a psychologist, he attributed the causes for 'mirror images' to such psychological mechanisms as the 'strain toward consistency' and the 'Asch phenomenon'.[27]

The study of American-Soviet mutual images was later developed into the broad topic of enemy images. There were parallel accumulations of literature on the subject in both international politics and psychology.[28] David Finlay and others hold that the idea of the enemy finds its most common expression in international politics. The idea of the enemy presupposes the existence of conflict between the nations. Nevertheless, sometimes the perception of conflict is 'not occasioned by the rival ends of the antagonists, but by the need for tension release of at least one of them'.[29] In their opinion, the enemy image can serve psychological, sociological, and political functions for politicians. The implication is quite clear: enemy images can sometimes be artifacts created and manipulated by political leaders to serve many ends, including establishing a country's identity, legitimizing its actions and programs, and providing rationales for attaining its goals. The enemy image, as they point out, tends to polarize 'we' and 'they' into black and white, good and evil. It endures for a long time, hence the habitual utilization of the 'inherent bad faith' model. The case study of J. F. Dulles' attitude toward the Soviet Union illustrates the rigidity and simplification of his enemy image and its negative impact on American foreign policy.

Cognitive studies of several major international issues haunting US-Soviet relations, such as the arms race, and the deterrence and conflict spiral, have illustrated the negative effect of enemy images.[30] These studies, to various degrees, point out that many erroneous assumptions about nuclear weapons were stimulated by the mutual images of the enemy. These enemy images exacerbated conflict, caused nations to overlook parallel interests, and increased the possibility of disaster through errors of judgement. For example, the debate about the nuclear strategy toward the Soviet Union turned out to be a debate about the image and intention of the Soviet Union. What counted as a 'rational' policy toward the Soviet Union depended critically on which image one believed best described American-Soviet relations.

Since the late 1970s, studies of American-Soviet mutual images as well as images of the international system gradually moved away from focusing exclusively on the rigidity and unanimity of enemy images. Such studies came to incorporate plausible perceptual adaptability and differentiation and to cover a wider range of international issues. While some scholars continued to explore the linkage between images and foreign policy, others paid more attention to the formation and change of perceptions per se.

Studies concerning the American image of the Soviet Union moved beyond analysis of individual decision-makers and endeavoured to map out broader American elite images of the Soviet Union and other international issues.[31] Ole Holsti and James Rosenau, for example, carried out a series of studies on changing American elite perceptions of the Soviet Union and a range of domestic and foreign policy issues.[32] Their extensive mail surveys of the American elite yielded some interesting results. They found that the broad foreign policy consensus that existed among American leaders during the post-war era was shattered by the Vietnam War.

Consequently, American elites' beliefs were divided into competing images concerning world affairs and the direction of American foreign policy: Cold War Internationalism, Post-Cold War Internationalism, and Semi-Isolationism.

More noticeable was the progress in studies of Soviet perceptions of American foreign policy and international relations in general.[33] Most studies, to various degrees, described a gradual differentiation and sophistication in Soviet perceptions of the United States. In his study of Soviet perspectives on international relations, William Zimmerman empirically illustrated the significant changes in Soviet perspectives on the structure of the international system, on state behaviour, and on the process and pattern of change in international relations with the emergence of the Soviet Union as a global power. Even their view of American foreign policy-making and motivation had to some extent changed with 'a shift in focus from Wall Street to Washington' and an appreciation of 'realistic elements within the American leadership'.[34] In sum, Zimmerman observed a marked tendency for Soviet perspectives on international relations to converge with American analysis. John Lenczowski's study of Soviet perceptions of United States foreign policy[35] examined the Soviet view of the shifting world balance of power and of a broad range of domestic and foreign issues confronting the US policy-makers. He discovered different 'schools of thought' in the Soviet perception of the United States and noted the tremendous growth in sophisticated Soviet analyses of American foreign policy. This trend was further noted in Robert Huber's study of Soviet perceptions of the United States Congress.[36] He concluded that a pluralist model could better explain the Soviet perceptions of the United States Congress.

The above selective literature review indicates that the study of the perceptual-psychological dimension of interstate relations has become an important and dynamic subject of inquiry in the field of international relations. Various theoretical and conceptual frameworks or models, based on interdisciplinary knowledge of human behaviour, have been produced for empirical research. A considerable quantity of studies dealing with diverse cognitive problems at different levels of interaction among nations (individual foreign policy decision-makers, elite groups, and the general public) have yielded useful findings for a better understanding of international relations. However, inadequacies continue to exist and further improvement is needed.

First, the perceptual-psychological approach to international relations, especially during the Cold War period, was dominated by the theoretical and empirical studies on 'enemy image' largely exemplified by the American-Soviet confrontation. A typology of national images incorporating other kinds of national images is yet to be fully developed. In the post-Cold War era, however, the study of black-and-white national images should be replaced with the study of more subtle and complicated national images.

Second, the study of national images in the broader sense has been sluggish compared to the study of perceptual problems in the narrow domain of foreign policy decision-making. In other words, the study of perceptions and images as independent variables has been more advanced than the study of perceptions and images as dependent variables. But if we do not have a sound understanding of perceptions and images per se, it is unlikely that we can use them as independent variables with confidence.

Furthermore, with the end of the Cold War, issues other than traditional national security, such as economic interdependence, human rights, and the environment, have gained salience on the agenda of national policy. Consequently, foreign policy-making is to a much lesser extent an exclusive privilege of top decision-makers. More domestic constituencies have been involved. Consequently, the study of broad national images has become more relevant.

Third, insufficient attention has been paid to the dynamic process of formation and change of perceptions. National images usually are taken as a given and the question of how these images are formed in the first place is seldom asked. Quite often, people elaborate on the difficulty of changing existing perceptions or images but make no parallel efforts to explore the way the stereotypes can be changed. Although terms such as 'process of sophistication' and 'conversion mechanism' have been used occasionally, real contributions in this respect are far from satisfactory.

The Evolution and Study of Sino-American Mutual Images

Compared with the advances made in the study of American-Soviet relations, the application of a perceptual approach to the study of Sino-American relations since the establishment of the People's Republic of China is underdeveloped.[37] Before the 1970s, the phenomenon could be partially explained by the years of open hostility and prolonged isolation between the two countries. For both sides, the dominant black-and-white 'enemy' images did not need much scholarly elaboration. Among very few studies on the subject, two books might be singled out for special attention. One is the Harold Isaacs classic study on American images of China in 1958.[38] In this book, Isaacs conducts a historical and empirical analysis of American elite images of China based on interviews with 181 respondents, covering a wide range of the American elite.

In articulating traditional American images of the Chinese people, Isaacs notices two sets of seemingly contradictory images: a cluster of admirable qualities such as high intelligence, persistent industry, filial piety, and peaceableness, widely associated with the greatness of the Chinese civilization, and quite another cluster of uncivilized qualities such as cruelty, barbarism, inhumanity, and the facelessness of an impenetrable mass. He argues that in the long history of the American association with China, these two different images rise and fall at the fresh calls of circumstances. Consequently, the American image of the Chinese people has shown both a timeless stability and an unlimited chaos, and a back-and-forth movement along the continuum of love–hate.

Isaacs maintained that historically, American admiration of China's ancient greatness and related high expectations seldom matched its real experience with the Chinese, both in the United States and China. In other words, while abstractly the Chinese were regarded as a 'superior people', in reality they always appeared as an 'inferior people'. From the conception of Chinese as inferior and weak people emerged the American mentality of looking upon the Chinese as 'wards' whom Americans always needed to help and protect. Isaacs found that most of his interviewees came to think of themselves as the benevolent guardians and benefactors of China. The emotion of parentalism made them view the hostility from the Communist regime of China as 'biting the hands that had fed them these many years' and made them regard the Chinese as 'the ungrateful wretches'.[39]

Isaacs pointed out that many Americans were quite emotional about China, but that they did not really understand what was actually happening in the country. The total separation of the two countries from the 1950s added to the difficulties in mutual understanding. As a result, 'our imaginations are left to supply the details of outlines we can hardly see'.[40] Therefore, America's 'new' images of China became large caricatures with little differentiation or substance. Furthermore, the emergence of Communist China as a world power following the Korean War created a new situation that did not 'fit' into traditional images of the Chinese, even for those who held deeply entrenched, admiring images of them. They were resistant to accepting these 'new' images as being 'Chinese' at all. Rather, they were described as 'Communist' or 'Russian'.

Isaacs' insights into the shaping of American elites' images of China have proved enduring. In the strict sense, however, he basically provided a picture of American images of traditional China only, rather than of Communist China. In his analysis, the elites' images of China were, in essence, images of individual Chinese people rather than of China as a state. Methodologically speaking, since his interviews were neither standardized nor well-structured, it was difficult to analyse the findings in a systematic and aggregate fashion. The book was a historical narrative rather than a systematic report of his interview data.

The unfortunate impact of Sino-American confrontation in the 1950s and 1960s on mutual perceptions was further reflected in A. T. Steele's study of American people's mentality about China in 1966. The data for Steele's study were collected primarily from a nationwide survey of public opinion and a series of more than 200 interviews by the author with Americans occupying responsible and leadership positions throughout the country.

His findings typically reflected the American 'enemy' image of China. First, the overwhelming majority of Steele's respondents picked China as a greater long-range danger to the United States than the Soviet Union in both bilateral and regional terms, although China was still seen as a weak country economically and militarily. The perception of China as a threat led people to reinterpret China's history, describing China as having been an expansionist power traditionally. Second, the 'enemy' image did not require much information to sustain. Steele found a disturbing lack of knowledge among the general public on even the most elementary facts about China. A large portion of the survey sample was not even aware that China was ruled by a Communist government. Steele attributed the problem to biased and insufficient coverage of China in news media and a lack of education about China in schools and universities. Third, Communist China rendered some basic assumptions about traditional China and Sino-American relations irrelevant (such as the idea that American Christianity and democracy were the cures for China's troubles, or the belief in special bonds of mutual affection). Nevertheless, Americans were reluctant to part with comfortable old notions and to accept the new reality: 'When stories conflict we often prefer to believe the version that fits best with our traditional thinking.'[41] Fourth, to reduce their cognitive dissonance, Americans tended to differentiate the Chinese people from the Chinese government: the Chinese people were still seen as good people and it was the Communist leadership that hated the United States. This perception was an important departure from the traditional image of China that was characterized by seeing China as individual people rather than as a state. The emergence of a strong state effectively governed by the Communists was a surprise to most Americans.

However, by the middle of the 1960s, reality finally forced Americans to realize that Communist China was not a 'passing phenomenon' and that they had to deal with China as a major power. Regarding American policy toward Communist China, Steele's study showed that American opinions were polarized between those who were no-compromise 'fundamentalists' and those who preferred to coexist with Communist China in the long run. While most Americans regarded the Beijing regime as ruthless, irresponsible, and hostile, they also favoured more communication with China. Steele came to the conclusion that by the middle of the 1960s a more favourable public opinion on China policy had been developing, and that this provided opportunities for a more realistic discussion and reappraisal of US China policy.

Steele's study differs from Isaacs' pioneering work in several respects. First, although Steele's book touched on the historical roots of America's image of China, the focus of inquiry was not on images of traditional China but rather on images of Communist China. Moreover, his focus was less on Chinese as individuals and more on China as a state. Second, where Isaacs was quite interested in determining the philosophical and cultural sources of and historical patterns in American images of China, Steele's book was more policy-oriented. Third, Isaacs' study was conducted in the aftermath of the Korean War, while Steele's research was done in the shadow of the Vietnam War. Both events strongly influenced American perceptions of China.

Deficiencies in Steele's study differ from those in Isaacs' study. Steele's study is too policy- and issue-oriented and, consequently, sacrifices the depth and richness of the images. While this is a common flaw of public opinion surveys, the author could have remedied it with his elite interviews. However, he did not try hard enough to connect and compare elite images with the public images of China.

In brief, parallel to the state of Sino-American relations in the 1950s and 1960s, mutual perceptions were characterized by enemy images based on ideological convictions. The polling data on American attitudes toward China further recorded this mentality.[42] During the 1960s, the intensity of the enemy image between the US and China was even stronger than that between the United States and the Soviet Union. For instance, the Gallup polls on public opinion show that in 1962, a majority of the American respondents (56%) considered China as a 'greater threat to world peace' than Russia (27%).[43] In 1967, only 5% of the American respondents indicated favourable feelings towards China, while 19% of them reacted favourably to the Soviet Union.[44] This unfavourable feeling was seen not just in American attitudes toward 'Communist China' but also in their opinions about the Chinese people. In a 1966 survey, among the top five words the respondents considered as best describing the Chinese people, four were negative. The Chinese people were perceived as 'ignorant', 'warlike', 'sly', and 'treacherous'.[45] At the same time, however, the emergence of China as a nuclear power moved American public opinion toward favouring recognition of China and changing the policy of no contact. By the end of the 1960s, a popular support for a more flexible China policy had taken shape.[46]

From the early 1970s, with Richard Nixon's historic visit to China, the United States and China touched off the long journey toward normalization. While the initial rapprochement was a product of the strategic calculation by the top decision-makers, the resumption of direct contacts between the two peoples gradually eroded the rigid enemy image, leading to broader perceptual changes, and in turn these perceptual changes helped sustain the dynamics of the relationship.[47]

In the 1970s, a number of scholars analysed the phenomenon of 'China fever' that sprung up in the United States after the initial American exposure to a 'new' China.[48] John Fairbank mentioned that the new relationship brought Americans to a high point in their interest in and idealization of China. For those whose feet touched Chinese soil for the first time since 1949, 'guided tourism' produced a remarkably uniform and positive set of impressions. 'The reports are as consistent as the astonishing consistency they describe.'[49] Warren Cohen noticed that during the months that preceded and followed Nixon's trip to China, American interest in things Chinese soared and Chinoiserie filled media stories in the early 1970s.[50] Stanley Karnow found that some prominent journalists' China images had been transformed dramatically.[51] In brief, with the thaw in Sino-American relations, the American image of China was suddenly reversed.

These authors, however, did not take this favourable image for granted. They realized that the American public's attitude toward China had a tendency to swing from one extreme to another: the 'good guy' Chinese could be turned into a 'bad guy' overnight. Although numerous reports about a 'new China' poured into the United States, Fairbank saw little that was new in the American image and viewed them as a mere revival of the other side of old images.[52] Cohen maintained that the American public's attitudes toward the Chinese remained superficial. Whether American images of China would remain positive or negative depended on the development of Sino-American relations. If the exigencies of international politics or China's internal politics led to renewed antagonism, public opinion surely would become negative again.[53] Karnow described the phenomenon as 'changing misperceptions of China' that portrayed the country in nothing but euphoric prose, thus substituting one set of illusions for another without coming substantially closer to any plausible understanding of China. He was worried about the potential danger that the pendulum would swing back again to jeopardize a stable relationship, because the American 'love–hate' syndrome is too emotional to remain in balance for a long period.[54]

The pendulum did start swinging back in the late 1970s and the early 1980s, when Sino-American relations had been normalized and interactions between the two countries had become routine. In his analysis of the change in the American image of China,[55] Harry Harding defined the 1970s as 'a period of pronounced fascination with China'. In the early 1980s, however, 'China fever' had given way to 'China stinks'. The same phenomena regarding the Chinese state, society, leadership, and economic development were described in very different terms in the 1980s than they had been a decade before. Harding explored the sources of the reappraisal. Americans tend to substitute today's 'truth' for yesterday's myth, only to discover that today's 'reality' becomes tomorrow's illusion. This is why American attitudes toward China have undergone regular cycles of romanticism and cynicism, of idealization and disdain. The reversal also had something to do with a change in patterns of interaction. The initial positive effects of 'revolutionary tourism' in the early 1970s were quite different from that of a long-term stay in China, which easily led to disillusionment. Ironically, as China's reality changed for the better, the American image of China actually changed for the worse. Harding noticed with unease the similarities between the reappraisal of China in the 1980s and the original romanticization in the 1970s: a persistent tendency to make sweeping moral judgements about China, an inclination to remedy misunderstandings by turning them upside down, and a strong tendency to apply Western values and social standards to interpret the situation in China.

For the American general public at that time, their knowledge of China remained quite limited, as reflected in Edward Hall's comparative study of American perceptions of modern and traditional China and Japan.[56] Methodologically replicating a previous pilot study on the American image of Japan in 1978, Hall interviewed 246 'adults living in the Seattle area', using a standardized questionnaire to elicit an American image of China and its sources. At the aggregate level, he found that the respondents' general images of China were best represented by their description of geographic (huge population, physical size, etc.), political (the communist nature of the government, the impression of political instability, etc.), and economic (poverty and starvation, rich natural resources, etc.) characteristics, as well as by descriptions of the Chinese as people (disciplined, intelligent, industrious, etc.). The author also tapped the difference between the American image of 'traditional China' and that of 'modern China', with a majority of his respondents using some aspects of culture or heritage to characterize the former, and mentioning China's communist government and its power or strength to describe the latter.

One merit of Hall's study is that it compared Americans' China image with their Japan image. The findings showed that the American image of Japan exhibited greater amounts of information and more detailed knowledge than the less specific impressions of their China image. Hall used the terms 'complex discrimination' and 'simple discrimination'[57] to discuss this difference in national images. The Japan image demonstrated a much higher percentage of complex discrimination. Hall attributed the smaller proportion of complex discrimination in the China image to the fact that Americans could not easily obtain information specific to the Chinese people and adequate in amount and depth for the exercise of complex discrimination. The author realized that these differences were due to the relatively recent reacquaintance with China after nearly a quarter of a century of mutually imposed isolation. In contrast, Americans had a continuous and close relationship with Japan during most of that same period. Thus, the author treated the degree of contact and information availability as an important variable to explain image differentiation.

Hall's study of the American image of China still falls into the category of public opinion survey, although it is methodologically more sophisticated. His improvements of the questionnaire by differentiating images of traditional and modern China, and between complex discrimination and simple discrimination, are effective in tapping the different dimensions of American images of China. His emphasis on the linkage between image and image sources yielded interesting findings. However, the capacity for generalization of his findings was quite restricted by the fact that his sample was drawn from a very limited population. Also, as the author's interest was mainly in improving survey instruments, he did not provide a sophisticated theoretical analysis of his findings.

These studies notwithstanding, until recently the subject of mutual images has not been vigorously pursued, in spite of the tremendous expansion in the volume of the literature on Sino-American relations. Although many authors in their studies of various aspects of China and Sino-American relations have touched upon, implicitly or explicitly, the topic, systematic and formal investigations of Sino-American mutual images and their impact on the bilateral relationship have been scant. This is even more the case regarding research on the Chinese image of the United States.[58] In 1973, Tu Wei-ming, a Chinese-American scholar, did an 'exploratory' study on the subject.[59] He argued that the traditional Chinese image of the United States was characterized both by admiration and by ambivalence, as a result of irreconcilable conceptual and experiential differences between the two countries. On the one hand, the United States was perceived as a model of science and democracy for China to emulate. On the other hand, the Chinese felt uneasy about the unequal nature of the relationship and about the American insensitivity and arrogance in dealing with Chinese. Tu found that since the establishment of the PRC, however, the Chinese images of America had been neither admiring nor ambivalent but outright negative: 'The earlier image of America as a model of science and democracy has thus been displaced by an image of a greedy and violent nation, struggling to remain the wealthiest and the strongest on earth.'[60] Whereas Tu did not explicate the linkage between the traditional and modern Chinese images of the United States, he did point out that there was still 'a thousand li' ahead on the road to mutual appreciation of cultural values between these two great peoples, even with the normalization of the relationship.

Before the 1980s, because of the difficulty of conducting broad-based research in China, the imbalance had been in favour of studying top Chinese policy-makers' images of the United States rather than broader elite or public images. Allen Whiting is one of the few American China scholars who have paid special attention to the Chinese policy-makers' perceptions about the United States. In his classic book on the Korean War[61] he investigated the problem of misperception in Sino-American relations. Contrary to the conventional American perceptions interpreting Mao's entry into that war as a function of an aggressive and expansionist communism, Whiting found that Beijing's decision to enter the war was actually the result of national security concerns that had been aroused by a pattern of American statements and actions that had been perceived within the image of a hostile power.[62] Whiting explored why both sides failed to understand the other side's intentions. After analysing the new Chinese leadership's frame of reference regarding world affairs in general and US policy in particular, he came to the conclusion that the misperceptions were caused by the difficulty each side had in projecting itself into the frame of reference within which the other operated.

The themes of perception and misperception have appeared throughout Whiting's later studies of Sino-American relations and Chinese foreign policy.[63] In all these studies he has focused on China's response to the behaviour of the United States and other governments, as mediated by the perceptions of policy-makers. For example, in his classic study of Chinese behaviour in three crises (the Korean War, the Sino-Indian border war, and the Indochina War), Whiting found that the patterns of Chinese conflict behaviour were determined by a unique Chinese deterrence calculus. Chinese leaders relied on propositions such as 'the worse our domestic situation, the more likely our external situation will worsen', 'the best deterrence is belligerence', and 'correct timing is essential'. These idiosyncratic perceptions of external threats and deterrence efficacy sometimes impeded China's effective interactions with the non-Chinese world.

In more recent years, the perceptual dimension of Sino-American relations has drawn more serious scholarly attention. Several topical symposiums have been convened to discuss the subject comprehensively.[64] As for empirical research on the topic, the target of inquiry has been extended from either public opinion or top policy-makers to elite groups between them. Some substantial studies of historical US-China mutual images have been published since the late 1980s.[65] However, in terms of contemporary US-China mutual images, two studies dealing with the evolution of American elite images of China and Chinese elite images of the United States merit special comment.

In *China Misperceived*, Steven W. Mosher articulated the evolution of American intellectual perceptions of the PRC (tracing it back to the early days of the Communist movement in the 1930s and the 1940s), with the focus on the period since Nixon's initiative in the early 1970s.[66] As the title of his book suggests, he believes that the PRC has been misperceived by American China-watchers and journalists in a repetitive cycle of hostility-admiration-disenchantment-benevolence. Basing his research on a selective pool of academic works, press reports, and the writings of tourists and professionals, Mosher divides the American image of the PRC into four periods: (1) The age of hostility (1949–1972); (2) The age of admiration (1972–1977); (3) The age of disenchantment (1977–1980); and (4) The age of benevolence (1980–1989). Although this periodization per se was not entirely new,[67] Mosher characterized these periods with some prevailing paradigms of perceptions.

Following the 'totalitarian paradigm' and 'modernizing communist regime' during the age of hostility, a new paradigm of revolutionary socialism was developed in the 1970s to describe China as an egalitarian and purposeful society from which Americans could learn how to solve their own problems. But Americans' rosy image of China was soon shattered by the revelation of the disastrous Cultural Revolution and the regime's own disowning of its past. American intellectuals then came up with a new paradigm of the 'authoritarian modernizing regime', in which the Deng regime was portrayed as a benevolent dictatorship committed to modernization and to moving toward democratization. This paradigm, however, was severely battered by the Tiananmen crackdown and Americans again shifted their view of China overnight, seeing the Chinese Communist government as a repressive and tyrannical regime with complete disregard for its people and world opinion.

As a whole, Mosher's study offers a well-articulated historical account of the evolution of the American image of the PRC. His advocacy of a cyclical interpretation of the American image of China, while intuitively bearing some historical truth, could be flawed in its excessive application. Mosher has declared that the 'authoritarian modernizing paradigm' lost its validity in the face of the 1989 crackdown, but he does not indicate what new paradigm has emerged. The logic of his cyclical model suggests that the next image should again be that of hostility, but clearly Mosher does not have enough empirical evidence to support this prospect. Second, this cycle, as Mosher describes it, evinces little perceptual sophistication: one misperception is replaced by another endlessly. In other words, Mosher seldom recognizes the valid elements in each paradigm, viewed from the then-prevailing historical conditions. Furthermore, Mosher treats China as an unchangeable subject around which American perceptions move up and down for artificial reasons, such as Nixon's or the Chinese regime's intentional cultivation or manipulation. In fact, the fluctuation of American images, to a significant extent, reflects the changes in Chinese reality. Methodologically, Mosher's selection of literature in the China field is limited and even biased. He neglected numerous sophisticated analyses of China by various scholars, and attached too much importance to the judgements of a few Chinese dissidents.

With regard to the other side of the dyad, David Shambaugh published a major study on Chinese elite images of the United States since the 1970s.[68] He devoted his attention to an important cohort of the Chinese elite—'America watchers' in the central government bureaucracy, professional research institutes, press, and universities. Using a mixed database of specialized professional publications, the print media and personal interviews, he articulated the evolution of China's America watchers' images of the United States over the period 1972–1990. Under an overarching framework of the Marxist school versus the non-Marxist school, Shambaugh pieced together the content and variation of their images of American economy, society, polity, and foreign policy. According to his definition, the Marxist school is characterized by an interpretation of the United States using coherent Marxist-Leninist categories of analysis and terminology, whereas the non-Marxist school is notable for its a-theoretical, non-ideological, ad hoc, and descriptive nature.

Shambaugh discovered a gradual shift of perceptions over time from the Marxist school to the non-Marxist school, with the latter becoming more prevalent in the 1980s. However, the competition between the two schools is still going on. In contrast to Mosher's study of Americans, Shambaugh noticed a trend among Chinese toward perceptual sophistication and differentiation over the period. Nevertheless, despite considerable progress, 'Chinese understanding of the United States remains shallow and seriously distorted. With a few exceptions, the vast majority of America watchers in China do not understand the United States very well'.[69] In other words, the ambivalent nature of the Chinese image of the United States remains unchanged. Like American perceptions of China, Chinese perceptions of the United States are also characterized by ambivalence, viewing the United States as a 'beautiful imperialist.'

Shambaugh has presented a solid and thorough literature survey of the Chinese elite image of the United States since the 1970s. His work has opened a new domain in the study of Sino-American relations. His analysis throughout the book is attuned to subtlety and nuances. Further refinement is nevertheless possible. Shambaugh's generalization in terms of Marxist and non-Marxist schools is conceptually sensible, but problematic in application. For instance, his effort to group America watchers into two schools in the context of institutional and professional affiliation is somewhat arbitrary. The different projections of opinions he described, for example, among university professors and specialists in some government-related think tanks could well be due to the division of labour rather than to different schools of thought. University professors are supposed to do more theoretical research, while specialists in research institutes are dealing with more concrete and empirical issues. Therefore the mere application of Marxist terminology is often not a reliable indicator for coding people into different schools. Moreover, although Shambaugh covers a range of dimensions of Chinese images of the United States in his study, his effort to link these various parts is inadequate. Consequently, his description of the Chinese image of the United States is somewhat fragmented and lacks overall structure.

The scholarly findings on Sino-American mutual images between 1970 and 1989 can also be supplemented by public opinion data on the American side. Overall, the American perception of China had greatly improved, albeit with a lot of ups and downs.[70] Following Nixon's visit, favourable ratings for China rose from 5% in 1967 to 23% in 1972.[71] In 1973, this figure almost doubled to 47%.[72] For the first time since the 1950s, the percentage with a positive feeling surpassed the negative (43%). This positive trend did drop back to some extent in the mid- and late-1970s, before the normalization. However, starting from the 1980s, the positive opinion of China steadily took hold.[73] It reached a climax before the Tiananmen crackdown in 1989. A Gallup Poll conducted in February 1989 indicated that 72% of the respondents held positive and only 13% negative opinions.[74] Apparently the Tiananmen Incident greatly shattered the

American public's good feeling toward China. Another Gallup Poll in August 1989 presents a quite different picture: 31% rated China favourably and 58% unfavourably.[75]

This latest twist in Sino-American relations and its ramifications for mutual images has not been subject to systematic scholarly examination. Although Mosher's and Shambaugh's studies touched upon the transition, their research had been largely conducted before 1989, and the impact of Tiananmen and other structural changes in the post-Cold War era were for the most part added as postscripts.

A review of the major studies of Sino-American mutual images indicates that most scholars usually focus only on one side in the perceptual equation. They do not examine the subject of mutual perceptions and images in a cross-national, comparative, and interactive mode. Because different authors consider different groups of people on different issues using different analytic tools, the results of these studies cannot always be compared. Even though some authors have made efforts to compare Sino-American mutual images, the available data are often too asymmetric to permit a real comparative study.[76] A study of Sino-American mutual images in a coherent theoretical framework based on a cross national database, therefore, might produce more interesting and comparable empirical evidence.

Furthermore, current studies do not pay sufficient attention to the structure of mutual images. They either deal with a single dimension of the images or fail to integrate various parts of the images. Thus, a great deal of the complexity and richness of perceptions may have been lost. In reality, a sophisticated national image is more likely to be multidimensional than unidimensional. Therefore, an exploration of the structure of mutual images may provide a more complete and self-sustained model of how the United States and China perceive each other.

Taking the Tiananmen Incident as a main reference point and the post-Cold War era as a broad background, this volume attempts to contribute along these lines. Several general intellectual themes can be drawn upon from the existing literature to serve as a road map for the following analysis of post-Cold War mutual images.

First, a traditional line of observation is to interpret ups and downs in the American image of China as a function of historical cycles, moving back and forth between the two poles of love and hate. The perceptual shift since 1989 seems to confirm this cyclic interpretation once again. Yet the inherent logic of this argument leaves very little room for perceptual sophistication. While the cyclic phenomenon reflects some historical truth, a more interesting question is whether such cycles represent simple repetitions of old stereotypes or upward spirals of perceptual sophistication.

A study of Sino-American mutual perceptions at a low ebb in the wake of Tiananmen can provide more valid empirical answers to this question.

Second, Sino-American mutual images before 1989 were in large measure a function of the ideological and geopolitical confrontation between the United States and the Soviet Union. For both sides, the Soviet factor was pivotal in making either the 'enemy' images in the 1950s and 1960s or the 'quasi-ally' images in the 1970s and 1980s. With the drastic diminishing of Soviet influence as common denominator for the relationship, to what extent are those Cold War assumptions about the target country during the Cold War still valid, and what are some of the new cognitive systems of reference in their places? In other words, how do Americans and Chinese perceive the nature of the relationship under new circumstances?

Third, the existing literature suggests that Sino-American mutual perceptions are not characterized merely by vertical flux but also by horizontal ambivalence, as reflected in cognitions such as 'beautiful imperialism' or 'benevolent totalitarianism'. How is this ambivalence reflected in the 'structure' of mutual images, namely the cognitive dissonance within or among various image dimensions at different levels of analysis? What are some of the new variations of the traditional ambivalence, and how do they contribute to the perceptual gaps between the two countries and hence the friction in the relationship?

Fourth, so far as the source of mutual images is concerned, no study has been done to explicitly investigate the impact of dynamic interactions since the 1970s on mutual images. The Tiananmen Incident provides a unique opportunity to explore the respective influence of 'reorganizing' big events and non-eventful daily contact on the formation and evolution of mutual images. Does the outburst of mutual resentment immediately after Tiananmen simply reflect short-term reactions dictated by the circumstances in both countries or long-held perceptions based on direct and indirect interactions? Stated otherwise, to what extent can mutual perceptions be modified or even reversed by a single event?

Notes to Chapter 1

1   For a general introduction to the field, see Herbert Kelman, 'Social-psychological Approaches to the Study of International Relations: Definition of Scope', in Herbert Kelman (ed.), *International Behaviour: A Social-Psychological Analysis* , New York: Holt, Rinehart, and Winston, 1965, pp. 3–39; Herbert Kelman, 'Assumptive Frameworks in International Politics', in Jeanne N. Knutson (ed.), *Handbook of Political Psychology,* San Francisco: Jossey-Bass, 1973, pp. 261–295; Christer Jonsson, 'Introduction: Cognitive Approaches to International Politics', in Christer Jonsson (ed.), *Cognitive Dynamics and*

International Politics, London: Frances Pinter, 1982, pp. 1–17; Steve Smith, 'Belief System and the Study of International Relations', in Richard Little and Steve Smith, *Belief Systems and International Relations,* Basil Blackwell: Oxford, 1988, pp. 11–82; James F. Voss and Ellen Dorsey, 'Perception and International Relations: An Overview', in Eric Singer and Valerie Hudson (eds.) *Political Psychology and Foreign Policy,* Boulder: Westview Press, 1992, pp. 3–30.

2   Kelman classified social-psychological studies of international relations into two main categories: the study of international politics and foreign policy that concerns the determinants of decision-makers' perceptions and behaviour and consequent foreign policies, and the study of the international behaviour of individuals that deals mainly with non-decision-making individuals' attitude and behaviour toward other nations. See Kelman, *International Behaviour,* p. 10, 65. He later made another distinction: studies focusing on attitudes relevant to international relations held by various groups of individuals; and studies focusing on psychological and social-interactional factors in international politics and foreign policy decision-making. He regards the former category as studies in which perceptual factors constitute the dependent variables and the latter as studies in which they serve as the independent variables. See Kelman, 'Assumptive Frameworks in International Politics', p. 263.

3   For a general introduction to the decision-making approach, see Richard C. Snyder, H. W. Bruck, and Burton Sapin (eds.), *Foreign Policy Decision-Making: An Approach to the Study of International Politics,* New York: Free Press, 1962; Glenn Snyder and Paul Diesing, *Conflict Among Nations: Bargaining, Decision-making and System Structure in International Crisis,* Princeton: Princeton University Press, 1977; Robert Jervis, 'Political Decision Making: Recent Contributions', *Political Psychology 2,* No. 2 (1980): 86–101; Alexander George, *Presidential Decisionmaking in Foreign Policy: On the Effective Use of Information and Advice,* Boulder: Westview Press, 1980; and Yaacov Y. I. Vertzberger, *The World in Their Minds: Information Processing, Cognition, and Perception in Foreign Policy Decisionmaking,* Stanford: Stanford University Press, 1990.

4   Harold Sprout and Margaret Sprout, 'Environmental Factors in the Study of International Politics', in James N. Rosenau (ed.), *International Politics and Foreign Policy, A Reader in Research and Theory,* New York: Free Press, 1969, p. 49.

5   Harold Sprout and Margaret Sprout, *Man-Milieu Relationship: Hypotheses in the Context of International Politics,* Princeton: Center of International Studies, Princeton University, 1956; 'Environmental Factors'.

6   J. David Singer, 'The Level-of-Analysis Problem in International Relations', in Rosenau, *International Politics and Foreign Policy,* p. 26.

7   Alexander George, comments on the back cover of *Perception and Misperception in International Politics* by Robert Jervis, Princeton: Princeton University Press, 1970.

8   Ibid., p. 28.

9   Among others, see Richard A. Brody, 'Cognition and Behaviour: A Model of International Relations', in O. J. Harvey (ed.), *Experience, Structure, and Adaptability,* New York: Springer, 1966, pp. 321–348; Michael Brecher, Blema Steinberg, and Janice Stein, 'A Framework for Research on Foreign Policy Behaviour', *Journal of Conflict Resolution 13,* No. 1 (1969): 75–101; Stephen G. Walker, 'National Role Conceptions and Systemic Outcomes', in Lawrence Falkowski (ed.), *Psychological Models in International Politics,* Colorado: Westview Press, 1979 pp. 169-210; Christer Jonsson and Ulf Westerlund, 'Role Theory in Foreign Policy Analysis', in Jonsson, *Cognitive Dynamics and International Politics,* pp. 122–157; Ole R. Holsti, 'The Belief System and National Images: A Case Study', in Rosenau, *International Politics and Foreign Policy,* pp. 543–550; Douglas Stuart and Harvey Starr,

'The Inherent Bad Faith Model Reconsidered: Dulles, Kennedy, and Kissinger', *Political Psychology* 3, No. 3/4 (1981–82): 1–33; Robert Axelrod (ed.), *Structure of Decision: The Cognitive Maps of Political Elites,* Princeton: Princeton University Press, 1976.

10   Nathen C. Leites, *The Operational Code of the Politburo,* New York: McGraw-Hill, 1951; *A Study of Bolshevism,* Glencoe (Ill.): Free Press, 1953.

11   Alexander George, 'The "Operational Code": A Neglected Approach', *International Studies Quarterly XIII,* No. 2 (1969): 201–216.

12   Ole Holsti estimated in 1982 that some two dozen follow-up studies have employed the OC approach to analyse the beliefs of political leaders, including several American Presidents and Secretaries of State, Western European leaders, and a few others. See 'The Operational Code Approach: Problems and Some Solutions', in Jonsson, *Cognitive Dynamics and International Politics,* p. 75.

13   Gordon D. White, 'A Comparison of the Operational Codes of Mao Tse-Tung and Liu Shao-Chi', Mimeograph, Stanford University, 1969; Ole Holsti, 'The Operational Code Approach to the Study of Political Leaders: John Foster Dulles' Philosophical and Instrumental Beliefs', *Canadian Journal of Political Science* 3, No. 1 (1970): 123–157; D. McLellan, 'The "Operational Code" Approach to the Study of Political Leaders: Dean Acheson's Philosophical and Instrumental Beliefs', *Canadian Journal of Political Science* 4, No. 1 (1971): 52–75; Kurt K. Tweraser, 'Changing Patterns of Political Beliefs: The Foreign Policy Operational Codes of J. William Fulbright 1943–1967', Sage Professional Papers in American Politics 2, series/No. 04–016, Beverly Hills: Sage, 1974; Stephen G. Walker, 'The Interface Between Beliefs and Behaviour: Henry Kissinger's Operational Code and the Vietnam War', *Journal of Conflict Resolution 21,* No. 1 (1977): 129–168; and L. Johnson, 'Operational Codes and the Prediction of Leadership Behaviour: Senator Frank Church at Mid-Career', in Margaret G. Hermann (ed.) *A Psychological Examination of Political Leaders,* New York: Free Press, 1977, pp. 80–119. Several scholars applied the OC approach in broader scope. For example, Daniel Heradsveit tested the OC approach in the context of decision-making in the Middle East; see 'Decision-Making in the Middle East: Testing the Operational Code Approach', Norwegian Institute of International Affairs, 1977; Stephen G. Walker and Lawrence S. Falkowski studied the operational codes of US Presidents and Secretaries of State in a collective fashion; see 'The Operational Codes of US Presidents and Secretaries of State: Motivational Foundations and Behavioural Consequences', *Political Psychology* 5, No. 2 (1984): 237–266.

14   For a summary of various studies using this approach, see Stephen G. Walker, 'The Utility of the Operational Code in Political Forecasting', *Political Psychology* 3, No. 1/2 (1981–82): 24–60.

15   Alexander George, 'The Causal Nexus Between Cognitive Beliefs and Decision-Making Behaviour: The "Operational Code" Belief System', in Falkowski, *Psychological Models in International Politics,* p. 95; Ole Holsti, 'The Operational Code Approach: Problems and Some Solutions', p. 75.

16   For a discussion of the merits and shortcomings of this approach, see the dialogue between Gunnar Sjoblom and Ole Holsti in Jonsson, *Cognitive Dynamics and International Politics,* pp. 37–90.

17   George, 'The "Operational Code": A Neglected Approach', p. 191; 'The Causal Nexus', p. 101.

18   David Finlay, Ole Holsti, and Richard Fagen, *Enemies in Politics,* Chicago: Rand McNally, 1967, pp. 86–89; and K. J. Holsti, *Change in the International System: Essays on the Theory and Practice of International Relations,* Aldershot: Edward Elgar, 1991, p. 10.

19   Jonsson, *Cognitive Dynamics and International Politics,* p. 9.

20   Gunnar Sjoblom, 'Some Problems of the Operational Code Approach', in Jonsson, *Cognitive Dynamics and International Politics,* pp. 60–64.

21   George, 'The Causal Nexus', pp. 95–96.

22   Jonsson, *Cognitive Dynamics and International Politics,* pp. 53–54.

23   Kenneth Boulding, *The Image Knowledge in Life and Society,* New York: Vail-Ballou Press, 1956, p. 6.

24   Kenneth Boulding, 'National Images and International Systems', *Journal of Conflict Resolution 3,* No. 2 (1959): 120–131.

25   Among other studies, see Raymond A. Bauer, 'Problems of Perception and the Relations between the United States and the Soviet Union', *The Journal of Conflict Resolution 5,* No. 3 (1961): 224–229; Anatal Rapoport, *The Big Two, Soviet-American Perceptions of Foreign Policy,* Indianapolis: Pegasus, 1971; Ralph K. White, *Fearful Warriors: A Psychological Profile of US-Soviet Relations,* New York: Free Press, 1984; Daniel Frei, *Perceived Images: US and Soviet Assumptions and Perceptions in Disarmament,* Totowa: Rowman and Allanheld, 1986; Michael D. Intriligator and Hans-Adolf Jacobson (eds.), *East-West Conflict: Elite Perceptions and Political Options,* Boulder: Westview Press, 1988; Deborah W. Larson, *Anatomy of Mistrust: US-Soviet Relations During the Cold War,* Ithaca: Cornell University Press, 1997. In addition to Soviet-American relations, another pair of bilateral relations that has drawn considerable attention in this direction is the Arab-Israeli conflict. See Ralph K. White, 'Misperception in the Arab-Israeli Conflict', *Journal of Social Issues 33,* No. 1 (1977): 190–221; Daniel Heradsveit, *Arab and Israeli Elite Perceptions,* Oslo: Universitetsforlaget, 1974; *The Arab-Israeli Conflict: Psychological Obstacles to Peace,* Oslo: Universitetsforlaget, 1979; Henry Clay Lindgren, 'Friends and Enemies' Enemies: Heider's Balance Theory and Middle East Relations', *Political Psychology 1,* No. 2 (1979): 104–105; and Herbert Kelman, 'Israelis and Palestinians: Psychological Prerequisites for Mutual Acceptance', *International Security 3,* No. 1 (1979): 162–186.

26   Uri Bronfenbrenner, 'The Mirror Image in Soviet American Relations: A Social Psychologist's Report', *Journal of Social Issues 17,* No. 3 (1961): 45–6.

27   Ibid., p. 50. His mirror image theory has been empirically tested by some scholars, e.g. William Eckhardt, 'A Test of the Mirror-Image Hypothesis: Kennedy and Khrushchev', *The Journal of Conflict Resolution 11,* No. 3 (1967): 325–332; and Gerald N. Sande and others, 'Value-Guided Attributions: Maintaining the Moral Self-Image and the Diabolical Enemy-Image', *Journal of Social Issues 45,* No. 2 (1989): 91–118.

28   For a general introduction to this topic, see Arthur Gladstone, 'The Concept of Enemy', *Journal of Conflict Resolution 3,* No. 2 (1959): 132–137; Finlay, *Enemies in Politics;* Jerome D. Frank, 'The Image of the Enemy', in his book, *Sanity and Survival in the Nuclear Age,* New York: Random House, 1982, pp. 115–136; and the special issue of *Journal of Social Issues* on enemy image 45, No. 2 (1989); and Noel Kaplowitz, 'National self-images, perception of enemies, and conflict strategies: psychopolitical dimensions of international relations', *Political Psychology 11,* No. 1 (1990): 39–81.

29   Finlay, *Enemies in Politics,* p. 5.

30   See Frank, *Sanity and Survival;* Jervis, *Perception and Misperception,* pp. 58–113; Philip E. Tetlock, 'Policy-Makers' Images of International Conflict', *Journal of Social Issues 39,* No. 1 (1983): 67–86; Richard Ned Lebow, 'The Deterrence Deadlock: Is There a Way Out?' *Political Psychology 4,* No. 2 (1983): 333–354; Robert Jervis, Richard Lebow, and Janice Stein, *Psychology and Deterrence,* Baltimore: The John Hopkins University Press, 1986; Scott Plous, 'Psychological and Strategic Barriers in Present Attempts at Nuclear Disarmament: A New Proposal', *Political Psychology 6,* No. 1 (1985): 109–133; 'Perceptual Illusions and Military Realities', *Journal of Conflict Resolution 29,* No. 3 (1985): 363–389;

'Perceptual Illusions and Military Realities', *Journal of Conflict Resolution 31*, No. 1 (1987): 5–33; and Alexander Gralnick, 'Trust, Deterrence, Realism, and Nuclear Homicide', *Political Psychology 9*, No. 1 (1988): 175–188.

31   See Alexander George and Richard Smoke, *Deterrence in American Foreign Policy: Theory and Practice*, New York: Columbia University Press, 1974; Ralph K. White, 'Empathizing with the Rulers of the USSR', *Political Psychology 4*, No. 1 (1983): 121–137; Richard K. Herrmann, 'American Perceptions of Soviet Foreign Policy: Reconsidering Three Competing Perspectives', *Political Psychology 6*, No. 3 (1985): 375–411; J. Philipp Rosenberg, 'Presidential Beliefs and Foreign Policy Decision-Making: Continuity During the Cold War Era', *Political Psychology 7*, No. 4 (1986): 733–751; Jerel A. Rosati, *The Carter Administration's Quest for Global Community: Beliefs and Their Impact on Behaviour*, South Carolina: University of South Carolina Press, 1987; 'Continuity and Change in the Foreign Policy Beliefs of Political Leaders: Addressing the Controversy over the Carter Administration', *Political Psychology 9*, No. 3 (1988): 471–505; Cheryl Koopman, Jack Snyder, and Robert Jervis, 'American Elite Views of Relations with the Soviet Union', *Journal of Social Issues 45*, No. 2 (1989): 119–138; Choichiro Yatani and Dana Bramel, 'Trends and Patterns in Americans' Attitudes Toward the Soviet Union', *Journal of Social Issues 45*, No. 2 (1989): 13–32; Keith L. Shimko, *Images and Arms Control: Perceptions of the Soviet Union in the Reagan Administration*, Ann Arbor: University of Michigan Press, 1991; Martha L. Cottam, *Images and Intervention: US Policies in Latin America*, Pittsburgh: University of Pittsburgh Press, 1994; and Stephen Twing, *Myths, Models, and US Foreign Policy: The Cultural Shaping of Three Cold Warriors*, Bounder: Lynne Rienner Publishers, 1998.

32   See Ole Holsti and James Rosenau, *American Leadership in World Affairs: Vietnam and the Breakdown of Consensus*, Winchester: Allen & Unwin, 1984; 'The Domestic and Foreign Policy Beliefs of American Leaders', *Journal of Conflict Resolution 32*, No. 2 (1988): 248–294; and 'What Are the Russians Up to Now: The Beliefs of American Leaders About the Soviet Union and Soviet-American Relations 1976–1984', in Intriligator and Jacobson, *East-West Conflict*, pp. 45–105.

33   See William Zimmerman, *Soviet Perspectives on International Relations, 1965–1967*, Princeton: Princeton University Press, 1969; Morton Schwartz, *Soviet Perceptions of the United States*, Los Angeles: University of California Press, 1978; John Lenczowski, *Soviet Perceptions of US Foreign Policy: A Study of Ideology, Power and Consensus*, Ithaca: Cornell University Press: 1982; Neil Malcolm, *Soviet Political Scientists and American Politics*, London: MacMillan Press, 1984; Richard K. Herrmann, *Perceptions and Behaviour in Soviet Foreign Policy*, Pittsburgh: University of Pittsburgh Press, 1985; and Robert T. Huber, *Soviet Perceptions of the US Congress: The Impact on Superpower Relations*, Boulder: Westview Press, 1989.

34   Zimmerman, *Soviet Perspectives on International Relations*, p. 278.

35   Lenczowski, *Soviet Perceptions of US Foreign Policy.*

36   Huber, *Soviet Perceptions of the US Congress.*

37   As early as 1974, Robert Boardman noticed this problem when he talked about the potential significance of perception theory in the study of Chinese foreign policy: 'In contrast to the vigor with which this subject [the study of perception] has been pursued by international relations' scholars in recent years, the approaches to Chinese foreign policy bear little sign of any substantial perception studies'. See his essay 'Perception Theory and the Study of Chinese Foreign Policy', in Roger Dial (ed.), *Advancing and Contending Approaches to the Study of Chinese Foreign Policy*, Halifax: Center for Foreign Policy Studies, Department of Political Science, Dalhousie University, Canada, 1974, p. 321. Unfortunately, the situation since then has not improved substantially.

38   Harold R. Isaacs, *Scratches on Our Minds: American Images of China and India*, New York: John Day, 1958.

39   Ibid., pp. 193–194.

40   Ibid., p. 215.

41   A. T. Steele, *The American People and China*, New York: McGraw-Hill, 1966, p. 57.

42   For a systematic study of American public opinion of China during this time period, see Leonard A. Kusnitz, *Public Opinion and Foreign Policy: America's China Policy, 1949–1979*, Westport: Greenwood Press, 1984.

43   See *The Gallup Poll, Public Opinion 1935–1971*, New York: Random House, 1972, p. 1,881. Also see Kusnitz, *Public Opinion and Foreign Policy*, p. 117; Richard G. Niemi, John Mueller, and Tom W. Smith, *Trends in Public Opinion, A Compendium of Survey Data*, New York: Greenwood Press, 1989, p. 60, Table 2.13.

44   See *The Gallup Poll, Public Opinion 1972–1977*, Wilmington: Scholarly Resources Inc., 1978, p. 918; Kusnitz, *Public Opinion and Foreign Policy*, p. 140.

45   *The Gallup Poll, Public Opinion 1935–1971*, p. 2015.

46   Benjamin I. Page and Robert Y. Shapiro, *The Rational Public, Fifty Years of Trends in Americans' Policy Preferences*, Chicago: The University of Chicago Press, 1992, pp. 245–251.

47   For a general survey of the evolution of Sino-American mutual perceptions since the 1970s, see Harry Harding, *A Fragile Relationship, The United States and China since 1972*, Washington, DC: The Brookings Institution, 1992, pp. 60–66, 100–106, 131–137,169–172, 207–214, 239–246, 290–296; also Kusnitz, *Public Opinion and Foreign Policy*.

48   John Fairbank, *China Perceived: Images and Policies in Chinese-American Relations*, New York: Alfred. A. Knopf, 1974; *Chinese-American Interactions: A Historical Survey*, New Brunswick: Rutgers University Press, 1975; Benson Lee Grayson (ed.), *The Image of China*, New York: Frederick Ungar, 1979; Stanley Karnow, 'Changing (Mis)Conceptions of China', in Grayson (ed.), *The Image of China*, pp. 284–304; Warren Cohen, 'American Perceptions of China'; in Oksenberg and Oxnam, *Dragon and Eagle*, pp. 54–86; Harry Harding, 'From China with Disdain: New Trends in the Study of China', *Asian Survey 22*, No. 10 (1982): 934–958.

49   Fairbank, *China Perceived*, p. XVI.

50   Cohen, 'American Perceptions of China', p. 83.

51   Karnow, 'Changing (Mis)Conceptions of China', p. 83.

52   Fairbank, *China Perceived*, pp. XVII, 169.

53   Cohen, 'American Perceptions of China', p. 86.

54   Karnow, 'Changing (Mis)Conceptions of China', pp. 285, 287.

55   Harding, 'From China with Disdain'.

56   Edward Payson Hall, Jr., 'A Methodological Approach to the Study of National Images: Perceptions of Modern and Traditional China and Japan', Ph.D. dissertation, University of Washington, 1980.

57   'Complex discrimination' was operationalized as the reported perceptions of both similarities and differences between the object country and the United States, while 'simple discrimination' was referred to as seeing only similarities or only differences of that country. Ibid., p. 111.

58   To be sure, there is a body of perception studies of Chinese images of other countries and international relations. Among others, see Jonathan D. Pollack, 'Chinese Attitudes Towards Nuclear Weapons, 1964–9', *The China Quarterly*, No. 50 (April/June, 1972): 244–271; E. Ted Gladue, Jr., *China's Perception of Global Politics*, Washington, DC: University Press of America, 1982; Yaacov Y. I. Vertzberger, *Misperceptions in Foreign*

Policy-making: The Sino-Indian Conflict, 1959–1962, Boulder: Westview Press, 1984; Gilbert Rozman, *The Chinese Debate About Soviet Socialism: 1978–1985*, Princeton: Princeton University Press, 1987; Shih Chih-yu, 'National Role Conception as Foreign Policy Motivation: The Psychocultural Bases of Chinese Diplomacy', *Political Psychology 9*, No. 4 (1988): 599–631; Harish Kapur (ed.), *As China Sees the World: Perceptions of Chinese Scholars*, London: Frances Pinter, 1987; Banning Garrett and Bonnie Glaser, 'Chinese Estimates of the US-Soviet Balance of Power' Washington, DC: *Occasional Paper*, No. 33, The Woodrow Wilson International Center for Scholars, 1988; and Allen S. Whiting, *China Eyes Japan*, Berkeley: University of California Press, 1989. For a succinct review of these and other related studies, see David Shambaugh, *Beautiful Imperialist: China Perceives America. 1972–1990*, Princeton: Princeton University, 1991, pp. 28–34.

59   Tu Wei-ming, 'Chinese Perceptions of America', in Oksenberg and Oxnam, *Dragon and Eagle*, pp. 87–106.

60   Ibid., p. 104.

61   Allen S. Whiting, *China Crosses the Yalu*, New York: Macmillan, 1960.

62   Whiting, *China Eyes Japan*, pp. 16–17.

63   See Allen S. Whiting, *The Chinese Calculus of Deterrence*, Ann Arbor: University of Michigan Press, 1975; 'New Light on Mao: Quemoy 1958: Mao's Miscalculations', *The China Quarterly*, No. 62 (June 1975): 263–270; Liao Kuang-sheng and Allen S. Whiting, 'Chinese Press Perceptions of Threat: The US and India, 1962', *The China Quarterly*, No. 53 (January/March, 1973): 80–97.

64   See Harold R. Isaacs et al., 'China and America: Looking at Us Looking at Them', Boulder: The China Council of the Asia Society, September 7, 1978; Michael Hunt et al., 'Mutual Images in US-China Relations', Washington, DC: *Occasional Paper*, No. 32, The Woodrow Wilson International Center for Scholars, 1988.

65   For instance, David R. Arkush and Leo O. Lee (eds.), *Land Without Ghosts: Chinese Impressions of America From the Mid-Nineteenth Century to the Present*, Berkeley: University of California Press, 1989; Patricia Neils, *China Images in the Life and Times of Henry Luce*, Savege: Rowman & Littlefield, 1990; Jonathan Goldstein, Jerry Israel, and Hilary Conroy (eds.), *America Views China: American Images of China Then and Now*, Bethlehem: Lehigh University Press, 1991, Christopher Jerspersen, *American Image of China 1931–1949*, Stanford: Stanford University Press, 1996. The image study of Sino-American relations has also drawn more attention among Chinese scholars in China. The most extensive and in-depth study in Chinese is Yusheng Yang's *Zhongguoren de meiguoguan, yige lishi de kaocha* (Chinese Images of the United States, A Historical Survey), Shanghai: Fudan University Press, 1996. Another book in this regard is Jishun Zhang's *Zhongguo Zhishifenzi de Meignoguan 1943–1953* (Chinese Intellectuals: Impressions and Views of the United States 1943–1953) Shanghai: Fudan University Press, 1999.

66   Steven W. Mosher, *China Misperceived: American Illusions and Chinese Reality*, New York: Basic Books, 1990.

67   For example, Warren Cohen periodized the changing American perceptions into 1784–1841: Era of Deference; 1841–1900: Era of Contempt; 1900–1950: Era of Paternalism; 1950–1971: Era of Fear; 1971–Present: Era of Respect. See 'Mutual Images in US-China Relations', pp. 31–36.

68   David Shambaugh, *Beautiful Imperialist*. This book is based on his earlier Ph.D. dissertation, 'China's America Watchers' Images of the United States, 1972–1986', University of Michigan, 1988.

69   Shambaugh, *Beautiful Imperialist*, p. 41.

70   For the general trend of American feeling toward China, see Harding, *A Fragile Relationship*, p. 372, Figure, A.1; Niemi, Mueller, and Smith,*Trends in Public Opinion*, p. 66, Table 2.20.

71   *The Gallup Poll, Public Opinion 1972–1977,* p. 40.

72   Karlyn H. Bowman, 'Public Attitudes toward the People's Republic of China', in James R. Lilley and Wendell L. Willkie II (eds.), *Beyond MFN, Trade with China and American Interests,* Washington, DC: AEI Press, 1994, p. 147, Table A.1.

73   Ibid.

74   *The Gallup Report,* May 1989, p. 3.

75   Ibid., August 1989, p. 13.

76   See Harding, *A Fragile Relationship.*

CHAPTER 2 ·
CONCEPTUAL FRAMEWORK AND
METHODOLOGY

The Significance of the Topic

The foregoing literature and historical review of the perceptual study of international relations in general and of Sino-American relations in particular, establishes the rationale for this study in both theoretical and practical terms. First, previous analyses of national images and perceptions in international relations leave much to be improved. In general, the advent of the post-Cold War era requires a new typology and focus of research. Second, most studies of Sino-American relations have been structurally, functionally, or policy oriented and have paid insufficient attention to psychological-perceptual dimensions of the relationship. The swift change in mutual perceptions sparked by the Tiananmen crackdown and its constraining effects on the well-being of the Sino-American relationship in recent years underscore the psychological fragility of the two peoples' images of one another. This phenomenon reinforces the relevance and importance of exploring the formation and evolution of Sino-American mutual images. Yet the change and continuity in mutual images since 1989 remain to be systematically investigated.

Of course, the question can be put in a more generic fashion: why study national perceptions and images in the first place? A simple answer is that the perceptions and images one country holds of another influence its policy and behaviour toward that country and, consequently, affect interstate relations. In addition, international behaviours 'become explainable only when we know, or can accurately guess, the subjective interpretations and beliefs of the people involved'.[1] Therefore, the primary objective of studying national images is to explain and understand international behaviour.

Nevertheless, as Alexander George notes, the 'causal nexus' between cognitive beliefs and foreign policy behaviour is not easily discovered.[2] The relationship is not consistently clear, even in the most controlled psychological experiments, not to mention in the more complicated and uncertain context of international relations. People's cross-situational consistency of behaviour tends to be low, and their attitudes frequently are poor predictors of their actions.[3] Efforts to establish a causal relationship between foreign policy decision-makers' belief systems and their policy behaviour have not always been satisfactory.[4]

The reasons are not difficult to discern. As Alexander George points out, perceptions influence, but do not unilaterally determine decision-making behaviour. They are only one variable-cluster within a rich and complex causal framework for explaining decision-making. At most, belief systems such as the operational code introduce 'diagnostic propensities' that influence policy-makers' diagnoses of situations in certain directions, and 'choice propensities' that lead them to favour certain types of action and alternatives over others.[5] In other words, it is extremely difficult to find a direct causal relationship between perceptions and behaviour unless these 'other influences' are minimized and the measured attitude is specific to the observed behaviour.[6]

Moreover, numerous psychological experiments have shown that attitudes and behaviour have a reciprocal relationship, each feeding upon the other. Whereas people's behaviour may be predicted by their attitudes under some conditions, under other conditions, behaviour also can have an impact on attitudes. In other words, attitudes quite often follow actions.[7] For instance, it is plausible to argue that the change in Sino-American mutual perceptions initially was triggered by Ping-Pong Diplomacy and Nixon's visit to China in the early 1970s. With this in mind, it can be said that the importance of studying national images or perceptions lies not only in their influence on national behaviour, but also in their tendency to be influenced by interactions among nation-states. The relationship between the two variables involves a process of constant reinforcement of and adjustment toward one another, rather than a deterministic, unidirectional movement.

In short, while the ultimate purpose of studying national perceptions and images is to explain international behaviour, it is impossible to find a one-to-one correspondence between perceptions and behaviour. Therefore the concept of causality in its narrow sense cannot be applied. The significance of the subject must be viewed more broadly. First, it is necessary to explore the explanatory power of national images using a long-term rather than a short-term perspective. The study of mutual perceptions between nations can enhance people's understanding of other countries as well as their own. A better understanding among nations surely will lead to more realistic foreign policies in the long run. Of course, more differentiated and sophisticated national images may not overcome real conflicts of interest that exist among nations. They are likely, however, to create a better perceptual environment under which conflict and cooperation are more sensibly handled. For that reason, relevant research on national perceptions and images is not necessarily devoted to the direct, short-term connection between perceptions and behaviour. Rather, a study that illuminates perceptions in themselves—their structures, evolution, and sources—can be important to the discipline of international relations.

Second, the interaction between national images and international behaviour should be viewed from a more dynamic and dialectical perspective. Interactions (either direct or indirect) between nation-states are not just conditioned by people's pre-existing images, but also modify and evolve these images. In other words, the sophistication of national images tends to be achieved through interactions with other countries. This dynamic relationship, however, has rarely been examined in the study of Sino-American mutual images.

The Scope of the Study

Although the importance of national images in international relations does not need much elaboration, the difficulties in operationalizing such images are considerable. Indeed, they 'have never been surrendered easily to empirical study or quantification'.[8] As implied in my previous analysis, the study of images or perceptions can be pursued from different angles. For analytical purposes, national images can be treated as independent, intervening, or dependent variables.[9]

(1) *National images as independent variables.* Under this scheme, images or perceptions of a foreign nation are used to explain national behaviour (whether foreign policy actions or other actions) toward that foreign country, either alone or together with other independent variables. The process can be represented diagramatically as in Figure 2.1.

Figure 2.1 National Images as Independent Variables

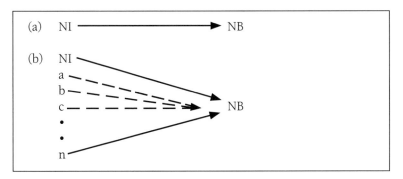

(2) *National images as intervening variables.* Under this research design, images are not directly related to policy outcomes. They nevertheless affect the information-gathering process of policy-makers. This mode of analysis focuses on how incoming information affects action after being 'filtered' through images or perceptions (see Figure 2.2).

Figure 2.2 National Images as Intervening Variables

(3) *National images as dependent variables.* This method explores the factors that determine the formation, structure, persistence, and change of national images or perceptions. This type of study could take a pattern similar to that of the first, but in a reverse direction (Figure 2.3).

Figure 2.3 National Images as Dependent Variables

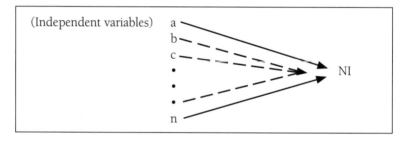

(4) *Reciprocal causation.* Under this scheme, the relationship between national images and behavioural variables (e.g. face-to-face contact, major events) is a dynamic process in which mutual reinforcement and adjustment can occur (Figure 2.4).

Figure 2.4 National Images and Behaviours as Reciprocal Causations

The first two modes of research very often are used in decision-making studies of foreign policy. In this study, the latter two modes will be the focus of inquiry. In other words, this study will not treat perceptions or images as independent variables to explain behaviour in Sino-American relations. Instead, Sino-American mutual perceptions per se—their structure, evolution, and sources—will be the subject for investigation, thus illuminating the nature, potential, and constraints of the relationship.

Any discussion of perceptions or images naturally gives rise to some problems of definition. First, whose images does this book want to investigate? When we talk about the American image of China or the Chinese image of the United States, what is generally being referred to is an image of the people in these two countries. People in either China or the United States, however, can be classified into different groups by various criteria. Each of these groups might have different images of the other nation. While it is convenient to talk about the American people's image of China or vice versa, such terms are meaningful only after the perceptions of major groups or classes in a country have been adequately assessed and aggregated from different levels. In fact, the term often is used in an impressionistic or sweeping manner. Nevertheless, to substantiate national images empirically, it must be made clear from the outset which categories of people provide the perceptions to be scrutinized.

Generally speaking, we can identify the national images of three groups: top decision-makers, the intermediate elite, and the general public.[10] In this study, the mutual perceptions of the intermediate elites in the United States and China will be the heart of enquiry. The term 'intermediate elite' is defined here as those people who usually are not directly involved in national foreign policy decision-making but who, nevertheless, are influential in forming the images held by the general public. This group also provides perceptual information concerning the other country to top decision-makers.[11] Of course, in reality, the boundaries among these three categories is by no means fixed.[12]

This choice is made for several reasons. First, the study of intermediate-elite perceptions is significant to an understanding of international politics because this group provides a bridge between the general public and top leaders. On the one hand, compared with the general public, their perceptions have much more influence on policy-making.[13] On the other hand, compared with a small number of top leaders, their perceptions are likely to be more representative of the general public's views and, therefore, to better reflect the general psychological mentality toward the target nation. Second, the intermediate elites have played an increasingly important role in Sino-US relations. The secret diplomacy of the 1970s involving a tiny number of top decision-makers has been replaced gradually by multi-channel and multi-level interactions in which intermediate elites, such as scholars, businessmen, and diplomats, are performing important functions; yet their perceptions and images have not been investigated adequately to date. Third, studying the perceptions of intermediate elites also has some methodological advantages. As previous studies have shown, data on the images of top decision-makers are the most difficult to obtain. Such studies, out of necessity, have relied primarily on public statements. The validity of these public statements as a representation of the real beliefs of top leaders is highly questionable.[14] These top leaders are usually unavailable for surveys or face-to-face interviews when they are in power. In this regard, intermediate elites are relatively more accessible for data-collection and are less self-censored in the expression of their true feelings and opinions. On the other hand, although data on the perceptions of the general public can be easily obtained in the United States, the theoretical generality of this data is uncertain, because the perceptions and images of the general public are less articulate and more subject to the influence of contingent events and manipulation. Moreover, the majority of public opinion surveys are oriented toward opinions on policy issues and do not specifically address factors that constitute primary images of a foreign country.[15]

The category of intermediate elite still represents a very large population that should be stratified. The following major clusters of Chinese and Americans are the foci of the study: intellectuals, business people, and diplomats. This study further narrows in on members of these three groups who are involved in Sino-American relations or who at least have a professional or personal interest in the target country. The decision to narrow the study in this way was made somewhat arbitrarily, but not without consideration.

Time and resource limitations are the most obvious reasons to exclude other categories of intermediate elite from my study. These three groups of individuals also have been the backbone of Sino-US interactions in the last two decades and are, therefore, of primary importance for this investigation. Relatively speaking, intellectuals have more sophisticated and systematic views of the other side and they play an important role in creating images of the other side in their own country. Business people are an increasingly important force in Sino-American interactions and yet their perceptions of the other side have seldom been examined carefully.[16] The same reasons also apply to diplomats, whose perceptions are virtually unknown to the public. The rationale for concentrating on the Chinese and American elites of these three groups is threefold. First, this study is not a simple-itemed public opinion survey that only elicits general knowledge about China or the United States. Rather, it attempts to tap the multi-dimensional structure of images, which may not be well-developed in the minds of those people who are not involved or interested in the target country. Second, a point to be elaborated on later, one of the plausible sources for perceptual changes to be explored, is cross-national interaction and contact. With Chinese and American elites' various degrees and types of involvement in Sino-American interactions, it is possible to examine the relationship between these two variables. Third, Chinese and American elites are supposed to be the most knowledgeable about the target country. Their images, therefore, may have greater impact in shaping the national mentality about the other side.

In summary, this book will endeavour to study Sino-American mutual images from the perspective of Chinese and American elites in three cohorts: intellectuals, business people, and diplomats. More specifically, intellectuals include scholars and professionals who have been active in various exchanges between the two countries. Business people are those people who have been involved in Sino-US economic collaborations. Diplomats consist of those governmental officials (active or retired) who have served in bilateral or multilateral settings related to Sino-American relations.

Modelling the Structure of Mutual Images

The next step is to define what kind of images or perceptions held by these three groups of elites will be examined. It seems that there is no universal definition for 'perception' or 'image' in either political science or psychology. Since it is difficult to reach an agreement on the hierarchy among such terms as 'belief system', 'operational code', 'image', 'perception', and 'attitude', many authors use these terms interchangeably in their studies.[17]

On a more abstract level, national images or perceptions belong to the philosophical dimension of George's operational code system. In George's terms, national image can be defined as a nation's perception of the fundamental character of its international political opponent.[18] Of course, national images encompass more than just images of an opponent or enemy. The following general categories of national image can be suggested: the national image of enemy, limited adversary, neutral, friendly non-ally, limited ally, and ally.[19] For instance, intuitively we may say that during the 1970s and 1980s, the mutual images of China and the United States were transformed from pure enemy images to those of friendly non-allies, or, for a short time, even those of limited allies.

How, then, can the concept of national image or perception be further substantiated and elaborated? In the simplest terms, national image can be defined as what the people of one country believe to be real or true of another nation.[20] Three basic characteristics of national image have been mentioned by various scholars. First, what accounts for a national image is not the objective reality of a foreign nation but the subjective construal of that country.[21] Second, national image is a set of ideas and thoughts about an objective country held fairly consistently by a subjective country.[22] Third, national image refers to the preconceived stereotype of a nation, state, or people that is derived from a selective interpretation of history, experience, and self-image.[23] In short, national images can be described by three S's: subjective, stable, and selective.

Having stated these basic characteristics of national images and perceptions, it is still necessary to find concrete indicators to facilitate empirical investigation. Certainly it is difficult to exhaust all the elements of national images in one study. At most this study can explore only a limited number of dimensions that are considered important. With this caveat in mind, a national image can be defined as consisting of three analytically distinct orientations toward a foreign country: cognitive, affective, and evaluative.[24] These perceptual dimensions can be applied to concrete attitude objects: specifically, Chinese or Americans as people; China or the United States as a society; China or the United States as a cultural identity; and China and the United States as a dyad in international relations. Thus, the attitudinal dimensions and object dimensions of Sino-American mutual images can be consolidated into the following 3 × 4 matrix.

Table 2.1 Dimensions of Mutual Images

	Of People	Of Society	Of Culture	Of Dyad
Cognitive				
Affective				
Evaluative				

While the four object dimensions are self-evident, the three attitudinal orientations need further elaboration before they can be used to measure national images. Cognitive orientation concerns the general knowledge one has of a foreign nation. This knowledge consists of both factual elements (such as geographic location, population, history, and form of government) and more abstract elements generalized from factual elements (such as the perception of a nation as strong or weak, democratic or totalitarian, benign or threatening). In this study, the main purpose is not to test the factual knowledge of 'Chinese elites' and 'American elites' but, more importantly, to determine the degree of structural or dimensional complexity of their mutual images. This structural complexity comprises two measurements: outer differentiation and inner differentiation. Outer differentiation measures the extent to which people perceive the target nation and their own nation as similar or different. Inner differentiation measures the degree to which people perceive the various objects within the target country as unitary or pluralistic.

Affective orientation concerns the general feeling one has about various aspects of a foreign country. This orientation can be simplified into the dichotomy of favourableness and unfavourableness with specific references. However, for this research, the importance of this orientation lies in measuring the degree of consistency or discrepancy in people's feelings concerning the four specified attitude objects of the target nation.

Evaluative orientation taps elites' judgements about the four objects of the target country. They 'typically involve the combination of value standards and criteria with information and feelings'.[25] In this study, they are reflected in people's positive or negative appraisal of the target country. This orientation also involves respondents' 'attribution' propensity, that is, how American and Chinese elites interpret the causes of the phenomenon in the target country. The attribution can be either 'disposition-based' or 'situation-based'.[26] The former tends to emphasize the importance of personal, societal, or cultural idiosyncrasies of the target country while the latter pays attention to the importance of objective situations under which various phenomena take place in the target country. Another characteristic of this orientation is people's 'reference' propensity. Stated otherwise, people tend to view the target nation in a dynamic rather than a static way, and will evaluate phenomena in the target country in either vertical (history) or horizontal (other countries) comparisons.

Cognitive psychology assumes that there is some degree of congruence among people's cognitive, affective, and evaluative propensities. Therefore, two standard models of mutual images can be hypothesized. Image I postulates that cognitively, people may perceive a high degree of outer differentiation and a low degree of inner differentiation regarding the target country. That is, they see big differences between China and the United States, but little difference among various objects within China or the United States. Because of their low inner differentiation, their feelings toward different objects in the target country are fairly consistent: either overall favourable or overall unfavourable. Moreover, due to a high level of outer differentiation, these people tend to make 'dispositional' attribution in evaluating phenomena in the target country. On the other hand, in Image II people may perceive a low degree of outer differentiation and a high degree of inner differentiation regarding the target country. Consequently, they tend to view developments in the subject country as 'situational' rather than 'dispositional'. The linkage among various components of these two image models can be highlighted by a diagram (see Figure 2.5).

Figure 2.5 Structure of Two Standard National Image Models

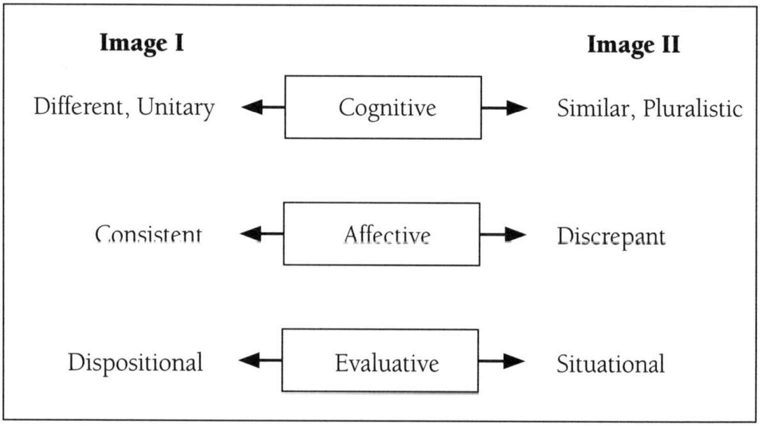

Image I		**Image II**
Different, Unitary	← Cognitive →	Similar, Pluralistic
Consistent	← Affective →	Discrepant
Dispositional	← Evaluative →	Situational

One major hypothesis of this study is that a transition from Image I to Image II has taken place in Sino-American mutual images since the 1970s, indicating perceptual sophistication. Of course, these two standard models greatly simplify the inherent complexity of reality. The actual attitudes of Americans and Chinese toward each other vary along the continuum of these three orientations. While some people may demonstrate a high degree of cross-dimensional consistency in their images, others may show inconsistency and ambiguity. For others still, it may be difficult to distinguish conceptually various dimensions of national images. The function of this conceptualization is to treat national images as a system in which various dimensions or elements are related to one another.

Modelling Interaction and Perceptual Change

Having conceptually defined the structure of Sino-US mutual images, we now turn to the task of modelling the change in Chinese and American elites' perceptions toward the other side and the sources of change since the 1970s. Of course, perceptual continuity and change are determined by numerous variables. As far as the Sino-US relationship is concerned, most of these variables can be placed under the heading of Sino-US interactions. The concept of interaction, however, needs more clarification. Although the term has been used pervasively in the perceptual-psychological literature of international politics, articulated definitions have been scant. In psychological terms, the concept of social interaction directs attention to 'properties of the feedback process by which organisms influence each other'.[27] Interaction can thus be regarded as a process of mutual influence upon participants' perception and behaviour.

This study will focus on two forms of interaction that are more likely to have an impact on the mutual images of selected Chinese and American elites. One form is indirect interaction, wherein one party learns about the other through third sources, such as reading, listening to the radio, watching television, etc. The second form is direct interaction: face-to-face interaction and person-to-person contact between mainland (PRC) Chinese and Americans in different institutional settings and with regard to different issues. Direct interaction was almost non-existent between PRC Chinese and Americans from 1950 to 1970, but has become a salient feature of the relationship since then, and thus deserving of particular attention. These two forms of on-going interaction can be upset by major events, either in bilateral developments (e.g. Nixon's visit to China in 1972), or in international developments (e.g. the Soviet Union's disintegration in 1991). Although the majority of people's images about the other side are not based on a single event but result from generalizations of experience over time, dramatic events such as the 1989 crackdown in China could lead to considerable readjustments in perceptions. The interesting question here is what impact 'reorganizing' events, such as the Tiananmen Incident, have on perceptions that have changed incrementally over long periods of contact.

To further elucidate the relationship between interaction and perceptual change, this study will draw upon literature in both political science and social and cognitive psychology concerning social interactions and attitude changes. Some caveats about the application of psychological theories in the study of international relations are in order. There is extensive literature on attitude and perception change in the field of cognitive and social psychology. While there have been some serious attempts to apply psychological theories to the study of international relations and foreign policy,[28] nothing similar has been done in the study of Sino-American relations. As many of these authors are well aware, the application of psychological theories to the study of international relations has certain limitations.[29] First, there is little consensus among psychologists themselves on important issues concerning belief systems, attitude change, and interaction dynamics. Different authors refer to different theories and empirical evidence for different purposes. Second, psychological theories are usually based on well-controlled and manipulated laboratory experiments that by no means can be replicated in the real world of international politics. Third, the subjects of most psychological experiments are American college students and the experiments are usually done in American settings. The cultural idiosyncrasies of the findings render their applicability to cross-national studies such as this one questionable. In short, the translation of psychological theories to the reality of international politics is no easy job.

Realizing that theories from psychology cannot be applied indiscriminately to the study of international politics, one still cannot deny the possibility that relevant psychological theories may shed important light on some aspects of the field. As Kelman argues, even though an experiment or simulation cannot establish with any degree of certainty that a relationship observed in the laboratory holds true in the real world, it can establish that such a relationship is at least plausible under certain circumstances. Therefore, psychological theories can make contributions to one's systematic thinking about international relations as opposed to providing final scientific verification of propositions about international relations.[30] Of course, the point of departure and the criterion of relevance must be the substantive concerns of international relations rather than those of experimental psychologists. Therefore, this study will not try to test systematically various psychological theories in the setting of Sino-American relations. Rather, the theories are presented as heuristic models for better conceptualizing and understanding the perceptual changes, as well as the relationship between interaction and perceptual evolution.

With cross-national interaction as the main explanatory variable, four heuristic models of the maintenance and change of Sino-American mutual images can be hypothesized to guide empirical research.

(1) *The static model.* This model, derived from assumptions about the inherent deficiencies of human inference and judgement, largely emphasizes the obstacles to profound change in established national images or stereotypes through interactions. Many psychologists stress the theory-driven nature of social perceptions and behaviour. They point out that too often people are obsessed by their pre-existing 'knowledge structures' or 'schemata' in interpreting new information. These 'schemata' are frequently incorrect and biased.[31] The well-known Bennington studies demonstrated that beliefs and perceptions formed under certain social circumstances could survive

for a very long time.[32] Prejudice and stereotypes, once established, have their own self-perpetuating dynamics which direct people's biased interpretation of disconforming information and create a selective memory for conforming information.[33] Festinger's cognitive dissonance theory[34] assumes that people feel tension when two of their perceptions or beliefs are psychologically inconsistent. In such cases, people quite often will reduce the dissonance by explaining away new evidence that runs counter to their pre-existing perceptions.[35]

In brief, as Boulding concludes, 'The national image is the last great stronghold of unsophistication.'[36] This model has found considerable empirical evidence in the study of international relations.[37] In light of this model, we can regard both Americans and Chinese as 'consistency-seekers' in their perceptions toward each other. Their characterization of the other side is often unduly influenced by prior beliefs and images that are very resistant to change. Therefore, it is the pre-existing images and perceptions which condition interactions rather than the other way around. While some superficial changes in peripheral mutual perceptions, induced or dictated by circumstances, can be observed between Chinese and Americans, the central or master concepts of an 'enemy image' shaped during the Cold War have remained intact in the last three decades. This can be approximately described as in Figure 2.6.

Figure 2.6 A Static Model of Perceptual Change

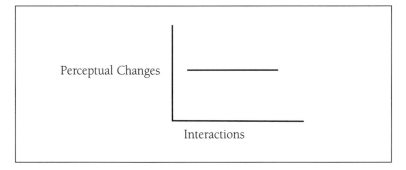

(2) *The linear model.* In contrast to the static model, this model assumes that there is a linear relationship between Sino-American interaction and perceptual change. The more interaction between the two peoples, the more likely it is that their distorted perceptions, forged by mutual hostility and isolation in the past, will alter. The school of communication and attitude change in social psychology underpins this model. This approach

is exemplified by the work of Carl Hovland and his associates at Yale University.[38] The main premise of this theory is that perception and attitude can change in response to persuasive communication through social interactions. It assumes that people are rational, information-processing organisms who can be motivated to learn and acquire new opinions and perceptions through structured communication. The process of communication and persuasion involves many functional variables, including source, message, and audience.[39]

Social psychologists have suggested two routes to persuasion and attitude change—central and peripheral routes. The difference between these two routes rests with people's motivation, ability, and involvement in the process of communication. The central route occurs when people are highly motivated and involved in the issue, and are able to comprehend and 'elaborate' on the message they are receiving. The peripheral route occurs when each of these three factors is low, and people use simple-minded heuristics to evaluate communication. Experiments indicate that persuasion via the central route is likely to produce an enduring attitude change. Moreover, the level of involvement is an important determinant of the quality of persuasion and consequent attitude change.[40]

In accord with this model, we may hypothesize that a learning process occurred during Sino-American interactions in the last three decades. Each side made attempts to persuade the other side to alter a formerly negative image of itself using various means. Because 'China elites' and 'America elites' usually are heavily involved in interactions and are intellectually capable of elaborating on messages from the other side, the central route of persuasion is most likely to occur. Although numerous independent factors may either facilitate or impede the effectiveness of a persuasive message, the on-going interaction process in itself has enough reinforcement dynamics to effectively open the mindset of the communicators. The great 'discrepancy' between American and Chinese elites' pre-existing images and the 'messages' they have received through interaction and observation expedites their attitude change. Of course this model alone cannot predict the direction potential perceptual changes may take. That depends on whether the information generated or received has been mostly positive or negative. In other words, the content of interactions could produce altered opinions and feelings toward one another with an upward or downward linear slope as shown in Figure 2.7.

(3) *The fluid model.* While the static model focuses on the restraining forces for perceptual changes, this model emphasizes the inconsistency and irregularity of perceptual change. It is supported by several important psychological theories. First, it is derived from the tradition of situationism

Figure 2.7 A Linear Model of Perceptual Change

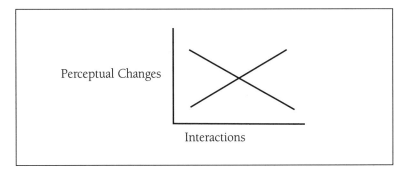

Perceptual Changes

Interactions

in social psychology starting with the work of Kurt Lewin. This approach stresses the power of social situations to produce attitudinal and behavioural changes.[41] It argues that people's perceptions and behaviours often are determined by circumstances, and their cross-situational consistency is very low. Sometimes apparently insubstantial manipulations of situational factors can change people's perception and behaviour dramatically. A related explanation is D. J. Bem's self-perception theory.[42] This theory postulates that people frequently do not have well-formed perceptions of an attitude object and therefore must derive attitudes from behaviour, which often is dictated by the situation. Moreover, people's perceptions often consist of a tension system in which various contradictory elements are precariously balanced.[43] Therefore, any external stimuli may topple this balance and compel perceptual changes. In sum, this model points to the fluctuation of human perceptions and behaviours, which are subject to the influence of situational variability. This model implies that people are not 'consistency-seekers' in their cognitive activities, but are 'problem-solvers' who seek to find perceptual attributions for practical purposes.

Using this model, Sino-American perceptions of each other can be assumed as unstable variables. Perceptions are contingent reflections of specific situations. As Sheila Johnson notes, 'National stereotypes are based on immediate impressions of people and events rather than upon some deep-seated, immutable force known as national character.'[44] Chinese and Americans do not seek to keep a consistent image of the other, rather they tend to adjust their perceptions to specific bilateral or international events. Therefore, a constant perceptual flux is observable in American and Chinese perceptions, and this flux is related to big events and major policy shifts in Sino-American relations. As a result, there is no persistent or enduring direction of change in mutual images. For instance, the hostile mutual perceptions resulting from the Tiananmen Incident have the potential to be replaced by opposite views if major positive events occur in the relationship. Of course, the perceptual flux might be asymmetric between the two countries, because the same event can be construed differently by Chinese and Americans. This model can also be described by a rough diagram (Figure 2.8).

Figure 2.8 A Fluid Model of Perceptual Change

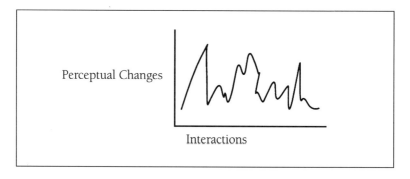

(4) *The curvilinear model.* Whereas the linear model describes Sino-American perceptual change as a linear function of interaction, this model draws people's attention to the possible regression phenomena in accounting for perceptual change.[45] The regression principle tells us that, in the long run, the values measuring the impact of a given phenomenon tend to return to the mean, since the mean is a baseline from which an index usually only deviates by a certain amount. For example, a study of foreign students studying in the United States found a U-shaped curve in their changing images of America. Foreign students typically started with a highly positive attitude toward the United States, but gradually became more disillusioned. Beyond a certain time, however, they gained a deeper and more sophisticated image of the United States that was closer to reality.[46]

In the case of Sino-American perceptual changes, instead of assuming a simple upward or downward trend, we may take into account some natural 'regression' through repeated on-going interactions. More specifically, we may hypothesize that in the early stages of Sino-American rapprochement, the mutual perceptual evolution moved in an upward direction. Both sides constructed an excessively positive image of the other side. Nevertheless, with the routinization and substantiation of interactions, the initial idealization of the other side started 'regressing' to perceptions closer to reality or even declining toward more negative images as a result of frustration from mutual disillusions. This process, however, could be either part of a spiral representing a growing sophistication of mutual images or simply a cycle eventually returning to the original starting point. The model is shown in an approximate diagram in Figure 2.9.

Figure 2.9 A Curvilinear Model of Perceptual Change

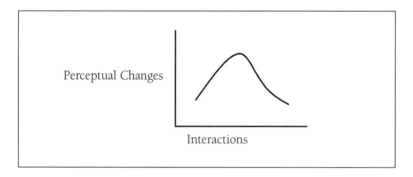

These four models are designed only for conceptual and analytic purposes. In reality, they are neither mutually exclusive nor typologically exhaustive. Nevertheless, each model may capture cognitive variables not included in the others. For example, the static model emphasizes the intransigence of pre-existing images; the linear model draws people's attention to the effective communication flow during interaction; the fluid model stresses the importance of situation; and the curvilinear model focuses on inherent tendencies in perceptual evolution. All these factors can be incorporated into a dynamic process of interaction. The main task is to determine which model is more powerful in explaining Sino-American perceptual changes, and to substantiate these general models with empirical evidence.

Methods and Data

The core of this study is a set of more than two hundred interviews conducted in both the United States and China. Given the nature of elite studies, some methodological problems need to be discussed.

Face-to-Face Interviews
The primary data-collecting method applied in this research was the structured, face-to-face interview with cross-sectional samples of three

clusters of Chinese and American elites: intellectuals, business people, and diplomats. Despite its limitations, this approach best served my research purposes.

First, I was interested in doing a comparative study of Sino-American mutual images. A structured questionnaire approach can yield comparable data sets by posing the same essential questions on both sides. This has an advantage over a literature or documentary survey in which a systematic comparison is more difficult. Second, an interview approach can elicit mutual images and perceptions of a wider range of Chinese and American elites than reliance on written materials. Both in the United States and China, the number of those who have the privileges and opportunities to articulate their images of the other side in public writing is limited. A literature survey, therefore, is more likely to be biased in that it only represents the opinions of those elites whose professions require published writing. The extent to which their views are representative of other elites is unknown. Interviewing, however, can provide opportunities for those who usually do not make their opinions known publicly to articulate their perceptions of the target country. Third, the interview method can provide insights into people's mindsets more directly than merely reading what people have written. In addition, as reviewed in Chapter 1, Shambaugh's and Mosher's studies of mutual images already made good use of written sources. On the Chinese side, Yusheng Yang's recent book conducted a fairly thorough survey of the literature in Chinese on the China image of the United States.[47] Therefore, instead of reusing the available materials, it is preferable to 'create' data that did not exist previously. This approach provides an original data set and a different lens through which readers can validate or falsify the inferences about mutual images from studies using other approaches.

Interviews aimed at eliciting people's images inevitably involve problems with the validity of data. People may not be willing to reveal their real perceptions or honest feelings about the other side. They simply may not know the answers and give off-the-cuff, uninformed reactions. While these problems cannot be ignored in using the interview approach, problems of the same nature also exist in other modes of data collection. For instance, it is common knowledge that what people write or say publicly may not fully reflect what they think privately. Perfect methodologies do not exist and researchers are forced to choose the one most suited to the analysis of their particular research problem. We can only minimize but not eliminate the problems of validity and reliability. By creating a private interview setting in which the interviewer and the respondent can establish a degree of rapport, the possibility of spontaneous thought-flow is higher than in other modes of data collection.

Sampling

As mentioned earlier, the main research subjects are three strata of intermediate elites in both countries. Ideally, one would like to draw a simple random sample from each stratum and then join subsamples to form the total sample. However, for technical reasons it is not feasible for this research. Among other things, as is often the case in elite studies, it is hard to determine the exact population for each stratum, especially in the case of business people and diplomats. It is nearly impossible on the Chinese side. Without a reasonably accurate account of the population, probability sampling is impossible and, consequently, a truly representative survey is out of the question. Even if the sampling problem was solvable, time and resource limitations prevent the application of such an approach, since potential respondents might be spread throughout the two countries. In addition, China's political situation at the time of this research made it even more unrealistic to carry out a standard survey of the elite's perception of the United States. Consequently, even if a random sample could be obtained in the United States, the failure of the same effort in China would have made a comparative study less valid because of the asymmetric database.

When probability sampling is not viable, 'softer' methods such as purposive and chain referral sampling have to be applied. Of course, such sampling techniques inevitably reduce the external validity of the data. That is, it limits the extent to which the findings from the sample could be used statistically to estimate population parameters. Still, the method may serve the research objective of this study reasonably well. As described earlier, this research attempts a preliminary exploration into the structure of mutual images, their social and psychological mechanisms, and their sources of perceptual change. In other words, while it is desirable to capture the mainstream of mutual images of Sino-American elites, this research does not intend to generalize beyond the sample to the larger populations. Given the nature of this study, a probability sample may not be as critical as is normally the case, since we are more interested in obtaining ideas, good insights, and the variety of image patterns.[48]

Questionnaire Development

The interview instrument is always crucial to the quality of data. In designing the questionnaire, the initial choice was whether to make the interviews structured or unstructured. A structured interview means that the interviewer asks the same basic questions of all respondents, while an unstructured interview allows circumstances to decide what kind of questions will be asked. Because unstructured interviews produce incomparable data, they are ill-suited to the research goal of doing a comparative study. In developing a structured interview instrument, the initial choice was to use closed-ended or open-ended questions. Each format has its advantages and disadvantages. Although closed-ended questions are easy to answer and code, they may impose constraints on respondents and impede the natural flow of their thoughts. As closed-ended questions only provide a limited number of choices, they are unlikely to elicit opinion in depth. On the other hand, open-ended questions allow respondents to convey the fine shades of their opinion in a relatively unconstrained way, and thus motivate respondents to produce richer and more valid answers. Nevertheless, it is highly demanding for post-interview coding and there is a risk of information loss or distortion due to the difficulty of pigeonholing responses into limited coding schemes.

A combination of closed-ended and open-ended questions was employed for several reasons. While closed-ended questions are more suitable to measure knowledge of facts and attitudes toward clear-cut policy issues, they are not well-suited to measuring general perceptions and images. The pretest[49] showed that intellectually sophisticated people often resisted closed ended questions because they believed their thoughts were too rich to be put into a few categories and turned into numbers. Given the elite nature of the sample and the subtlety of the subject, closed-ended questions alone were inadequate to tap mutual perceptions. On the other hand, an entirely open-ended instrument and typical Lane-type intensive interviews were too time-consuming for the respondents, who were usually very busy, and for the post-interview data analysis. A combination of the two modes of questions, therefore, produced a desirable balance for the needs of this research. Closed-ended questions provided base-line data for comparison and open-ended responses produced more differentiated information to interpret closed-ended responses and to help formulate new hypotheses.

The content of the interview instrument was built on the three major research questions defined earlier: the underlying structure of mutual images, the patterns of perceptual change, and the sources for perceptual formation. Specifically, it incorporates, among other things, respondents' basic views on the target country concerning the four attitude objects: people, society, culture, and international behaviour; their perceptual changes since the 1970s along these four dimensions; their sources of image formation; and some demographic information.[50] The American and Chinese versions of the questionnaire were designed with the same structure and format. For most of the questions, only the name of the target country was changed. However, the content of some questions had to be redefined to accommodate the different conceptions and stereotypes in the Chinese image of the United States.

Cross-National Comparability

As discussed earlier, relatively few studies in the field of international relations have conducted interviews with respondents from both sides of an important dyad. While the approach immediately puts the findings in a comparative perspective, making them intellectually more illuminating and interesting, it also complicates the study methodologically. The main challenge is to achieve 'comparability'. In other words, if the two data sets are not comparable in some important ways, the subsequent comparative analysis will be invalid. There are several aspects to this problem.

First, interviewees must be as comparable as possible. That is, it is necessary to elicit perceptions and images from the same kinds of people in both countries. If an interviewer talks to high-level officials in one country but talks to people on the street in the other, the data thus obtained will not be comparable at all. To secure matched subgroups cross-nationally is always a difficult business. In this research, the overall comparability lies in the fact that the respondents in each country were composed mainly of individuals who had been involved in Sino-American affairs in various fields. To further increase the comparability, people from comparable professions in both countries were interviewed. The three groups defined as study targets provided a basic check for comparability.[51] More specifically, the intellectual subgroup in both countries consisted of professors in universities, scholars in research institutions, and a small number of other professionals, such as exchange officials, writers, and journalists. Of course, the percentage of each cluster within each sample was not exactly the same. For instance, I interviewed more professors and fewer think-tank researchers in the United States than in China. Nevertheless, the intellectual respondents were comparable at least in some aspects. For example, most of them studied social science rather than natural science and many of them were so-called China or America watchers in their respective countries. For the business people subgroup, the majority of respondents were involved in Sino-American economic relations. In this sense, they were counterparts. The most salient difference between them was that most American business people were working in the private sector, while their Chinese counterparts tended to work in the public sector. This is why many Americans do not think there are many genuine business people and entrepreneurs in China.[52] This difference may well affect the comparability between the two subgroups. However, the divergent nature of the two countries' political and economic systems restricted the ability to control for this difference. In any event, functionally, they were still comparable. The diplomats were the most comparable, since both groups functioned in an official capacity within the foreign service.

Second, interview stimuli should be as comparable as possible for both Chinese and American respondents. As described above, except for some questions that reflect different characteristics of each society, most questions were direct translations with changes only in the country's name. Naturally, the Chinese and American respondents might have different understandings of the same concepts. For this reason, no survey instruments can be made precisely comparable. For Chinese and American respondents, the same definition could mean different things. It is assumed, however, that elites in both countries share more, on a conceptual level, than ordinary people do. This is particularly the case among this set of respondents, whose frequent contact with the other side helped them acquire some common vocabulary to facilitate communication. Moreover, most questions were phrased in quite general rather than specific terms. It could be argued that the more general a dimension is, the more likely it is to have cross-national validity, since people's understanding of it could well overlap.

Another source for inequivalent stimuli is language. Chinese and English are very different languages. Some English words and expressions are hard to translate accurately into Chinese. Nuances might be lost in translation. Yet the fact that I did interviews with both samples and can speak both languages fluently allowed me to clear up or prevent misunderstandings. When questions were confusing, I could rephrase them or paraphrase their content to the respondent. This increased the comparability of the interview instruments despite the difficulties in achieving equivalent stimuli in cross-national studies.

The problem of instrument incomparability may not be as critical in this study as it could be in other studies. For one thing, this is not a comparative study of people's attitudes toward an identical subject. Rather, it concentrates on Chinese and Americans' perceptions of one another. Therefore, as long as the concepts serve roughly the same functions in their respective structure of image and tend to form parallel cognitive relationships, an identical understanding of concepts is not necessary.

Finally, interview environments should be as comparable as possible. This issue has both spatial and temporal dimensions. While interviews were carried out in two different countries, the specific interview settings were quite comparable. Most interviews were conducted in respondents' offices. Some respondents preferred to be interviewed in their homes. Usually the surroundings were private enough to avoid being interrupted or monitored by others. Another possible source of non-equivalence is the time when the interviews were conducted. Temporal comparability can be maximized by conducting the interviews within approximately the same time frame. If the interval between field research in the two countries is too long, many events could take place and they might affect people's perceptions. My entire fieldwork covered a period of 16 months, during which no dramatic intervening events took place in Sino-American relations. The aftermath of the 1989 crackdown still could be felt among the respondents. However, after more than a year, people were much less emotional in their reflections. The only big international event during this period was the Gulf War. If the Tiananmen crackdown had a greater impact on the American image of China, the Gulf War affected the Chinese image of the US considerably. Since formal interviews in China did not start until June 1991, however, the recency effect might not be as strong as it would have been if the interviews on the Chinese side had been carried out in the midst of the war.

With these methodological questions in mind, I conducted my fieldwork in the United States and China during 1990–1992. In the United States, I interviewed 141 respondents, located in Washington DC, New York City, San Francisco, and Los Angeles. In China, I interviewed 127 Chinese respondents, located in Shanghai, Beijing, and Guangzhou.[53] The results of these interviews constitute the primary database for this study.

All in all, while no efforts were spared to make the research as rigorous as possible, some compromises had to be made to render the study feasible and to keep a balance between cost and benefit. I am convinced that the necessity for rigour ought not to undermine a willingness to tackle problems of significance. We should follow our intellectual interests wherever they lead, while fully realizing that even the best available methodology is far from perfect. All the limitations notwithstanding, the data collected represent an effort never before attempted, and provide a rich source for a solid and novel study of Sino-American mutual images.

Notes to Chapter 2

1 Lee Ross and Richard Nisbett, *The Person and the Situation: Perspectives of Social Psychology*, Philadelphia: Temple University Press, 1991, p. 60.
2 See his analysis in 'The Causal Nexus'.
3 Richard Nisbett and Lee Ross claim that the inability to bridge the gap between cognition and behaviour 'is the most serious failing of modern cognitive psychology'. See *Human Inference: Strategies and Shortcomings,* Englewood Cliffs: Prentice-Hall, 1980, p. 10.
4 For example, Cheryl Koopman's study on American elite views of relations with the Soviet Union shows that no belief factors can explain more than about a third of the variance in policy preferences. See Koopman, 'American Elite Views of Relations with the Soviet Union', *Journal of Social Issues 45*, No. 2 (1989): 119–138.
5 George, 'The Causal Nexus', p. 103, pp. 109–111.
6 David Myers, *Social Psychology,* New York: McGraw-Hill, 1983, p. 41.
7 For a summary of this reciprocal relationship, see Ibid., Chap. 2.

8   Philip Converse, quoted in George, 'The Causal Nexus', p. 104.

9   This conceptualization draws heavily on Sjoblom's essay, 'Some Problems of the Operational Code Approach', pp. 40–41.

10 For discussions on this issue, see Boulding, 'National Images and International Systems', and Kelman, *International Behaviour*, pp. 3–39, 565–607.

11 These people are usually called 'national leaders' or 'opinion-makers', defined by Rosenau as 'those members of the society who occupy positions that enable them to transmit, with some regularity, opinions about foreign policy issues to unknown persons'. See James Rosenau, *National Leadership and Foreign Policy: A Case Study in the Mobilization of Public Support*, Princeton: Princeton University Press, 1963, p. 13. Robert Putman calls them the 'influential elite', defined as people with 'substantial indirect or implicit influence; those to whom decision-makers look for advice, whose opinions and interests they take into account, or from whom they fear sanctions'. See *The Comparative Study of Political Elites*, Englewood Cliffs: Prentice Hall, 1976, p. 11.

12 Under some circumstances, the intermediate elite could become either a part of the general public (for example, in a nationwide probability survey), or a part of top decision-makers (when some of them are recruited into the governmental foreign policy-making apparatus).

13 As Kelman says, when decision-makers speak of public opinion, they generally think in terms of influential congressmen, newspaper editors, or leaders in various non-governmental organisations. See *International Behaviour*, p. 584.

14 Lenczowski, *Soviet Perceptions of US Foreign Policy*, p. 20; Whiting, *China Eyes Japan*, p. 19.

15 Hall, *A Methodological Approach to the Study of National Images*, pp. 15–16.

16 In recent years, there emerged some studies about the American business experience in China, e.g. Jim Mann, *Beijing Jeep: the Short, Unhappy Romance of American Business in China*, New York: Simon & Schuster, 1989; and Randall Stross, *Bulls in the China Shop and Other Sino-American Business Encounters*, New York: Pantheon Books, 1990.

17 For discussions on the conceptual relationship among these concepts and their different usages among some political scientists, see Finlay, *Enemies in Politics*, p. 29; Rosati, *The Carter Administration's Quest*, p. 16; George, 'The Causal Nexus', pp. 96–97; and Whiting, *China Eyes Japan*, p.18.

18 The first question of George's philosophical beliefs regarding OC includes: 'What is the fundamental character of one's political opponents.' See George, 'The "Operational Code": A Neglected Approach', p. 201. Later, David Lampton and Ole Holsti further operationalized this question. See Lampton, 'The US Image of Peking in Three International Crises', p. 29, and Holsti, 'The "Operational Code" As an Approach to the Analysis of Belief Systems: Final Report to the National Science Foundation Grant, No. SOC75-15368', pp. 61–65. Their operationalization, however, was basically done in the framework of enemy image.

19 In his refinement of the OC system, George had already mentioned the concept of 'limited adversary'. See 'The "Operational Code": A Neglected Approach', p. 221. Ole Holsti in his efforts to develop a codebook for OC added 'other significant political actors'. Nevertheless, he did not conceptually differentiate the image of political opponents and of other actors. See '"The Operational Code" As an Approach', p. 61. In his critique of the OC approach, Sjoblom points out that the limitation to the opponents is arbitrary and unnecessarily narrow. See 'Some Problems of the Operational Code Approach', p. 61.

20   See Hall, *A Methodological Approach to the Study of National Images,* pp. 20–21.

21   Boulding, *The Image,* p. 6.

22   Rosati, *The Carter Administration's Quest,* p. 16.

23   Whiting, *China Eyes Japan,* p. 18.

24   I adopt this typology largely from Gabriel Almond and Sidney Verba's conceptualization of political culture. See *The Civic Culture: Political Attitudes and Democracy in Five Nations,* Princeton: Princeton University Press, 1963, pp. 12–26. Many authors who study national images have more or less followed this tradition, e.g. William Scott, 'Psychological and Social Correlates of International Images', in Kelman, *International Behaviour,* pp. 72–77; and Finlay, *Enemies in Politics,* pp. 31–32.

25   Almond and Verba, *The Civic Culture,* p. 15.

26   Individuals' attribution tendencies have become a keen subject of inquiry in the field of social psychology in recent decades. A variety of attribution theories have been developed to explain how people make inferences about others' behaviour. In general, people tend to attribute others' behaviour either to internal causes (for example, the person's disposition) or external causes (for example, something about the person's situation). These theories draw attention to various attribution fallacies in social thinking. See David Myers, *Social Psychology,* New York: McGraw-Hill, 1990, pp. 70–81; Harold H. Kelley and John L. Michela, 'Attribution Theory and Research', *Annual Review of Psychology,* Vol. 31 (1980): 457–501; and John H. Harvey and Gifford Weary, 'Current Issues in Attribution Theory and Research', *Annual Review of Psychology,* Vol. 35 (1984): 427–459.

27   Robert B. Cairns (ed.), *The Analysis of Social Interactions: Methods, Issues, and Illustrations,* Hillsdale: Lawrence Erlbaum Associates, 1979, p. 4. Kelman points out: 'By social interaction I do not simply mean the behaviour of individuals in one another's presence, but their mutual attempts to assess and affect one another's goals, images, expectations, and evaluations, as they act and react vis-à-vis each other.' See Kelman, *International Behaviour,* p. 22.

28   See Finlay, *Enemies in Politics;* Jervis, *Perception and Misperception;* Deborah Welch Larson, *Origins of Containment: A Psychological Explanation,* Princeton: Princeton University Press, 1985; and Rosati, *The Carter Administration's Quest.*

29   See Jervis, *Perception and Misperception,* pp. 3–6; Jonsson, *Cognitive Dynamics and International Politics,* pp. 6–7; and Kelman, *International Behaviour,* pp. 596–597.

30   Kelman, *International Behaviour,* pp. 599–600.

31   Nisbett and Ross, *Human Inference,* Chap. 2, 8.

32   This is a classic study of social influence conducted in the late 1930s by Theodore Newcomb. It shows that originally conservative women students formed more liberal political preferences after having been exposed to the environment of Bennington College. Their political orientation remained unchanged even after more than 20 years. See Ross and Nisbett, *The Person and the Situation,* pp. 35–38, and Theodore M. Newcomb et al., *Persistence and Change: Bennington College and its Students after 25 Years,* New York: Wiley, 1967.

33   Finlay elaborated on various ways to reject new information. See *Enemies in Politics,* pp. 31–36. Also see R. Vallone, L. Ross, and M. Lepper, 'The Hostile Media Phenomenon: Biased Perception and Perception of Media Bias in Coverage of the Beirut Massacre', *Journal of Personality and Social Psychology* 49, No. 3 (1985): 577–597; and Myers, *Social Psychology* (1983), pp. 458–459.

34   L. A. Festinger, *Theory of Cognitive Dissonance,* Stanford: Stanford University Press, 1957.

35 This theory has been applied widely to explain discrepancies between people's behaviour and attitudes. People can either adopt a new attitude to fit their behaviour or can change their behaviour to fit their perception. See Myers, *Social Psychology* (1983), p. 58.

36 Boulding, *The Image,* p. 130.

37 See the literature review in Chapter 1.

38 Carl I. Hovland, Irving Janis, and Harold Kelley, *Communication and Persuasion,* New Haven: Yale University Press, 1953.

39 Philip Zimbardo and Ebbe Ebbesen, *Influencing Attitudes and Changing Behaviour,* Menlo Park: Addison-Wesley, 1969, pp. 15–20.

40 Robert B. Ciadini, Richard Petty, and John Cacioppo, 'Attitude and Attitude Change', *Annual Review of Psychology,* 32 (1981): 365–366; Joel Cooper and Robert T. Croyle, 'Attitude and Attitude Change', *Annual Review of Psychology,* 35 (1984): 415–416; and Sharon Brehm and Saul Kassin, *Social Psychology,* Boston: Houghton Miffin, 1989, pp. 446–449.

41 Ross and Nisbett, *The Person and the Situation,* pp. 27–58.

42 D. J. Bem, 'Self-Perception: An Alternative Interpretation of Cognitive Phenomena', *Psychological Review,* No. 74 (1967): 183–200; and 'Self-Perception Theory', in Leonard Berkowitz (eds.), *Advances in Experimental Social Psychology,* Vol. 6, New York: Academic Press, 1972, pp. 2–62.

43 Ross and Nisbett, *The Person and the Situation,* pp. 13–17.

44 Sheila K. Johnson, *The Japanese Through American Eyes,* Stanford: Stanford University Press, 1988, p. 166.

45 Nisbett and Ross, *Human Inference,* pp. 150–154.

46 Ithiel de Sola Pool, 'Effects of Cross-National Contact on National and International Images', in Kelman, *International Behaviour,* pp. 115–117.

47 Yusheng Yang, *Chinese Image of the United States.*

48 For a more detailed discussion of sampling procedure, see Appendix A.

49 The pretest is described in Appendix A.

50 Details about the interview instrument can be found in Appendix C.

51 For statistical profiles of American and Chinese respondents, see Appendix B.

52 This situation, however, has been changing in recent years with the boom of the private sector in China.

53 For a detailed description of fieldwork, see Appendix A.

CHAPTER 3 ·
MUTUAL IMAGES OF PEOPLE

As Chapter 1 showed, during the Cold War era, the perceptual-psychological study of international relations focused on the cognitive problems of foreign policy decision-making rather than on national images in a broader sense. Furthermore, within the domain of national image studies, the perception of 'people' was seldom treated as an important subject of inquiry. Instead, national images were articulated in an abstract and narrow fashion. More often than not, national images, especially those of antagonistic countries, formed around a target country's government or its prominent national leaders. This was particularly the case in Sino-American relations. Owing to the lack of direct contact and interaction, the American image of 'Red China', as Isaacs pointed out, was very abstract and had little differentiation and substance.[1] This was equally true on the Chinese side. The Chinese image of the US was preoccupied with a very abstract concept of 'American imperialism', which was symbolized by a few notorious American politicians such as John Foster Dulles. In both countries, the images of Chinese or Americans as people were submerged in a black and white projection of government and ideology. They tended to be negatively stereotyped.[2]

The primary assumption of this chapter is that in terms of cognitive structure, perceptions of the people of a target nation provide a necessary, albeit insufficient, foundation for understanding and evaluating other more abstract dimensions of the target country. Therefore, a complete inquiry into national images should start with the study of images of people in both aggregate and individual terms. Most studies of Sino-American mutual perceptions since the 1970s have ignored this important dimension.

It can be hypothesized that with ever-increasing multi-channel and multi-level interactions between American and Chinese elites since the 1970s, their mutual images of people will show a considerable degree of concreteness, complexity, and sophistication. This process of sophistication may be reflected mainly in the following three respects. First, as elaborated in Chapter 2, their mutual images may demonstrate a lower degree of outer differentiation and a higher degree of inner differentiation. Second, their attribution of difference or similarity between them and the target people may be more discriminating in terms of 'disposition' (personality) and 'situation' (social traits). Third, while the general trend of perceptual evolution has been positive, the euphoria during the 'China fever' or 'America fever' period may have been replaced by more balanced and critical viewpoints. With regard to perceptual change, social psychology theories assume that processes of communication and cooperative interactions generally will increase the level of interpersonal liking.[3] An upward linear model, therefore, may better 'fit' this image dimension. We assume that the dramatic Tiananmen event did not disrupt this upward trend. Rather, the mutual images of heroic Chinese demonstrators for democracy and spontaneous American support of this movement may have reinforced positive mutual images.

General Cognitions of People

Throughout this study the four dimensions of mutual images have been measured by a set of questions structured to elicit cognitive, affective, and evaluative orientations of the American and Chinese respondents. For each dimension, respondents on both sides were first asked to articulate some general cognitions of the target country in an open-ended fashion. The purpose was to elicit some of their most salient image components spontaneously. In the image domain of people, respondents were initially asked: 'When you think about the Chinese/American people, what comes to your mind first?' Although their immediate reactions to this question may not necessarily reflect their image in its entirety, their responses are likely to convey their most memorable or retrievable impressions. Table 3.1 summarizes the American respondents' general cognitions of the Chinese people.

Table 3.1 General Images of the Chinese People (Sample Size = 141)

Subjects	Number of Cases	Proportion (%)
Personality Traits		
Hard-working	45	31.9
Friendly, warm	31	22.0
Intelligent	26	18.4
Goal-oriented	16	11.3
Humorous	14	9.9
Resourceful, pragmatic	13	9.2
Easy to deal with	12	8.5
Reserved	11	7.8
Open, frank	10	7.1
Cruel, selfish, rude, etc.	10	7.1
Attractive	8	5.7

Table 3.1 (*cont.*)

Subjects	Number of Cases	Proportion (%)
Confident, patient	7	5.0
Trustworthy, committed	6	4.3
Helpful, concerned	6	4.3
Curious, inquisitive	5	3.5
Social traits		
Cultured, courteous	22	15.6
Disciplined, conformist	16	11.3
Family and education-oriented	12	8.5
Poor, peasantry	12	8.5
Suffered a lot	12	8.5
Sophisticated human relations	7	5.0
Eager to join the world	7	5.0
Patriotic	3	2.1
Demographic traits		
Many of them, numerous	18	12.8
General remarks		
Diversified	17	12.1
Positive feelings	12	8.5
Specific images	10	7.1
Very different, no image	9	6.4
Not very different	7	5.0

Note: Since each respondent could mention more than one feature, the percentages in the table represent the proportion of respondents who mentioned each subject. Therefore the total of percentage distribution does not add up to 100%. This also applies to other tables of the same kind.

The responses were coded into two broad categories: personality traits and social traits,[4] along with demographic traits and general remarks. The table suggests that for most American respondents, their initial cognition of the Chinese people focused on personal dispositions rather than on social traits. These personal traits are mostly positive rather than negative. Many of these traits can be found in traditional American images of the Chinese. They apparently have re-emerged under the new conditions of Sino-American relations.[5] Several dimensions of these dispositions can be delineated. One dimension is about the attitudes toward work, career and life. Almost one-third of the respondents described the Chinese as 'hard-working', 'industrious', 'diligent', and 'productive'. Related to that, Chinese were seen as 'highly motivated' and 'very achieving' people.[6] Some American respondents were particularly impressed by the resilient attitude of the Chinese toward life. They portrayed the Chinese as 'resourceful', which means they have extraordinary capacity to deal with difficulties and sufferings.[7] Many Americans perceived the Chinese as having had quite a bitter life experience, either from historical or contemporary perspectives. In their contact with Chinese, they were often told personal ordeals in such episodes as the Cultural Revolution. For Chinese, these stories were nothing more than common experience. But for Americans, they were no less than legends. It is often the case that what was regarded by the Chinese as normal living conditions was perceived as unbearable for the Americans.

Another dimension of the Chinese personality that emerged concerns the way they deal with other human beings. In this respect, many American respondents saw the Chinese as 'friendly', 'warm', 'concerned', and 'trustworthy'. The third dimension incorporates some dispositions the American respondents found admirable and pleasant in the Chinese such as being 'intelligent', 'curious', 'attractive', 'humorous', and 'self-confident'.[8]

Owing to these qualities, the American respondents usually found the Chinese 'easy to deal with'. However, they seemed to have different opinions regarding whether the Chinese are 'open' or 'reserved'. Some respondents perceived the Chinese as 'outgoing', 'straightforward', and 'forthcoming', while others described them as 'enigmatic', 'suspicious', and 'self-contained'. This perceptual gap can be found in their answers to other questions as well. As the subsequent analysis will demonstrate, at least three explanations can be suggested for this phenomenon. First, Americans found Chinese more open when compared with Japanese and other Asian peoples, but more reserved when they were compared with Americans themselves. Second, Americans saw the Chinese as quite open in initial contact or superficial social functions, but quite reserved in more substantial relations. Third, the Chinese were viewed as quite open in personal relations but quite reserved in official capacities.

In all these dimensions, only a handful of the respondents mentioned some unpleasant qualities of the Chinese such as 'cruel', 'rude', 'selfish', and 'lazy'. As their responses to other questions will show, this does not necessarily mean that most respondents did not have any negative images in their minds. Rather, it only indicates that for most American elites, what came first to their minds were positive rather than negative traits.

A smaller proportion of the American respondents mentioned some social traits of the Chinese people. In this category, cultural, political, and developmental themes were touched upon to characterize the Chinese socially. The most frequently mentioned trait is the 'cultured' or 'civilized' quality of the Chinese. This quality does not just mean that Chinese are 'polite', and 'courteous', but more importantly, contains the historical and cultural accumulation of wisdom and sense. In the words of a professor: 'You can really see the influence of four thousand years of civilization, even on uneducated Chinese. You don't quite see that anywhere else in Asia.' This 'cultured' quality is reflected in the 'highly developed social skills' and 'sophisticated human relations' among the Chinese.[9]

If American elites perceived the Chinese as rich in cultural heritage, they also considered them poor and backward in terms of modern development. A professor noted, 'At all levels of sophistication, from the lowest to the highest, I am aware that the country contains a lot of people of low skill.' This gap might be even greater perceptually than in real terms for some respondents. A businessman declared that the Chinese 'always project a feeling of not being up to date—backward—although I know in many areas, it tends to be different from what you later learn'. This cognition about the 'backwardness' of Chinese also has some political connotations. Chinese were described as 'surviving the system' in their daily life, which is 'more time-consuming and looms larger' than in the United States.

The Chinese were seen by some to be partially responsible for their suffering, because politically they possess a conformist tendency toward government and authorities. Some American respondents apparently found this a paradox: 'On the one hand, Chinese are competent and resourceful, on the other hand, they are weak due to their lack of individual integrity and confidence, and easily shaped by social and political processes.' While Chinese have 'a great sense of responsibility toward people they know and their family members', they have 'less sense of duty toward public things' and 'don't care much about politics, big politics, high politics'. As the subsequent data will demonstrate, this cognitive dissonance of perceiving the Chinese as culturally superior but politically and economically inferior is a major configuration of ambivalence in the American image.

A considerable proportion of respondents cast their perceptions of the Chinese in more general terms. Some respondents demonstrated intrinsic positive feelings toward the Chinese, which has always been part of the traditional American image.[10] More importantly, these remarks reflect a certain degree of perceptual sophistication and differentiation through personal contact and interaction with Chinese. On the one hand, some respondents expressed a low level of 'outer distinctions'. They did not see the Chinese as 'distinct from everybody else'.[11] On the other hand, they showed a high degree of 'inner distinctions' and found that 'Chinese are more diversified than people realize'. The ambivalence, as often seen in their remarks, indicates a resistance to stereotypes and hence perceptual sophistication. A diplomat had the following comments:

> It's hard to say because it's a whole jumble of ideas. The more one learns about China, the more time one spends in China, the more difficult it is to answer that question. Images get flooded in my mind, but sometimes very contradictory ones. The cliché of inscrutable Orientals is something I just don't believe in. It comes to my mind, but I don't agree with that. Inevitably I think of friends, colleagues, and people I met. The problem is that I think Chinese have been very hard-working because many of the people I know have been. Yet I also visited far too many offices and factories where no one did any work. It's difficult to characterize.[12]

The initial reactions of the American respondents indicate that their perceptions of the Chinese are multidimensional rather than unidimensional, including dispositional, cultural, political, economic as well as demographic aspects. This cognitive complexity is also reflected in their 'outer' and 'inner' differentiation, and their cognitive dissonance in perceiving the Chinese as open versus reserved; culturally rich versus materially poor; personally resourceful versus politically weak, and so forth.

Does a similar cognitive pattern of discrimination and multidimension apply to Chinese perceptions of Americans? What kind of distinctive 'American character' impresses the Chinese elites most? Table 3.2 presents their general cognitions.

At first glance, several compatible trends are evident. First, the initial Chinese perceptions of Americans also focus more on personal traits. Second, most traits mentioned are positive rather than negative. Third, many personal traits were also mentioned by the Americans in their perception of the Chinese. However, the social traits Chinese respondents had in mind are essentially opposite to those the Americans ascribed to the Chinese.

The two most frequently mentioned words about the Americans are 'frank' (*tanshuai*) and 'open-minded' (*kaifang*). In contrast to the American perception of Chinese reservedness, almost four out of ten respondents described Americans as 'frank'.[13] This characteristic basically means two things to the Chinese respondents. First, it implies that Americans do not conceal their views but tell you what they think (*xiangshenme shuoshenme*). Second, it means that Americans are direct and give you 'yes' or 'no' answers.

Table 3.2 General Images of the American People (Sample Size = 127)

Subjects	Number of Cases	Proportion (%)
Personality traits		
Frank, candid	46	36.2
Open-minded	30	23.6
Easy to deal with	24	18.9
Friendly, warm	22	17.3
Hard-working	16	12.6
Pragmatic	15	11.8
Enterprising	13	10.2
Naive, shallow	12	9.4
Honest	10	7.9
Sanguine	9	7.1
Kind, generous	9	7.1
Vigorous, energetic	7	5.5
Easy come, easy go	6	4.7
Social traits		
Arrogant	19	15.0
Civilized	16	12.6
Poor understanding of China	10	7.9
Individualistic	9	7.1
Never suffered	5	3.9
Treating people as equal	5	3.9
Law-abiding	4	3.1
Demographic traits		
Immigrants	7	5.5
General remarks		
Diversified	14	11.0
Specific images	12	9.4
General good feelings	4	3.1
Not very different	4	3.1
Very different	2	1.6

Some Chinese considered that 'Americans have square heads and they don't know how to turn around'. When Chinese spoke of Americans as 'open', it meant that Americans are broadminded and not bothered by different opinions. Unlike dealings with the Japanese where 'you have to consider whether what you say will make them unhappy', 'you can argue with Americans in the first meeting'. 'Even if you argue with him until you are red in face, you can still be a good friend of his.' Some respondents even held that 'if you don't argue with Americans, they will not take you seriously'. Mainly because of these two traits, a portion of the respondents found that 'Americans are easy to deal with' compared to other foreigners.

A more complicated trait perceived by Chinese is so-called 'naivety' (youzhi). As we will see in the following discussion, many Chinese applied this term in a positive sense to indicate that Americans are not as 'complicated' as Chinese are. However, to some Chinese respondents, 'naive' might also mean something not so attractive. It could imply that Americans are 'immature' and 'emotional'. As a researcher put it: 'Americans are people of moods. . . . When they think everything is OK, they have a very high mood. When they think things are bad, their mood suffers a sharp decline.'

'Naive' may also mean 'shallow'. Chinese found Americans 'easy to deal with', but difficult to make 'real friends' with by the Chinese definition. They used the term yijiao yiwang ('easy come, easy go') to describe the American style of dealing with Chinese. Again comparing Americans with other foreigners, they found that 'Americans are easy to get into contact with and easy to get to know, but they also tend to forget you very quickly', whereas the British and French are usually cool at the beginning but 'could become lasting friends eventually'. Therefore, some respondents even discovered the reserved side behind the apparently outgoing Americans. A professor remarked:

> I think Americans have a stronger defensive device than the Chinese do. The Chinese, as soon as they know you well, don't care talking about personal affairs. Yes, Americans are outgoing on the surface, but in their heart, they have a very clear boundary. For foreigners like me, it's hard to lay one's heart bare with Americans.

So here we can see the function of a 'mirror image': both Americans and Chinese saw each other as open and easy-going, yet they found it difficult to turn the superficial acquaintanceship into a deep friendship. Their cognitive attributions for this trait, however, are somewhat different. While American elites perceived the Chinese as too 'deep' (reserved), Chinese respondents perceived the Americans as too 'shallow' (fuqian).

Some of the personal traits listed in the table, such as 'hard-working', 'friendly', 'warm', 'honest', and 'kind', can also be found in American cognition of the Chinese. In contrast to the American image of the Chinese, few Chinese respondents described Americans as 'intelligent'. This might have something to do with their perception of American 'naivety'. For some Chinese respondents, 'naive' could mean 'dumb'.[14] The Chinese elites were more impressed by the American 'enterprising' (*jinqu*) and 'pragmatic' (*wushi*) spirit. Yet American pragmatism could also contain both positive and negative connotations: on the one hand Americans were seen as practical (*shiji*) and 'seeking truth from facts' (*shishi qiu shi*); on the other hand Americans are 'short-term-oriented' and only see 'interests under their noses'. In this regard, conflicting perceptions arise and a cognitive balance is not easy to maintain for Chinese.

Like their American counterparts, the Chinese respondents also perceived Americans as 'civilized'. For both sides, the term implies 'politeness' and 'courtesy', but a subtle perceptual difference exists. In American eyes, Chinese are 'civilized' in terms of historical and cultural background. It is more an observation of mindset than of behaviour, and is not necessarily related to people's formal education or training. For the Chinese respondents, what they had in mind was the 'civilized' quality of Americans in terms of their education and behaviour, often citing things such as not spitting, not pushing around in public, and observing public order.

While Americans might be 'civilized' in their personal behaviour, psychologically they were also perceived as 'arrogant' and 'swollen with pride'.[15] This 'arrogance', as we will see in following chapters, is one of the core images held by the Chinese elites and has a trans-dimensional function in their image-articulation. The sources of this image could either come from personal experience or simply be a deduction from predisposition. Some respondents had had tough negotiation experiences with Americans and found them 'often taking a commanding position' and displaying 'a mentality of a superpower'. Others simply concluded that Americans 'have a smell of arrogance in their bones'. Such an assertion apparently did not have to be supported by direct evidence. With regard to the manifestation of this trait, American arrogance could be expressed either consciously or unconsciously. A foreign affairs officer held that Americans, including 'friendly personages' (*youhao renshi*) often showed a mentality of 'bestowing a favour on you' (*enci*): I come here to help you, even though 'many things are mutually beneficial'. By doing so, 'Americans hurt people unconsciously'.[16]

What makes this trait more unattractive to the Chinese elites is that Americans 'lack an understanding of China'. Here we can see another 'mirror image'. While some American respondents perceived the Chinese as 'lacking an understanding of the world', some Chinese respondents concluded that Americans 'lack an understanding of other countries'. As a foreign affairs official asserted, 'Some Americans are ignorant of China. I think generally speaking the Chinese have a better understanding of the United States than Americans have of China.' Chinese businessmen also found that Americans 'are far less informed than the Japanese are about China'. Interestingly enough, both sides tended to believe that they understood the target country better than the other way around. This cognition, of course, leads to a propensity to blame the other side for the problems in relations.

In contrast to the 'arrogance' image of Americans, however, some Chinese respondents perceived that 'Americans treat people as equals' (*pingdeng*). What they had in mind was not the American attitudes toward other nations, but rather the fact that within the United States, Americans treat people from all over the world 'equally' in relative terms. American intellectuals particularly were perceived as more 'liberal and internationally-oriented' and 'not caring too much about race and nationalities'. This 'equality' image represents another cognitive orientation that often is in tension with the 'arrogance' image.

In their initial image articulation, not many Chinese respondents mentioned political and economic traits of Americans. However, two traits contrary to what Americans observed of the Chinese were touched upon. First, Americans were perceived as 'individualistic'. While some Chinese respondents appreciated the high value Americans placed on individual character and freedom, others perceived Americans as 'slack' and 'random'. As the analysis in the rest of this chapter and following chapters will demonstrate, the 'individualistic' perception provides another important source of cognitive ambivalence for the Chinese respondents in their evaluation of American society and culture.

Second, in historical and developmental terms, Americans were perceived as 'lucky people' who 'have never suffered'. In the words of a scholar, 'They are like children from wealthy families (*fujia zidi*) and don't know what hardship is.' This trait, as a foreign trade official put it, leads to a tendency for Americans to 'seek pleasure and avoid hardship'. This 'lucky Americans' image, as we will see in Chapter 4, provides a cognitive source to explain the socio-economic gap between the two countries.

With the demographic traits of 'immigrants' and 'United Nations' in mind, Chinese elites also expressed a considerable degree of cognitive differentiation in their general remarks. Compared to the United States data, the Chinese respondents were more sensitive to 'inner differentiation' of the

American people. While some respondents still applied a traditional Marxist method of dividing Americans into 'ordinary people' (*laobaixing*) and 'ruling class' (*tongzhi jieji*), others preferred non-political differentiation. They found Americans 'very diversified' (*duoyanhua*) and 'miscellaneous' (*za*). They felt it was hard to tell 'what a typical American is'. An intellectual offered the following comments:

> As for Americans, in the past the Party always warned us to watch out for 'the American lifestyle' (*meiguo shenghuofangshi*). We have been told for many, many years that the American lifestyle is not decent and a reflection of the most corrupt part of the bourgeois way of life. As if there was indeed an American way of life. After my contact with Americans, I found it didn't exist because Americans are so diversified. Many immigrants have maintained their traditional way of life such as the Chinese in Chinatown. There is no such thing as a unitary American lifestyle.

With their routinized contact and interaction in academic, social, and business environments, some Chinese no longer perceived Americans as 'foreign devils' or 'people from another planet'. Despite different political and cultural backgrounds, they found 'the ordinary people (*laobaixing*) under heaven are the same'. A university professor who dealt with American experts teaching in China concluded: 'I don't feel that they have some evil intentions in mind and attempt to influence me. Not at all. They are just scholars as we are. They are not different from us.'

Overall, the Chinese elites displayed the same type of positive and discriminative orientation in their primary image of Americans. The spectrum of their perceptions is wide. Cognitive inconsistency and dissonance also exist in their perceptions: candid Americans versus shallow Americans; open-minded Americans versus ignorant Americans; arrogant Americans versus egalitarian Americans; civilized Americans versus dissipated Americans. This cognitive complexity is further reflected in their responses to other questions posed in the interviews.

Degree and Content of Cognitive Differentiation

One hypothesis set out in Chapter 2 is that with the on-going contact and interaction between American and Chinese elites, their outer differentiation of the other side should decrease and their inner differentiation of the other side increase. The open-ended data in the previous section reveals this trend regarding mutual images of people. In this section, a more systematic effort was attempted to measure and elicit the degree and substance of outer differentiation of people perceived by American and Chinese respondents. Respondents were asked to indicate their outer differentiation along a 7-point scale in answering the following question: 'Considering Chinese/ Americans as individuals, would you say that Chinese/Americans are very different from or very similar to Americans/Chinese?' Table 3.3 compares American and Chinese responses.

Table 3.3 Percentage Distribution of Cognitive Differentiation of the Chinese and American Peoples

Cognitive Differentiation	Percentage (%)	
	US Respondents	**Chinese Respondents**
1 (very different)	2.8	14.3
2	20.0	29.4
3	24.3	19.8
4	20.7	26.2
5	22.1	7.9
6	10.0	2.4
7 (very similar)	0	0
Total	100.0	100.0
Sample size	140	126
Mean/SD	3.73/1.37	3.00/1.26

Looking at Table 3.3, it is quite clear that for both samples, more respondents chose points on the 'different' rather than the 'similar' side of the scale. This indicates that they perceived more differences than similarities between the Americans and Chinese. Apparently the American elites had a considerably lower degree of outer differentiation than the Chinese elites did. While more than six in ten Chinese respondents opted for 1–3 points, less than half of the American respondents selected the same numbers. Moreover, only about 3% of the American respondents went as far as 1, whereas about 14% of the Chinese respondents selected this number. On the other hand, about one-third of the American respondents picked numbers from 5 to 7, while only about one in ten Chinese respondents made the same choice. This perceptual gap can be further verified by comparing the two means. For the American sample, the mean score almost cancels out the difference and similarity, whereas the average view of the Chinese elites is definitely on the more different side.[17] Many Chinese respondents were only willing to go as far as the mid-point 4 and cognitively they were unable to think that Americans and Chinese shared more similarities than differences. On the other hand, the proportion of American elites who chose 5 is almost the same as those who chose 3.

This interesting phenomenon may be explained by several factors. First, it was not until the late 1970s that China started opening to the outside world. For most Chinese elites in this sample, contact with foreigners, including Americans, was a recent experience. But for many American respondents, even though they did not have the chance to contact Chinese from the Mainland until China opened up, they nevertheless had opportunities to contact Chinese in Taiwan, Hong Kong, or South-East Asia. Second, the Chinese became a part of the American community a long time ago. A sizeable population of Chinese in American society routinized American perceptions of the Chinese and thus possibly reduced their consciousness of outer differentiation. Third, of course, for historical reasons, the Chinese perception of foreigners (*waiguoren*) implies more difference than similarity by definition. The boundary between foreigners and natives is very clear-cut. For Americans, however, in a sense they are all 'foreigners'. The boundary between 'we natives' and 'they foreigners' is more ambiguous. Having said this, however, given their distinct historical and ethnic background and their recent exposure to foreigners, there is good reason to assume that the Chinese elites significantly reduced their outer differentiation between Chinese and Americans during 1970–1990. The fact that nearly 60% of the Chinese respondents selected points 3 and higher in part reflects this perceptual sophistication.

When the American and Chinese elites chose numbers on the scale, what kind of specific differences and similarities did they have in mind? Of course, choosing a number merely expressed a subjective feeling. It might be unrealistic to completely translate this feeling into empirical indicators of similarities and differences. Yet the scale does provide a point of reference with which respondents could sort out some concrete indicators to support their outer differentiation. So in a follow-up question, the respondents were asked to list some of the most important differences and similarities between Chinese and Americans.

In their specification, both American and Chinese elites tended to attribute the similarities to personality traits rather than to social traits. Consistent with the data in Table 3.1, a portion of Americans considered Chinese 'easy to get along with'. They attributed this to somewhat compatible personalities or, as some respondents put it, to 'some natural chemicals' leading to 'easy affinity'. A business person observed: 'If you put a group of Chinese in a room with a group of Americans, even if they don't speak the other's language, pretty soon they all are laughing and getting along well. I think the Japanese are very jealous of the way Americans and Chinese get along.'

For many American respondents, the perception of this similar personality is not a conclusion drawn from a direct comparison between Chinese and Americans. Rather, it is a function of 'reference power', which implies that people use other agents as a frame of reference in making cognitive judgements.[18] The American respondents often perceived this similarity by comparing Chinese with other peoples, such as Japanese and Russians.[19] The similarity became more salient given the profound historical and cultural differences between the two peoples. As a professor remarked: 'I might say, given the fact that the Americans and British shared very much the same history, I am more impressed with how different they are, while the Chinese are more similar though with a different history.' Some respondents tended to suggest that Chinese and Americans are different simply because of the social circumstances. As soon as they get out of China, they 'become different people' and 'very much like us'. Corresponding to the data in Table 3.3, this pattern of attribution seems to be more popular among the American elites.

What kind of perceived similar personalities did American respondents have in their minds? Interestingly enough, the most frequently mentioned similarity is 'humour'. Americans view humour as a highly desirable quality in human relations, and the perception that Chinese share this disposition with Americans contributed greatly to their affinity toward Chinese. The intriguing thing is, however, that Chinese seldom think of themselves as humorous. In their answers, no Chinese respondents mentioned 'humour' as a trait they share with Americans.[20] One possible explanation is that Chinese may become more 'humorous' when they stay with Americans. It seems that Americans were not so aware of the Chinese adaptability to circumstances and that their outward behaviour might not reflect their inherent disposition. This cognitive inclination to overemphasize 'situational factors' in China but neglect the same factor in the United States contributed to the Americans' tendency to attribute the difference between the Chinese and Americans solely to the Chinese social system.

In terms of social traits, the most frequently cited similarity is that Americans and Chinese both care about family, education, children, and so forth. Furthermore, as human beings, Americans and Chinese share some common social desires and goals such as, in the words of a businessman, 'economic security—our rice bowls should be filled every day; dignity— not be kicked around by authorities too much; and pride in being whatever they are'. Some respondents also mentioned that Chinese, like Americans, are quite individualistic, and 'have a healthy disrespect for authority' and 'a certain resistance to being packed into moulds'.[21]

As a function of 'reference power', Chinese elites also stated that Americans are more approachable and easy to get along with compared to other foreigners. It seems that an important theoretical proposition about national image articulation can be surmised: people perceive the similarities between themselves and the people of a target country indirectly by comparing the target people with others belonging to the same category. The interesting phenomenon, however, is that although Chinese and Japanese share the same cultural heritage, quite a few Chinese respondents found Japanese less approachable than Americans. As a businessman put it, 'Chinese and Americans can trigger sympathy in each other; you don't feel such things when dealing with the Japanese.'

Chinese respondents also echoed American perceptions on some shared qualities such as 'hard-working', 'friendly', 'open', and 'pragmatic'. In terms of being 'pragmatic', some respondents believed that Americans and Chinese 'all pay attention to this life rather than an afterlife' and 'deal with human relations on a practical basis'. In talking about openness, some Chinese respondents also attributed the outward difference between Chinese and Americans to social system. As a young scholar saw it, 'Americans and Chinese are both open. But Chinese cannot express their openness under China's social system. So when they find that Americans are open, they naturally like Americans, just as a father finds that his son has some characteristics he himself is unable to demonstrate.'

In social terms, some respondents also considered that Chinese and Americans share values on family, but they usually limited this similarity to intellectuals and scholars. Similar to the American perception of Chinese 'national pride', Chinese respondents saw both Chinese and Americans as 'patriotic' and 'seeking to enhance the power and wealth of our respective nations and trying to maintain a decent position among nations'. One important trait absent from the Chinese perception of similarity is 'individualism'. Although American respondents believed they shared some of the Chinese traditional values on family and children, Chinese respondents usually did not think they shared the Western value of 'individualism'.

Some American and Chinese respondents emphasized greater compatibility between certain groups of Chinese and Americans, such as intellectuals and Chinese who received Western or missionary education. A Chinese businesswoman, who went to a missionary school before 1949 and now was working in a joint venture, found that 'many old Chinese intellectuals are very similar to highly educated Americans' as they 'do things earnestly, are responsible, say things according to facts, keep promises, and value reputation'. An American educator also found that those Chinese who had been to missionary schools had a 'Judaic-Christian ethic' that makes them 'just a lot easier to work with'.

When it comes to the differences between Americans and Chinese, does the same attribution pattern apply? In contrast to the articulation of similarities, American elites preferred to attribute the differences primarily to social rather than to personal traits. The only personal quality that drew a sizeable response is 'reservedness'.[22] Here the point of reference often is Americans rather than other Asians. As a business person remarked: 'I would say an American, typically speaking, tends to be very open and tell you everything he knows. A Chinese typically tends to keep his cards very close to his chest and not tell you what he knows until he knows a little bit more first.' Although it is 'easy to get along with them on the surface', it is hard to understand them well due to their 'reluctance to let outsiders into their private thinking and their private work'. As another American businessman put it: 'After spending five two-hour meals with someone from Iowa [an American], I think I can understand what makes that person tick, a lot better than some of my Chinese friends. Although I can predict how they will react to most things, I don't know why they react that way.' From these remarks, we can see the remains of the traditional image of the 'inscrutable Chinese'.

More of the American elites attributed differences between the Chinese and Americans to their political, economic, and cultural backgrounds. They considered that 'the strongest difference is the different response to authorities'. There are two different modes of attribution. The first mode emphasizes the political control by the system in which 'Chinese authority is totally unlimited' and 'everything is top-down'. More respondents, however, applied the second mode of attribution: the Chinese tend to accept political control and pressure, and often fail to 'stand up to whatever society is delivering upon them'. In this regard, 'The average Chinese is less concerned, feels less direct responsibility for changing the political and social environment; Americans have the sense that if the social and political environment is not to their liking, they have the ability and even the responsibility to do something about it. . . . The Chinese direct their energy more to their families than to the social environment.'

This trait of political passivity is related to two other salient differences mentioned by many American respondents: the Chinese are more family- and group-oriented. While, in articulating similarities, some American respondents took family-orientation as a similarity, more respondents recognized the differences in the relationship between family and individuals, family size, the way children are raised, and the attitude toward elderly people. The group-orientation, according to some respondents, contributed to the Chinese political passivity and weak individualism at the conceptual level. As a scholar put it: 'Chinese are in some ways as individualistic as Americans are, but tend culturally to believe that is not a good thing. Americans are not only individualistic but accept individualism. China is a more collectivist society made up of individualists and America is an individualistic society made up of individualists.' The difference between the Chinese 'individualists' and American 'individualists', according to a diplomat, is that 'Chinese see themselves much more as part of large organizations. Their own personal goals and aspirations are important, but important in a different way, fitting into a large complex', while Americans 'can be focused much more on themselves and their own ideas apart from the general society'.

The stronger group-orientation anticipates another social difference between the Chinese and Americans—the nature of human relations. First, personal relations are more important for the Chinese. The Chinese social relationship 'is governed by *guanxi* (network) rather than by a legal framework', and the Chinese 'rely on informal relations rather than on institutions and law'. Second, the personal relationship is more complicated from the American perspective. While Americans are 'relatively unconcerned about the consequences of their interactions with other people', the Chinese 'are highly calculating.' As a professor put it: 'If I say good morning to that [Chinese] person, he is going to come back to me as an old friend and ask me to do something; in which case I can ask him three or four stages down the line'. Consequently, the Chinese concept and practice of friendship are more 'exclusive' and 'reciprocal'. As a researcher said: 'With regard to friendship, Americans tend to have a large number of shallower friendships, or better yet acquaintanceships. The Chinese tend to have a smaller number of more intense and exclusive friendships.'

To what extent did the Chinese elites share American perceptions on the differences between the Americans and Chinese? Does a similar pattern of attribution apply to the China data? Apparently Chinese respondents attributed differences more evenly to both personal and social traits. This pattern also confirms an earlier observation that American elites had a stronger inclination to attribute differences between Chinese and Americans to social environment, while Chinese elites saw more intrinsic differences in personalities.

In contrast to Americans' perception of the Chinese as more reserved, one in four Chinese respondents considered that Americans are more 'extrovert-oriented' (*waixiang*). 'Extrovert' is a neutral term in Chinese and it has both positive and negative connotations. Most Chinese respondents applied the term in a positive sense. They appreciated Americans' 'outgoing, frank, and sometimes even naive' personalities that, as a business person saw it, 'can reduce unnecessary frictions and channel people's energy to where it should be'. For some respondents, however, the word conveyed a somewhat negative connotation. They thought that Americans have a tendency to show off, 'even though they don't know very much'. In Chinese eyes, a thoughtful or sophisticated person is seldom *waixiang*. Only those who are not very knowledgeable would show off.

Some respondents found that 'the Chinese have a more complicated inside world (*fuza*), whereas Americans are more shallow (*qian*)'. While *qian* meant 'superficial' and 'ignorant' for some respondents, it meant 'simple' and 'transparent' for others. They conveyed the impression that 'in dealing with Americans, you don't have to guess what they think. What they are thinking will be reflected on their face'. In contrast, Chinese often 'think too much and make things too complicated' in dealing with Americans. This difference between 'shallow' and 'deep', according to some respondents, can cause a cognitive gap between the Chinese and Americans. As a young scholar phrased it: 'Chinese intellectuals do not have difficulty in understanding Americans, but American intellectuals have greater difficulty in understanding the Chinese.' This comment further underlines the earlier Chinese complaint that Americans have a poor understanding of China.

As mentioned earlier in their original images, the Chinese perceived Americans as 'more pragmatic' or 'short-term-oriented'.[23] As a researcher put it: 'The Chinese like to say how great the future will be and how brilliant the past was; Americans only pay attention to today and how to make life better today.' This different way of thinking is also reflected in many Chinese idioms such as 'study hard for ten years' (*shi nian hanchuang*), 'it is not too late to have revenge after ten years' (*junzi baochou, shi nian buwan*), and 'using ten years to make a knife' (*shi nian mou yi jian*).

This dispositional difference appears in social relations. For instance, with regard to the attitude toward friendship, 'Chinese expect long-term and eternal friendships. Americans do not have that concept.' As an intellectual perceived, 'If you want to have a long-term relationship, you will be disappointed. So when you make American friends, you cannot expect a friendship for life (*sheng shi zhi jiao*).' This difference is also manifested in business practices. Some Chinese businessmen found that Americans 'just pay attention to the current deal and have no consideration for the next time'. Moreover, the difference finds its way into life and work style: 'Americans eat up and expend what they have', while for the Chinese, 'if you make ten dollars today, you save nine for the time you cannot make any'. On the other hand, some respondents appreciated that Americans handle work and life in a more efficient way. While Americans 'work when they work, play when they play', Chinese tend to 'mix work with play' and 'just drag on and have no sense of efficiency'.

The social differences perceived by the Chinese elites primarily focus on the role and function of individuals in a social context. This cognitive orientation somewhat matches the American perception about the group-orientation and political passivity of the Chinese. The first difference cited by the Chinese respondents is that Americans are much less 'inhibited' as individuals.[24] They attributed this difference to the political, economic, as well as cultural constraints. Some respondents believed that politically 'Americans can say everything they want, while we have to worry about the repercussions of our words'. In the words of a professor: 'Chinese don't say what they think. What you say at a meeting is different from what you think privately. You have to be a double-dealer. Is it because Chinese are naturally so? Not necessarily. It has something to do with the system.'

Yet this difference also has its cultural roots: 'Americans respect history, but do not rigidly adhere to history, while the Chinese 'rigidly adhere to history and tradition' and 'have a heavy burden on their backs'. One manifestation is that Chinese are too sensitive about social norms and 'first have to consider the outside reaction to what they are going to say and do'. In contrast, Americans 'worry less about others' reactions', and 'are living easily without restraint'.[25]

Finally, the difference has something to do with the more impoverished economic conditions that impose limits on the freedom of action of the Chinese. As a diplomat put it: 'Chinese are more restrained (*fang bu kai*)— pondering and guessing too much. That has something to do with their economic condition. Chinese cannot afford to be generous. Sometimes, you have to think twice. Americans don't have to.'[26]

The second difference lies in the relationship between individuals and the collective. In this respect, Chinese elites perceived a normative difference. In China, at least in terms of social norms, collective rights and values are above individual values, whereas in the United States, 'people value individual rights more highly than collective rights'. However, as the data on evaluation will show, Chinese respondents had divergent value judgements about this difference. Some had a negative evaluation of the Chinese collective orientation and considered that in China 'individuals are almost neglected, including individual rights and personalities'. But more Chinese respondents did not particularly embrace the 'excessive' American individualism. They found Americans 'more selfish and self-centred' and 'too fussy about privacy'. Yet others thought both American individualism and Chinese collectivism are two extremes. While Americans sometimes 'don't care about others', 'we Chinese are too concerned with others' affairs', as reflected in a mentality of '"red eye disease": either we move up together or I will drag you down'. A third difference involves social independence in relation to family, work unit (*danwei*), and society. In the opinion of a businessman: 'In China, everyone is a member of a big societal family, while in the United States everyone is an independent unit.' One manifestation of this difference is political dependency: 'Chinese don't have very distinct individual opinions on issues; they just follow traditional, parental, or official lines.' A second configuration is social dependency. It used to be the case that 'your whole life was arranged by your unit from the cradle to the grave'. A third expression is family dependency: 'Chinese youths are more and more relying on their parents for marriage, for jobs, and for other things.' Chinese respondents regarded this 'dependency' character as 'the most striking difference between Americans and Chinese'. While some respondents attributed this trait to social systems and argued that Chinese 'are not born that way', others pointed out that 'it is beyond ideology and is something in your blood'. A scholar did not think that Chinese are willing to abandon this dependency easily. 'Chinese dependency on society is much bigger (compared to that of Americans). Although Chinese do not like the Communist Party very much, when their practical interests are involved, they will ask everything from their unit. Their demand on the government and unit is unlimited.'[27] The on-going structural economic reform has been chipping away at this 'social dependency' as reflected in the loss of life employment, medical insurance, and so on, thus creating a lot of social tension and insecurity.

Finally, the Chinese respondents perceived Americans as having a stronger democratic tradition. As some respondents put it, 'Chinese do not have the democratic habit (*minzhu xiguan*).' Historically, 'Chinese did not even value life, not to mention political rights'. Yet some respondents pointed out that a difference exists between 'big democracy' and 'small democracy'. Associated with the perceptions that Chinese are politically passive, but socially quite demanding, they argued that Chinese 'have too little big democracy and too much small democracy', while Americans are just the opposite. A manager noted: 'In American companies, the subordinates do what their boss tells them to do. It's a clear-cut relationship. We cannot do that here. We managers and workers are supposed to be equals. You can not order your subordinate to do things, you have to consult (*shangliang*) with him.' On the other hand, Chinese, as American elites perceived, are quite indifferent to big politics. A Chinese researcher had an interesting comparison: 'Chinese argue on the street, but are polite in the People's Congress; Americans are polite on the street, but argue in Congress.'

The mutual perceptions of differences between Americans and Chinese evince some noticeable patterns. In discussing differences, it seems the 'power of reference' was replaced by more direct comparisons between the subject and object peoples. In contrast to the perceptions on similarities, both sides tended to attribute differences to social traits rather than to personal traits, with the American elites demonstrating a stronger inclination in this regard. Also in contrast to the data on similarities, which is positively oriented, articulation of differences reveals more negative qualities of the other side. However, the American and Chinese elites manifested different cognitive patterns. The Chinese elites tended to articulate the differences in terms of discussing their own problems. The American elites had a stronger propensity to articulate the differences in terms of discussing the other side's problems rather than their own. [28]

Affective and Evaluative Orientations

The articulation of cognitive similarities and differences by the American and Chinese elites reveals to some extent their affective and evaluative inclinations. For most respondents, however, their affective and evaluative orientations toward the target people are still implicit, partial, or unknown. Therefore it is desirable to make a further effort to tap these two dimensions of mutual images of people. For this purpose, respondents were asked to answer the following question: 'I would like your overall opinion of the Chinese/American people. Would you say that your overall opinion of the Chinese/American people is very favourable, somewhat favourable, somewhat unfavourable, or very unfavourable?' Table 3.4 provides a comparison of mutual affective orientations between the two samples.

In accordance with our hypothesis, most American and Chinese respondents had favourable feelings toward the target people. More than 95% of the American respondents chose points on the 'favourable' side, and over 90% of the Chinese respondents also chose 'favourable' options. However, a closer look at the data indicates a telling difference between Chinese and American elites in the intensity of feeling. More than half of the American respondents had a 'very favourable' feeling toward the Chinese people, whereas the parallel percentage for the Chinese respondents was less than 10%. Instead, a majority of the Chinese respondents defined their attitude toward Americans as 'somewhat favourable'. Moreover, while no one on the American side selected 'unfavourable', three Chinese respondents did so.[29]

Table 3.4 Percentage Distribution of Affective Orientation Toward the
Chinese and American Peoples

Affective	Percentage (%)	
Orientation	US Respondents	Chinese Respondents
1 Very favourable	59.0	6.5
2 Somewhat favourable	36.7	85.5
3 In the middle	4.3	5.6
4 Somewhat unfavourable	0	2.4
5 Very unfavourable	0	0
Total	100.0	100.0
Sample size	139	124
Mean/SD	1.45/0.58	2.04/0.47

This perceptual gap is consistent with an earlier observation that more
American respondents spontaneously expressed their strong affection for
the Chinese. Two possible explanations for this difference can be suggested.
First, Chinese elites as a whole had a less favourable opinion of the Americans
than American elites had of the Chinese. This conclusion cannot be verified
by the previous analysis, because Chinese respondents generally talked about
Americans positively, especially in making comments on differences between
the two peoples. Second, this pattern may simply mirror the different
personalities of the Chinese and Americans. American respondents tended
to convey their feelings in a more emotional and even exaggerated style,
whereas Chinese respondents were more reserved in expressing their feelings
and reluctant to go to extremes, even though they might have quite high
opinions of Americans in their hearts. This pattern will manifest itself again
in other dimensions of mutual images.

In order to elicit respondents' positive and negative evaluations of the
target people based on their cognitive and affective orientations, they were
asked to identify qualities they liked most and least about the target people.
In their responses, both American and Chinese elites evinced a stronger
inclination to attribute them to personal dispositions. On the American
side, frequently mentioned traits included 'friendly', 'frank', 'intelligent',
'committed', and 'humorous'. It is interesting to note that more respondents
(about 25% compared to about 7% in their initial images and about 11% in
their perceptions of similarities) liked the 'openness' and 'frankness' of the
Chinese. Relating it to the subsequent data on negative evaluation, 'openness'

and 'reservedness' constitute a constant dichotomy in the American image of the Chinese.

Another likeable quality is the Chinese sense of commitment. Although quite a few American respondents complained about the Chinese reluctance to make a commitment in the first place, they nevertheless admitted that 'once they make a commitment to somebody, there is an absolute commitment there'. While it might not be easy to open a Chinese heart, 'when a true relationship is established, it's deep and lasting and can stand up to a lot of pressure'.

The qualities such as 'honesty', 'sensitivity', 'curiosity', and 'resourcefulness' were also emphasized in the Americans' positive evaluation. Some respondents appreciated the Chinese ability to 'retain a real humanist quality at a personal level despite an oppressive system, which might otherwise turn people into a bunch of animals'. A diplomat had a 'tremendous admiration for many Chinese I have known who suffered very deeply over the years, but have come out of suffering without great bitterness'. These remarks are quite different from the traditional image of describing the Chinese ability to endure hardships as 'an absence of nerves'.[30]

When it comes to positive social attributes of the Chinese, American elites apparently did not have much to say. The cultured quality, and the related courtesy and 'sophisticated' human relations, coupled with family-loving orientation, stand out as the main attributes Americans could appreciate.[31] Although some Americans were impressed by the 'subtlety' and 'sensitivity' of Chinese human relations, the data on negative evaluation will show that more Americans were alienated by it.[32]

On the Chinese side, the quality that Chinese respondents liked most is American 'frankness'. Nearly half of the respondents cited this trait, as compared to about 36% who mentioned it in articulating initial images and 25% in describing differences. Taking into account that many American respondents also liked the Chinese 'openness', we may conclude that the mutual perception of 'frankness' is an important factor to draw Americans and Chinese together. Some Chinese respondents were particularly impressed by American 'frankness' in business practice. Americans 'get to the point and do not talk in a roundabout way', and they 'think bargaining is not honest'. 'Chinese businessmen generally think it is easier to do business with Americans, and more difficult to do business with the Japanese.' Chinese respondents particularly appreciated that Americans do not offer bribes in business dealings. A Chinese foreign affairs officer observed: 'Chinese like to talk about business at a dinner table. The Japanese exploit our habit very well. Americans are more honest. Even if you invite them for a dinner, they will decline to attend.' A businessman even suggested that because 'Americans are honest and do not know how to treat people with gifts and meals, they cannot compete with the Japanese in China'. Another attribute that did not appear often in previous comments is 'helpfulness'. Quite a few Chinese respondents told stories about their experience in the United States to illustrate the willingness of Americans to help foreigners and strangers, which sometimes surprised them in a 'society of money and no human sensitivity'.

In the category of social attributes, more Chinese respondents liked the 'civilized' quality of Americans. This is similar to the American responses. As analysed earlier, the meaning of 'civilized' is somewhat different for the Chinese and American respondents. While Americans admired the ancient 'civilized' quality of the Chinese, Chinese appreciated the modern 'civilized' quality of the Americans. This complementary cultural attraction between the Chinese and Americans, as we will further see in the analysis of mutual images of culture, is another important factor contributing to their positive feeling for one another.

Chinese elites endorsed more American social values than the other way around. As mentioned earlier, Chinese respondents appreciated the American tendency of treating individuals as equals (*pingdeng*). Some appreciated the equality in a family: 'Children can call their parents by their names and they treat each other as equals.' Others favoured the equality in a group. They found that American visitors 'do not care about protocol and are quite informal' and that they 'don't like our way to treat the head and the members of a delegation differently, such as letting the head have a limousine and putting the others in a bus'. Yet others appreciated the equal treatment in utilizing human resources: 'Americans value talented people. No matter what race you are, from which country, low-level or no background, so far as you are qualified, they will appreciate your ability.' This 'egalitarian' image of Americans is at odds with the 'arrogant' image of Americans to be seen in Chinese negative evaluation of Americans, further illustrating the perceptual ambivalence.

Consistent with their articulation of differences, some Chinese respondents had a very positive evaluation of the 'independent' quality of Americans. Given the prevalent 'social dependency' in China, they particularly appreciated that 'Americans have a high view of themselves and think it is a shame to depend on parents when they have grown up'. Even the children of very wealthy families usually work while attending school. 'In our Chinese eyes, they do not have to work at all.'

A number of respondents also envied the individual freedom of Americans. However, as their negative evaluation will show, more Chinese respondents felt uncomfortable with the 'excessive freedom' of Americans. The phenomenon reflects a cognitive dilemma in the minds of Chinese respondents. They could perceive it as a big difference between Americans and Chinese and even felt that is something Chinese lack. Yet this does not necessarily mean that they would conceptually embrace this quality and give it a definite positive evaluation. As we will see in Chapter 4, this cognitive tension is also reflected in their perceptions of American society.

Another quality that drew some positive evaluation from the Chinese respondents is 'dedication' (xianshen jingshen). First, Americans 'have a strong dedication to what they believe' and 'will try every means to realize them', whereas the Chinese, including intellectuals, are losing 'the sense of justice' and tend to be 'cynical' (wan shi bu gong) and to 'speculate' (touji). Second, Americans are devoted to their careers. A foreign affairs officer was impressed by the American journalists who 'are not afraid of hardships in order to do their jobs'. Ironically, a professor of Marxist political economy had a favourable memory of American Christians: 'Those Christians are really devoted people and they do not try to cultivate you for their own interest, but rather for your own interest.'

The data on positive evaluation show that the American and Chinese respondents had parallel positive evaluations of many personal attributes that they found attractive in one another. In the domain of social traits, except for some mutual affections in cultural terms, American and Chinese elites did not share many 'mirror images'. There is an important difference in their evaluative orientation. For American respondents, what they found positive about the Chinese was more related to traditional cultural values, whereas Chinese respondents embraced some contemporary social values held by Americans.

In terms of negative evaluation, both American and Chinese respondents, as in the case of cognitive differentiation, again turned to social attributes rather than to personality attributes. Compared to positive evaluation, the negative evaluation of personal traits is less diversified. For American respondents, many pointed to the trait of 'reservedness'. Some American respondents realized the contradiction in describing the Chinese as both 'frank' and 'reserved' people. They tried to reconcile this cognitive dissonance by drawing a distinction between the Chinese tendency to be 'frank' in initial contact and 'reserved' in substantial relations. They found that in dealing with the Chinese, 'you can go some distance, then, politely, a kind of curtain pulls down, making it difficult to deal with them'.[33]

A number of American respondents went one step beyond 'reserve' to describe Chinese as 'devious'. Many respondents seemed to be struggling to draw a line between 'indirect', 'subtle', 'devious', and 'dishonest' in their comments about the Chinese. The typical perception is that Chinese have a tendency to say 'what you want to hear, not what they want to say or what they think'. A former American visa officer in China found the Chinese had 'little compulsion to tell me the truth', but reported 'whatever was needed in order to get whatever they needed out of me'. Again, some American respondents tended to attribute this quality to 'a kind of system under which the Chinese work'. Especially in official dealings, some diplomats found 'a tendency [for the Chinese] to be less than honest about sensitive matters'.

These observations are closely linked to the social trait viewed negatively by many American respondents—political dependency. It seems that the Tiananmen Incident in 1989 did not dramatically change the American perception in this regard. They still found that the Chinese are unable 'to break out of prevailing political norms' and 'expect too little out of their government'. A diplomat regretted 'the [Chinese] willingness to be a part of something that is hypocritical'. Chinese officials 'will say things they do not believe and will be very rude and uncooperative simply because they are told to do so or they haven't been told to do otherwise.'

While in their positive evaluation some American respondents appreciated the 'sophisticated' side of Chinese personal relations, in their negative evaluation they were annoyed by the 'manipulative' or 'exploitative' side of personal relations. They were also turned off by 'the relative lack of attempt on the part of the Chinese to build institutions necessary to order their world, to accomplish personal objectives in an orderly, regularized, sometimes legal fashion'. This nature of personal relationship, according to some respondents, creates unnecessary constraints in their dealings with the Chinese and creates 'a situation where you have a lot of undercutting of each other'.[34]

This leads to another social trait American respondents found distasteful in the Chinese—their narrow loyalty toward family and close friends and 'a tendency to not see people who are outside of their commitment'. They found that the Chinese had 'two different standards of behaviour' in dealing with human relations. As an American professor put it: 'If you are close to somebody [a Chinese], my Chinese friend will have a very real degree of trust, honesty, and openness. But with [Chinese] people you don't know so well, I often have the feeling that they have been very circumspect, not manipulative exactly, but not entirely straightforward, as reflected in their willingness to be opportunistic or even to be exploitative.' These perceptions may further explain why American elites often saw Chinese as both 'open' and 'reserved'.

As a manifestation of another 'mirror image,' some American respondents were also irritated by Chinese 'arrogance'.[35] They asserted that 'fundamentally most Chinese instinctively are a little arrogant about their own culture' and 'feel most others are barbarians'. That kind of mentality sometimes led to a behavioural pattern of 'treating foreigners like a child'. As a former diplomat described: 'They will lie to you in a way they lie to a child. They expect foreigners to behave according to Chinese standards of proper behaviour. But they don't feel reciprocal obligation to foreigners because foreigners are not the same. In negotiations, it's quite common that they treat you like a child in a sense that there is a deliberate attempt to embarrass you, to make you feel inadequate. . . . . That's the way Chinese treat children. Chinese wouldn't treat other Chinese adults this way.' As a result of this 'ethnocentrism', Chinese were perceived as 'stubborn' and reluctant to 'lose face' in official dealings. Some diplomats commented that Chinese often feel 'they are absolutely right' and are unwilling to 'acknowledge the validity of the other side's position'.

Another expression of this 'arrogance' is that the Chinese are quick to form biases about foreigners. A young banker found that the Chinese 'without any personal experience, are very quick to generalize and to develop prejudice and bias'. 'I am always surprised how racist many Chinese that I know were, who had very little experience with blacks, yet they were very racist.'

As in the case of Chinese articulation of American 'arrogance', for some American respondents this perception is a feeling, a predisposition rather than a cognition based on empirical evidence. As subsequent chapters will show, this 'mirror image' is pervasive among some American and Chinese elites, albeit Chinese respondents showed a higher intensity of feeling.

Some respondents, especially business people, were frustrated by the Chinese 'slowness in taking decisions,' and by their 'reluctance in making commitments'. A business person complained about the Chinese negotiating habit: 'Just when you think you have got an agreement on the whole thing, there is always a "by the way", something which cuts another piece of your deal, always a sort of chiselling away the deal that has been made.' In some American respondents' eyes, this behavioural trait is an expression of the 'tough-mindedness' or 'polite aggressiveness' regarding their own interests. In this regard, Chinese were not seen as being as long-term-oriented as they claimed to be.[36]

In comparison to the American dislike of 'deep' (reserved) Chinese, Chinese elites did not appreciate the 'shallowness' of the Americans. They mainly discussed two aspects of this trait. One is the 'shallowness' in perceptions. Throughout their comments, some Chinese respondents asserted that Americans do not have a profound, objective, and cool-minded perspective on many issues, including their views on China. Americans often take a 'one-sided approach to things in China'. 'When they identify with you, everything is good; when they don't, everything becomes bad.' They are 'too fragile in their emotions' and too easily carried away by the media that tends to 'agitate sensation and make false images'. While some Americans felt humiliated that Chinese 'treated Americans like children', some Chinese did think that Americans are like 'children'. An America watcher found that Americans had difficulty comprehending 'those issues you have to turn around to understand'. 'Sometimes I feel dealing with Americans is like an adult dealing with children. No matter how you explain the thing to them, they just could not understand.' The 'shallowness' can also be observed in behaviour. Americans tend to 'exaggerate their words and gestures', and their 'thanks' and compliments sometimes are just 'a ritual'. As a business person put it, 'Americans are fond of talking big (chuiniu), but they do not always deliver what their words promise.'

Although some Chinese respondents saw Americans as occasionally 'insincere' and 'affected', few of them attributed this quality to dishonesty or deviousness. 'Shallowness' is just the other side of 'openness' and 'frankness'. it appears that Chinese respondents had less cognitive dissonance in describing Americans as both 'open' and 'shallow'.[37]

In terms of social attributes, three major negative evaluations can be delineated from Chinese responses. The first concerns the American attitude toward foreigners, including Chinese. In this respect, the Chinese respondents seem to have a 'collective schema'. About four out of ten respondents perceived Americans to be 'overbearing' and 'arrogant'. Compared to their previous responses, the stimulus of negative evaluation induced a higher frequency for this comment. For some respondents who worked in American consulates or in joint ventures, their 'arrogance' cognition is based on their personal experience. They found that Americans 'have mixed feelings of sympathy and contempt' toward Chinese and 'often make jokes about Chinese among themselves'. For others, there is a shift in their frame of reference. When they took Americans as individuals, they found them quite amiable and easy to approach. But when they perceived Americans in a collective fashion or as representatives of a country, they found in them arrogance and lack of sensitivity toward other nations. As they put it, Americans are 'like upstarts' who 'look down upon poor, backward nations'. In their positive evaluation, some Chinese respondents considered that Americans could not beat the Japanese in economic competition in China because Americans are 'too honest'. Here the perception was that they failed to do so because they 'do not investigate and understand different situations in different countries'.

Some respondents, however, thought that the Chinese were partially responsible for the American 'arrogance'. As a professor said: 'The American superiority is boosted by Chinese. You treat them with too high standards and make them arrogant. Some Americans are just ordinary professors. But when they come to China, they become VIPs. It's unequal treatment.' Therefore, these respondents advocated dealing with Americans on an equal footing. A manager in a joint venture declared that his way of dealing with American arrogance was 'tit-for-tat': 'If you are arrogant, I am even more arrogant than you are.' He warned, 'Americans should have a correct understanding of the Chinese. Indeed, China as a whole is economically behind the United States. But China has a group of people who are no worse than Americans in their intelligence and knowledge. So Americans can not deal with the Chinese as if they are teachers.'

This 'teacher' mentality on the part of Americans, according to some respondents, is reflected in their official and business behaviour. While Americans saw the Chinese as 'stubborn', the Chinese perceived Americans as 'inflexible'. In official dealings, Americans are too 'ideological'. A former Chinese government official remarked: 'We can get along quite well without talking about ideology. As soon as we are touching upon ideology, they immediately display a kind of supercilious and patronizing mentality.' Chinese business respondents found Americans 'too rigid' in business dealings: 'whenever there is a deadlock in negotiations or a dispute in transactions, they just stick to their own concepts'.

The second dimension to emerge concerns Americans' attitudes toward individual freedom. In the context of positive evaluation analysed earlier, apparently more Chinese respondents did not appreciate the 'excessive freedom' of Americans. The Chinese attitudes on this issue were divergent as well as ambivalent. The mentality is that it might be a good thing for Chinese to have more freedom, but the 'excessive' freedom Americans have is not very desirable. Of these 'excessive freedoms', 'random sex' is the most undesirable, leading to what some Chinese respondents called the 'befuddled life' of Americans, and it was viewed as leading to many unresolvable social problems.

This 'excessive freedom' is linked to a third dimension of negative evaluation, namely what some respondents called 'excessive individualism'.[38] This dimension concerns the way Americans deal with human relations. Some Chinese respondents considered Americans to be too 'profit-oriented' (*zhongli*). Consequently, they felt that Americans lack 'human sensitivity' (*renqingwei*). A Chinese researcher considered this propensity to be reflected at both individual and national levels:

> Americans are too profit-oriented. There is a Chinese saying, if you
> just make friends for profit, the friendship will be over when the

opportunity for profit disappears. Chinese value personal loyalty. Americans value interests and profit. They talk a lot and are very polite, but do not help friends much in practice. When somebody is not even concerned with his parents, how could you expect him to be concerned with his friends? So you can not depend too much on Americans for loyalty and friendship. It is the same thing in dealing with other countries. They say some nice things, such as human rights, but these are just means to pursue interests.

This 'insensitive' image is in contrast with the 'helpful' image mentioned in Chinese positive evaluation of Americans. Related to the comment of 'easy come, easy go', the initial American warmth often raised Chinese expectations for what they could get from Americans. When the 'indifferent' side of the Americans emerged in daily interaction, Chinese were naturally disappointed.

The negative evaluations in mutual images demonstrate both 'opposite images' and 'mirror images'. As far as the former is concerned, Americans perceived the Chinese as too 'deep', while the Chinese perceived Americans as too 'shallow'; Americans perceived the Chinese as having too little political freedom, while the Chinese perceived Americans as having too much individual freedom; Americans perceived the Chinese as having excessively complicated human relations, while the Chinese perceived Americans as being indifferent to human relations. 'Mirror images' exist as both sides saw each other as 'arrogant', 'stubborn', and 'interest-oriented', albeit with different attributions.

As the following chapters will demonstrate, many of the above findings regarding Sino-American mutual images of people are further manifested in mutual images of society, culture, and international behaviour.

The Trend of Perceptual Change

It is hypothesized in Chapter 2 that Sino-American mutual images have undergone significant changes since the opening of the relationship in the 1970s. Since no longitudinal data are available to permit a more rigorous analysis of perceptual evolution, the measurement of these changes and the testing of the theoretical models of perceptual change become a difficult task. As a substitute method, the respondents were asked to make a self-evaluation of their perceptual changes over the last two decades. Needless to say, the reliability problem of the data thus generated can be quite considerable, given the fact that people typically have very short memories and have a tendency to justify and rationalize their previous attitudes and behaviours according to their present cognition. However, it is still worthwhile to collect data of this kind, mainly for two reasons. First, we did not ask our respondents to recall specific details of what they perceived or did in the last two decades. Rather, what we tried to track was their general feeling about their perceptual changes on some broad conceptual issues. It is easier for people to retrieve their general feelings than details of their perceptions. For this reason, the reliability problem can be alleviated to some extent. Second, understanding how American and Chinese elites perceive their own image changes is an interesting subject by itself. Other researchers may compare what we have found here to alternative sources to test their validity. At the very least the data can serve the purpose of offering a point of reference for future studies.

We anticipated that since the 1970s, Sino-US mutual images of people would provide evidence of an upward trend of evolution in a more positive direction, mainly because increasing contact and interaction between elite Americans and Chinese in a dynamic fashion have led to better understanding of, and stronger personal bonds with, the target people. It was also suggested that compared to mutual images of society and international behaviour, the general positive feeling toward people is less likely to be negated by a macro-event such as the Tiananmen Incident, since the image of people could be more personally rather than collectively oriented. The foregoing analysis largely confirmed these propositions. To further explore them from another angle, the respondents were asked to describe their perceptual change in the past twenty years or so. The first question was cast in a more generic fashion: 'With regard to your current image of the Chinese/American people, how does it differ from that which you held before the 1970s?' Table 3.5 is a comparison of American and Chinese responses along a 7-point scale of perceptual change.

It is evident from the table that a majority of the American and Chinese elites considered that their image of the target people had changed significantly since the 1970s. While close to two-thirds of the American respondents opted for points 1–3, six out of ten Chinese respondents made the same choice. The mean score indicates that on average Chinese respondents again exhibited a more conservative tendency.[39] Nearly 30% of the Chinese respondents chose numbers 5–7, whereas the corresponding percentage for the American elites is slightly over 20%.

Combining this finding with the data in previous sections, it can be said that compared to the Chinese image of the American people, the American image of the Chinese people evinced a lower outer differentiation, more positive affective orientation, and greater perceptual change. Yet we have to wait and see whether the same trend applies to other dimensions of mutual

Table 3.5 Percentage Distribution of Perceptual Change Regarding the Chinese and American Peoples

Perceptual Change	Percentage (%)	
	US Respondents	Chinese Respondents
1 (changed greatly)	28.6	16.9
2	29.2	26.3
3	10.7	18.6
4	8.6	8.4
5	6.4	10.1
6	9.3	14.4
7 (no change at all)	7.1	5.1
Total	100.0	100.0
Sample size	140	118
Mean/SD	2.93/1.95	3.39/1.85

images to determine that the Chinese elites had an overall more negative, stable, and alien perception of the United States.

The data in Table 3.5 indicate the intensity of perceptual change, but not its direction. However, if we put the data on affective orientation from Table 3.5 and Table 3.4 together, it can be said with reasonable confidence that the evolution is upward-oriented in a positive direction. To further test this observation, a specific attitudinal question was designed. It is assumed that the perception about the target people's attitude toward foreigners may typically reflect respondents' overall opinion. American respondents were then asked to describe the attitude of Chinese toward foreigners along a 7-point scale, with 1 representing 'very xenophobic' and 7 'very cosmopolitan', across three temporal points of reference: the 1970s, 1980s, and 1990s (the present). Table 3.6 summarizes the findings.

The data further verify the earlier proposition that the American perception of the Chinese has changed significantly toward the more positive side since the 1970s. In the 1970s, more than eight out of ten American respondents in the sample perceived Chinese as very xenophobic (points 1–2). This dropped to less than 10% in the 1980s. At the same time more than 40% of the respondents located Chinese on the more 'cosmopolitan' side (numbers 5–7). Apparently this trend was not reversed by the Tiananmen Incident. Rather, the number of holders of the 'cosmopolitan' image increased to more than 50% in the 1990s. Some respondents did

Table 3.6 Percentage Distribution of Perceptual Change Regarding the
Attitude of the Chinese Toward Foreigners

Scale	Chinese Attitude Toward Foreigners (%)		
	1970s	1980s	1990s
1 (very xenophobic)	44.0	2.1	0.7
2	41.1	7.1	10.7
3	8.2	19.3	12.1
4	2.2	28.3	22.9
5	3.0	29.3	37.9
6	1.5	10.0	13.6
7 (very cosmopolitan)	0	2.9	2.1
Total	100.0	100.0	100.0
Sample size	134	140	140
Mean	1.85	4.22	4.40

regress in their judgement, as seen from the slight increase in percentage for respondents who selected 2 compared to the same category in the 1980s. But on the whole, an upward linear model as set forth in Chapter 2 holds.

Similarly, the evolution of Chinese perception regarding American attitude toward foreigners was measured by a 7-point scale, with 1 representing 'very discriminatory' and 7 'very egalitarian'. Table 3.7 represents the distribution over time.

As expected, in the 1970s more than seven in ten Chinese respondents perceived Americans as 'discriminatory' rather than 'egalitarian' in treating foreigners. Often when Chinese said Americans were 'discriminatory', they also included the American attitudes toward blacks. The interesting thing is, however, while very few American respondents saw Chinese as 'cosmopolitan', more than 20% of the respondents (points 4 and above) had the belief that Americans treated foreigners fairly equally, even at that time. Some respondents were aware of the fact that the United States was a place for immigrants from all over the world. Some respondents who had contact with Americans before 1949 still held favourable impressions of Americans as individuals. In the 1980s, the perceptions of Americans on this issue changed significantly. Only about 20% of the respondents stuck to the more 'discriminatory' side, while about four in ten respondents selected points on the more 'egalitarian' side. Still, approximately 30% of the respondents preferred to take a middle stance rather than move to the

Table 3.7 Percentage Distribution of Perceptual Change Regarding the
Attitude of the Americans Toward Foreigners

	American Attitude Toward Foreigners (%)		
Scale of Attitude	**1970s**	**1980s**	**1990s**
1 (very discriminatory)	11.8	0.8	0.8
2	39.3	5.0	5.0
3	23.6	18.6	17.8
4	16.7	33.9	30.5
5	5.9	29.6	32.2
6	1.0	11.0	11.8
7 (very egalitarian)	2.0	0.8	1.7
Total	100.0	100.0	100.0
Sample size	102	118	118
Mean	2.83	4.29	4.36

more 'egalitarian' side. They often described Americans as having 'both sides', further reflecting the previously analysed perception of American 'arrogance'. As with the United States sample, Chinese perception in this regard was not affected much by the American reaction to Tiananmen and the subsequent souring of the relationship. Instead, the perception has been largely stabilized in the 1990s. Consistent with the data in Table 3.5, Chinese respondents demonstrated less perceptual change compared to their American counterparts. Overall, an upward linear model approximates the data reasonably well.

Differentials of Mutual Images

In Chapter 2 we presented a theoretical model that assumes that there is a linkage between contact, 'big' events, and perceptual formation and change. For instance, the intensity of interaction and contact with one another may affect cognitive and affective orientations toward the target country. A 'reorganizing' event such as the Tiananmen Incident may also have a negative or positive influence. Moreover, socio-demographic variables such as occupation and age may have a bearing on respondents' perceptual propensities toward the target country too.

In this section, some of these variables are applied to test their associations with mutual images of people. The variable of contact is measured by the following questions: first, whether a respondent had contact with the target people or visited the target country before 1949;[40] second, whether a respondent had contact with the other side during the period 1950–1970; third, whether a respondent had contact with the other side during the 1970s; fourth, the frequency of contact during the 1980s;[41] fifth, the number of times respondents visited the target country during 1970–1990. The impact of the Tiananmen Incident[42] is also used as an explanatory variable. Moreover, the variables of profession and age are added because these two factors often condition respondents' historical experience, value orientations, and psychological propensities.

Accordingly, crosstabulations were made between these explanatory variables and data on cognitive differentiation, affective orientation, and perceptual change in terms of mutual images of people. These cross tabulations yielded mean scores for each attitudinal dimension.[43] We hypothesize that variables of personal contact, especially the contact since 1970, could decrease people's outer differentiation and facilitate their perceptual change regarding the target people. But the impact of personal contact on affective orientation may vary in different time periods. Big events such as Tiananmen are unlikely to have a strong influence on respondents' perceptual orientations toward the target people, since the incident and the reaction to the incident are more likely to be associated with the target government. Due to different intellectual backgrounds and value systems, the same profession in the two samples could point to different cognitive orientations. The respondents' age, however, may have a parallel function for both American and Chinese respondents in terms of their perceptual orientations.

The crosstabulation indicates that as far as the association between variables of contact and outer differentiation is concerned, some patterns can be delineated, although inconsistency exists. Apparently, American respondents who visited China before 1949 on average manifested the lowest outer differentiation. This could be attributed to their familiarity with the Chinese due to their initial visits or stays before 1949. When they resumed their contact with the Chinese during the 1970s or 1980s, they might have found some connections in the Chinese they saw then with those they met before 1949. Contact with Americans before 1949 does not make a big difference for Chinese respondents' average score on differentiation, although those who met Americans also had the highest mean score, indicating lower outer differentiation.

However, contact during the period 1950–1970 and in the 1970s, as well as the frequency of contact during the 1980s, do not make a straightforward difference for either sample. It appears that the number of visits to the target country explains the differentials relatively better. For both sides, the difference between those who visited the target country more than six times and those who did not visit at all is quite obvious. The former displayed the highest mean score, indicating their lower outer differentiation. It might be said that living among the target people is more likely to reduce the outer differentiation than is contact with the target people on the respondents' own soil.

The Tiananmen Incident demonstrates an intriguing impact on cognitive differentiation. For both sides, the 'greatly affected' respondents perceived more similarities between the two peoples. On the American side, American respondents might have perceived more similarities between Chinese and Americans by witnessing the aspirations of the Chinese for democracy. The same thing cannot be said about the China sample since the 'greatly affected' respondents usually referred to the American reaction to the event in a negative tone. A plausible explanation could be that their lower level of outer differentiation was determined by other factors such as contact, and the American reaction to Tiananmen did not affect their views in this respect.

Profession has a similar impact on cognitive differentiation on both sides. Intellectuals, on average, had the lowest outer differentiation of the target people. Relatively speaking, American diplomats and Chinese business people displayed the highest cognitive differentiation. It could be inferred that intellectuals, generally speaking, had more opportunities to have substantial contact with the ordinary people in the target country compared with diplomats and business people. Diplomats often had official contact that might reveal more attitudinal and behavioural differences between Americans and Chinese. Business people usually did not stay in the target country very long. Intellectuals could stay in target countries for years, doing research and teaching, which might help them find more common ground between Americans and Chinese.

Age has a fairly consistent association with the degree of outer differentiation. On average, the older a respondent was, the more similarity he or she perceived between the two peoples. Older respondents on both sides might have had more direct and indirect contact (not necessarily in the 1980s, and including that prior to 1949) with the target people, thus leading to their perception of more similarity. Another factor could be that older respondents had a natural tendency to perceive that 'ordinary people under Heaven are the same', due to their life experience.

The same set of explanatory variables is also crosstabulated with respondents' affective orientation toward the target people in Table 3.4. It should be pointed out that in both samples, a majority of respondents had a favourable opinion of the target people and the variation of opinion was minimal. Consequently, we can only compare the difference in intensity of positive feelings. Again, contact before 1949 yields a telling difference. On both sides, the respondents who had contact with the other side, on average, had a more favourable view of the target people. In interviews, some American respondents mentioned their 'brotherly' friendship with Chinese at that time. Chinese respondents, especially those who attended missionary schools, had favourable impressions of American teachers and missionaries. Contact during the period 1950–1970 and even in the 1970s generally had the opposite effect. One might argue that the circumstances for contact during these periods were not particularly conducive to personal amiability. Looking at the relationship between respondents' affective orientation and the frequency of contact in the 1980s or the number of visits since the 1970s, one might be hesitant to simply apply the social psychological proposition that familiarity usually causes mutual liking. Rather, those who had more intensive contact could have a somewhat less favourable opinion of the target people. It can be argued that contact may reveal both good and bad things about the target people. During interviews, those respondents who only had superficial contact frequently had difficulties in articulating the negative aspects of the target people. On the other hand, some respondents who had substantial contact were more able to discover the shortcomings of the other side and therefore were less likely to express emotionally positive feelings.

The Tiananmen Incident does not have a great impact on respondents' affective orientation toward the target people. One might argue that for both sides, the event has affected the affective orientation toward the target government rather than the people. However, the 'greatly affected' respondents, especially in the China sample, on average, did show a higher mean score, indicating a less favourable attitude. The reason might be that these respondents tended to see the inherent weakness of the other side. The 'greatly affected' Chinese respondents perceived American 'emotionality' and 'arrogance'. As the earlier analysis implied, there is no strong evidence suggesting that the incident greatly enhanced the American view of the Chinese.

The influence of profession seems to differ between the two samples. On the American side, intellectuals demonstrated the least favourable mean score, and diplomats the most favourable mean score. Apparently, the lower outer differentiation of American intellectuals is not associated with a more positive feeling toward the Chinese. Their comments in interviews indicate that some of them tended to discover the ugly side of the Chinese through their research and observation. Interestingly, diplomats had, on average, a more positive view. It seems that American diplomats were more inclined to draw a comparison between their official dealings and contact with the ordinary Chinese people. Taking their official dealing as a reference point, their affinity with ordinary Chinese might increase. On the Chinese side, intellectuals had the most favourable mean score. Chinese intellectuals were more inclined to identify with Americans and American values. On the other hand, Chinese business people and diplomats tended to be more sensitive to the American 'arrogance' and 'excessive individualism'.

Association between age and affective orientation displays different patterns for American and Chinese respondents. On the American side, the respondents younger than 40 had the most favourable mean score for the Chinese, while those of 60 and older had the least favourable score. This pattern further reveals that American respondents' cognitive and affective orientation often did not go hand in hand. It could be the case that young Americans tended to view the Chinese in a more idealistic way, while older respondents had a more balanced view. However, for Chinese respondents, it is the respondents aged 60 and older who had the most favourable mean score, while the middle-aged respondents had the least favourable one. It seems that some older Chinese respondents held favourable memories formed before 1949 of Americans. Middle-aged respondents tended to be more conservative in their perceptions, due to the ideological image-making process in their formative years.

The third analysis variable crosstabulated with explanatory variables is the respondents' perceptual change regarding the target people in Table 3.5. Contact before 1949 again makes a difference. In both samples, those who had contact before 1949, on average, claimed less perceptual change. Their image of the target people, although formed a long time ago, displayed greater stability. Apparently, contact during both the years 1950–1970 and the 1970s impaired, rather than facilitated, people's perceptual change. It might be suggested that the image produced by contact during these time periods tends to persist. Those who did not have contact then were more likely to have perceptual changes, since they did not have many predispositions. The function of contact in the 1980s, however, is quite different. The intensity of contact seems to be positively associated with greater perceptual change. On both sides, the respondents who visited the target country six or more times evinced greater perceptual change than those who had not visited. In the Chinese case, respondents who visited the United States once claimed on average a 1.3 point greater perceptual change than those who never visited the United States. There is reason to believe that respondents who had contact with the other side before 1980 were less likely to change their pre-existing images, whereas respondents who began their contact in the 1980s were more likely to experience perceptual change.

The impact of Tiananmen is not significant for either side, indicating that the perceptual evolution of American and Chinese respondents is not contingent upon this event. As suggested earlier, the incident might have affected respondents' perceptions of other dimensions of the target country rather than that of people.

With regard to profession, it is noteworthy that for both sides, business respondents displayed the lowest mean score, indicating greater perceptual change. On the other hand, American intellectuals and Chinese diplomats displayed the least perceptual change. It could be argued that many American 'China' elites formed their perceptions of the Chinese a long time ago. Chinese diplomats, as reflected in their image articulation, often exhibited stronger predispositions about Americans.

The relationship between age and perceptual change is fairly straight. On average, the younger the respondent, the greater the perceptual change he or she had experienced. As some young respondents mentioned in the interviews, what they often experienced was an accumulation of knowledge and understanding of the target people through interactions and contact. Understandably, the well-established image of older respondents was less susceptible to change.

To sum up, the applied explanatory variables display some observable associations with respondents' cognitive, affective, and evolutionary orientations. Among the variables of contact, contact before 1949 has the most visible impact. It tends to decrease respondents' outer differentiation and perceptual change, and to enhance their positive feelings toward the target people. Other variables of contact have more mixed influence. Respondents who had contact during the period 1950–1970 and during the 1970s did not evidence a clear difference in their cognitive differentiation, but they did have a less positive affective orientation and experienced less perceptual change. The frequency of contact in the 1980s does not necessarily decrease outer differentiation, but the number of visits has this effect. More contact with and visits during 1970–1990 are instrumental in more perceptual change, but do not produce more favourable attitudes toward the target people. The impact of Tiananmen does not increase 'greatly affected' respondents' cognitive differentiation or cause more perceptual change, but it does seem to have brought about more negative feelings. Profession often has a divergent impact on Chinese and American respondents. In the American case, intellectuals were prone to have the lowest cognitive differentiation, the least favourable feelings, and the least perceptual change. Diplomats were inclined to have the highest cognitive differentiation, but the most positive affective orientation. Business people evinced more perceptual change. On the Chinese side, for intellectuals, lower cognitive differentiation and more positive feelings go together. For business people, higher outer differentiation and less positive feelings coexist. Chinese diplomats experienced the least perceptual change regarding the American people. For both sides, age tends to be associated with lower outer differentiation and less perceptual change. However, younger American respondents and older Chinese respondents, respectively, seemed to have the most favourable opinions of the target people.

These findings, however, are suggestive rather than conclusive, since explanatory variables could confound each other in uncontrolled crosstabulations. Therefore, the relationships will be further tested by multivariate analysis in Chapter 7.

Notes to Chapter 3

1　See Isaacs, *Scratches on Our Minds*, pp. 215–216.
2　See *The Gallup Poll, Public Opinion, 1935–1971*, p. 2015.
3　See J. Richard Eiser, *Social Psychology: Attitudes, Cognition and Social Behaviour,* Cambridge: Cambridge University Press, 1986, p. 22.
4　Of course the boundary between personality traits and social traits is by no means clear-cut. In reality, they interact in a dynamic way. On the one hand, personal characters are influenced by specific social traditions and circumstances. On the other hand, human dispositions have their biological and hereditary origins that are not necessarily products of social conditions. Therefore, some traits could be coded either as personal or social, depending on how respondents made attributions.
5　See Isaacs, *Scratches on Our Minds*, pp. 72–73. He considered that the image of 'the friendly, attractive, admirable individual Chinese had almost completely disappeared' during his time, p. 238.
6　Some Americans particularly appreciated Chinese entrepreneurship. As a business person said: 'The most striking thing [about Chinese] is their natural sense of business in an environment where a great many people of your age and my age [30–40] didn't have any formal business training.'
7　As a business person put it: 'Wonderful people! Full of joy, happiness, optimism, laughing and eating, and their living in tragic, difficult conditions means that they are all the more remarkable. They can laugh, eat, and be cheery despite difficult conditions to prove just how wonderful they are.'
8　The American respondents usually described these traits in an abstract fashion and did not elaborate on them. While some of them could be seen as clichés, they nevertheless represent their conceptualization or generalization of the Chinese people.

9   As we will see, American respondents also had different opinions on this issue. While some respondents were fascinated by the strong motivation and skill of the Chinese for personal relations, others saw China's network of *guanxi* as an unhealthy feature that 'complicates the process of social interactions'.

10   A professional said: 'When I am born again, I want to be a Chinese.' An intellectual remarked: 'For whatever reasons, I tend to be much more emotionally inclined to respond favourably to Chinese. . . . I don't know why.' A foundation official declared: 'My friendship with the Chinese is so deep that I even don't know they are Chinese.'

11   A small number of respondents, however, still demonstrated a high degree of outer differentiation. As a business person put it: '[Chinese] are alienated people to me, in terms of not being able to fit to the logic of my way of thinking.'

12   As a result, some respondents came up with specific images of the Chinese they contacted such as 'Chinese in the Northeast', 'people in Beijing', or even 'peasants at a train station'.

13   They used terms such as 'forthright' (*haoshuang*), 'outright' (*shuangqi*), 'straightforward' (*zhishuang*), 'straight' (*zhi*), and 'clear-cut' (*gancui*).

14   A business person said: 'I find while some Americans are smart, some of them are quite naive and even dumb. Americans are not like Orientals, so shrewd and circumspect.'

15   This trait could also be considered as a personal disposition, but many Chinese respondents attributed it to the American political and economic background rather than to their personalities.

16   A scholar commented: 'Some Americans love to say, "I have a very good feeling toward China. Ever since my childhood, my mother asked me to save a mouth of food for China's poor children." They think they are saying so out of good intentions, but I feel hurt.'

17   A significant test of the two means supports the argument that the American respondents on average displayed a lower degree of outer differentiation (t = -4.51, p < 0.0005).

18   See Eiser, *Social Psychology,* p. 39.

19   Some even suggested that Chinese 'are more like Americans than some Europeans in this respect'.

20   That does not mean that the Chinese did not think that Americans are humorous. Rather they did not think of themselves as being as humorous as Americans are. A young business person observed: 'We Chinese usually lack a sense of humour, which is so pervasive among Americans. It's a fashion for Americans to make some jokes in their speeches and talks. Of course, some jokes are made for jokes' sake. Nevertheless, they create an atmosphere of relaxation.'

21   This cognition seems to be at odds with what some respondents observed earlier, that the Chinese are 'conformist' politically. This 'defiance' image might have been shaped by the recent developments in China. Nevertheless, there is no strong evidence in this data set to suggest that this image has become prevalent among the American respondents.

22   They described this trait in terms such as [the Chinese] 'don't express openly', 'more cautious', 'less direct', 'not outspoken', and 'closed rather than open'.

23   Although some respondents cited 'pragmatic' as a similarity, more Chinese respondents thought that the Chinese spend too much time on unnecessary social rituals (*ketao*) and ideological matter (*wuxu*).

24   They thought that Americans are more 'uninhibited' (*bushou shufu*), 'free' (*ziyou zizai*), and less 'depressed' (*yayi*) and 'conservative' (*baoshou*).

25   These comments coincide with the observation made by another Chinese scholar elsewhere. He pointed out that Americans tend to think the restrained Chinese character

is a result of government 'repression'. In fact, Chinese restraint is partly political and partly cultural. Liancheng Duan, 'Chinese-American misunderstanding, their cultural roots, the China difference', *Beijing Review*, July 11, 1988, p. 33.

26   This remark may provide a footnote for the American perception about the 'calculating' nature of the Chinese.

27   These perceptions contradict American perceptions on the same subject. While some Americans saw Chinese as asking too little politically from the government, some Chinese respondents thought that Chinese asked too much socially from their unit and government.

28   To a large extent, the Chinese perception of the United States indeed reflects their critique of their own country. This cognitive tradition started as early as the late Qing dynasty. Yusheng Yang's recent study of the Chinese image of the United States touched upon this important theme. See Yusheng Yang, *Zhongguoren de meiguoguan* (Chinese Images of the United States). The Americans, on the other hand, usually do not use their own country as a system of reference.

29   A t-test of the two means indicates that American respondents held significantly more positive feelings toward the Chinese people than the other way round ($t = 8.96$, $p < 0.0005$).

30   See Isaacs, *Scratches on Our Minds,* pp. 101–104.

31   As a former government official remarked: 'It's hard not to like them if they want you to like them. They are so cordial, so polite when they choose to be that way. . . . That's culture, not just human nature.'

32   A banker expressed this conflicting mentality: 'I like their subtlety most, but the subtlety sometimes reaches a point where there is more ambiguity than Americans are used to, leading to misunderstanding.'

33   As a researcher observed: 'It's possible to establish a frank and open basis for conversation. This permits us to speak quite freely about our difference of views. . . . But something I am uncertain about is that I am not quite sure that, it sounds like a contradiction, but I don't think it is, Chinese colleagues have told the full range of their views when they disagree.'

34   As a scholar commented: 'If you have ties with one *guanxi* network, members of that network will tend to mistrust you if you have ties with many other networks. Sometimes you get frustrated by your tendency to get locked into a particular relationship, while as a scholar or specialist of China, you want to have as universal access as possible.'

35   Not every American respondent, however, considered this trait as necessarily bad. It could turn into a self-confidence that makes Chinese 'more pleasant to deal with' because 'it's easier to deal with someone who is self-confident than with people who are insecure'. As a diplomat put it: 'I think Russians are more difficult to deal with because they are more paranoid and insecure than Chinese.'

36   A business consultant commented: 'Chinese are more global-minded and more universalistic than Japanese in dealing with global issues in high political circles. However, an average Chinese business guy is not so long-term oriented, but is a short-term guy. It's a problem because we Americans are also short-term oriented. That means nothing could get done. Somebody has to take the long-term view.'

37   Some respondents did perceive a tendency for Americans to be excessively frank—'blunt' or even 'rude'. They described Americans as 'ill-tempered', 'crude', and 'scatterbrained' (*madaha*).

38   In the minds of many Chinese, individualism means egotism and selfishness by definition, therefore implying a negative connotation. A famous saying in the Mao era was 'individualism is the root cause of all evils'. Tsomin Wang, 'Chinese-American misunderstandings, their cultural roots, the America difference', *Beijing Review*, July 18–24, 1988, pp. 32–34.

39   The difference is statistically significant at a probability level of 0.05 (t = 1.92).

40   American respondents were asked whether they had visited mainland China before 1949. Chinese respondents were asked whether they had had contact with Americans before 1949. The reason for the difference in wording is that there was much less chance for Chinese respondents to visit the United States prior to 1949 than for their American counterparts to visit China.

41   Whether a respondent had contact with the other side every week, once or twice a month, a few times a year or once or twice in several years.

42   This variable was measured by asking respondents the following question: 'Some people say that the Tiananmen Incident (the American reaction to Tiananmen) entirely changed their image of China (the United States), others say that their general image was affected little by the event, what was your situation?' The responses fell into three categories: great effect, some effect, and no effect.

43   The crosstabulation data on this and other dimensions of mutual images are not presented here due to the space limit.

CHAPTER 4 ·
MUTUAL IMAGES OF SOCIETY

In international relations, the core of national images consists of cognitive, affective, and evaluative orientations concerning, among other things, the nature and function of a target country's political and economic systems, governmental structure, and social configurations. In this study, we define them as mutual images of society to distinguish them from images of people, culture, and international behaviour.

Before the 1970s, Sino-American mutual images of society were primarily projected in an undifferentiated and rigid framework of ideology that defined the other side as 'monolithic totalitarian communism' or 'rotten monopoly capitalism'.[1] Consequently, the Americans and Chinese perceived high incompatibility between the two societies. From the 1970s, the mutual images of society evolved considerably.[2] Chinese and American societies were no longer seen as ideologically so alien and functionally so incompatible. Indeed, during the heyday of US-China reconciliation, Americans and Chinese perceived one another's society as a kind of model from which they could learn something for their own social and economic development.[3] While some basic assumptions about the nature of the target society remained unchanged, and disillusionment occasionally occurred,[4] mutual images of society were reasonably positive and on an upward track with the on-going political and economic reforms in China before June 1989.

Apparently, the Tiananmen crackdown and the collapse of world communism reversed this positive trend. The differences in values, ideology, and social systems between the two countries seemed to be magnified and to become the main point of reference in perceiving the target society. An interesting question, then, is how much of the perceptual sophistication, accumulated before June 1989, survived the blow of this 'reorganizing' event and its aftermath? This chapter tries to provide some insights by first articulating the current mutual images of society in the conceptual framework set out in Chapter 2, then tracing their evolution since the 1970s, and finally tapping into some of the factors that might have influenced their configurations.

Several broad hypotheses can be suggested to guide the following empirical analysis. First, American and Chinese respondents may show greater outer differentiation in comparison with their outer differentiation of people given the divergent nature of their political, economic, and social systems. Second, some basic assumptions about the target society that had been submerged before the Tiananmen Incident could have been revived or reinforced by the event, which particularly re-conceptualized people's overall opinions of the target government. Third, the effect of this single event may not completely negate the perceptual sophistication and differentiation achieved during the last two decades of interaction and contact. That is to say, even with the Tiananmen Incident and its negative influence, the mutual images of society held by American and Chinese elites are still more sophisticated than they were twenty-odd years ago. Fourth, the Tiananmen Incident and its aftermath may have asymmetric impact on American and Chinese elites in terms of their perception of the target society, and hence produce different patterns of perceptual configuration and evolution.

General Images of Society

As in the dimension of people, a spontaneous image profile of the target society was obtained by asking the following question: 'When you think about China/the United States as a society, what comes to your mind first?' The image profiles of Chinese society articulated by the American respondents is summarized in Table 4.1.

They were coded into the categories of political, social, economic, geo-demographic, and historical features. The percentage distribution shows that a majority of the American respondents referred to some political characteristics of Chinese society. Two different, albeit related, dimensions concerning the nature and dynamic of Chinese society emerged. Not surprisingly, for many American respondents, what first came to their minds was the authoritarian and bureaucratic nature of Chinese society.[5] Related to that, some respondents immediately perceived conflict between the state and the people. In the opinion of some respondents, those admirable traits and potentials mentioned in their image of the Chinese people were 'killed and wasted' by this undesirable political and social system.[6] For these respondents, the Tiananmen Incident revived or reinforced their original assumption about the inherent nature of the Chinese political system to which they attributed China's problems. As a former diplomat pointed out, 'One of the reasons for the strong (American) reaction after the Tiananmen crackdown was just an outpouring of American fear of a highly centralized system in a big country.'

While the Chinese state was perceived as repressive and harsh to its people, American respondents also noticed the other side of the coin: China is a very difficult country to govern. A good portion of respondents touched upon various aspects of this issue of governance. They pointed out that the

Table 4.1 General Images of Chinese Society (Sample Size = 141)

Subjects	Number of Cases	Proportion (%)
Political features		
Authoritarian	44	31.2
Difficult to govern	24	17.0
Unstable	18	12.8
People's potential wasted	16	11.3
Well-managed	13	9.2
Ungovernable	12	8.5
Bureaucratic	11	7.8
Uninstitutionalized	10	7.1
Social features		
Collectively oriented	17	12.1
Resisting state control	17	12.1
Complex	13	9.2
Economic features		
Poor, less developed	14	9.9
Diverse	10	7.1
Modernizing	7	5.0
Geo-demographic features		
Most populous	25	17.7
Massive	16	11.3
Historical features		
Enduring	19	13.5
Burdensome historically	10	7.1
Lacking democratic tradition	8	5.7

Note: Since each respondent could mention more than one feature, the percentages in the table represent the proportion of respondents who mentioned each subject. Therefore the total of percentage distribution does not add up to 100%. This also applies to other tables of the same kind.

Chinese political system has so far been unable to modernize and institutionalize itself. The major symptom of this failure is the chronic political turmoil and instability, once again illustrated by the Tiananmen upheaval. As they saw it, both historically and presently, China 'has been constantly struggling between order and chaos'. The Tiananmen turmoil formed a rather fatalistic perception for some American respondents. A scholar remarked, 'My basic view is that China is ungovernable. The political order in China is in a state of perpetual and periodic chaos because the country is too big, too populous, and too poor to be governed. Therefore it is an oxymoron. . . . You really cannot have a Chinese state.' This 'difficult to govern' perception involves a somewhat different attribution process from the 'people suppressed' perception aforementioned. The latter attributes the problem solely to the nature of the Chinese political system, whereas the former pays more attention to the objective factors retarding effective governance of China, such as huge population, massiveness, poor infrastructure, high complexity, and diversity of Chinese society.[7]

Some American respondents even perceived a rationale for a totalitarian government due to the political weakness of the Chinese. An American diplomat remarked: 'The thing which comes to my mind as a country, is the difficulty that it had in pulling together except under a very strong central leadership. Chinese make comparisons between themselves and the Japanese: why did the Japanese do so well? They work together. Why is it we Chinese don't do so well? We always have little factions, squabbles and frictions among ourselves. . . . You can almost say that China needs a dictatorship. That is not a very pleasant thing to say.' So while some respondents felt 'sorry' for the Chinese people who have to suffer under the totalitarian regime, some others expressed 'sympathy' for those who have tried to govern China, and even appreciated their 'successful management'. It can be said, therefore, that while Tiananmen intensified some American respondents' disgust towards the Chinese political system, it also made some sophisticated some respondents' views about Chinese society. This cognitive complexity is mirrored in some respondents' propensity to attribute the political turmoil in China not merely to the subjective 'evil nature' of the Chinese regime, but also to the objective constraints under which the Chinese government must operate.

This perceptual complexity can further be seen in some respondents' conceptual distinction between the Chinese 'state' and 'society'. For them, while the Chinese 'state' is repulsive and rigid from the American viewpoint, Chinese 'society' is more human, dynamic, and even progressive. The spontaneousness of the democratic movement in 1989 reinforced their convictions that Chinese society and the Chinese state are 'going in several different directions at the same time', and that society is not under the complete control of the state. This cognitive differentiation between 'state' and 'society' allows American elites to have a more realistic and less ideological observation of how the social system really works in China.[8]

In contrast to the mutual images of people analysed in the previous chapter, which converge on many accounts about the other side, the mutual images of society evince a sharper contrast between what American and Chinese elites perceived in one another's countries. Table 4.2 presents a profile of the Chinese respondents' images of American society.

Table 4.2 General Images of American Society (Sample Size = 127)

Subjects	Number of Cases	Proportion (%)
Political features		
Stable and effective	15	11.8
Political system successful	12	9.4
People's potential utilized	12	9.4
Having more freedom	9	7.1
Social features		
Various social problems	28	22.0
Polarized, racial issues	25	19.7
Full of energy, vigor	16	12.6
Civilized and educated	9	7.1
Excessively individualistic	9	7.1
Geo-economic features		
Highly developed	28	22.0
Rich and wealthy	11	8.7
Living standard high	11	8.7
Richly endowed by nature	9	7.1
Cities clean, service good	6	4.7
Economically declining	6	4.7
International features		
Open and diverse	15	11.8
Powerful	12	9.4
Overbearing	11	8.7

The table reveals that for the Chinese respondents, the most frequently mentioned topic areas are the social and economic aspects of American society. In the political domain, Chinese elites saw quite the opposite of what Americans perceived in Chinese society. In their initial reaction to the question, almost all the features mentioned in this category are positive rather than negative. On the whole, the American political system was regarded as a great success.[9] Two dimensions of this 'success' were more frequently mentioned. First, Chinese elites were impressed by the political stability of American society: no nationwide political turmoil, no succession crisis, and no ups and downs. They attributed this stability primarily to the built-in mechanisms of the political system, which, in the words of some respondents, 'has a great capacity to make self-adjustments' (zhiwo tiaojie). An academic administrator said: 'Although we criticize the division of three powers as having three governments, the checks and balances prevent policies from going to extremes. As a function of the system, Americans know when to compromise and to what extent.' Second, the political system provides room for individual opportunities and initiatives, and hence gives free rein to, rather than suppresses, people's 'enthusiasm' (jijixing). Equal opportunity and free competition, among other things, are the driving forces that push American society ahead.[10]

A kind of consensus on the merits of the American polity, however, does not necessarily mean they agreed on the replicability of this system. While some respondents considered that the American system 'made contributions to the progress of mankind' and could play an 'exemplary role' for other countries, others insisted that the United States is a 'unique' country, and that—as good as the system might be in the United States—it by no means can be transplanted to other countries such as China. A university professor said: 'The American political system fits the local conditions well. It is the best. But it won't work if you transplant it to China. It doesn't fit China and other Asian countries. "Bourgeois democracy" is very expensive and the Chinese cannot afford it. No way out. It is determined by fate. Whether you like it or not, you are Chinese. Even if Bush comes here to lead the country, he will be unable to solve the problems.'

Political stability, according to the Chinese respondents, contributes to the highly developed economy of the United States. Living in a relatively poor country, Chinese elites showed a greater cognitive awareness of the economic configuration of American society. For many respondents, their first impression of the United States was its being 'the wealthiest and most powerful country'. The cognitive attribution in this respect, however, is not merely politically oriented. Quite a few respondents adopted a more 'situational' explanation. They applied the term *de tian du hou* ('exceptionally richly endowed by nature') to describe the natural, as well as historical, advantages of the United States and concluded with envy that in this respect 'other countries, including China, were no comparison'.[11]

Chinese elites were less appreciative of the social features of the United States. Conceptually, they usually did not distinguish the 'state' from 'society' as did their American counterparts when discussing China, but some of them also perceived discrepancies between 'state' and 'society'. On the one hand, American society was seen as politically stable, full of vitality and energy, and civilized. On the other hand, this society was regarded as polarized, dangerous, and abnormal. These conflicting perceptions created a cognitive dissonance in the minds of some respondents.[12] The recognition of the coexistence of political success and social malfunction reflects a structural complexity of their cognition that was nonexistent before the 1970s.[13]

Cognitive Differentiation of Societies

It is anticipated that, compared to respondents' mutual images of people, the degree of their outer differentiation of the two societies will be higher due to divergent political and economic systems. To test this hypothesis, respondents were asked to choose a score along a 7-point scale in answering the following question: 'Considering Chinese/American society as a whole, would you say that Chinese/American society is very different from or very similar to American/Chinese society?' Table 4.3 presents a comparison of their cognitive differentiation of the societies.

The table indicates that both American and Chinese elites demonstrated a very high degree of outer differentiation. Almost all Chinese respondents (98%) chose scores below 4 and about 90% of the American respondents made the same choice. As in the case of mutual images of people, Chinese respondents again demonstrated a higher level of differentiation compared with their American counterparts. While nearly one in ten American respondents chose 4–5, only about 2% of the Chinese respondents selected 5. Among those who chose points below 4, 42% of the Chinese respondents went as far as point 1, whereas the equivalent figure for the American side is 28%.[14] However, on both sides, about half of the respondents preferred 2 rather than 1, and that implies that conceptually American and Chinese respondents perceived some minimum similarities between the two societies.[15]

Table 4.3 Percentage Distribution of Cognitive Differentiation of Chinese and American Societies

Cognitive Differentiation	Percentage (%)	
	US Respondents	**Chinese Respondents**
1 (very different)	27.8	42.1
2	46.4	47.6
3	15.7	8.7
4	6.4	0
5	2.8	1.6
6	0.7	0
7 (very similar)	0	0
Total	100.0	100.0
Sample size	140	126
Mean/SD	2.19/1.01	1.81/0.82

Presumably, when people are asked to offer impressions of another country, their initial reactions are likely to focus on those features different from their own. We can assume that those topic areas covered in their general images of the target society will be further elaborated in their answers to the following question: 'What are the most important differences and similarities between the two societies?'

American respondents touched upon an array of political, social, economic, cultural, and geographic differences between the two societies. The articulation of political differences maintains its salience. Approximately four out of ten American respondents mentioned the less democratic nature of the Chinese political system. They found the Chinese state system far more 'intrusive' and 'pervasive' in social life.[16] As a result, 'the ability of an individual to control his or her destiny' and 'to choose their own life' is very limited in China.

The political ecology in these two societies is also different. American respondents perceived two seemingly contradictory features. On the one hand, they raised the question of 'stability versus upheavals', with the implication that Chinese society is less institutionalized and legalistic. On the other hand, they raised the issue of 'stagnation versus change', implying that American society is more receptive to political changes. In other words, it is a difference between 'negative versus positive' or 'institutionalized versus uninstitutionalized' changes. A diplomat found a linkage between these two characteristics: 'Maybe because China has had too many upheavals in history and therefore the great goal is to have another option to upheavals. In the United States, sure Americans want peace, but they also want change, innovation. They want fulfilment. Americans like a little bit of turmoil, but not too much.'

This observation is further strengthened by another dichotomy in the American perceptions. While Chinese were perceived as family- and group-oriented in social terms, they were described as more 'selfish' and 'passive' in political terms and lacking a 'civic culture'. The difference lies in 'the [Chinese] inability to join in a common effort without it having been imposed from the top'. One respondent had this comparison: 'Americans tend to do things together without having somebody force them to do it. Americans also have a way of knocking off the rough edges when they get together. People always have different ideas, but Americans tend to agree on main things and forget about small differences, whereas with Chinese, it seems to me, these small differences get magnified and make it impossible for people to work together.'

Compared to their initial reactions, more American respondents mentioned the economic gap between the two societies. Many of them, especially those who had not been to China or visited only in the 1970s, still perceived China as quite a primitive society. They were struck by the 'lack of infrastructure', 'massive poverty', and consequent 'immobility' of Chinese society. An intellectual who visited China in the 1970s and had not been back since observed: 'Chinese are perhaps more like Americans of two hundred years ago in their level of expectation about how many different suits you have to have in order to be considered acceptable and so on.' These respondents might well have been surprised if they had revisited China in recent years. However, as seen in Chapter 3, some Americans are still more accustomed to the image of a primitive China and backward Chinese.

Quite different from their image of the Chinese people, only about 18% of the American respondents spontaneously mentioned some similarities between the Chinese and American societies (compared to 98% who mentioned differences). That does not necessarily mean they did not perceive any similarities, but it does indicate differences had a higher degree of 'salience' in their images.[17]

Chinese respondents displayed a similar pattern in their articulation of societal differences and similarities. While almost 97% of the respondents mentioned at least one difference, only about 16% of them mentioned similarities. Apart from noting the similar aspirations of people, some also perceived a parallel function of the government and social system.[18]

Apparently, more Chinese respondents were aware of the shortened distance between the two societies in terms of values and social problems since China's opening toward the outside world.[19] It can be said that for both sides, although functionally the social similarities had been increasing with China's modernization and marketization, American and Chinese elites had not been able to conceptualize them into definable categories by the time of this research.

The Chinese articulation of differences matches the American images quite well. In general they were more sensitive to the different 'nature' of the two societies. Nearly 40% of the respondents immediately responded to the question with a term—social system (*shehui zhidu*). The term usually means that China is a 'socialist country' and the United States is a 'capitalist country'. They were also more aware of the difference in 'ownership of the means of production' (*suoyouzhi*), which is 'private' in the United States and 'public' in China. However, for many respondents, it was just a habitual reflection of their 'schema' rather than a value judgement of 'good' and 'bad' as used to be the case in the past.

This can be seen from their more concrete comments about the political differences between the two societies. Three major differences were frequently mentioned. The first involves the structure and process of the political system. The division of three powers, the direct election of top governmental officials, and the decentralization (separation of government from enterprises, the autonomy of state governments, etc.) were cited as indicators. The second big difference is that of 'uniformism versus pluralism' (*yiyuan* versus *duoyuan*). As a professor saw it, 'Chinese society, like a pre-set machine, is moving at a constant speed in a designated direction, while American society is an entity in which apparently different forces are moving in different directions.'[20] The third difference lies in 'rule by men' and 'rule by law'. It is the legalistic nature of American society that, according to some respondents, contributes to its political stability. A senior professor who studied in the United States in the 1940s made the following observation:

> China needs a person like Zhou Enlai to govern. But people of his quality are too few and you can not have them all the time. Who is Ronald Reagan? He is an actor! He doesn't know anything about international affairs. Yet he still can be the President. Was the country in chaos under his leadership? No. Harding in the 1920s was really an idiot. Coolidge was not very smart either. It is said that among all the American presidents, only about five were outstanding. Most of them were mediocre. For a country with a history of more than 200 hundred years, you only have had five outstanding presidents; how can you

explain the American success? Because it is a country ruled by law and institutions. Even if you are not so intelligent, so long as you are not mad, you can be the president. A country ruled by men is very sad. When he dies, his policy ends. If he is wrong, hundreds and thousands suffer.

Chinese respondents had a consensus about the democratic nature of the American political process, but different voices can be heard on the representativeness of the government. One opinion holds that the American system can better reflect the will of the majority of the people. The two systems are different in the sense that 'the Chinese government controls the people while the American government serves the people.' Another view believes that in the final analysis, the United States is still 'a country ruled by the propertied class, and it does not represent the ordinary people'. Even for these respondents, they usually did not deny the merits of the democratic process of American politics.[21] A Marxist economist offered a very interesting view:

I often say that the nature of the American political system is bourgeois. Even though you have elections, those with money and power are more likely to be elected. It is a bourgeois dictatorship. No question about that. Yet if you talk about process and form, it is very democratic. Those who did not have formal training in Marxism will easily believe that their system is better than ours. We have a people's democratic dictatorship here, and its nature is different. But people's feeling about democracy is not so strong. I think it is a contradiction that needs to be resolved. If we can improve our process and form of doing things, we could have a better political system.

This perceptual gap is also reflected in their articulation of social differences. Chinese respondents agreed with their American counterparts that one fundamental difference between the two societies is the position of, and values attached to, individuals in society. There are two consequences resulting from this difference. On the one hand, in American society, individuals are less constrained by society and the political system; therefore talented people can fully explore their potential. On the other hand, in a very competitive society such as the United States, individuals are less protected by society and government and thus 'less safe'. Chinese respondents tended to appreciate the weak socio-political constraints placed on individuals in the United States. However, they also saw a downside to the competitiveness in American society. This lends an ambivalence to their opinion on 'freedom' and 'justice'. They were nervous about the 'huge gap between the rich and the poor' and 'the big rise and fall' of individuals in

American society. While the 'iron rice bowl' or 'big pot' in Chinese society may produce inefficiency and dependency, nevertheless they also reduce inequality.[22] From these comments, one can understand better the potential social consequences brought by the increasing distribution disparity in China.

Affective Orientation Toward the Target Society

The data in Chapter 3 show that as people, Americans and Chinese share a sort of 'special feeling' toward each other. Behind this feeling, however, is the backdrop of long-time political and ideological hostility and confrontation between the two 'incompatible' social systems that continue even today. The Tiananmen episode is just the latest manifestation of it. It can be reasonably predicted that, in contrast to their highly positive mutual images of people, American and Chinese elites would display a very negative affective orientation toward one another's government, which are often seen as symbols of social systems. To test this proposition, the following question was asked: 'I would like your overall opinion of the Chinese/American Government. Would you say that your overall opinion of the Chinese/American Government is very favourable, somewhat favourable, somewhat unfavourable, or very unfavourable?' Table 4.4 presents their responses.

Table 4.4 Percentage Distribution of Affective Orientation Toward the Chinese and American Governments

Affective Orientation	Percentage (%)	
	US Respondents	**Chinese Respondents**
1 Very favourable	2.9	0.8
2 Somewhat favourable	11.5	47.5
3 In the middle	11.5	28.0
4 Somewhat unfavourable	43.2	21.2
5 Very unfavourable	30.9	2.5
Total	100.0	100.0
Sample size	139	118
Mean/SD	3.88/1.07	2.77/0.88

As it turns out, the hypothesis about the negative affective feeling toward the target government is confirmed only partially. More than 70% of the American respondents held a 'somewhat' or 'very' negative feeling toward the Chinese government. Only about 14% of them had a 'somewhat' or 'very' favourable opinion, along with another 12% taking a middle stance. The pattern on the Chinese side is quite the opposite. A full 48% of the respondents had a favourable opinion of the American government. A much smaller portion (about 24%) described their attitude as 'somewhat' or 'very unfavourable', along with another 28% of the respondents 'sitting on the fence.' The two divergent trends can be further illustrated by the following graph.[23]

Figure 4.1   A Graph of Affective Orientation Toward the Target Government

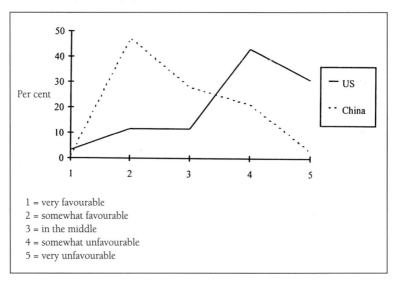

1 = very favourable
2 = somewhat favourable
3 = in the middle
4 = somewhat unfavourable
5 = very unfavourable

The graph reveals that the two curves are skewed toward opposite directions. For the United States sample, the curve leans toward the negative side and the mode is 4, 'somewhat unfavourable'. In contrast to this, the Chinese line is skewed toward the positive side with a mode of 2. It can be reasonably argued that the more negative trend on the American side demonstrates the impact of the Tiananmen crackdown and its aftermath. If the study had been conducted before that event, the result could have been quite different. In effect, many respondents qualified their answers by saying 'at this moment' or 'right now'.[24] There is evidence that not all respondents adopted this attitude out of 'intrinsic' motivation. Instead, some respondents' affective orientation in this respect was 'extrinsically' motivated.[25] This outward negative feeling toward the Chinese government, as the subsequent analysis will show, does not necessarily prevent American respondents from making some more discriminating and positive evaluations of the Chinese government. The very reason that the mode of the American data is located on 4 (somewhat unfavourable) rather than 5 (very unfavourable) is that many respondents still saw good things about this government. The curve on the Chinese side suggests that the Chinese opinion of the American government was affected little by the Tiananmen Incident (or at least did not have much negative impact). We can deduce, therefore, that for Chinese respondents, the more positive opinion of American society shaped in the last decade or so remained unchanged.[26] As Chapter 6 will illustrate, the animosity between the United States and China following the Tiananmen Incident did influence many Chinese respondents' opinions on American international behaviour. However, their negative feelings in that regard did not spread into their affective orientation toward the American government concerning its domestic management.

Evaluative Orientation

The data in Table 4.4 displays a general trend of affective orientation of American and Chinese elites toward the target society. These numerical data nevertheless fall short of revealing the perceptual complexity and subtlety. To further elicit their positive and negative evaluations combining cognitive knowledge and affective feelings, respondents were asked: 'Based on your personal experience, which aspects of the Chinese/American system impress or irritate you most?' Differentiation, balance, and sophistication emerged from their responses.

In their positive evaluation, American respondents demonstrated a considerable degree of inner differentiation of the Chinese government and society. Although in general many respondents had a negative view of the Chinese government, about one-third of the respondents described their personal experience in China as 'very comfortable'. Some respondents were particularly impressed by the effectiveness of their Chinese hosts in dealing with foreigners.[27] They realized that, as foreigners, they were privileged in China, and did not have to deal directly with the Chinese system or to experience the hassles that ordinary Chinese people had to suffer in their daily life.[28] So they were able to differentiate what they had experienced personally from what they observed or learned from other sources. As a diplomat said: 'I personally feel quite comfortable. . . . But there is a certain sense of discomfort too, because of the sympathy for other people. I feel quite uncomfortable just observing the society, not that it affects me personally.'

While many respondents affectively felt disgusted by the Chinese government, their knowledge of Chinese history and of the difficulty in governance enabled them to have some positive evaluations. Some respondents could differentiate their negative feelings at the moment from their evaluation of the record of the Chinese government since 1949. A portion of the American respondents mentioned the 'accomplishments' of the Chinese government since 1949, and the political openness and economic progress since the 1980s.[29] For these respondents, the Tiananmen Incident did not completely negate their previous images of the Chinese government, which they believed had greatly improved the basic welfare of Chinese people in terms of feeding, clothing, and sheltering a billion people, providing order, basic health and education, and so on. This is particularly the case for those who had some personal experience with pre-1949 China, which was in sharp contrast to what they saw after the 1970s.[30] Quite a few respondents experienced great psychological dissonance in answering the question because their affective and evaluative orientations seemed to be in conflict. As a retired diplomat put it: 'It's mixed. When put in the historical Chinese context, I would lean to a somewhat positive side. But if I am applying American standards, I would say somewhat negative.'

The perceptual complexity is further reflected in their inner differentiation of Chinese society. Obviously American elites had positive views of the Chinese people. Even with regard to the government, their views were quite discriminating. Although many respondents had negative views of the Chinese government as a whole, they held quite favourable views of the government officials, whom they found 'competent', 'dedicated', 'intelligent', 'serious-minded', and 'well-motivated'. They made various differentiations between the party and the government, between the top political leadership and professionals, between the central government people and local government people, between young and older officials, and between hard-liners and reformers. These differentiations demonstrate very well that their perceptions of Chinese society and government are more complicated and sophisticated than as reflected in the quantitative terms in Table 4.4.

In quantitative terms, Chinese elites evinced more positive feelings toward the American Government. This tendency manifests itself more concretely in their positive evaluation of American society. Their appreciation is more concentrated on the political and economic aspects of American society. In the political domain, Chinese elites were most impressed by what they called the 'good governance' (*zhili youfang*). This perception of good governance is reflected in several ways. The political stability of the United States is an indicator often mentioned in their comments. They recognized that the American government is not trouble-free: it has scandals, political crises, and personnel reshuffles. What the Chinese appreciated is the stability of the basic systems and institutions, which prevent the country from 'falling apart'. As a result, the political struggles at the top do not affect the economy and social life nationwide.[31] Another dimension they mentioned is the democratic process, including its checks and balances, elections, and public supervision, which makes the government more accountable to the people. Departing from their traditional separation of the American people from the government, some Chinese respondents found that the political system 'fits the situation there' and 'is supported by the American people'.[32]

Some Chinese respondents found the decentralization in American management very attractive. In their words, 'The American Government takes care of what it should take care of and does not take care of what it should not'. The divisions of power between the federal and state governments, the autonomy of local government and grassroots organizations were very much appreciated. Chinese managers of factories and companies particularly liked the independence of enterprise in American society. A joint-venture manager said: 'I like the separation of the Government and enterprise. The Government only employs economic means to influence the enterprises, but does not interfere in their decision-making and daily operation. It is symbolic that when American businessmen came here to visit, the government officials, the mayors, and the governors met them. When we went there to visit, we seldom dealt with these guys.'

Understandably, Chinese respondents were more impressed by the economic aspects of American society. Coupled with the generally mentioned advanced (*fada*) economy and science and technology are things such as a clean environment, magnificent urban development, convenient service, high living standard, and developed infrastructure. Although they kept 'polarization of wealth' in mind, they recognized the high living standards of 'ordinary people'. The highly developed transportation and service systems left deep impressions on those Chinese who travelled or toured in the United States. A business person asserted that the only things that impressed him in the United States were 'the highway and the restroom beside the highway'. Other respondents observed that in the United States, people can buy good service with money: 'When you go to a shopping mall, even if you don't have money, you still enjoy service. In China, even when you are buying, you often receive anger and unpleasantness anyway.'

In their positive evaluation, Chinese respondents also demonstrated a certain degree of inner differentiation of American society. They made a differentiation between the basic political system and a particular policy, the political system and the administrative system, the government as a whole and individual government officials, and the government in general and a particular administration or leaders. These differentiations somewhat enabled them to reconcile their first-hand observations and their political predispositions. Like some of their American counterparts, while Chinese respondents were aware of the problems in American society, some of them also realized the 'situational' difficulties in governance. A scholar remarked, 'As a Chinese, I am never very favourable toward the American Government. But this Government is leading a very complicated country. Although many Americans are complaining, as an outsider, I find the task is not easy.' A business person echoed: 'The United States is such a big country, you have people from all over the world, good and bad, black, yellow, and all kinds of people. But it still can maintain a rapid development of economy and culture. It is admirable.'

The negative evaluation by American and Chinese respondents displays different patterns. The complaints from the American respondents focus on the political and bureaucratic control and the 'regimentation' of Chinese society.

Although American respondents recognized some accomplishments of the Chinese Government, they were aware of the high human costs involved. As some respondents put it, the goals are not bad, but the means applied are not always 'human'. The perceived tight control exerted by the Chinese government and its harsh treatment of the Chinese people are, in American elites' opinion, 'unnecessary' and no longer 'justifiable'. While some respondents were impressed by the organizational and mobilizing ability of the Chinese Government, it is the very same capacity that disgusted or even scared some American respondents. They found 'the idea that certain things could be sacrificed for a large goal intimidating and almost chilly'.[33]

As analysed earlier, the Tiananmen upheaval was a great shock to many American respondents and dramatized for them the instability of Chinese politics. The PRC's failure to institutionalize the political system drew contempt and regret from American respondents. Some respondents, especially those who had limited experience and knowledge about China, had a hard time understanding the 'ups and downs every 10 or 15 years', and 'how Deng had come so far, then went all the way back'.

For the American 'China' elites, the regimentation and erraticism of Chinese society was not just something theoretical, but also a part of their personal experience. Foreigners were 'treated as a special group' in China.

While this brought some privileges to them, it also could mean they were 'constantly under supervision, control, and direction'. Some respondents, especially those who had official capacities such as diplomats, were frustrated in 'the difficulty of getting close to anybody in human terms'. Their actions were restricted in terms of travel, visiting friends, and so on. They were 'watched, monitored, or even followed'.[34] Because of the volatility of Chinese politics, American elites sometimes found it hard to generalize their experience. 'It depends on time', they declared. A China scholar described his experience since 1989 in the following words: 'My sense is, while things have not gone all the way back to the late Mao period, for the first time, I began to wonder if I would be watched or followed.' This sense of alertness does not always derive from direct evidence, but rather from their predisposition that China is a totalitarian or authoritarian country in which 'foreigners should assume that they are being observed'.

Ironically, while politically Chinese society was viewed as regimented and tightly controlled, administratively it was seen to have a 'lack of planning', to be 'totally disorganized' and 'the most inefficient'. More than 20% of the respondents complained about various aspects of the Chinese bureaucracy. The typical manifestation is the term 'not convenient' (*bu fangbian*), which 'drives Americans nuts'. As a professor said, 'The entire Chinese society is permeated by a bureaucratic mentality and bureaucratic organizations.' Those Americans who lived in China were especially annoyed by the so-called 'petty bureaucrats' such as the service people in hotels, taxi drivers, and store clerks who had control over people's daily life. They noted that 'the most irritating thing was trying to get help from service people', and 'no one had an incentive to do anything beyond their minimum assignment'. However, in their view, if you had some connections (*guanxi*), if you could establish a kind of personal bond, the outcome could be totally different. A lawyer who had had intensive dealings with the Chinese bureaucracy described the system as 'highly regimented, yet at the same time arbitrary. . . . That sounds like a dichotomy that is not possible. But in the context of the Chinese Government, it is an accurate description'.

The negative evaluations of American society by the Chinese respondents exhibit a different pattern, concentrating heavily on social aspects of American society. While many Chinese respondents had a high opinion of the American system in its capacity to maintain political stability, they were not so sure about its capacity to maintain social stability. A majority of the Chinese respondents listed various social problems such as polarization, urban decay, crime, homelessness, pornography, and drugs. Just as many American respondents felt politically and psychologically insecure in China, Chinese respondents felt physically unsafe in the United States.[35] They attributed these problems to several factors. The American legal system is 'too soft' and 'benign' in dealing with crime and criminals. As Chinese elites saw it, 'The United States needs a little bit of "proletarian dictatorship".' On the other hand, the overemphasis on privacy, freedom, and individualism encourages what some respondents called a 'self-indulgence', which leads to many social abnormalities such as homosexuality and pornography. As for the 'polarization of wealth' (*pinfu xuanshu*) manifested in numerous homeless and poor people, the phenomenon was partially attributed to the excessive competition and a lack of mechanisms for social equalization. A diplomat who served in Europe remarked: 'I like those socialist democratic countries such as Switzerland and Denmark better. They have more equality there. You don't see homeless people and shabby places as you can find in the United States.' A politically stable but socially chaotic American society is a puzzle to many Chinese respondents. Just as many Americans could not understand why the Chinese failed to pull together to work out a viable political system, Chinese respondents found it hard to believe 'why such a rich and powerful country is so impotent in eliminating social evils'.

Although some Chinese respondents did not consider racial discrimination a serious problem in American society, others still saw it existing, albeit in a more subtle way. They admitted that compared to other countries, American society is more open and international, but invisible barriers and discriminations are there. It might be easy to make a living in the United States, but it is another matter to make a successful career and to 'enter the mainstream of American society'. A veteran diplomat who used to study in the United States said: 'They describe American society as a "free society". Actually "free society" is not that free and the social pattern is very strong. You can make good friends. But it is impossible to become a part of the American society unless you are born and grow up there. Even then, it is still difficult.' Psychologically, some respondents described their experience in the United States as 'living under another's roof', even though they felt more comfortable materially.

It is interesting to note that few Chinese respondents criticized discrimination against blacks. This used to be a common Chinese perception of American society. Chinese respondents were aware of the 'black problem'. Some even described it as a 'cancer' or 'time bomb' in American society.[36] Yet they did not simply blame the American Government for the problem. For many Chinese respondents who had first-hand experience of American society, they tended to have a 'dispositional' explanation of the problem and considered it largely one of the blacks' own making. They often applied the term 'being fond of eating and averse to work' (*hao chi lan zuo*) to describe blacks. One reason for their negative impression of blacks is that 'while blacks are discriminated against, they also discriminate against others. They think they are No. 2 [below whites but above everyone else] in the United States'.

Chinese respondents' negative evaluation also reflects a more critical perception of the American political system. Two question marks were in some respondents' minds. First, to what extent can the American political system represent ordinary people? In some respondents' eyes, monopoly capital, powerful interest groups, and money were crucial in American politics. They also found some 'formalism' or 'affectations' in the American political process: 'Politicians often make big promises during campaigns but can do little to deliver them after they take office,' and therefore 'American politicians are better at saying than doing.' Second, some Chinese respondents wondered whether the outcome of national policy is always in the best interest of the country. While the checks and balances may avoid political disasters, they also can 'eat up' good policies due to endless partisan struggle and political gridlock. An America scholar observed: 'The good thing about the American political system is that it has a bottom line which keeps the worst from happening such as dictatorship or *coup d'état*. Above this line, however, anything could happen. . . . The vital national interest sometimes could be easily liquidated by a single vote in Congress.' But she hastened to add: 'It might be a necessary price.'

In short, American and Chinese elites showed quite distinct patterns in their evaluative orientation toward the target society. Generally speaking, American respondents had a negative orientation regarding the Chinese state but a more benign view of Chinese society. In contrast, Chinese respondents held a positive image of the American polity, but a more negative opinion of American society. Of course, in each dimension, many respondents mentioned both positive and negative elements, but the basic pattern is clear. This perceptual discrepancy is a manifestation of increased inner differentiation on both sides and thus a sign of perceptual sophistication. Nevertheless, the gap also creates new sources for perceptual ambivalence. The Americans wondered why such talented Chinese people have been unable to produce a viable political system. The Chinese asked why such a politically sophisticated American Government appears to be quite helpless in dealing with social problems. These fundamental questions remain unanswered in most respondents' minds and are potential sources for conflicting expectations and misperceptions. The essential problem for both sides still is that many Americans and Chinese applied their own system of reference to view socio-political phenomena and events in the target country. Only when American and Chinese elites have learned to view the target society on its own terms and to more fully understand the different political, economic, cultural, and even geographic bases of these problems, as some respondents in this study already demonstrated, can the relationship between the two countries be less susceptible to damage from either unrealistic wishful thinking or dehumanizing cynicism.

Evolution of Mutual Images

We proposed at the beginning of this chapter that Sino-American mutual images of societies could have been affected adversely by the Tiananmen Incident, since this tragedy and the American reaction to it typically reflect the different natures of these two countries' social systems. However, the impact of this event might not be so overwhelming as to completely negate the image ingredients accumulated over the last two decades. This hypothesis has been largely confirmed by the previous contextual analysis. To further test this assumption in quantitative terms, respondents on both sides were first asked to measure their attitudinal changes in general terms, and then along more specific conceptual issues. The first question asked is: 'With regard to your current image of Chinese/American society, how does it differ from that which you held before the 1970s?' A 7-point scale was given to measure their perceptual change. Table 4.5 provides a comparison of the American and Chinese responses.

Table 4.5 Percentage Distribution of Perceptual Change Regarding Chinese and American Societies

Perceptual Change	Percentage (%)	
	US Respondents	Chinese Respondents
1 (changed greatly)	18.6	10.1
2	38.6	21.1
3	25.7	26.3
4	5.7	10.1
5	3.6	15.2
6	7.1	11.9
7 (no change at all)	0.7	5.1
Total	100.0	100.0
Sample size	140	118
Mean/SD	2.64/1.39	3.61/1.72

A parallel pattern for both sides can be detected from the table. A majority of the respondents considered their perception of the target society to have changed significantly. The intensity of perceptual change is greater on the American side. More than eight out of ten American respondents chose the points 1–3, and among them more than half preferred 1 or 2. Only some 17% of the American respondents chose numbers 4 and above. Chinese respondents were more conservative. About 60% of them took numbers from 1 to 3, while about 40% chose 4 and above. The difference between the two means is statistically significant.[37]

The greater perceptual change on the American side can be explained by several factors. The single most important factor, as some respondents mentioned during the interviews, is the shock of the Tiananmen Incident, but it is not the whole story. It also reflects the greater volatility of Chinese society itself during 1970–1990. Some respondents described their perceptual evolution as a zigzag course that followed the ups and downs of Chinese society. The flatter curve of change on the Chinese side may mirror the more conservative disposition of the Chinese respondents, but it can also reflect their deeper ideological 'schemata'. Chinese respondents were more inclined to distinguish between 'nature' (benzhi) and 'appearance' (xianxiang). Some respondents in their comments demonstrated considerable perceptual change, but could still assert that their understanding of the 'nature' of American society remained the same.

The data report something about the intensity of perceptual change, but the direction of these changes remain to be defined. Respondents on both sides were then asked to describe their perceptual changes concerning the 'nature' and the 'successfulness' of the target society across three time-points: the 1970s, 1980s, and 1990s (the present). American respondents were asked to describe the nature of Chinese society along a 7-point scale, with 1 indicating 'very totalitarian' and 7 'very democratic', and to appraise communist rule along a similar scale, with 1 meaning 'a complete failure' and 7 'a complete success'. Table 4.6 presents their responses.

The table indicates that American perceptions about the 'nature' and 'successfulness' of Chinese society have experienced significant changes over the last 20 years. With regard to the nature of Chinese society, in the 1970s, almost nine out of ten respondents perceived China as a very totalitarian society (points 1–2). In the 1980s, this percentage decreased to about 30%, with only 3% selecting 1. At the same time, more than 40% chose the number 4 and above, indicating a cognition that China was moving in a more 'democratic' direction. However, this perceptual trend reversed itself to some extent in the 1990s. The percentage of respondents who chose points on the 'totalitarian' side again increased, but apparently most respondents did not go all the way back to their position held in the 1970s.

Table 4.6 Percentage Distribution of Perceptual Change Regarding the
'Nature' and 'Successfulness' of Chinese Society

Scale	Nature (%)			Successfulness (%)		
	1970s	1980s	1990s	1970s	1980s	1990s
	Totalitarian vs Democratic			Success vs Failure		
1	66.7	2.9	10.7	3.8	1.4	3.6
2	23.0	28.1	23.5	19.0	5.0	10.7
3	5.9	24.5	34.3	28.0	20.2	23.5
4	2.2	28.8	21.4	17.4	22.3	37.1
5	0.7	14.4	9.3	23.5	39.6	23.5
6	1.5	0.7	0	6.8	11.5	1.4
7	0	0.7	0.7	1.5	0	0
Total	100.0	100.0	100.0	100.0	100.0	100.0
Sample size	135	139	140	132	139	140
Mean	1.53	3.32	3.01	3.70	4.32	3.75

A parallel, but more moderate, pattern applies to their evaluation of the successfulness of communist rule in China. Even in the 1970s, almost 50% of the respondents (points 4 and above) considered the communist rule in China to be somewhat successful. Only 4% of the respondents considered it a complete failure. The pattern is consistent with a slight idealization of China at the initial stage of the Sino-American thaw. Over half of the respondents chose scores on the more 'successful' side (points 5–7) in the 1980s, while only slightly more than 25% preferred the points 1–3. However, in the 1990s, this number again increased to about 38%. On both issues, so to speak, what was described in Chapter 2 as a curvilinear model can be used to approximate the actual data. The American perceptions of Chinese society improved significantly in the 1980s, but regressed in the 1990s.[38]

The apparent 'regression' on these two issues can be explained by two major factors. The first is the Tiananmen Incident, which for many respondents dramatically demonstrated the totalitarian nature of Chinese society and failure of communist rule. Stated otherwise, the event did revive some of the previous 'schemata' of Chinese society that had faded away before the event. Another factor is the natural process of disillusionment that started long before the Tiananmen Incident through in-depth contact and interaction with China. Some respondents lowered their evaluation of Chinese society through their own business or research experiences. Others had a rosy image of Chinese society in the early 1970s, but became disillusioned by their direct or indirect observation. Nevertheless, the data also indicate that the degree of 'regression' is limited, and that the Tiananmen Incident did not totally reverse the perceptions they had built up in the last two decades. Most American respondents still considered China much less 'totalitarian' than it was in the 1970s. As the previous analysis of positive and negative evaluation reveals, many American respondents were still able to see some good aspects of the communist rule.

Chinese respondents were asked to describe their perceptual evolution along the same dimensions of 'nature' and 'successfulness' of American capitalism. The former was measured along a 7-point scale, with 1 indicating 'very monopolistic' and 7 'very democratic'. The latter was measured along the same scale, with 1 representing 'a complete failure' and 7 'a complete success'. The data are summarized in Table 4.7.

Table 4.7 Percentage Distribution of Perceptual Change Regarding the 'Nature' and 'Successfulness' of American Society

Scale	Nature (%)			Successfulness (%)		
	1970s	1980s	1990s	1970s	1980s	1990s
	Monopolistic vs Democratic			Success vs Failure		
1	25.0	1.7	1.7	6.4	0	0
2	38.4	11.0	11.0	18.4	0.8	0
3	13.4	11.8	8.5	21.1	8.4	6.8
4	12.5	28.8	26.2	30.3	29.7	29.7
5	8.0	30.5	30.5	14.6	37.3	38.1
6	1.8	15.3	21.2	8.3	19.5	22.0
7	0.9	0.8	0.8	0.9	4.2	3.4
Total	100.0	100.0	100.0	100.0	100.0	100.0
Sample size	112	118	118	109	118	118
Mean	2.54	4.30	4.45	3.62	4.87	4.93

The Table demonstrates a pattern of perceptual change somewhat different from the pattern for the American respondents. From the 1970s to the 1980s, Chinese perceptions regarding the 'nature' and 'successfulness' of American society also improved greatly. In the 1970s, almost four-fifths of the Chinese respondents regarded American society as very 'monopolistic' (points 1–3). In the 1980s, this percentage was reduced to about one-fourth.

Instead, nearly half of the respondents found American society more 'democratic' than 'monopolistic' (points 5–7). The estimation of the 'successfulness' of American capitalism, just like the United States data, showed a less dramatic change. Over 20% of the Chinese respondents declared that even in the 1970s they viewed American society as quite successful in terms of economy and science and technology (points 5–7).[39] The percentage with this view increased to 60% in the 1980s, and few respondents chose points below 3. The major distinction between the American and Chinese data is that we see little 'regression' in the latter. Compared to their images in the 1980s, Chinese elites' current perceptions of American society were either further improved or stabilized. For the whole period, therefore, the upward linear model of perceptual change proposed in Chapter 2 fits the data better than a regression model.

Evidently the United States' strong response to the Tiananmen unrest did not result in a visible regression in the Chinese perception of American society, at least not on the two issues we measured. Compared to the American respondents, fewer Chinese respondents mentioned cognitive regression through their personal experience with the United States. One possible proposition is that Chinese elites might have had lower expectations than their American counterparts from the very beginning of the relationship. As a result, they experienced less cognitive disillusionment later on. However, their perceptions have flattened out since the 1980s, and that also can be perceived as a function of mutual interactions, which allowed their images to mature in the sense of providing the Chinese with a more balanced view of American society. Thus, from the data available, it appears that the Chinese perception of American society demonstrated a higher degree of stability since the 1980s.

Accounting for Variations in Mutual Images

In Chapter 3, on mutual images of people, we crosstabulated respondents' cognitive differentiation, affective orientation, and perceptual change with a set of explanatory variables to examine their bivariate relationships. In this section, the same procedure was conducted to account for variations in American and Chinese elites' mutual images of society. We predict that variables of contact may explain respondents' cognitive differentiation and perceptual change to some extent, since these factors could reflect respondents' exposure to the target society in different time periods and, hence, their familiarity with and preconceptions of the target society. The Tiananmen Incident could well influence respondents' affective orientation toward the target government, given the emotional reaction of both sides to this dramatic episode. As in the previous chapter, age is likely to be positively associated with a decrease in outer differentiation and negatively related to perceptual change. The impact of profession will not be unitary for American and Chinese respondents, given the different value orientations of the three professional groups in the two societies.

The crosstabulation of the data of cognitive differentiation in Table 4.3 and explanatory variables yields some interesting findings. A caveat has to be kept in mind before looking at these findings, however. As Table 4.3 shows, a majority of respondents on both sides had a high degree of outer differentiation and the variation of the data is not very large. Yet, some subtle differences still emerge when their scores are crosstabulated with source variables. Contact before 1949 seems to explain the degree of outer differentiation fairly well. For both American and Chinese elites, those who had contact with the target people or visited the target country prior to 1949 on average had higher scores than those who did not, indicating that they perceived the two societies as more similar. It might be the case that the two societies those respondents saw before 1949 shared more similarities.[40] Simply because they had some first-hand knowledge about that country, when the interaction was resumed in the 1970s, the target society was not totally strange to them, even though the social system had become drastically different.[41] However, contact with the other side during the period 1950–1970 has a somewhat adverse impact. Those who had contact showed a lower mean score than those who did not. It could be assumed that during the Cold War period and the Sino-American confrontation, the political and ideological differences between the two societies were sharpened and that experience might still influence their current cognition. This function reversed itself during the 1970s. For both samples, respondents who had contact with the other side then, on average, had a higher mean score. One might attribute this difference to the change of circumstances under which these contacts occurred.

A high intensity of contact in the 1980s does not significantly decrease respondents' outer differentiation, suggesting the possibility that more contact could lead to discovery of more differences between the two societies. Those who had not visited the target country did show a higher degree of outer differentiation. It seems that for both sides, those who visited the target country only once have a jump in their mean scores compared with those who did not, indicating a lower degree of outer differentiation. It is interesting to note, however, that the United States data display an inverse U-shaped pattern. When respondents visited China more than five times, their mean score tends to decline again. Similar to the function of contact in the 1980s, this trend may suggest that although the initial visits and contact could help bring out a sense of similarity for both sides, further visits could bring more differences between the two societies to the surface.[42]

The impact of the Tiananmen Incident on cognitive differentiation is quite understandable for the American respondents. There is a sort of linear relationship between the two variables. The 'greatly affected' American respondents had a lower mean score compared to those who considered it relatively non-consequential to their images of China. People who were shocked by the Tiananmen crackdown must have thought that Chinese society was very different from their own. For those respondents who were affected very little, the incident did not increase their degree of outer differentiation.[43] The data on the Chinese side are somewhat puzzling. The trend is just the opposite. Those who were greatly affected by the American response to the crackdown also had the higher average score in their outer differentiation. Why is that the case? On the whole, Chinese respondents were less affected by the event so far as their perception of American society was concerned. As the data on perceptual changes showed, it is more likely to affect the American perception of Chinese society than the other way around. Even though some Chinese respondents were not pleased with the American response to the event, as discussed earlier, that might influence their perceptions of American international behaviour rather than that of American society. In other words, the formation of their outer differentiation was based on factors other than the American reaction to Tiananmen. Another possible explanation is that the higher mean score reflects some respondents' state of mind in responding to American condemnation: do not just criticize us; if we killed people this time, you did the same thing in the past, you are no better than we are. Both governments may use force to deal with the population when necessary.

Associating respondents' professions with their outer differentiation also produces different results for the American and Chinese elites. On the American side, it seems that intellectuals had the lowest degree of outer differentiation, with diplomats having the highest. On the Chinese side, however, diplomats exhibited the lowest degree of outer differentiation, with intellectuals and business people following in that order. How is this difference explained? It can be assumed that American intellectuals had more opportunities to interact directly with Chinese society and ordinary people. For many of them, it was their professional job to learn about and experience the daily life of Chinese society. Therefore, they might find more similarities in certain aspects of life in the two societies. For business people and diplomats, their contact with the target society could be more formal and shallow. Especially for diplomats, government-to-government contact in official capacities might reveal more of the differences between the two systems. For the Chinese respondents, the situation was quite different. Generally speaking, Chinese intellectuals and business people did not have as many opportunities as their American counterparts to visit or interact with the other side. Among the three cohorts of Chinese respondents, diplomats had more frequent contact with American society, which might have contributed to their lower degree of outer differentiation.

In regard to the relationship between age and cognitive differentiation, again we find different patterns for the two data sets. The United States data display an upward trend in cognitive differentiation corresponding with increasing age. Respondents younger than forty had the highest degree of outer differentiation on average. That may well indicate that the young American respondents were more aware of the political and ideological differences between the two societies. Respondents older than sixty had the lowest degree of cognitive differentiation. That may reflect their past experience, including their contact before 1949, as well as their memory of the artificial exaggeration of the societal difference during the Cold War period. The Chinese data show a sort of U-curved trend. In contrast to the young American respondents, Chinese respondents younger than forty had the lowest degree of cognitive differentiation. It could be argued that they were more sensitive to the social changes of the last decade or so, which have made Chinese society closer to American society. It may also reflect the fact that the young Chinese respondents themselves were more inclined to identify with the United States in terms of values and individual aspirations. The middle-aged respondents (between the ages of forty and fifty-nine) showed the highest degree of cognitive differentiation in this regard. The impression obtained from the interviews is that some respondents in this age group had the most difficulty in trying to reconcile the concepts of 'socialism' and 'capitalism'. It may well be the case that the political and ideological indoctrination received during their formative years still had a bearing on their current images. For the respondents sixty or older, however, the average score increases again. That may also have something to do with those respondents' experience with the United States before 1949, when the PRC was established. Most of these Chinese who had contact with Americans before the 'liberation' fall into this age group. As some of them declared in interviews, the United States was never a strange country to them, even though this image was submerged by the official Chinese image of the United States before the 1970s.

The same explanatory independent variables are applied to the respondents' affective orientation toward the target government in

Table 4.4. Here is the summary of the findings. The earlier discussion showed that American and Chinese elites had quite an opposite affective orientation toward each other's government. The American elites primarily had a negative image of the Chinese Government, while the Chinese elites primarily had a positive image of the American Government. Yet within each sample, variations in opinion exist, and the crosstabulation may help us to understand these differences. The variable of contact before 1949 yields a different influence on American and Chinese elites. On the American side, consistent with the earlier analysis, those who had visited China before 1949 seemed to have a more favourable image of the Chinese Government. From their positive and negative evaluations, we can see that the contact they enjoyed then formed a frame of reference that was different for those who did not have first-hand knowledge of 'old China'. For the Chinese respondents, however, those who had contact with Americans before 1949 on average had a more negative image of the American Government. From their comments during the interviews, it seemed that contact with Americans before 1949 produced mixed feelings for some Chinese respondents. Their images were positive in terms of the American assistance to China during the War against Japan, American teachers in missionary schools, and so on, yet their images were negative in terms of the American intervention in the Chinese Civil War, drunken American solders in jeeps dashing around madly, and so forth. Some respondents, who had a missionary education background or who studied in the United States, later joined the CCP partially due to disillusionment with the United States during the Chinese Civil War. These people tended to have a split mentality in their perception of the United States. Personally, they had favourable memories of their American teachers and friends. Politically, they were more sensitive to what they perceived as American 'interference' or 'arrogance' in dealing with the Chinese.

The more negative affective orientation largely holds true for the Chinese respondents in associating their affective orientation with contact during 1950–1970, the 1970s, and the 1980s. Those who had contact or a higher frequency of contact turned out to be less favourably inclined toward the American Government. The American data in these categories show a rather opposite tendency, albeit inconsistently. American respondents who had contact with the other side more often seemed to have more positive feelings. For instance, respondents who had contact with the other side least frequently in the 1980s, on average had the most unfavourable image. One thing that appears to be common to both sides is that the mean score goes down somewhat (more favourable) with the increase in number of visits to four or five, but goes up (less favourable) after more than five. This may suggest the possible 'regression' in images of the other side as analysed in the previous section. But as a whole, the intensity of contact since the 1970s does not dictate respondents' affective orientation toward the target government. One may argue that respondents' affective orientation toward the target government could be determined more by their overall value system rather than by frequency of contact.

As predicted, the Tiananmen Incident seemed to produce a visible impact on people's affective orientation for both sides. Respondents who were greatly affected by the event generally had more negative views of the target government in comparison with those who were not. It can be said that, compared to the relatively non-consequential daily interaction, 'big' events could have a more salient effect on people's affective orientation toward the target country.

The relationship between profession and affective orientation demonstrates different patterns for the American and Chinese elites. On the American side, intellectuals and business people had more negative views of the Chinese Government than diplomats did. This could be a result of several factors. First, intellectuals and business people were more conscious of certain values and ideas that made them feel repulsed by a Government that massacred students. Diplomats could be less emotional and more cool-minded. They might better understand the difficulty and dilemma of the Chinese G129overnment, given their own official capacities. Second, as mentioned earlier, some American diplomats tended to have quite favourable impressions of the Chinese officials, and that might affect their overall opinion of the government. Third, quite a number of diplomats visited China before 1949, and they could have a more favourable view of the Chinese Government from a historical perspective.

For the Chinese elites, the picture is just the opposite. It is the diplomats who had the most negative views of the American Government. First, Chinese Government officials usually evinced more orthodox views in their comments, although that might not fully reflect their private thoughts.[44] Second, since some of them had to directly deal with US-China relations after the June 4th Incident, they could have a deeper resentment against American 'interventionism'. Understandably, intellectuals and business people had a more favourable view of the American Government among the three cohorts, as reflected in their comments about the 'good governance' of the American political system. In particular, Chinese intellectuals were more likely to endorse American values of democracy and freedom as manifested in the democratic movement in 1989.

The relationship between age and affective orientation is very clear for Chinese respondents. On average, the younger a respondent was, the more favourable view of the American Government he or she held. That might reflect, as a scholar put it, a 'pro-American feeling' among the Chinese young generation. Respondents older than sixty, however, had the most negative view of the American Government. That might mirror, as the same scholar pointed out, an 'anti-American feeling' toward the United States following the Tiananmen episode among the old generation. These two conflicting trends compete to form the general public image of the United States in China. A complete assessment of the Chinese attitudes toward the United States should take both trends into consideration.

The pattern on the American side, however, is less straight forward. It seems that respondents either younger than forty or older than sixty, had a less unfavourable image in comparison with middle-aged respondents. For the younger American respondents, a higher degree of cognitive differentiation apparently does not mean a more negative affective orientation in their perceptions. The older respondents tended to show both a lower degree of outer differentiation and a less negative orientation toward the Chinese society and Government.[45]

Finally, we try to associate the explanatory variables with the levels of perceptual change presented in Table 4.5. The data indicate that the variable of contact before 1949 can explain the differentials fairly well. Both American and Chinese respondents who had contact with or visited the other side before 1949 had a lower rate of perceptual change in comparison with those who did not have contact, not to mention those who were either not born yet or were too young to have meaningful contact at that time. The data suggests that images of the target society shaped then have an enduring impact and are quite resistant to change. The pattern applies quite consistently to those who had contact both during the period 1950–1970 and in the 1970s. However, this effect is reversed during the 1980s. Both American and Chinese respondents who had a high intensity of contact generally expressed a greater degree of perceptual change. This might be attributed to the different nature of contact in the 1970s and 1980s. In the 1970s or earlier, the contact was usually formal, brief, and superficial. Such contact might confirm, rather than change, the preconceptions of the other side. In the 1980s, however, the contact gradually became more individual, regular, and deep. This might well facilitate the discovery of new grounds able to overturn their pre-existing images. Many respondents initiated their contact in the 1980s, and for them, perceptual changes were more likely to take place.

The impact of the Tiananmen Incident on the perceptual change is more mixed. The pattern in the Chinese data is somewhat to be expected. Those Chinese respondents who were not affected by the event evinced less perceptual change and vice versa. On the American side, the pattern is quite the opposite. The 'greatly affected' respondents displayed the highest mean score, indicating least perceptual change. Some American respondents might have reasoned that since the Tiananmen Incident made them regress in their perceptions, their overall opinion of the Chinese Government did not change that much across the entire time period.

The relationship between profession and perceptual change again goes in a different direction for the American and Chinese elites respectively. On the American side, diplomats had the highest degree of perceptual change and intellectuals had the lowest degree. On the Chinese side, diplomats had the lowest rate of change while intellectuals had the highest. This interesting pattern could be related to their affective orientations. On both sides, the group that had the most negative view of the target government claimed the least perceptual change, while the group that had the most favourable view of the target government asserted the most perceptual change.

The variable of age has a conventional impact on respondents' perceptual changes. Younger respondents on both sides demonstrated greater perceptual changes, while older respondents were more reluctant to change their pre-existing 'schemata' shaped by their life experience.

The above analysis indicates that contact, the Tiananmen Incident, profession, and age do have some influence on respondents' perceptions of the target society. Contact before 1949 is apparently associated with lower outer differentiation and less perceptual change. Its impact on affective orientation is different for the American and Chinese respondents. Contact during the period 1950–1970 and during the 1970s did not facilitate perceptual change, but the frequency of contact in the 1980s and of visits since the 1970s tend to expedite perceptual change. Nevertheless, their associations with cognitive differentiation and affective orientation could go either way. It is possible that respondents found more different and negative sides of the target society when their contact and visits attained a certain level.

The Tiananmen Incident has the most visible effect on people's affective orientation toward the target government. For both sides, the 'greatly affected' respondents were inclined to have the most unfavourable opinion of the target government. Profession appears to bring different perceptual orientations to the American and Chinese respondents. On average, American intellectuals expressed the lowest outer differentiation and the least perceptual change. In contrast, American diplomats evinced the highest outer differentiation and the greatest perceptual change. Compared to intellectuals and business people, American diplomats also had the least unfavourable affective orientation toward the Chinese Government. The pattern is almost reversed on the Chinese side. Chinese intellectuals experienced the greatest perceptual change, while Chinese diplomats expressed the least perceptual change. Although Chinese diplomats exhibited the lowest outer differentiation, their affective orientation toward the American Government is the most unfavourable of all. These patterns indicate that a low level of outer differentiation is not necessarily related to more positive affective feelings. Increased age is negatively related to perceptual change on both sides. Yet, its impact on cognitive differentiation and affective orientation could be curved. For instance, both younger and older Chinese respondents perceived more similarity between the two societies than did the middle-aged. The younger and older American respondents tended to have less unfavourable feelings toward the Chinese Government than did the middle-aged.

Notes to Chapter 4

1   For China's perception of American society before the 1970s, see Yusheng Yang, *Zhongguoren de meiguoguan* (Chinese Images of the United States), Chapter 10.

2   For a detailed discussion about the perceptual evolution in the scholarly and intellectual communities in both countries, see David Shambaugh, *Beautiful Imperialist*, Chapters 2, 3, 4, 5; Steven Mosher, *China Misperceived*, Chapters 7, 8, 9; Yusheng Yang, *Zhongguoren de meiguoguan* (Chinese Images of the United States), Chapter 11.

3   See Harry Harding, *A Fragile Relationship*.

4   Henry Harding analysed the process of this disillusionment on the American side. See his essay, 'From China with Disdain.'

5   They applied terms such as 'authoritarian', 'totalitarian', 'repressive', 'bureaucratic', 'police state', 'highly centralized', 'dictatorship', and 'tightly controlled'.

6   A former government official observed: 'I guess what comes to my mind most of all is sadness, in the sense that the Chinese people are such an extraordinarily talented people and the Government is sort of extraordinarily untalented.'

7   They described these difficulties as 'mind-blowing'. Some respondents mentioned that they used to have a very 'naive' view of China, and Tiananmen made them realize the 'complexity' of China that is not yet fully understood by most Americans.

8   American respondents often were impressed by how the Chinese people can 'get around the system.' As a professor observed: 'The system theoretically controls you very tightly, but as long as you understand how to get along with the system, you could avoid some of the worst aspects of it.'

9   For many respondents, what came to their minds first were the 'division of three powers', 'the Declaration of Independence', and 'democratic republic system'. They pointed out that, as far as the capitalist system is concerned, the American system is 'the most typical', 'most successful', and 'most developed'.

10   Some respondents considered that *laobaixing* (ordinary people) have a greater degree of freedom and the government is more benign to them', and 'as long as you work hard and make an effort, making a living is not a problem'.

11   According to one Chinese observer, many Chinese think that American wealth is largely a windfall—a result of the rich natural resources, commercial exploitation abroad, and geographical immunity from the two world wars. Chinese tend to say that 'the Americans are *tientien guonie* (enjoying Spring Festival every day)'. That means that the Americans earn so much easy money that they can relax and have fun every day. Tsomin Wang, 'Chinese-American misunderstanding, their cultural roots, the America difference', *Beijing Review*, July 18–24, 1988, p. 32.

12   Reflecting this dissonance, they described American society as a 'mixture of contradictions', 'having two equally salient sides', 'coexistence of both "fragrant flowers" and "poisonous weeds"'.

13   As a researcher put it: 'This society is not going to collapse as we used to think, yet it is neither ideal as we once imagined.'

14   A significance test supports the observation that American respondents displayed a lower degree of outer differentiation ($t = -3.32$, $p < 0.005$).

15   As a Chinese respondent put it: 'Societies are composed of human beings. After all, we are all human beings'.

16   A diplomat held a perception that 'the [Chinese] Government is very much in control all the way down to the smallest level, the street neighbourhood and even the family. You have to get permission to do anything. The American reaction is if you want to do something, go ahead and do it unless they told you not to. The Chinese reaction, it seems to me, is not to do anything unless you are told to do it'.

17   Some American respondents referred to the similar political, economic, and national desires of the Chinese and American people. As seen in their images of Chinese as individuals, some respondents considered that the value of family and education is something shared by the two societies. Some respondents did see a trend of convergence of these two societies in the recent decades. On the whole, respondents were much less inclined to discuss similarities between the two societies.

18   A business person believed that 'both governments are tools and representatives of certain social groups'. A trade official held, 'In a fundamental way, both societies want to develop the economy and increase production, although they take different paths.' A foreign service staff member declared: 'If you talk about the operation of the government, the United States and China do not have big differences. They also have a huge bureaucratic system that functions in a surprisingly similar way.'

19   Respondents mentioned various social problems, such as crime, pollution, drugs, and unequal distribution of wealth. They also touched upon the value changes in the areas of money, family, marriage, and sex.

20   This difference, however, cannot be perceived in an absolute way. A young scholar who lived in the United States for several years had a more sophisticated view: 'The United States is pluralistic on the surface, but you still can see uniformity underneath. China is uniform on the surface, but you can see pluralism underneath.'

21   A Marxist economist offered a very interesting view: 'I often say that the nature of the American political system is bourgeois. Even though you have elections, those with money and power are more likely to be elected. It is a bourgeois dictatorship. No question about that. Yet if you talk about process and form, it is very democratic. Those who did not have formal training in Marxism will easily believe that their system is better than ours. We have a people's democratic dictatorship here, and its nature is different. But people's feeling about democracy is not so strong. I think it is a contradiction that needs to be resolved. If we can improve our process and forms of doing things, we could have a better political system.'

22   This view was held across three groups of respondents. A business person said: 'In American society, if you are successful, you are the "king" (*wang*), but if you fail, you become a "bandit" (*kou*). We here advocate working together with one heart in difficult times (*tong zhou gong ji*) .' A university president said: 'The American society advocates individual struggle (*geren fendou*). We here share a big rice bowl (*daguofan*). Of course things are changing now, but we cannot afford to have their way of doing things entirely. If a factory cannot sell its products on the market, Americans will close it and fire the workers. We cannot do that, but keep producing with the result that you have an inventory piled up.' A diplomat said: 'Social justice is neglected in the United States. If you cannot survive, that's your problem. We here must help each other out. Food for three people could be shared by five.'

23   A significant test of the two means indicates that the Chinese respondents on average had much more positive feelings about the target government (t = -9.1, p < 0.0005).

24   A university professor expressed this mentality: 'How could anybody at this point favour the communist regime in China?'

25   What the term implies is that after Tiananmen, there formed a social norm on the issue that they morally and psychologically felt compelled to comply with. A former government official had this reaction: 'Oh, dear, I guess I have to say "very unfavourable".' When asked why, she said: 'Every time I read anything about China in newspaper, there is a big difference between now and before Tiananmen. Now everything appears to be a problem.'

26   This inference will be further verified by the analysis on perceptual changes.

27   They found that Chinese are quite good at 'using protocol to make you comfortable' and are very skilful in making foreigners 'feel friendly and sympathetic to Chinese viewpoints'.

28   As some respondents put it, they were always 'intermediated by somebody else', and there was a 'buffer' between them and the Chinese system.

29   Some respondents chose 'somewhat unfavourable' rather than 'very unfavourable' because they realized that the Chinese Government 'has done some good things'. A diplomat said: 'The real difference is, I think that most Americans probably will answer "very unfavourable". I moved it up to the next category because I realized the enormous problems the government has to deal with, the very sincere effort many people in the Chinese Government made to solve these problems, and the great accomplishments they have made, particularly through early and mid-1950s, and again through the early and mid-1980s.'

30   A diplomat who served in China before 1949 commented: 'The transformation of China from 1949 to 1989 is one of the miracles in economic world history.' He declared, 'I don't think it is a good government, but I think it's wonderful if they have a government at all.' A musician who used to be a soldier in China responded: 'The Chinese Government has done a miraculous job in one or two major areas. I think that they have somehow been able to alter the previous cycles of famine and death by famine, the rank and disparity between those with property and money and those without.' A writer said: 'Compared to the situation before 1949, I was very impressed with how much better things are than I saw: the general state of people's health, the general outlook.'

31   A joint venture manager found that in American society, 'political changes do not necessarily bring about economic changes. China is different. If you have a new leader, then you have a new set of policies'. A university professor said: 'They can have crises and scandals at the top level: Watergate, Irangate. But these things do not affect production and economy. Politics has little influence on the social life.'

32 To reduce their cognitive dissonance, some respondents expressed this perception indirectly, using official terminology. They considered that American leaders 'are doing very well in playing the "false democracy".' As an intellectual put it, 'The Government makes the majority of the people believe that the system is good, and if you have problems, it is just because some individuals are bad. You always see many posters and demonstrations. In reality, they have little effect. But the trick is that people believe they can make a difference and affect government policy.'

33 A diplomat observed: 'The tendency of the Chinese Government to put certain principles and objectives first and foremost over all others, even at the risk of the Chinese people, is a very unfavourable tendency. . . . Deng Xiaoping has his famous comment that if people want to emigrate from China, fine. America could take hundreds of thousands, that sort of idea. China has lots of people and some of them are not useful and just get rid of them, let them go. . . . That's something that as an American who has a different view of the individual and individual life, I find disturbing and hard to deal with.'

34 This perception is particularly salient for those who served in China during the 1970s and the early 1980s. Various stories were told about their unpleasant experience.

35 Especially those who lived in big cities complained about the 'lack of safety'. A business person observed: 'In New York City, I am nervous. I have to constantly worry whether I carry too much or too little money in my pocket, whether it is too late to go out, which route I should take, whether I should take the subway. Too nervous.'

36 They were concerned about the future of the United States when the proportion of the black population will increase to a certain level. A scholar said: 'I don't know what will happen in the future. The birth rate of blacks is very high. I don't know what will happen ten years from now.'

37 $t = 5.03$, $p < 0.0005$.

38 On the 'nature' issue, the percentages of respondents who chose 1–3 for the 1970s, 1980s, and 1990s are 95.6%, 55.5%, and 68.5%, respectively; the parallel figures for the 'success' issue are 50.8%, 26.6%, and 37.8%.

39 During that period, the Chinese public media seldom reported positive news about American society, only descriptions of the 'economic crisis' and 'social degeneration'. Some respondents learned more objective information from the *Reference News*, a daily paper internally circulated for cadres.

40 At least, they did not perceive a clear-cut ideological difference between the two societies. Some American respondents who stayed in China then recalled that they had more freedom travelling around and interacting with the Chinese people.

41 Some American respondents mentioned that when they visited China again after the opening of the relationship, they found the place familiar. Some Chinese respondents also mentioned that their contact with Americans before 1949 made them feel closer to Americans and American society.

42 A preliminary examination of another variable—the length of executive stay in the target country—also indicates that for those who lived in the target country for two years or more, their mean score of outer differentiation is relatively low.

43 Some respondents even suggested that similar episodes could happen or happened in the United States.

44 In fact, several Chinese diplomats declined to give their affective orientation in interviews.

45 If we split the group of 60 and older into two of 60–69 and 70 and older, we find that the respondents who were 70 or older had the highest mean score of outer differentiation (2.46) and the lowest mean score of affective orientation (3.36).

CHAPTER 5 ·
MUTUAL IMAGES OF CULTURE

Compared to other dimensions of mutual images covered in this study, an exploration of mutual images of culture is a more onerous endeavour. It is very hard to find a generally recognized definition of culture and a reliable device to measure and describe culture.[1] Since our purpose here is not to study American and Chinese cultures per se, but to elicit American and Chinese elites' general perceptions of one another's cultures, we define it as a rather broad entity within which is embedded sociological, intellectual, artistic, and material dimensions. In other words, cultures is treated as, in this case, an all-encompassing concept that serves as a catalyst to elicit respondents' perceptions about the target nation at a cognitive level broader than people, society, or international behaviour.

As in the case of other dimensions of mutual perceptions, before the 1970s, Sino-American mutual images of culture were distorted, uninformed, and fragmentary. As Isaacs' study revealed, the American image of Chinese culture was dominated by stereotypes largely derived from their experience of 'Chinatown' in the United States. During the 1950s and 1960s, Americans perceived the communist regime in China as something totally 'alien' to Chinese culture and imposed by an outside force. The Chinese image of American culture was heavily contaminated by ideological propaganda and bias. The term 'American lifestyle' (*meiguo shenghuo fangshi*) was being equated with a 'dissipated' and 'extravagant' culture that was not only alien to the communist way of life, but also at odds with human nature and dignity.

The flourishing of mutual cultural exchanges between the United States and China accompanying the opening of the bilateral relationship in the 1970s gradually produced a more objective and less ideological re-examination of one another's way of life, and of the material and spiritual expressions of the target culture. Americans, at least in the early 1970s, discovered some merits in the 'puritanical' Chinese way of life. Chinese realized that the American way of life is not so 'corrupt' as they once thought. The initial 'China fever' in the United States and the ensuing 'America fever' in China promoted intensive interest and interactions between the two cultures and facilitated better understanding, even a convergence, of reciprocal cultural values, artistic styles, and human behaviour. While many Americans and Chinese still believed their own culture and life-style to be somehow 'superior' to the other's, they began to understand and appreciate the rationale and underpinnings of the target culture.

In this chapter, we will first try to provide a profile of mutual images of culture along the cognitive, affective, and evaluative dimensions set forth in the conceptual framework of Chapter 2. The evolution of the mutual images since the 1970s will then be explored. Finally, a set of explanatory variables will be applied to account for image differentials. It can be assumed that because of the divergent epistemological and ontological origins of the two cultures, American and Chinese elites may display a higher degree of outer differentiation in their cognitions. For the very same reason, however, the difference may enhance rather than reduce their intrinsic fascination with the target culture, and thus yield a positive affective orientation. In terms of perceptual change, we believe respondents in our samples may demonstrate more perceptual continuities, in comparison with other dimensions of mutual images, because culture per se is characterized by stability and does not change as quickly as social structures or international behaviour. Therefore, theoretically, a static model may be a better approximation to the evolutionary trend. Likewise, we do not anticipate that mutual images in this regard would have 'regressed' dramatically due to a single event such as the Tiananmen Incident.

General Images of Culture

In accordance with the structured research design, the first step is to obtain a spontaneous profile of mutual images of culture. Tables 5.1 and 5.2 represent general images of one another's cultures developed from responses to the question: 'When you think about China/the United States as a cultural entity, what comes to your mind first?'

The features mentioned by both American and Chinese respondents were coded into three broadly defined topic areas: (1) general characteristics, (2) specific forms of culture, and (3) values and inclinations. Apparently, two trends of thought characterize the American image concerning the basic features of Chinese culture. What strikes half of the American respondents is the 'antiquity' of Chinese culture. For most of them, this perception mainly conveys two traits—'continuity' and 'richness', for which many respondents could not resist expressing their admiration and respect.[2] As a lawyer remarked: 'No other place, no other culture, no other people have maintained so much cultural stability for so long in the same geographic area.' This continuity and cohesiveness can transcend time and space, as well as ideology and political regimes.[3]

The vertical dimension of longevity is further enhanced by the horizontal dimension of Chinese culture. It is the 'richness', 'depth', 'complexity', and 'sophistication' that attract and fascinate many American respondents. They found that in this 'treasure house', 'there is almost nothing primitive' and

Table 5.1 General Images of Chinese Culture (Sample Size = 141)

Subjects	Number of Cases	Proportion (%)
Basic features		
Ancientness, sophistication	71	50.4
Gap between ancient and modern	34	24.1
Powerfulness, vitality	9	6.4
Homogeneity	6	4.3
Specific forms of culture		
Traditional art	44	31.2
Traditional philosophy	15	10.6
Traditional literature	12	8.5
Traditional performing arts,		
Music	9	6.4
Language	6	4.3
Food	4	2.8
Science	3	2.1
Values and inclinations		
Emphasis on family and education	14	9.9
Sense of history	10	7.1
Pride, arrogance	7	5.0
Unique interpersonal relations	6	4.3
Tendency toward centralization	5	3.5

Note: Since each respondent could mention more than one feature, the numbers of cases and percentages in the table represent the proportion of respondents who mentioned each subject. Therefore the total of percentage distribution does not add up to 100%. This also applies to other tables of the same kind.

'the historical parallel is almost endless'. Yet American respondents had different opinions about the merits of this 'complexity'. For some respondents, although 'it is a difficult culture we foreigners can never know very well, it rewards all the efforts you make'. For others, the complexity is a burden, even for the Chinese, let alone for the Americans.[4]

The endurance and sophistication formerly made Chinese culture a 'powerful civilization'. It became a 'dominant culture in East Asia', and its influence also 'spread to other parts of the world'. Nevertheless, for many American respondents, Chinese culture is a concept attached to the past

Table 5.2 General Images of American Culture (Sample Size = 127)

Subjects	Number of Cases	Proportion (%)
Basic features		
Diversity, pluralism	32	25.2
Shallowness	29	22.8
No tradition and identity	15	11.8
Being dynamic and influential	15	11.8
Having basic way of life	8	6.3
Christian culture	5	3.9
Specific forms of culture		
Movies, traditional music	15	11.8
Science and technology	14	11.0
Pop music, sports, etc.	12	9.4
High level of education	12	9.4
Philosophy, literature	4	3.1
Values and inclinations		
Creativity, independence	17	13.4
Decadence, extremes	12	9.4
Freedom, having choice	10	7.9
Respect for history & culture	9	7.1
Pragmatism, commercialization	7	5.5
Modernness	5	3.9
Others	6	4.7

rather than to the present.[5] Nearly one in four respondents mentioned the discrepancy between traditional and modern Chinese cultures in terms of economy, art, literature, science, and scholarly accomplishments. This gap is reflected in the mentality of the Chinese, who are 'extremely proud of their own cultural achievements over the years, but increasingly frustrated that its past has exceeded its present'. This cognitive ambiguity also exists in the minds of American respondents. Whereas traditional Chinese culture frequently elicits their admiration, the current condition of Chinese culture often incurs their contempt.[6]

To reconcile this cognitive dissonance, American respondents offered both 'situational' and 'dispositional' explanations in their ensuing cognitive differentiation and affective evaluation. The 'situational' attribution blames the communist regime and ideology which 'destroyed' and 'contaminated' the traditional culture. The 'dispositional' explanation argues that Chinese culture 'lost its dynamics' due to its own inherent weakness: lack of creativity and adaptability.

The historical orientation of the American image of Chinese culture was also reflected in their references to specific forms of Chinese culture. Most respondents mentioned traditional art, philosophy, literature, performing arts, and so on. The most frequently mentioned form of culture is traditional art, in its various expressions of painting, calligraphy, bronze, porcelain, ceramics, and architecture. Obviously, quite a few American respondents equated traditional Chinese art with Chinese culture. Another salient feature of their images is the heavy weight given to art and humanity over science and technology.

While American respondents regarded the vertical dimension of Chinese culture, namely its history and continuity, as 'unmatched' in the world, Chinese respondents perceived the horizontal dimension of American culture, namely its diversity and openness, as 'without comparison' in the world.[7] When it comes to the implications of these 'horizontal' characteristics of American culture, however, Chinese respondents expressed subtle differences in their opinions. Parallel to the cognition of the 'shallowness' of Americans as people, about one-third of the respondents described American culture as 'shallow' and lacking 'tradition' and 'identity'.[8] Two frames of reference were employed in their remarks. Naturally, by comparing American culture with Chinese culture, some respondents perceived the former as a 'cultural desert' due to its short history. Here are some of their remarks: 'Just look at their museums. Things two hundred years old are regarded as treasures. In China, whose family cannot show you something from two hundred years ago?' 'They take things of several hundred years ago as antiques. We Chinese cannot help laughing.'

Another frame of reference often used is European culture. Especially for some Chinese intellectuals, they had greater admiration for European cultures in terms of literature, music, and art. They perceived that European culture 'is deeper, more serious, and brings about aftertaste', and asserted that 'the United States does not have first-class philosophers, writers, and artists'. Some respondents were influenced by their specialities and experience during their school years. A business person said: 'When I was studying foreign languages in school, we did not study American literature at all, but British literature. If I spoke English with an American accent, my teacher would criticize me for "speaking English like an American sailor".' A scholar recalled: 'When I was in school, I thought it didn't make any sense to study in the United States. . . . We never talked about American literature. When I studied music, there was nothing special about American music. We felt their stuff was too crude and primitive.'

The other facet of the Chinese image, however, finds that American culture has its own unique 'basic life-style', and 'collective American spirit', which are distinguishable from European and other cultures.[9] More importantly, American culture is a dynamic and functioning one. As a senior intellectual observed: 'If you use European or Chinese standards to judge the United States, it doesn't have much culture. But I think culture has nothing to do with the past, you should see its function and influence at present and in the future. If you use that criterion, American culture is very competitive.'

Applying this standard, Chinese elites found that American culture is 'influential' and 'has irresistible penetrating power'. Although some respondents were puzzled why 'stuff like pop music and blue jeans have such great appeal', they could not deny the fact that 'young people are crazy about these things'. 'There must be reasons for it to win so many young people over', a foreign affairs official concluded. For this phenomenon, Chinese elites also had both 'dispositional' and 'situational' explanations. The former suggests American culture is powerful because it can 'better reflect human nature and human desires'. The latter argues that it does not reflect the power of American culture per se, rather that the power is merely a manifestation of an advanced economy and science and technology. A trade official elaborated:

> Many aspects of American culture, such as Coca Cola, KTV, jeans, and pop music, in the final analysis are expressions of its powerful economy. Because economically the United States is powerful, its culture is also admired by many people. Because China is backward economically, its culture is looked down upon. So there is a relationship between economy and culture. For example, the Shanghai dialect used to be quite popular because Shanghai used to be the most advanced city in the country. Now Cantonese has become more popular. Japanese culture originated from China, but it is more influential in the world now. I think that once China has modernized itself, probably the *dabing youtiao* (a typical breakfast in Shanghai), like McDonalds, will be popular throughout the world.

This may explain why Chinese elites expressed a greater appreciation for the so-called 'material civilization'—science and technology. Even in the case of the more frequently mentioned 'cultural' form—the American movie—for some respondents, it is 'a combination of culture and technology'. Just as some American respondents equated traditional Chinese art with Chinese culture, some Chinese respondents found that 'there is nothing in American culture except movies'. In particular, senior Chinese respondents held a very deep impression of American movies and music of the 1930s and 1940s, and described them as 'worth watching a hundred times' and 'worth hearing a hundred times' (*baikan buyan, baiting buyan*).

Cognitive Differentiation

It is hypothesized that because of the fundamental differences in origins, components, history, and evolution between Chinese and American cultures, respondents in our samples may display a very high level of outer differentiation in their comparison of the two cultures. In this regard, we should expect no great discrepancies between the two data sets. Respondents on both sides were asked to locate themselves on a 7-point scale of differentiation. Table 5.3 provides a comparison of their outer differentiation.

Table 5.3 Percentage Distribution of Cognitive Differentiation of Chinese and American Cultures

Cognitive Differentiation	Percentage (%)	
	US Respondents	**Chinese Respondents**
1 (very different)	25.0	37.3
2	51.4	36.5
3	14.3	16.7
4	7.1	6.4
5	2.1	3.2
6	0	0
7 (very similar)	0	0
Total	100.0	100.0
Sample size	140	126
Mean/SD	2.14/0.92	2.09/1.04

The data show a parallel pattern of cognitive differentiation for the American and Chinese elites. In both samples, about 90% of the respondents selected points falling on the 'different' side (1–3). For the American respondents, this percentage is about the same as their differentiation of the two societies. For the Chinese respondents, surprisingly, the percentage is slightly lower.[10] In other words, Chinese respondents perceived a lower degree of difference between Chinese and American cultures than that between the two societies. The only noticeable difference is that in the United States sample, about 50% of the respondents chose 2, while on the Chinese side the percentage is more evenly split between 1 and 2 (37.3% versus 36. 5%). This implies that there are still more Chinese respondents who considered these two cultures as virtually having nothing in common.[11]

Mutual images of culture, as broadly defined, will inevitably involve respondents' perceptions of people and society as discussed in previous chapters. American and Chinese elites could attribute differences or similarities between peoples and societies to their cultural roots. As a result, their distinctions between Chinese and American cultures will reconfirm some of their observations about people and society, albeit at a different level of generalization.

In terms of historical and intellectual origins, American respondents referred to the dichotomy of 'continuity versus transience'. They found that Chinese culture 'is a much more defined and refined culture, which goes back to antiquity, and has a thread that brings you right up to today', while American culture 'is always changing, always very different'. For Chinese culture, because of historical accumulation, 'there is really nothing new; somewhere in Chinese history, there have been similar episodes one can draw lessons from'. For American culture, there is nothing old, due to its ever-evolving nature. In this respect, some American respondents felt uneasy that 'we have little culture here'. As a magazine editor put it: 'I feel somewhat uncomfortable about how new everything is here and our willingness to rip up things that are only 40 years old and consider them too old.' Different historical origins, as some respondents mentioned, are reflected in different intellectual approaches, including philosophy and religions.

In terms of modern culture, American respondents touched upon some political and economic factors pertinent to cultural configurations. They cited the different 'material and ecological bases', which contribute to cultural differences. Some respondents pointed out that differences between the two cultures 'mainly stem from poverty, lack of availability of consumer goods, and the leisure opportunities that a rich society has'.[12] In American culture, 'the population enjoys physical and geographical resources as well as an environment of almost infinite potential. Whereas the Chinese population has, from the very beginning, been constantly reminded of limit and the need for renewal'. These differences lead to different life style and value orientations, manifested in family policy, attitudes toward education and gender, and sanitary habits.

A full 25% of the American respondents related the political difference between the two societies to China's cultural sources, including its political structure, control, and attitudes. Indeed, the relationship between Chinese culture and politics is a causality working in both directions. On the one hand, the tendency to have a 'centralized government', and 'the willingness to accept central control' are the manifestations of an 'authoritarian political culture'. On the other hand, in modern China, cultural activities are heavily controlled and directed by the state. As a result, some respondents found it hard to 'separate communist culture from traditional Chinese culture'. In the social domain, nearly a third of the American respondents described their perceptions of Chinese people and society, such as group-orientation, family values, and norms in human relations, as value and behavioural expressions of different cultural propensities.

The historical legacy, coupled with the political and social configuration of Chinese culture, has a bearing on the more purely 'cultural' activities discussed by the American elites, including both high and popular cultures. As a diplomat put it, culture 'is a drag on Chinese society, whereas in the United States, it tends to be the cutting edge for experimentation and generational differences'. American respondents perceived two major differences in this respect. Nearly 20% of them mentioned a dichotomy of 'imitation versus originality'. They found that in Chinese culture the norm for artistic work is 'to meet a standard' and 'to recreate the greatness of the past'. Even 'innovation is established on continuity'. In American culture, the norm is 'to liberate, to break new ground, to overthrow the past'.[13]

Another tendency on the part of the American elites is to perceive 'a sharp division between high culture and popular culture'. Some respondents recognized that Chinese high culture is more refined and sophisticated than its American counterpart. Nevertheless, the Chinese traditional culture 'was dominated by an aristocracy' and 'was really accessible to only a small proportion of the Chinese population'. As a result, the mass culture was seen as underdeveloped. 'There is not really much relationship between them [high and popular cultures].' In other words, even though the Chinese high culture is more refined, that does not necessarily mean that 'China is a more cultural society than American society'.

Articulation of differences between American and Chinese cultures by the Chinese elites demonstrated some convergence as well as divergence. Nearly half of the Chinese respondents noticed various differences in the historical and intellectual roots of the two cultures: 'several hundred years' versus 'several thousand years' is a dichotomy often cited. Embedded in this primary difference are several distinctive features. In terms of origins, it is a difference between 'Oriental' and 'Occidental' cultures. Some Chinese respondents tended to view Chinese culture and American culture as representatives derived from these two origins.[14] Another dichotomy is that of homogeneity versus heterogeneity. In the words of a Chinese scholar, 'American culture is the one with the greatest hybridization, whereas Chinese culture is the one with the least degree of hybridization.' The verticality and homogeneity of Chinese culture led to another perceived difference: 'The United States is a sheet of blank paper, whereas China bears a heavy historical burden.' Some American respondents may have felt their culture inferior to the Chinese cultural tradition of thousands of years, yet Chinese respondents did not feel all that lucky with the heritage from their ancestors: not a few respondents defined their cultural legacy as a 'feudal tradition' or 'feudal burden', which carries negative connotations. We may recall, from Chinese elites' previous articulation of differences between Chinese and American societies, that they tended to attribute China's problems partially to this 'historical burden'.

Chinese respondents also observed differences in the political, economic, and social expressions of the two cultures. It is notable that only a very few respondents formally attributed the difference to the 'socialist' and 'capitalist' natures of the two cultures. Chinese respondents were inclined to define the political differences as that between 'laissez-faire versus control', or 'free competition versus everything-should-be-guided'. Echoing the American observations analysed earlier, some Chinese respondents recognized that the Chinese 'are accustomed to applying a fixed criterion to judge everything else', while in the United States, 'whether a cultural form or activity can develop depends on social needs rather than on pre-set criteria'. The Chinese tendency toward control is not merely a result of the communist ideology, but has its origins in traditional Chinese culture. In the final analysis, some respondents considered that Chinese culture tends to 'depress or constrain human nature and aspirations', while American culture tends to 'release or reflect human nature and human aspirations'. This ontological difference can partially explain those dichotomies in social norms and practices such as 'individualistic versus group-oriented' and 'independent versus dependent'.

In discussing other differences in cultural propensities, Chinese respondents paid attention to the dichotomies of 'conservative versus revolutionary' and 'exclusive versus inclusive', which are two dimensions of the same issue. As one professor put it, it is a difference between a 'static culture' and a 'mobile culture'. American culture is 'the most revolutionary' or 'rebellious' one, in which 'you can see new things every day'. Chinese culture, on the other hand, is a 'closed system', which 'tends to reject outside cultures'. Some respondents pointed out that since the Tang Dynasty, Chinese culture had gradually become 'something neither alive nor dead' (bu si bu huo). The repeated cultural debates about essence (ti) and function (*yong*) demonstrated the impotence of Chinese culture in finding a way to absorb perceived fine elements of foreign cultures while maintaining its own identity.[15] Stated otherwise, 'American culture has the capacity to positively absorb outside civilizations, while Chinese culture barely manages to passively assimilate them.'

Regarding cultural functions and forms, Chinese respondents discussed the differences through the use of dichotomies such as 'subtle versus direct', 'entertaining versus reflective'. A joint venture manager who personally witnessed the interaction and conflict between Chinese and American cultures in his enterprise had a very interesting metaphor: 'Chinese culture is something like a cloud in the sky, while American culture is like a sword in hand. A cloud in the sky is obscure, hazy, and has deep and sometimes undefinable connotations. A sword in hand is clear, concrete, and very definable.' Such perceived differences extend to cultural forms, content, and practices. With regard to forms of expression, Chinese respondents viewed their culture as much more 'subtle' and 'implicit', asserting that 'there are some things you are unable to speak out but can only feel'.[16] With regard to content, some Chinese respondents considered American culture more 'entertaining' and Chinese culture more 'reflective'. As a Chinese diplomat put it, because of its refinement and deep connotations shaped by thousands of years of history, 'Chinese culture does not just make your body and heart happy, but it also moulds your temperament. American culture is very direct and you can feel the effect immediately. But it is mainly for entertaining purposes and satisfying the needs and desires of sense organs.' Consequently, Chinese and American cultures have very different approaches in practice. Some respondents found that American culture pays more attention to 'operationalization' and 'efficiency', with an emphasis on science and technology rather than on humanities. As some respondents generalized, 'The core of American culture is its pragmatism'. It is this pragmatism that helped Americans to 'create the most rational culture in the shortest time period, while the Chinese are still searching for a rational culture'.

As in the case of mutual images of society, only a small portion of respondents in both samples mentioned concrete similarities between Chinese and American cultures. Interestingly, more Chinese than Americans mentioned similarities between the two cultures (28% of the Chinese respondents as compared to 14% of the American respondents). The percentage of the Chinese respondents is considerably higher than in the case of references to the similarities between the two societies, and is consistent with the lower outer differentiation reflected in Table 5.3. This may indicate that Chinese respondents attached fewer political connotations to the concept of culture compared with their orientation toward society. Without that constraint, they felt freer to talk about similarities. Throughout their image articulation of American culture, political considerations were not very salient. This is another indication of perceptual sophistication.

In both samples, respondents referred to the similarities in personality, human aspirations and social values embedded in the two cultures. It seems that Chinese respondents, gave more weight to the inherent similarities between the two cultures in terms of values and ethics, including patriotism, pragmatism, openness, and enterprising spirit. American and Chinese elites also noticed the 'increasing convergence' between the two cultures in terms of 'TV culture', 'materialism', and 'popular culture'.[17] Some American respondents observed so-called 'creeping cosmopolitanism' in Chinese culture, which indicates that 'it is moving in the right direction'. Some Chinese respondents also noticed that 'the distance between American and Chinese cultures has been shortened' and that 'both sides are absorbing the culture of the other side, especially among the young people', as reflected in the value placed on money, knowledge, sex, and marriage, and in forms of literature, music, painting, and so on. They realized, however, that this is an asymmetric process. 'Chinese culture is moving more toward American culture and the penetration of American culture in China is very deep.' It can be referred as a 'cultural trade deficit' in Sino-American exchanges, in which there is greater movement of cultural goods from the United States to China than vice versa.

Affective Feelings

Earlier we hypothesized that while American and Chinese elites displayed a high degree of outer differentiation regarding the target culture, they might also have a high degree of affection toward one another's cultures resulting from intrinsic mutual attraction. It was also anticipated that the Tiananmen Incident had less effect on Sino-US mutual images of culture than on other dimensions of mutual images, since cognitively people are less likely to associate a specific event with a subject as abstract as culture. Thus we expect that positive affective orientation will prevail in both samples. As in other dimensions of mutual images, respondents were asked to give an overall opinion on the target culture along a continuum of five affective choices. Table 5.4 presents a comparison of the American and Chinese responses.

Table 5.4   Percentage Distribution of Affective Orientation Toward
Chinese and American Cultures

	Percentage (%)	
Affective Orientation	**US Respondents**	**Chinese Respondents**
1 Very favourable	38.1	4.9
2 Somewhat favourable	41.7	54.9
3 In the middle	9.4	30.3
4 Somewhat unfavourable	10.8	9.8
5 Very unfavourable	0	0
Total	100.0	100.0
Sample size	139	122
Mean/SD	1.93/0.95	2.45/0.74

Parallel to their mutual image of people, American and Chinese elites' feelings toward the target culture are fairly positive. On both sides, only about one in ten held a 'somewhat unfavourable' opinion of the target culture. No respondent chose 'very unfavourable'. For Chinese elites, this is a remarkable perceptual sophistication. However, a difference in positive intensity still exists. Evidently, American respondents demonstrated stronger positive feelings toward Chinese culture than the other way round. Almost four-fifths of the American respondents had a positive opinion of Chinese culture (numbers 1 and 2), among which about 38% described their feeling as 'very favourable'. The parallel proportion for Chinese respondents is just 60%, with only 5% choosing 'very favourable'.[18] Instead, a majority of the Chinese respondents preferred the next choice of 'somewhat favourable'. While only about 9% of the American respondents took the middle ground, as many as 30% of the Chinese respondents did so. This difference can be further verified by comparing the two mean scores.[19]

Apparently, the traditional American positive attitude toward Chinese culture was not affected significantly by the Tiananmen upheaval. Compared with their image articulation of Chinese society, fewer American respondents mentioned the incident in their comments. They tended to blame the communist system rather than the culture for the tragedy. No evidence indicates the Chinese perception of American culture was considerably affected by the event either. Chinese elites' relatively weaker positive feeling toward American culture might indicate that while they did like certain values and practices of American culture, it is still too 'shallow' to be greatly appreciated as a cultural system or tradition.[20] American elites demonstrated just the opposite cognitive tendency. Although many American respondents did not particularly appreciate, and even felt disgusted about, some specific values and practices in Chinese culture, as a historical or abstract concept, they still had a strong fascination with and admiration for Chinese culture.[21]

Evaluative Orientation

The above two contrasting perceptual patterns can be further confirmed from the positive and negative evaluations of one another's cultures made by the American and Chinese elites in answering the following question: 'What are the things that you feel are most fascinating or distasteful [in Chinese/American culture]?

In their positive evaluation, what American respondents liked about Chinese culture were those things more or less connected with traditional Chinese culture. To many American respondents, the traditional Chinese culture provides them with 'strong intellectual stimulation'. On the one hand, fascination comes from China's intellectual sophistication and accomplishments, as reflected in 'the ability to strike a balance in a very sophisticated way', 'the ability to appreciate things in their simplicity', 'the intellectual dimension of the society', 'understatement', 'a lot of nuance', and 'the way in which language, painting, and music all are related to one another'. Some respondents were particularly impressed by ordinary Chinese people's 'strong sense of history and tradition in their daily life and customs'. On the other hand, American elites were fascinated by Chinese culture 'simply because it is different'. They argued that for Americans, the power of Chinese culture lies in its difference. If it is Westernized, it will lose its attraction. By studying Chinese culture, as a professor said: 'one gets new consciousness of one's own culture and sees it from a different perspective. In a sense, one not only learns about China, but one has the opportunity to learn from China about oneself. China's culture is so rich and highly developed that almost any phenomenon of human experience has some Chinese counterparts. . . . Almost anything you try to study, there is a Chinese version of it'.

When coming to the concrete forms of Chinese culture, again the most frequently mentioned is traditional Chinese art, coupled with other forms of high culture including literature, philosophy, and performing arts. Some respondents were fascinated by Chinese language. To them, it is not just a tool for communicative purposes, but a vessel conveying 'Chinese history and human experience'. For other American respondents, Chinese cuisine seemed to be the main thing in Chinese culture they could attach some good feeling to. An intellectual commented: 'Food. I suppose I could say art, but I am not so fascinated with it as I used to be. Literature is not so special. Probably the outstanding part is food.'

In terms of cultural orientations and values, some American respondents were impressed and fascinated by 'the social skill of interaction', including the configuration of 'social networks'. That does not necessarily mean Americans liked 'personal networks'. Rather they were fascinated by them. As a professor said: 'I would not personally want to be enmeshed in a Chinese family network. I am impressed by it. I think it's quite remarkable. It has many plusses and many minuses. But I am impressed by how important it is to hold China together.' As already mentioned in their images of the Chinese people, Americans could not help admiring the cultural inclination of their 'absolute and indestructible will to survive' and their 'ability to bear hardships'. These qualities, American respondents indicated, are reflected in the Chinese intellectual and artistic pursuits, that are characterized by 'the determination of great scholars and great artists to continue their purpose and efforts without rewards from the state, and sometimes in very ugly circumstances', and 'the extent to which the Chinese are willing to postpone gratification'.

In the Chinese positive evaluation of American culture, a noticeable feature is a departure from traditional stereotypes about an inherently 'decadent and moribund' American culture. A portion of the Chinese respondents asserted that, regarding the American cultural system, there is nothing they felt 'unacceptable' or 'incompatible with'. Some even declared they 'feel at home with American culture'. That does not imply that they had a positive evaluation of everything in American culture. The perceptual breakthrough is that many Chinese respondents had ceased to hold a Marxist deterministic view of American culture as a reflection of a 'bourgeois lifestyle'. They began to view it as simply another way of life that has both its good and its bad aspects. Even though they could not accept some values and practices in American culture, they felt they could 'understand them'.[22]

Many Chinese respondents expressed their appreciation of what they called the two forms of 'core spirit' of American culture: 'constantly blazing new trails' and 'take in everything'. This American spirit, according to Chinese elites, has been nurtured under specific social and material conditions. One important condition is 'a free and tolerant environment' for cultural and intellectual activities and creation. Chinese intellectuals particularly appreciated the 'academic freedom' and 'the separation of academia and politics'. For them, freedom of speech and expression is very attractive.[23] Such a cultural and academic freedom is supported by material conditions. Some respondents declared that they were not enamoured of American culture per se, but were impressed with 'the material conditions for creating culture', including libraries, research facilities, and access to information and data. Thus, both 'software' and 'hardware' provide an ideal environment for cultural activities. A scholar expressed this mentality: 'I feel envious at the "freedom of thinking" in American culture, they have such good material conditions. The libraries and data are so rich. You can do whatever you want. I sometimes think if we just had half of their freedom and conditions, our accomplishments could be much greater. I think Chinese intellectuals are trying to jump with a sandbag on their feet. If we could get rid of the sandbag, we could jump much higher than Americans do.'

In terms of people's cultural life, the merits of American culture are 'freedom of choice' and 'availability of choice'. Some respondents appreciated that 'American culture can meet the cultural needs of all levels, high and low'. 'After eight hours of work, you can do whatever you want and you can have very colourful and rich entertainment'; 'carrots or cabbages, you can make your own choice and no one will tell you which to choose'. One implication of this 'freedom of choice' is that American culture can better 'reflect and satisfy human needs and desires'. However, as we will shortly see, Chinese respondents cognitively found it difficult to draw a boundary between the 'appropriate liberation of human nature' and 'self-indulgence'. Although conceptually they could appreciate the American values in this regard, psychologically they felt uncomfortable accepting the practice of 'the liberation of personality' (*gexing jiefang*).[24] A business person conveyed this cognitive dissonance: 'I appreciate the liberation of personality. Even though I desire it, as a person raised in this society, I have to pay attention to the environment. Consequently, if you allow me to do things according to American culture, I dare not. So reflecting in myself, I feel it is the most attractive thing but the thing hardest to realize.'

While American elites favoured the intellectual and artistic aspects of traditional Chinese high culture as against the 'modern' forms of Chinese culture, Chinese respondents were inclined to appreciate the 'material' and 'popular' components of American culture. Simultaneously, they valued aspects of American culture that they perceived to be somehow compatible with traditional Chinese values and ethics. This complexity is reflected in their evaluation of specific forms of American culture. Some Chinese respondents asserted that what they appreciated in American culture were just 'science and technology', not 'literature and art'. Other respondents were split in their appreciation of 'traditional' and 'modern' American culture. One group of respondents evinced a particular fondness for

American movies and music of the 1930s and 1940s, because they reflect 'ethics very similar to Chinese culture' and 'are full of the human touch' (*renqingwei*). Other respondents had more 'sympathy' with modern American movies, novels, and music because they are 'creative', 'imaginative', 'super-realistic', 'convey a feeling of openness', and 'reflect the tension and depression in the minds of people in modern society'. The Chinese perception of American popular culture, however, is in the process of evolving. A middle-aged business person described his perceptual change: 'Our concept and visions are changing. I used to find things like disco, rock and roll, and pop music weird. I did not appreciate them. In recent years, it has become popular in China. You have more contact with these things. Gradually you get used to that and begin appreciating them. So those things you disliked before, you may like now.'

The general positive feelings toward one another's cultures, however, did not prevent American and Chinese elites from scrutinizing the target culture in a negative fashion. It is interesting to note that even in their negative evaluations, American respondents did not have much impression of the modern Chinese culture. What they perceived as negative is actually the lack of modern Chinese culture, the suppression of traditional culture by the communist regime, and some political and social aspects of the traditional culture that are at odds with American values.

As in their evaluation of Chinese society, American elites demonstrated a strong political orientation in their image of Chinese culture. In their perceptions of Chinese society, American elites blamed communist ideology for the 'bad government' in China. Here some respondents discovered a deeper source for this phenomenon—traditional political culture. The Chinese bureaucratic and authoritarian systems, according to some respondents, 'grew out of a culture which is repressive in nature'. It is not just the rulers but also the ruled who are influenced by this political tradition. As a professor pointed out: 'There is a relationship between culture and the nature of a political system. For example, people say that no one in China wants to see people run over by tanks. But at the same time they also say most Chinese people are so afraid of chaos (*luan*) that they would tolerate an authoritarian government if given a choice between democracy, *luan*, and organized authoritarian government.'

Although most American respondents favoured Chinese culture on a personal level, some of them cognitively were able to differentiate what they subjectively felt about that culture and its objective function for China's development. Personally, American respondents had a very positive view of traditional Chinese culture. However, from the perspective of China's future as a nation, they realized this tradition 'has been a barrier in many respects, interfering with the adaptation the Chinese must make to upgrade to the standards of the modern world'.[25]

As discussed earlier, American respondents felt that traditional Chinese culture had 'stagnated' or 'declined' in the modern age. As a result, China lacks 'a modern culture'. They tended to dramatize the gap between Chinese 'traditional culture' and 'modern culture'. A diplomat remarked: 'I cannot quite understand why people who as individuals I respect a great deal for their minds, imagination, vision, and energy, when aggregated together produce nothing. That's a frustration; China should be the leader of culture for the world by any reason or standard, and it is not.'

To this 'why' question, American elites had two attributions. One is the 'dispositional' explanation. Holders of this view believed the problem lies in a 'lack of originality, lack of creativity' and the 'poor adaptability' built into Chinese culture, which made it 'increasingly bankrupt' since 1800. 'It is not restrictively related to a socialist ethic and a communist ethic; it goes back through the entire time period.' Other American respondents leaned toward the 'situational' explanation. They emphasized that the fine traditional Chinese culture had been 'destroyed' or 'contaminated' by communist ideology and control. These respondents drew a clear line between 'traditional culture' and 'party culture',[26] and found that 'these two cultures are disjoined'.

In social terms, American respondents attributed those negative aspects to what they called 'a mean culture to outsiders'. The term conveys that Chinese culture adopts a 'particularistic attitude' in handling social relations. In the words of some American respondents, the Chinese 'are quite insensitive to the suffering of other Chinese', 'so jealous of each other', and there is a mob tendency among Chinese to 'attack anybody or anything said to be an enemy or villain, no matter what the facts are'. This cold side of human relations also finds its way into personal style. American respondents found distasteful the 'hypocrisy in Chinese dealings' under the name of 'face', namely, 'they say one thing even though they believe another'.

In a related inclination, Americans perceived an 'elite-oriented' nature of Chinese culture. Some respondents found 'a gap between the literate and illiterate'. Chinese intellectuals 'look down upon people who are working their ass off to get things going' and they 'don't have great interest in working with their hands, naturally doing things'.

In terms of cultural forms, apparently many American respondents were unable to enjoy Chinese performing art and music, such as Beijing Opera, which was cited by some as 'the most distasteful'. In terms of life style, American respondents felt uncomfortable with the sanitary habits of Chinese.

In the words of a researcher: 'There is an extraordinary sensitivity to beauty, but there is a kind of extraordinary insensitivity to ugliness, particularly in terms of sanitation.'

Unlike American elites, Chinese elites were less inclined to consider the political implications of American culture. While appreciating the cultural environment and conditions in the United States, Chinese found that, as a civilization, American culture is 'shallow'. This shallowness has several dimensions. One indicator is its short history. As a scholar put it, it 'is all on the surface, and lacks aftertaste. In this culture, you can hardly walk into history'.[27] Another indicator is the lack of a 'sophisticated high culture'. According to some Chinese scholars, academic research in the United States is 'good at quantitative analysis but poor at qualitative analysis'. American music, art, and literature more often 'only release people's emotion' and 'do not help people think far and deep'. A third one is that American culture is 'both modern and primitive': 'You can feel modernity when you are on a highway. But when you go to small towns, you always feel the smell of countryside.' A young scholar found that some American intellectuals 'have a strong desire to own land', which 'is quite a primitive feeling'. Finally, although Chinese elites normally appreciated the cultural tendency 'to start something new in order to be different' (*biaoxin liyi*), some respondents pointed out that to be 'new' or 'different' is not necessarily positive. A diplomat argued: 'If you are different as well as superior, that's good. But if you are different just for the sake of being different, that's not good. You take a piece of gunnysack as an artwork. Well, it is very different. But is it better? I don't think so.'

Chinese elites felt that, given the 'shallowness' of American culture, American 'cultural egotism', or its self-proclaimed mentality of 'special mission' is not justified. Some respondents declared that 'the most disgusting thing in American culture is its self-righteousness' and they 'can tolerate anything in American culture except the mentality of "manifest destiny".' As a diplomat remarked, 'On the one hand, you have to compare your culture with other cultures. On the other hand, you advocate your own culture. You should draw a balance. You cannot export your culture like "exporting revolution".'

Other American cultural inclinations Chinese respondents considered unacceptable included what they called 'self-indulgence' and 'commercialization'. As analysed earlier, Chinese elites had an ambivalent attitude toward cultural freedom and control. While some respondents were disturbed about censorship and the leve of orthodoxy in Chinese culture, other respondents thought it is necessary to have criteria to distinguish good cultures from bad ones. A professor commented: 'They [Americans] don't differentiate good from bad. Something bad to you might be good to me. There are some good things about it [American culture]: tolerance. But I think, objectively, you should have some criteria to distinguish good things from bad things, good quality from bad quality.' Therefore, in cultural activities, it is undesirable to 'let market dictate everything' and to 'let everything flow unrestrained under the slogan of freedom'. The problem with American culture is that 'there is no mechanism to mobilize good cultures to effectively check bad ones'.

The negative evaluation of American culture along the lines of 'different, but not good' and 'self-indulgent' was also reflected in the Chinese elites' references to specific forms of culture. Nearly one-fourth of the respondents mentioned pornography, violence, and homosexuality, which, in the words of some respondents, 'regressed American culture to a primitive state and the level of an animal'. Other Chinese respondents did not appreciate such things as pop music and modern art, which either made people feel 'restless and perturbed' or 'are simply beyond anybody's comprehension'.

Change of Mutual Images

We anticipate that among the four dimensions of mutual images, that of culture is the most stable and the least susceptible to change. Because the concept of culture tends to be all-encompassing, it is more difficult to elicit longitudinal data along specific subject scales, as we did in the study of other dimensions of mutual images. Given these considerations, respondents' perceptual change regarding the target culture was measured in a more general fashion. Table 5.5 compares their perceptual changes, developed from responses to the question: 'With regard to your current image of Chinese/American culture, how does it differ from that which you held before 1970?'

Looking at the table, we can detect somewhat different patterns of perceptual changes for the United States and China samples. For the American elites, the hypothesis of image stability has been confirmed to some extent. Less than 40% of the respondents chose points 1–3, indicating that their perceptual change was greater than their level of continuity. Only less than one-fourth of the respondents considered that their perception of Chinese culture had changed greatly (points 1–2). On the other hand, nearly half of the respondents chose points 5–7 to indicate that their perceptions of Chinese culture had not changed much. In the China sample, however, the hypothesis of stability does not hold. Nearly 60% of the respondents chose numbers 1–3, among whom 37% had changed their perception of

Table 5.5 Percentage Distribution of Perceptual Change Regarding
         Chinese and American Cultures

Perceptual Change	Percentage (%)	
	US Respondents	**Chinese Respondents**
1 (changed greatly)	10.0	8.5
2	14.3	28.0
3	13.6	22.8
4	14.3	9.3
5	12.1	14.4
6	26.4	14.4
7 (no change at all)	9.3	2.5
Total	100.0	100.0
Sample size	140	118
Mean/SD	4.21/1.89	3.52/1.69

American culture greatly (points 1–2). At the same time, only about 30% of them opted for points 5–7 on the scale. Interestingly enough, this is the only dimension of mutual images in which Chinese respondents had experienced greater perceptual changes compared to their American counterparts.[28] Figure 5.1 further illustrates this difference.

The graph clearly demonstrates the above analysis. For the United States sample, the mode is located on 6, whereas the mode for the China sample is 2. This indicates that in the United States sample, the group with the

Figure 5.1 A Graph of Perceptual Change Regarding the Target Culture

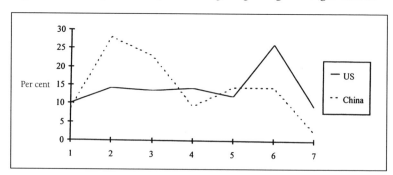

largest number of cases consists of respondents whose images did not change much. In contrast, the respondents making up the largest group in the China sample are those who considered their perceptions to have changed significantly. It can be inferred, therefore, that while a static model of perceptual change, set forth in Chapter 2, fits the United States data better, the same thing cannot be said about the China data. Some possible explanations for the difference come readily to mind. As the earlier analysis shows, for most American respondents, their core image of Chinese culture was oriented toward traditional art, philosophy, literature, and so forth. They perceived a discrepancy between 'traditional culture' and 'modern culture', and for some, Chinese modern culture does not exist. Therefore, in their eyes, Chinese culture is characterized by continuity rather than by change. Likewise, their perceptions of this culture also tended to be static.

For Chinese respondents, however, it is a different story. Many Chinese respondents saw American culture to be in constant evolution. Chinese elites found it difficult to identify mainstream American culture, owing to its multifarious nature. They tended to form new perceptions since the subject itself is undefinable. While the American perception of traditional Chinese culture could plausibly be the same before and after the 1970s, what Chinese elites were told or had learned before and after the 1970s was in sharp contrast. As soon as Chinese elites started having direct contact with American culture, their distorted image of American culture, forged by official propaganda, frequently one-dimensional or lacking structural complexity, began to collapse in response to persuasive new messages and information. Some Chinese respondents mentioned that before they visited the United States, they thought everything in American culture was 'a mess' (luanqibazao). They soon realized this was not true, or at least, not the whole picture.[30] Combing the data from Table 5.4 on affective orientation and from Table 5.5 on perceptual changes, it can be said with some confidence that an upward linear model approximates the change in the Chinese image of American culture in the last two decades.

Explaining the Image Variations

As in previous chapters, we want to know something about the determinants of the variations in American and Chinese respondents' cognitive, affective, and evolutionary orientations toward one another's cultures. In light of the theoretical assumptions about the relationship between contact, big events, and image articulation and evolution, several tentative hypotheses are suggested here for empirical testing. First, on the whole, direct contact still serves as an important factor affecting respondents' cognitive, affective, and evolutionary propensities toward the target culture. The impact may be less significant since to a greater extent people can learn and sustain an opinion about the target culture through indirect means, such as reading, visiting various exhibitions, and so on, without going to a foreign country or having direct contact with foreigners. Second, big events such as the Tiananmen Incident may also have less impact on reciprocal perceptions of culture, since images of culture are most likely to grow out of accumulation of knowledge over an extended period. As culture is a fairly abstract and broad concept, fewer American respondents would attribute a single event to the target culture. Third, age and profession have greater influence on images of the target culture, since these two variables encompass individual and professional values and the extent of exposure to the target culture upon which respondents base cognitive inference.

We first tabulate the bivariate relationship between the set of explanatory variables and respondents' outer differentiation of the target culture. With regard to the relationship between the several variables of contact and the respondents' outer differentiation toward the target culture, it seems that for American respondents, except for the frequency of contact in the 1980s that does not yield a consistent trend, other variables explain Americans' cognitive differentiation reasonably well. As in their images of Chinese people and society, American respondents who had visited China before 1949 again evinced a lower outer differentiation, presumably because their experiences revealed more similarities between the two cultures. It could also simply be a function of their general familiarity with China, which affected their overall outer differentiation across various dimensions. American respondents who had contact with China during the years 1950–1970 and in the 1970s also demonstrated a relatively lower degree of outer differentiation compared with those who did not have contact. The number of visits American respondents made to China after 1970 had the same effect. Those respondents who had not visited China had the highest degree of cognitive differentiation, while those who had visited China more than five times had the lowest degree of cognitive differentiation. It could be argued that those who frequently visited China witnessed more cultural changes in China toward the direction of American or Western standards in the last two decades, hence they perceived more similarities between the two cultures.

The same effect is not so consistent in the China sample. The difference in mean scores between those who had contact with Americans before 1949 and those who did not is almost insignificant. The frequency of contact in the 1980s apparently has a reverse impact on people's cognitive differentiation. The higher the intensity, the lower the mean score, indicating the higher degree of outer differentiation. This pattern is also reflected to some extent in the relationship between the number of visits and outer differentiation. The respondents who visited the United States more than five times had a relatively lower mean score. One possible explanation could be that American culture, in contrast to a Chinese culture that has been experiencing Westernization, did not show the same degree of Orientalization. As a result, Chinese respondents discovered increased differences as they had contact with or visited the United States more frequently.

As predicted, the Tiananmen Incident does not show a big impact on respondents' cognitive differentiation of the two cultures. However, for both sides, those who said they were greatly affected by the event showed a lower mean score than those who did not say so, suggesting that these respondents saw more differences between these two cultures.

Interestingly, profession demonstrates a similar impact on American and Chinese elites. On both sides, intellectuals had the highest mean score (low outer differentiation), while diplomats had the lowest mean score (high outer differentiation). Intellectuals, through their professional studies or research, might have a better understanding of one another's cultures, at least from the intellectual viewpoint. That could help them find more common ground between the two cultures. The people whom they had contact with more frequently were intellectuals of the other side. Some respondents, especially Chinese respondents, mentioned during the interviews that they perceived more similarity of cultural dispositions in their counterparts. Diplomats, on the other hand, might be inclined to see more cultural differences due to their official dealings.

The association between age and outer differentiation reveals a U-shaped curve for the American respondents. The respondents younger than 40 had a higher mean score than those aged 40–59, while those 60 and older displayed the highest mean score. Young respondents might be more sensitive to the rapid changes in Chinese culture in recent years. On the other hand, older respondents were inclined to view the two cultures as more similar, which parallels their perceptions in other image dimensions. Their cognitive sophistication might help them see through some superficial 'differences' between the two cultures. In the China sample, those respondents aged 60 and older also demonstrated a lower outer differentiation.

The next step is to associate the same set of variables with respondents' affective orientation in Table 5.4. As in the case of affective orientation toward the target people, most respondents on both sides expressed fairly positive feelings toward the target culture. What we try to find here, therefore, are differences of intensity rather than of type. The data indicate that contact before 1949 seems to have opposite effects on affective feelings for the Americans and the Chinese. American respondents who visited China before 1949 evinced a more positive orientation toward Chinese culture than those who did not. For Chinese respondents, however, those who had contact with Americans before 1949 had, on average, less favourable feelings toward American culture. This opposite pattern may actually suggest that the American and Chinese respondents in this category have more in common regarding Chinese traditional values.

Contact during the period 1950–1970 and during the 1970s apparently has a parallel effect on respondents' affective orientation. For both sides, those who had any contact during these two time periods displayed less favourable feelings toward the other side's culture. This pattern does not change much with regard to the intensity of contact in the 1980s. More contact seems to be associated with less favourable feelings. The trend is more salient on the Chinese side. The number of visits again shows a sort of non-linear function for affective feelings. It seems that on average, the Chinese respondents who visited the United States only once had a more positive image of American culture than those who did not visit at all. On the American side, it is the respondents who never visited China that had the most favourable feelings about Chinese culture. For both samples, those who visited the target country more than five times had, on average, the least favourable feeling toward the target culture. Again, these patterns demonstrate a possible perceptual 'regression' with an increase in contact and number of visits.

Unexpectedly, the impact of Tiananmen has quite a consistent relationship with the affective orientation of both American and Chinese elites. Respondents affected greatly by the event, on average, showed the least favourable feelings toward the target culture. It could be suggested that some respondents did attribute the event and the American response to it to some distasteful cultural proclivities, and therefore evinced less favourable attitudes to the target culture.

Respondents' professions demonstrate an opposite impact on American and Chinese elites. While American intellectuals had the highest mean score of cognitive differentiation, they also had the highest mean score pointing to more negative affective orientation. It could be the case that familiarity with Chinese culture coming from close observation or repeated contact reduced Americans' original fascination with Chinese culture.[31] This point could be indirectly supported by the fact that although diplomats displayed the highest degree of outer differentiation, they had the strongest affection toward Chinese culture. Perhaps the perception of Chinese culture as 'exotic' increased their fascination. More often, diplomats chose their careers in China out of their intrinsic interest in Chinese civilization.[32] Consistent with their affective orientation toward American society, Chinese intellectuals, on average, had more positive views of American culture. One explanation could be that, as reflected in their positive evaluation, they had a greater appreciation of the 'intellectual freedom' in American culture. Chinese diplomats had the least favourable feeling, probably because they were more turned off by the 'sense of a special mission' in American culture.

Regarding the relationship between age and affective orientation, in the United States sample, the respondents aged sixty and older had the most positive feelings while the age group of forty to fifty-nine had the least favourable. In contrast, Chinese respondents younger than forty on average had the most favourable mean score, while the older respondents had the least favourable figure. This pattern is similar to their affective orientation toward the target society. It seems that for older American respondents, their lower outer differentiation and higher degree of affection go together; but for older Chinese respondents, a lower outer differentiation does not bring out a more positive affective orientation.

We expect that in terms of perceptual change, variables of contact and age would have stronger explanatory power. The crosstabulation of the same set of variables and the data on perceptual change in Table 5.5 shows that variables of contact explain the perceptual change in both samples quite consistently. Apparently, contact before the 1980s has a negative effect on the perceptual change regarding one another's cultures. Respondents who had contact before 1949, during the period 1950–1970, and in the 1970s more or less all demonstrated less perceptual change. This might suggest that these contacts either produced quite stable perceptions or confirmed respondents' predispositions. However, such is not the case when considering the frequency of contact in the 1980s. The general trend is that more contact brought about more perceptual change. Similarly, an increase in the number of visits tends to facilitate perceptual change. In the United States sample, those who had not visited China or visited just once have higher mean scores, indicating less perceptual change, but the mean score declines when the number of visits increases further. For the Chinese respondents, the association is somewhat non-linear. However, those who visited the United States once have a big jump in their perceptual change compared to those who did not. The data suggest that while visiting the target country once or twice might not make a consistent difference, the gap in perceptual change between those who did not visit the target country and those who did visit the target country four or five times or more is quite significant.

The association between the Tiananmen Incident and perceptual change is quite intriguing regarding the American respondents. The 'greatly affected' respondents on average displayed the least perceptual change regarding Chinese culture. Considering the relationship between this variable and their affective orientation, we might infer that the event further verified some of their preconceptions of Chinese culture. On the other hand, the event did not have a strong impact on Chinese respondents' perceptual change regarding American culture.

Among both American and Chinese elites, intellectuals demonstrated the most perceptual change regarding the target culture, and diplomats the least. A plausible explanation is that intellectuals tended to search for cultural interpretations of social phenomena, while diplomats and business people were more likely to separate culture from other dimensions of the target country. Even when their images of other aspects of the target country have changed significantly, their image of the target culture remains quite stable.

As in other dimensions of mutual images, association between age and perceptual change regarding one another's cultures is quite straightforward. Younger respondents were inclined to have greater perceptual change than older respondents. For respondents younger than forty, their image of the target culture had been forming during the last two decades and therefore experienced greater perceptual change. For those who were sixty and older, their pre-existing 'knowledge structures' about the target culture were more deeply rooted, and consequently less susceptible to change.

The analysis above reveals some distinct, albeit sometimes inconsistent, associations between each of the explanatory variables and respondents' cognitive, affective, and evolutionary orientations toward one another's cultures. In general, personal contact decreases American respondents' outer differentiation between their own culture and Chinese culture, but the same effect is not obvious on the Chinese side. Some respondents might find more differences when their contact attains a certain threshold. The impact of contact on affective orientation depends specifically on the form and the time of contact. It also could have opposite influences on American and Chinese elites. More likely, fascination with the target culture is reduced with increased contact. With regard to perceptual change, contact before the 1980s tends to reduce perceptual change, whereas contact during the 1980s and the number of visits enhance perceptual change regarding one another's cultures. The Tiananmen Incident does not reduce the degree of outer differentiation, but increases the negative feelings toward one another's cultures. The variable of profession often yields divergent associations for American and Chinese respondents. Intellectuals on both sides demonstrated a lower degree of outer differentiation and a greater degree of perceptual change, but their affective orientations were just the opposite. Diplomats evinced a higher degree of outer differentiation and a smaller degree of perceptual change. Again, this was in contrast to their affective orientations. Business people usually occupied the middle ground along these three dimensions. As far as the cognitive and evolutionary orientations are concerned, the variable of age has a fairly consistent and parallel bearing on both sides. Older respondents on average had a lower degree of outer differentiation and perceptual change, while younger respondents displayed just the opposite inclination. In terms of affective orientation, relatively speaking, older American and younger Chinese respondents expressed more positive feelings toward the target culture, whereas younger American and older Chinese respondents held less positive attitudes.

Notes to Chapter 5

1   There is a variety of anthropological, sociological, and even artistic definitions of culture. As Elkins and Simeon point out, culture 'is often hard to disentangle from structural or psychological variables'. It is 'an abstract concept, not a concrete thing'. Finally, it is 'unconscious, unexplicit, taken for granted'. David Elkins and Richard Simeon, 'A Cause in Search of Its Effect, or What Does Political Culture Explain?', *Comparative Politics 11*, No. 2 (1979), p. 137.

2   They tended to use the highest adjectives to describe these attributes, including terms like: 'one of the greatest civilizations', 'unbelievable complexity', 'tremendous accomplishments', 'enormous heritage', 'fantastic culture', 'incredibly rich tradition', 'the richest, most profound civilization on the earth', and so on.

3   Some respondents mentioned how this cohesive culture enabled Chinese immigrants to 'stay together in Chinatown for several generations'. A diplomat who served in both Taiwan and the Mainland described her feelings in the following words: 'When I went to Beijing, suddenly the whole business of saying "Republic of China" or "People's Republic of China" and so forth seemed almost irrelevant. It was so obvious in Beijing that you were in China. I mean, it was more than a government; it was obviously the culture.' Some respondents pointed out that the communist regime failed to transform the traditional Chinese culture using a foreign ideology. As an intellectual put it, 'Mao himself was a kind of captive of Chinese culture'.

4   As a professor expressed: 'Although Chinese are born into their culture, it must take them an enormous amount of effort to learn about it. I think it is a shame, in a way, because you have so many other things to learn.'

5   A lawyer recalled his impression of Chinese culture as 'mostly history', and mentioned that 'it is very hard to see the modern manifestation of Chinese culture'. A government official declared, 'When I think of Chinese culture, I don't think of the PRC; I think of the dynastic time.' A professor opined that Chinese culture is 'not a strong, living culture'.

6   Some respondents described the Chinese complacency with their past glory as 'unwarranted self-satisfaction'. A diplomat even asked: 'Does China even have a culture today?'

7   They applied such terms as 'take in everything' (*Jianshou bingxu*), 'all-encompassing' (*baoluo wanxiang*), 'international', 'melting pot', 'filter', and 'kaleidoscope' (*wanhuatong*).

8   Some defined American culture as 'a subculture', 'a cocktail culture', 'without tradition', 'nothing of its own', and 'incomplete'.

9   Some respondents pointed out that although American culture 'incorporates things of diverse nature, it adheres to its own basic way of life'. As a diplomat put it: 'Whether you like it or not, Americans indeed created a way of life.' Through their personal experience, some respondents discovered 'a collective American spirit' reflected in American movies, architecture, and a citizen's reaction to the national anthem.

10   In their outer differentiation of the two societies, as many as 98% of the Chinese respondents chose points 1–3.

11   However, a t-test of the two means indicates the difference is not statistically significant (t = -0.43, the null hypothesis can not be rejected).

12   This cognition is an echo to the Chinese perception of 'naturally endowed' in the previous chapter.

13   As a diplomat saw it, in the United States, 'how different one is, even how outrageous one is, tends to be a mark of ability, standing, greatness, and influence; where in China how good one is depends on how imitative one is'.

14   A university professor described them as 'two extremes': 'China is the peak of the Oriental civilization and the United States is the peak of the Occidental civilization. They have two totally different origins, flows, and orbits.'

15   As a government official observed: 'We Chinese have advocated "making foreign things serve China" and "weeding through the old to bring forth the new" for a long time. But we have never succeeded and these things remain a slogan and a zigzag course. The United States never purposefully advocates these things, but they do so in practice.'

16   A scholar asserted: 'The nuances and subtleties in Chinese culture are what the American culture absolutely lacks. . . . There are some things you can only comprehend but can not convey. . . . American culture has not matured to this level, so they cannot understand Chinese mentality very well.' Such kind of 'understatements', as mentioned by some American respondents, might increase the difficulty in mutual understanding and communication.

17   An American China scholar suggested that the difference between the two cultures only lies in 'the structural constraints on various cultural expressions and activities'. He argued: 'If Chinese culture, arts, and literature were unconstrained by the state, God knows what would happen, probably they would not be so different from American culture. There would be more pornography, more low culture, probably even greater interest in Western influence. But the state is constraining what the society would like to do in cultural terms. What happens is that the state tends to magnify the difference and limit the expression of similarity.'

18   As we can recall, this apparent reluctance to show strong positive feelings was also present in their attitude toward the American people.

19   A t-test supports the observation that American respondents evinced stronger positive feelings toward Chinese culture (t = 4.90, p < 0.0005).

20   Some Chinese respondents mentioned that in purely cultural terms, American culture 'has little to be really appreciated or admired'. In their positive and negative evaluations,

they displayed a mindset that American culture was 'acceptable, but not particularly likeable'.

21 Some American respondents made it very clear that what they appreciated was 'traditional culture' rather than 'modern culture' or 'communist culture'. Others understood Chinese culture in quite an abstract sense. They admitted that their positive feeling might not be based on a sound knowledge of Chinese culture.

22 As a researcher said: 'Basically, I can tolerate American culture. . . . I think everyone has the right to make a choice so far as he does not bother others. There are lots of things I don't like in that culture. But so long as they do not bother me, I don't care.'

23 Even a devoted Marxist economist had the following observation after he spent time in the United States as a visiting scholar: 'Under the condition of social stability and the relaxation of class relations, the environment is favourable for exploring issues. Academic discussion is not interrupted by outside interference. The cultural atmosphere is good.'

24 A business person conveyed this cognitive dissonance: 'I appreciate the liberation of personality. Even though I desire it, as a person raised in this society, I have to pay attention to the environment. Consequently if you allow me to do things according to American culture, I dare not. So reflecting in myself, I feel it is the most attractive thing but the thing hardest to realize.'

25 A business person said: 'I think many Chinese people feel their own culture has held them back in the 20th century. Some people have done a good job of describing some shortcomings in the culture. From my perspective, I think the culture is wonderful. I feel very good about it, but I recognize that some Chinese don't feel that way.'

26 They often expressed very positive views of the former and very negative views of the latter. They described the 'party culture' or 'current culture' as 'a strange plant from a greenhouse', 'a sort of cliché', 'sloganeering', and 'cartoon-like'.

27 Some respondents realized that given China's historical background, this feeling of 'shallowness' might reflect their own prejudice. As another scholar said: 'I am too preoccupied with traditional Chinese culture. Therefore, I tend to feel other cultures are crude. It is my bias.'

28 A t-test shows that the Chinese respondents experienced significantly more perceptual change than their American counterparts ($t = -3.08$, $p < 0.005$).

29 As a business person described his experience: 'Before I went to the United States, I was told that American media was full of obscenity. For the first few days, I watched TV through midnight, but I found nothing bad.'

30 Some respondents touched upon this tendency in their comments. A foundation official said: 'I think that many Americans grew up with the image of China all the way back to the missionary movement. There is a deep fascination with China, which just comes out of childhood. I think the more often I go, the less fascinated I am. I mean the more I see China, it is just another place, not fascinating.'

31 As a diplomat remarked: 'You couldn't work in China and have a negative attitude toward the culture, impossible. You couldn't be effective unless you have a positive view of the culture. Anybody who committed himself to working in China and being serious about it would have to have a positive view of the culture.'

CHAPTER 6 ·
MUTUAL IMAGES OF INTERNATIONAL
BEHAVIOUR

The preceding chapters have explored Sino-American mutual images of people, society, and culture, primarily involving various internal dimensions of the target country. Logically, a further step of this inquiry is to investigate an external dimension of mutual images—international behaviour—which to some extent is a function of the internal dimensions elaborated upon earlier. For many respondents in both samples, what the target country is doing internationally could have a higher salience in and relevance to their image articulation.

During the heyday of the Cold War, in the 1950s and 1960s, mutual images in this regard were characterized by a pure 'enemy' schema.[1] Each side saw the other as an imminent threat to its security and interests. The target country's international behaviour was perceived indiscriminately as being driven by evil intentions, with the ultimate goal of eliminating the opponent and dominating the world. Consequently, everything the other side did in the world was ill-disposed by nature and condemnable by definition.[2] With the rapprochement of US-China relations in the early 1970s, this rigid 'enemy' image became invalid and was gradually replaced by an image of de facto allies against Soviet expansionism. During this period, the evaluation of the other party's international behaviour in its own right was not necessary when a common enemy loomed large. A simple criterion was applied when making foreign policy judgements: are they conducive or not to containing and crippling the Soviet influence worldwide? This point of reference, however, lost its validity following the disintegration of the Soviet Union and subsequently the end of the Cold War. The dramatic changes in the international power structure coupled with the Tiananmen crackdown in 1989 brought forth new systems of reference for Sino-American mutual images of international behaviour.

In light of the theoretical construct developed in Chapter 2, it can be hypothesized that mutual images of international behaviour may display some distinctive attributes. Compared to their mutual images of society, the American and Chinese elites may show a lower degree of outer differentiation regarding the target country's international behaviour. This underlying assumption is grounded in the traditional *realpolitik* argument that every nation-state acts under universal systemic constraints that render domestic differences irrelevant. In affective and evaluative terms, while respondents' perceptions of the target domestic system may influence their cognitive orientations toward the target country's international behaviour, these perceptions may not be sufficient determinants of their mutual images of international behaviour. We can assume that images of the international behaviour of a target country are shaped primarily by a respondent's perceived national interest rather than a value judgement about the target country's society and culture. As a result, we may witness endogenous inconsistency between respondents' mutual images of society and of international behaviour.[3] With regard to perceptual change, it can be postulated that mutual images of international behaviour are more changeable, given the volatile nature of international relations, and therefore more susceptible to influence by big events such as the demise of the Soviet Union or the Gulf War. However, domestically confined events such as the Tiananmen Incident should not have such a compelling power to change the cores of the mutual images of international behaviour.

General Cognition of International Status and Behaviour

As with other dimensions of mutual images, primary mutual perceptions of international behaviour were elicited by asking respondents a general question: 'When you think about China (the United States) as a power in world politics, what comes to your mind first?' The bulk of American responses are presented in Table 6.1.

The responses were grouped into two broad categories: perceptions of China's international power status and perceptions of China's behavioural features in international relations. In the first category, three distinct cognitions emerge from the Table. The first cognition can be called an 'overrated' image, which was held by about one-third of the American respondents. The main idea shaping this image is that China was not a world power or even a major power and that it had been perceptually overrated.[4] While China may still have some role to play in regional affairs, it can bring very little to the table in the formation of a new world order. This 'overrated' image represents a significant revision to the 'triangular' image prevalent in the 1970s and 1980s.

For the Americans who held this image, the proposition that 'China is a major power' is a myth and an illusion that was nurtured and cultivated either intentionally by the Chinese or unintentionally by the Americans themselves. Some respondents attributed this notion to China's traditional 'Middle Kingdom' mentality, reflected in the frustration of many Chinese over the 'disparity' between the 'subjective continuing illusions of great power status' and 'objective declining power and influence'. As a scholar

Table 6.1 General Cognitions of Chinese International Status and
         Behaviour (Sample Size = 141)

Subjects	Number of Cases	Proportion (%)
Power status		
Not a world power	49	34.8
Discrepancy between 'is' and 'could'	34	24.1
Important power	30	21.3
Behavioural feature		
Inward-looking	22	15.6
Erratic, uncertain	22	15.6
Disruptive	14	9.9
Not expansionist	13	9.2
Clever in diplomacy	11	7.8
Sensitive to sovereignty	7	5.0
Third World-oriented	4	2.8

Note: Since each respondent could mention more than one feature, the percentages in the
table represent the proportion of respondents who mentioned each subject. Therefore
the total of percentage distribution does not add up to 100%. This also applies to other
tables of the same kind.

put it: 'China as a world power is a paper tiger (*zhilaohu*) I think Chinese
leaders for a couple of decades thought of China as a world power. I think
for the last couple of years they have been disturbed by the fact that they
have been virtually ignored by the rest of world.' Other respondents,
however, attributed China's 'illusive' power status more to the American
exaggeration of China, either as a threat or as an ally.[5] Why should American
politicians help in creating this myth? A diplomat explained the logic: 'Let's
treat China like it's important. If we treat it like it's important, maybe it will
act like it's important. If it acts like it's important, maybe it will change and
eventually become important.'

If this 'logic' was valid and necessary during the 1970s and 1980s, some
American elites saw little reason for maintaining it in the post-Cold War
era. This change in the subjective construal of China's power status reflects
the change in some objective factors, which led American elites to apply a
different standard in estimating China's international status.

Many respondents mentioned that militarily China does not have great
reach beyond its own borders. Moreover, in the post-Cold War era, economic
success and political influence were seen as even more important in assessing

China's international power status. In these areas, 'China is not a model for any other country' and 'has no chips'.[6] A scholar had a more sophisticated analysis of the impact of the post-Cold War structural changes on China's international posture:

> China had extraordinary leverage in the 60s, 70s, and early 80s because of its ability to play a balancing role between the United States and the Soviet Union . . . China did benefit from turmoil internationally, as long as it did not result in a major war. As superpower tensions have reduced and economic considerations increased, China does tend to lose position.

The second cognition can be described as the image of 'discrepancy', which was touched upon by about one in four American respondents. This image shares with the 'overrated' image the view that China is not a world power at present, but it pays more attention to China's material or physical potential to become a world power. In other words, people with this image perceived a discrepancy or a gap between what 'could' be and what 'is', regarding China's international position. The assumption is that given China's size, population, and natural resources, China could play a much larger role in the international arena. The recent changes in world situation have not obliterated this potential.[7] ·American elites were inclined to attribute the gap to the failure of the Chinese system and leadership, and offered some prescriptions to fill this gap. Some respondents predicted that a developed domestic market economy in China would help it become a real 'Central Kingdom'. Internationally, China should forgo the 'Middle Kingdom' mentality, join the mainstream world community, and 'behave on the world scene the way other powers do'.

The third cognition can be defined as the image of 'importance'. Irrespective of the twists and turns in Chinese domestic politics, the collapse of the Soviet Union, and the communist bloc in Eastern Europe, and the disappearance of the triangular relationship between the United States, the former Soviet Union, and China, about one-fifth of the American respondents believed that China 'still has a role to play' and 'can not be ignored due to its basic mass, absolute dimensions of power, and longevity of civilization, as well as the quality of its people'. Because of these factors, they argued, China 'must be involved in all the issues that affect the world', including solving various pressing world problems, regional conflicts, and the effective functioning of international regimes.

Indeed, for some respondents, China's importance lies more in its future potential than its present status. They were convinced that even with all the ups and downs in China's domestic politics, 'there is nothing stopping it from being a world leader', or 'a giant power' eventually. A senior diplomat disagreed with the 'overrated' image: 'At some points in the US, it's fashionable to downgrade China's importance. I think that's a mistake, particularly when you look at the next century.'

This long-term perspective contrasts with the previous two images, which focus on either the past (overrated) or present (powerless and discrepancy). It seems that, at least in this sample, the 'important' image is a minority view. Both the 'overrated' and 'discrepancy' images do not primarily perceive China as a world power. If the percentages for these two images are put together, they comprise almost six in ten respondents, while only about one in five held the image of 'importance'. The data thus suggest that downgrading China's international status was a prevailing cognition among American elites at the time the research was conducted.[8] Obviously, some American respondents were affected by the Tiananmen turmoil in China, which seriously eroded their confidence in China's ability to put its house in order, let alone its international power. This image of China as a weak international player has been remarkably modified in recent years. If the interviews had been conducted today, the perception would have been much different due to China's rapid economic growth, as reflected in the recent concerns about the 'China threat'.[9] From 'China as a paper tiger' to 'China as a threat', the perceptual change and continuity are equally evident. The contingent variables such as the Tiananmen Incident and economic boom may alter people's short-term estimation about China's power status, but the conceptual framework within which the perceptions fluctuate is still the gap between China's potential and reality as a world power.

The trend of downgrading China's international power status also manifested itself in American perceptions of Chinese international behaviour. On the positive side, few respondents explicitly perceived China as a threat to the United States at that time. The pure enemy image of the 1950s and 1960s was not in evidence. Instead, some respondents pointed out that although China is very sensitive about national sovereignty, it does not have 'any territorial or political ambitions outside its own borders'. On the other hand, even with a low estimation of Chinese power, some respondents were impressed by China's 'remarkable skill of turning weaknesses into strengths', which enabled it 'to exert its influence beyond its economic and military power'.

The perception of China as being non-threatening does not necessarily mean that Americans saw China's international behaviour as positive, benign, or harmless. About 40% of the American respondents referred to three negative features of China's international behaviour: erratic, inward-looking, and disruptive.

American respondents characterized Chinese international behaviour as 'erratic', 'uncertain', 'changeable', and 'unpredictable'. They primarily attributed these traits to China's power status. Some respondents considered that the unpredictability came from the fact that China was still an emerging power, and they were 'very concerned about what China wants to do when it becomes a real power'.[10] This intermediate power status contributed to China's being caught up between the so-called 'great power complex' and the 'Third World country complex'. As a state department official commented: 'It deals with areas where it has influence like a great power. It deals with areas where it doesn't have great influence like a Third World country. The result is an inconsistent foreign policy.' In Americans' eyes, this double identity is confusing as well as self-serving. Another source of instability in Chinese international behaviour comes from the instability in Chinese domestic politics. In other words, they saw China's foreign policy as a function of its domestic political swings.[11]

A seemingly paradoxical theme embedded in American perceptions is that China is too 'inward-looking', 'obsessed with itself in its foreign policy', and consequently 'a non-player' in world affairs.[12] This 'inward-looking' cognition is paradoxical in several respects. First, one might point out that in the 1960s and part of the 1970s, China was perceived as being too aggressive in international affairs by supporting various 'movements of national liberation', and Americans hoped to see a more restrained and inward-oriented China. Now China was criticized as being too uninvolved in international affairs. Second, while many American respondents did not see China as a world power, they still, maybe unconsciously, applied a 'great power' standard to judge China's international behaviour, and they did not think it was appropriate for China to behave just as an ordinary country. Third, although most American respondents no longer perceived China as a direct threat to American interests, they did not think that 'non-threatening' is a sufficient condition to endorse Chinese international behaviour. Rather, a new system of reference had been set up: to what extent does China positively contribute to international governance, presumably under American leadership? The fact that China seems to remain at the margin of this process has become a new source of frustration.[13]

Applying this criterion, some American respondents found that China continued to do things that were 'not constructive', 'irresponsible', and 'disruptive' for its own 'selfish' and 'narrowly defined' national interest. One cognition is that China 'only has the power to screw things up, to complicate things. It has no power to make things better'. Citing China's policy on Iraq and arms sales as examples, some respondents concluded that 'China refuses to act responsibly as a world power'. As a think-tank researcher put it:

'What really matters is China. What happens in the rest of the world is not of any importance unless it has direct impact on China.'

While American elites were developing a new system of reference in viewing China's international behaviour, Chinese elites were also trying to make sense out of American international behaviour and to establish their 'operational code'. Table 6.2 summarizes Chinese elites' general cognitions of American international power status and behaviour.

Table 6.2 General Cognitions of American International Status and Behaviour (Sample Size = 127)

Subjects	Number of Cases	Proportion (%)
Power status		
Powerful	55	43.3
Declining	6	4.7
Mixed feelings	6	4.7
Behavioural feature		
Hegemonic	71	55.9
Leadership desirable	46	36.2
Interest-, not moral-oriented	26	20.5
Upholding justice	14	11.0
Lacking historical vision	7	5.5

The Chinese responses were coded into the same two broad categories: power status and behavioural features. In the first category, Chinese respondents, like their American counterparts, also had three different perceptions of American power status. However, the majority (nearly one in two) of the Chinese respondents in this category held a 'powerful' image of the United States.[14] By contrast, only 5% of the respondents thought that the United States was a declining country, with another 5% expressing a more mixed feeling.[15] Compared with the United States sample, Chinese elites displayed less disagreement in their estimation of American power status.[16] This 'powerful' image was greatly enhanced by the American performance in the Gulf War. Many respondents took it as a showcase to demonstrate 'the undisputed American military superiority', and 'the successfulness of American strategy'.[17] Unlike the United States perception of China's power status that experienced dramatic change in recent years, this 'powerful' image of the United States has remained quite stable since the time of this research.

The more critical question is, however, how did they perceive the relationship between American power and American behaviour? Stated otherwise, how did they evaluate the United State's role in world affairs? Table 6.2 indicates an array of Chinese views on American international behaviour, but two major cognitions stand out.

One is the more traditional 'hegemony' image.[18] This image generally perceives the United States as a country seeking a sort of hegemony or pursuing 'power politics' (*qiangquan zhengzhi*) in world affairs, and taking advantage of its unique power status. Looking at Table 6.2, it can be said that the anti-hegemony mentality is quite strong, if not overwhelming, among Chinese elites. More than half of the respondents expressed their dissatisfaction with American interventionist policy in recent years.[19] For some of them, the perception might be merely a reflection of their long-time internalization of official lines and doctrine. For others, however, the resentment appeared to be genuine and personal.[20] They found Americans 'are too fond of poking their noses into others' gardens (*aiguan xianshi*)' and 'taking up the cudgels for all injured parties' (*da baobuping*).[21] With their ingrained concept of supreme and absolute national sovereignty, holders of this image thought it was morally unsustainable to try to impose a country's values and systems, no matter how good they were, on other countries.[22] Moreover, for some Chinese respondents, these kinds of attempts seem to be in conflict with those values Americans claim to cherish. Here a big cognitive question Chinese respondents often had in their minds is why the United States, a country proud of its pluralism at home, should even try to promote a monolithic world. Such a world, presumably under United States leadership, is not only unjustifiable according to American values, but also impossible given the fact that 'as powerful as the United States is, it is still unable to solve problems for other countries'. Therefore some respondents described the United States as 'lacking historical perspective' and 'lacking self-knowledge'.

Another philosophical theme running through many Chinese respondents' remarks is something like a Confucian creed: don't do to others what you would not have them do to you (*ji shuo bu yu, wu shi yu ren*). From this perspective, they accused American international behaviour of having double standards or of being hypocritical. First, the United States adopted different standards for its own domestic affairs and for those of other countries. Some respondents demanded that the United States clean its own backyard first: 'If you want others to follow your lead, you'd better solve your own domestic problems first. . . . If you can't, that shows your system is not perfect. How can you ask others to follow you blindly?' Second, Chinese elites saw the United States applying 'double standards too explicitly' in international affairs. Different policies toward Iraq and Israel were often cited as an example. Third, the United States applied different standards of treatment to one country in different time periods. A scholar pointed out: 'The real catch here is whether your policy or behaviour is at odds or in accordance with the American strategic interest. When China was useful in serving its anti-Soviet strategy, the problem of human rights could be put aside. When China seems to have no important place in the post-Cold War blueprint of a new world order, the issue of human rights has become a bargaining chip.' So in the final analysis, holders of the 'hegemony' image concluded that 'the United States actually is a country no different from others, but because of its strong sense of mission it tends to present itself as a country for some abstract values it can not consistently hold due to its national interest.'

Some Chinese respondents, while they might not generally oppose American intervention in international affairs, became very emotional when touching upon the American 'interference' in Chinese internal affairs. Even for some Western-educated respondents who generally had good feelings about the United States, this nationalistic mentality was inescapable. A veteran diplomat expressed this 'inferiority complex' emotionally:

> To tell you the truth, a large number of Chinese intellectuals I know feel sickened about the way the United States brandishes MFN trade status as a weapon to push down China. China's $10 billion trade surplus is nothing in the whole American foreign trade. If you Americans are sincere in helping China, why do you keep picking on it? The behaviour of the American Congress hurts Chinese feelings badly. To put it bluntly, you Americans are rich and strong, we Chinese are poor and weak. Therefore you feel free to bully us. I have very favourable feelings about some aspects of the United States, but on this issue I am disgusted. You take China as a piece on the chessboard of domestic politics, kicking it here and kicking it there. How do we Chinese feel? Some Americans also assert that Sino-US relations are not important any more because of the relaxation of US-Soviet relations. You simply play the China card in politics at home and abroad. We Chinese cannot stand this. Are you Americans advocating fair play? Where is the fair play? The only reason is that China is still poor so that you can kick me around. They are mistaken. We Chinese will not stomach this insult (*yanbuxia zhekouqi*). We are prepared for the worst. China will not disappear. In the future, Chinese people will remember what you Americans did to us when we were in difficulties.

According to some respondents, American 'interference' is based on some false and ignorant assumptions about the Chinese mentality and Chinese reality. First, external pressure has limited influence and could backfire. As a senior editor put it: 'If you do not let China back down with grace, you can not expect that China will change. China will fight to the last breath.' Second, American policy-makers should realize that 'the United States has no ability to master the political development in China. It has not had this ever, it will never have it in the future'. 'Any attempt to directly support certain political forces from within is out of touch with reality.' Third, in this respect, the American assumption of separating the Chinese Government and people is self-deceiving. As a business person put it: 'Americans should remember that although we could have many differences with our government and we complain a lot, when we face external pressures, we will forget these differences and share the same feeling with the government. . . . If you Americans think that you can kick around the Chinese Government without hurting ordinary people's feelings, you are deceiving yourselves.' Fourth, China has a different situation and Americans can not treat China like any other country. An economist declared:

> I can not understand American views on two things: Tibet and family policy. The American criticism makes absolutely no sense to me. Do they want to have a Tibet ruled again by slave owners? Do they believe Tibetans had a better life before 1949? Do they wish to see a population explosion leading to political and economic disasters in China? Americans, especially those Congressmen, sometimes do not know what they are talking about. It is easy to talk about beautiful things. Let them try to rule one billion people, then they may be able to put their minds back into their heads.

While the 'hegemony' image still holds true, another, more cosmopolitan trend regarding the American role in world affairs has emerged. About four in ten respondents expressed their appreciation of or support for American leadership in world affairs, albeit to different degrees. Their comments revealed several perceptual rationales behind this 'leadership' image.

The first rationale is situationally oriented: in the post-Cold War era, world leadership is a necessity. Many respondents evinced a mentality that 'you should have somebody to take care of matters in the world'. This argument follows the logic that the world, like a family or a country, has to 'have somebody to maintain order' and 'to stand up when something happens'. This idea is quite novel in the PRC's thinking about foreign affairs. Mao Zedong and his associates for a long time asserted that 'world affairs should be taken care of by all countries and can not be monopolized by one or two countries'. The current Chinese leaders also shy away from recognizing publicly the increasing interdependence and the necessity of governance in world affairs. However, a trend of post-Cold War 'new thinking' apparently is emerging among intermediate Chinese elites. To some extent, this image is closer to the traditional Chinese concept of politics. Traditionally, Chinese were fearful of chaos (luan) in domestic politics but seemed to care less about the chaos in the outside world. With the increase of Chinese economic dependency on and integration into the world economy, some Chinese respondents realized that China had a high stake in maintaining the stability of the international system and that a chaotic world was not in China's interest. From the perspective of economic globalization and interdependence, 'American leadership is not something you like or dislike. It is an objective necessity. If China desires to be a part of the international community, it should recognize this reality.' Moreover, during this period of transition toward a new world order, 'we need a country to take the lead'. As a business person put it: 'The United States is indeed an "international policeman". We used to use the term in a negative sense. But I think in a period of international turbulence, it is necessary to have a policeman to stand up and do something to maintain stability.'

The second rationale sustaining this 'leadership' image is more 'dispositional': compared to other major powers, the United States is the best candidate for world leadership. Related to their estimation of American power status, some respondents held that only the United States has the comprehensive power to exert leadership and to 'match its goals with its power'. For others, however, American leadership is not based just on power but also on merit. They argued that the question is not whether the world needs a leader, but rather who is going to be that leader. As 'overbearing' as the United States might be, it is 'the best candidate for the position'. A portion of the Chinese respondents believed that 'generally speaking, the United States can uphold justice' in world affairs, as reflected in its war against Iraq. Some Chinese respondents displayed sensitivity and understanding of American international behaviour. They agreed that Americans sometimes could be very arrogant and commanding, but to be a world leader is not an easy job.[23] An influential America specialist made a very interesting historical comparison:

> The United States is not necessarily a hegemonic country by nature. The United States is the best major power compared with Britain, France, and Japan. The style of its international behaviour is similar to China's rule of the East in history. Prior to the Industrial Revolution, China was the most benign major power, whereas the United States is the most benign major power since the Industrial Revolution.

Conceptually the 'hegemony' image and the 'benign leadership' image have very different systems of reference. Yet for some Chinese respondents, these two points of reference have interwoven to create some cognitive dissonance or ambivalent feelings toward American international behaviour. On the one hand, they realized the necessity for the United States to play a leading role in maintaining the stability of the international system and appreciated American efforts to solve hot international disputes. On the other hand, they were uneasy with the prospect of a 'unipolar world' and worried about possible abuses by American leadership and its excessive interference in other countries' internal affairs.[24] Some respondents were apprehensive that 'there exist no comparable forces to balance the United States after the Soviet disintegration', and consequently 'the United States gets too dilated'. A young business person described his ambivalent feelings toward the American international role in the following words:

> The United States is an important and irreplaceable force in the development of history. Of course, the United States does not just maintain world order for selfless purposes. Rather, it does so largely for its own national interests. Sometimes the United States goes too far. But on the other hand, the world would be unrecognizable without the United States. . . . So I have a very ambivalent feeling for American international behaviour. It is a conflict between head and heart.

Cognitive Differentiation

Following the structure of national image developed in Chapter 2, American and Chinese respondents were further asked: 'Would you say that China's/ America's international behaviour is very similar to or very different from that of other major powers?' This question was designed to measure the outer differentiation of their mutual images of international behaviour. Unlike the parallel question in measuring other dimensions of mutual images, the respondents were asked to compare the target country with a broader range of countries rather than just their own country. The consideration is that given the indirectness of the subject to most respondents, it may be more difficult to make a comparison strictly in bilateral terms. Also, the term 'other major powers' is able to provide a broader but still limited system of reference, which is unavailable in other dimensions of mutual images. Table 6.3 provides a comparison of outer differentiation by American and Chinese elites along a 7-point scale, with 1 meaning 'very different' and 7 'very similar'.

Table 6.3 Percentage Distribution of Cognitive Differentiation of Chinese
and American International Behaviour

Cognitive	Percentage (%)	
Differentiation	US Respondents	Chinese Respondents
1 (very different)	5.0	3.3
2	25.9	16.3
3	14.4	30.1
4	19.4	21.9
5	19.4	20.4
6	12.2	7.3
7 (very similar)	3.6	0.8
Total	100.0	100.0
Sample size	139	123
Mean/SD	3.77/1.61	3.72/1.31

The Table indicates that the general pattern of distribution for United
States and China samples is fairly similar. For both samples, there are more
respondents who selected points on the 'more different' side. In the United
States case, 45% of respondents chose points 1–3, while 35% selected points
5–7. The parallel distribution for the China sample is 50% versus 29%.
However, on both sides there is a considerable proportion of respondents
who viewed differences and similarities as cancelled out. Evidently the degree
of outer differentiation is relatively low compared to mutual images of society
and culture. Thus one hypothesis set forth at the beginning of this chapter
is confirmed. As the subsequent analysis will show, many respondents
perceived a fundamental similarity in the international behaviour of the
two countries—maximizing national interest. The mean score shows that
on average, American respondents still demonstrated a slightly lower degree
of outer differentiation.[25] One interesting phenomenon is that Chinese
responses cluster around the range 3–5, while American responses are more
dispersed. For instance, almost half of all American respondents chose either
1 and 2 or 6 and 7, whereas less then 30% of the Chinese respondents
made the same selection. The difference suggests that more Americans
tended to regard Chinese international behaviour as either very similar to
or very different from that of other countries. The Chinese were more
inclined to take the middle stance.

In the minds of the Chinese respondents, most 'major powers' were Western countries, and they usually did not put China itself into this category. Comparing the United States to other Western countries, they might find the differences not so striking. But considering the difference between the United States and, say, the former Soviet Union, as well as the gap in power and status between the United States and other Western powers, more Chinese respondents still preferred to choose 3 or 4. On the other hand, those American respondents who chose 2 might see sharper behavioural differences between China and the Western countries, including the United States. However, those who discarded the political and social difference between China and other major powers and just took into account the nature of international behaviour tended to find more similarities. In any event, the fact that very few respondents went all the way to 1 may indicate that in international relations, more respondents saw the target country as an outlying country in the international order.

As a follow-up question, the respondents were invited to list what they perceived to be the most important behavioural similarities and differences between the target country and other powers. Altogether, over half of the American respondents touched upon various similarities in international behaviour between China and other major powers. More than 4 out of 10 respondents considered that China 'pursues its national interest just as any other power does'. The 'fundamentals of Chinese policy are not that different from the fundamentals of Japanese policy or Soviet policy or American policy or European policy', and include safeguarding its own security and sovereignty, making alliances, and manoeuvring in the balance of power, engaging in international economic interactions, and applying diplomatic protocols. This cognition of perceiving China as 'a normal power' or 'just another big country' is a substantial sophistication compared to the American image before the 1970s. It contributed to the lower outer differentiation expressed by the American respondents in Table 6.3.

Some American respondents argued that ideology did not figure as largely in their images of China's foreign policy as used to be the case. Chinese leaders may 'disguise' their interests with an ideological flavour, but 'if you look at practice, this is a power that does certain things that are quite understandable from the point of view of international security and development interests'. Some respondents even suggested that China is less ideological than the United States in international behaviour. A former diplomat observed: 'I think I would give higher marks to China than I would give to the United States, because I think Americans tend to be rhetorical, ideological, and emotional in the way they talk. The Government usually behaves quite practically, but the American style of discussion has a great deal of emotion. China is nearer to normal than the United States. China has a *realpolitik* type of policy, which, to me, is the correct way.' Other respondents also noted that China's international behaviour had undergone remarkable changes since the 1970s and that 'they are behaving better and better as a world citizen'. As a professor described: 'In the 1960s, China acted as if it had its own system of international relations, did not need to pay attention to anyone else, and did not care whether it returned to the UN. Now, formalistically, China has been actively involved in the international process.'

However, American elites still perceived an array of differences between China and other major powers. Most of them were already touched upon in their initial articulation of China's international behaviour. The most frequently mentioned theme is that China is the most 'inward-looking' or the most 'introspective' country of all the major powers.[26] Underlying this characteristic of inwardness is what some respondents called 'a fortress mentality' that the 'Middle Kingdom is more important than the rest of the world and does not need the world really'. They found that China had 'a very, very great suspicion of interaction with foreigners'.

This mentality leads to some unique propensities in China's international behaviour. First, China pursues a more independent foreign policy. China 'has not tended to follow the lead of other countries' nor has it been 'unduly influenced by other countries'. Second, China has shown a defensive rather than offensive tendency in its foreign policy. China is 'more fearful of interference from other countries than interfering in others'. The most aggressive thing China will do is to 'teach a lesson' to its neighbours. China may occasionally be in an offensive mood, but it is really defensive in nature to 'protect what it has' rather than to realize 'some grand conquering goals'.

Third, the inwardness also implies that China often has a narrow definition of its national interest, which tends to lead to 'irresponsible' behaviour. China, in a scholar's words, 'has a more European notion of interest: foreign policy serves national interest purely'. 'Chinese foreign policy does not want to make the world better.' As a result, some American respondents found it very difficult to communicate with China on issues such as arms sales, because China 'has a hard time seeing, in a sense, that what is good for the world is also good for China'. A related phenomenon is that China pays very little attention to world opinion and does not recognize international standards on issues such as human rights. Some respondents held that as a major power, China should be more responsive to world opinion and can not 'hide what it is doing'.[27]

Another major source of difference between China and other powers, as mentioned earlier, lies in some unique characteristics of Chinese diplomacy as a reflection of the gap between means and goals. China has a tradition of 'manipulating the affairs of other countries'. Some American respondents were impressed by the Chinese 'ability to influence the majority of nations in the world positively toward China at minimum costs to China'. In some respondents' views, given China's limited power base, what its diplomacy has accomplished is a 'miracle' and 'their influence is beyond their real power'. But other respondents found this 'unconventional diplomacy' no longer acceptable. As a White House official put it: 'China is very unwilling to accept the norms of give and take. China tries to have everything to be in a win-win arrangement, never give and take, always take-take. It's a kind of one-sided exchange, a one-way relationship.'

Lack of national power, coupled with a distinctive domestic system, led to another attribute of China's international behaviour—inconsistency or uncertainty. Some respondents attributed this trait to the fact that 'Chinese national interest is defined by a relatively small elite group and is not defined in response to popular pressure or any kind of national consensus'. That is why sometimes China's international behaviour 'seems to be rather strange, seems to be irrational', as reflected in what a social celebrity called 'the constant closing and opening of the society to the outside world'. This instability is also reflected in China's diplomatic approach. According to a scholar, 'China moves from its pragmatism to ideology all the time in rather an extreme way. If an issue of principle comes up, it produces enormous passions and angers. However, if you find another formula, China can also deal with some of the most principled issues in a rather pragmatic way.'

In their articulation of similarities and differences between American international behaviour and that of other major powers, Chinese elites evinced both parallel and distinctive cognitions compared to their American counterparts. In the domain of similarity, the pattern of cognition is quite similar to the United States sample: the United States, like other major powers in the world, is a maximizer of national interest. When Chinese respondents were asked to compare the United States and 'other major powers', often their system of reference was 'Western powers', including the United Kingdom, France, Germany, and Japan. For both historical and geopolitical reasons, they tended to view the United States as one of the 'Western countries', which by definition share more similarities than differences in international behaviour. Another term of reference often applied by the Chinese respondents is 'great power' (*daguo*), which is broader than 'Western powers' and may include the former Soviet Union and occasionally even China. Comparing the United States with the USSR and

China, Chinese respondents naturally perceived more differences. This conceptual differentiation between 'Western powers' and 'great powers' could further explain their perception on outer differentiation in Table 6.3. In the final analysis, however, irrespective of their national idiosyncrasies, Chinese respondents found that 'great powers share striking similarities'. Above all, they 'take national interest as their first priority'. In this respect, Chinese respondents were more cynical than their American counterparts. Few respondents believed that the United States, as well as other major powers, would pursue certain abstract values or moralities as their ultimate national goals. As a diplomat put it: 'Nationalism is still the mainstream in today's world. I don't believe that some abstract concepts or values will prevail over nationalism.' Moreover, a portion of Chinese respondents emphasized an inherent impulse of great powers to pursue 'great-nation chauvinism' (daguo shawenzhuyi). In a business person's words, they all have a 'long arm' in international affairs, namely the tendency to define national interest in an all-encompassing fashion. It is understandable that for historical reasons, Chinese elites had a greater mistrust of great power conduct. The notable perceptual sophistication, however, is that they related this behavioural trait exclusively to national power rather than to particular social systems or ideologies. As a result, they no longer singled out the United States, as they used to, as the only 'hegemonic' power. Rather, some respondents suggested that other countries would do the same thing if they had the same capacity. Put differently, the chauvinistic tendency for great powers is 'situational' rather than 'dispositional'.

Along this line of realpolitik, there is a more cosmopolitan argument about the similarity. Some respondents pointed out that globalization of international affairs and the integration of the world economy had brought about much greater similarity in the agendas and behaviour of great powers. Regarding many global problems, great powers 'share many burdens, even though they offer different solutions'. Under these circumstances, while previously the United States had been regarded as a country persistently seeking dominance in the world, it was now increasingly perceived by some Chinese respondents as a normal power. A think-tank researcher observed: 'The general tendency is that the United States is moving from a superpower to a normal country. It is a long-term tendency. I do not believe that the United States wants to establish a unipolar world and seek absolute hegemony.'

Many Chinese respondents perceived that the power gap between the United States and other major powers is the most important source of their different international behaviours. What distinguishes the United States from other powers is its 'comprehensive power' that leads to 'comprehensive' and 'global-oriented' international behaviour. Unlike other countries, the United States is the 'leader', 'boss', 'master', and 'overlord'. As a writer put it, 'In today's world, only the United States can publicly express its independent will, other countries can not.' On many international issues, 'the American attitude is decisive', and 'as soon as the United States makes its attitude known, the dust settles'. A think-tank researcher concluded: 'If the United States wants to do something and mobilizes all its resources, in most cases it can achieve its objectives, as long as the adversary is not a major power or a whole region.'

When it comes to the comparison of behavioural traits and style, two apparently conflicting perceptions have emerged. One cognition perceives American international behaviour as assertive, arbitrary, and simple-minded. As in the answers to previous questions, the Chinese respondents described American behaviour as 'overbearing' and 'high-handed'. Some were fond of comparing American international behaviour with that of other powers in stylistic terms. They often described American behaviour as more 'blunt' (*lugu*), 'forthright' (*tongkuai*), and 'naive' (*youzhi*). In a somewhat negative tone, they found that 'Americans sometimes do not know how high the sky is and how thick the ground (*buzhi tiangao dihou*), and they 'stick to their own way of doing things and do not care about others'. In a more positive sense, they considered that the United States 'is willing to take the lead' and 'has the guts to do things.' Americans might be more 'blunt' and 'tougher', but they are not as 'slick and sly' as the British, as 'stealthy' as the Japanese, or as 'awkward' as the Russians.

An opposite perceptual trend found American behaviour to be more sophisticated and farsighted than that of other major powers. Some Chinese respondents thought that American foreign policy is more broadminded and sometimes has 'vision'. As a professor put it:

> Other countries, like France, the Soviet Union, and Japan, are more narrow-minded. Americans are more broadminded. For instance, usually businessmen do not want to sustain losses in their business dealings and they want to make money. Of course Americans want to make money too. But sometimes they are willing to sustain losses for long-term benefit. Russians are different. They are unwilling to lose a single penny. Americans do not care about small things. That's why people who studied in the United States often have good feelings about the country. Those who studied in the Soviet Union, Japan, and Germany do not have that kind of feeling toward their host countries. In this respect, Americans are wiser.

Some Chinese respondents also saw the United States applying more subtle and less coercive means to accomplish its foreign policy goals. In a professor's words, 'Americans have higher political skills and they know how to win people's support' (hui zuo ren). They noted that historically the United States employed economic and cultural means more than military means in its foreign policy.[28] In a comparison with the Soviet Union, they perceived the United States as 'much less brutal' in its international behaviour. This cognitive trend about American international behaviour further explained why some Chinese respondents considered the United States the best candidate for world leadership.

Affective and Evaluative Orientations

How is the cognitive dimension of mutual images analysed above related to the affective orientation held toward each country's international behaviour? To obtain systemic data on respondents' affective inclinations, they were asked to convey an overall opinion about the target country's international behaviour. Table 6.4 is developed from American and Chinese responses to the following question: 'I would like your overall opinion of China's/America's international behaviour. Would you say that your overall opinion of Chinese/American international behaviour is very favourable, somewhat favourable, somewhat unfavourable or very unfavourable?'

At first glance, it is a little surprising to find that more American respondents selected a 'positive' (45%) than a 'negative' (39%) orientation, even though many negative features were mentioned in their previous

Table 6.4 Percentage Distribution of Affective Orientation Toward Chinese and American International Behaviour

Affective Orientation	Percentage (%)	
	US Respondents	Chinese Respondents
1 Very favourable	2.9	1.6
2 Somewhat favourable	42.1	23.0
3 In the middle	15.7	29.5
4 Somewhat unfavourable	33.6	43.4
5 Very unfavourable	5.7	2.5
Total	100.0	100.0
Sample size	140	122
Mean/SD	2.97/1.05	3.22/0.89

articulation. This is a big contrast to their affective orientation toward the Chinese Government. The pattern for the China sample is reversed. More Chinese respondents (46%) had a 'negative' opinion of American international behaviour, compared to only 25% of the responses found on the 'positive' side.[29] The positive image percentage is smaller compared to their affective orientation toward the American Government. Instead, a larger group of respondents (30%) took a stance in between. The difference between the two data sets can be highlighted by Figure 6.1. The graph illustrates that while the curve for the Chinese data leans clearly toward the 'negative' side, the American responses are clustered around 2 and 4, indicating two distinct perceptual trends.

Figure 6.1 A Graph of Affective Orientation Toward the Target Country's International Behaviour

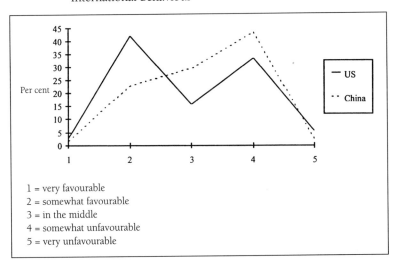

1 = very favourable
2 = somewhat favourable
3 = in the middle
4 = somewhat unfavourable
5 = very unfavourable

Unlike the study of other dimensions of mutual images, we did not formally ask respondents to give positive and negative evaluations. From their side comments we still can find some evaluative criteria or reference points guiding their affective judgement, which reflect both perceptual continuity and change.

On the American side, the first criterion can be called a 'traditional' perspective. The primary assumption of this criterion is that compared to its past behaviour, China has largely become a non-aggressive, non-threatening normal power in international politics. Respondents applying this criterion based their judgement either on a re-evaluation of China's foreign policy since 1949, or on a comparison of recent Chinese international performance with its past or with its domestic politics or with other superpowers. Some respondents in retrospect concluded that China in the past had not behaved as badly as it was once thought it had. As a China specialist pointed out: 'We often tend to forget how much the rest of the world did to China, especially the United States in the 1950s.' Although China 'made a lot of angry rhetoric, they didn't do that much that was so terrible'.[30] Others found that China's foreign policy in the recent decades had become 'much more sophisticated and rational' compared to its radical and irrational behaviour during periods such as the Cultural Revolution. More important, in terms of inner differentiation, is the fact that some American respondents had the cognitive ability to separate Chinese domestic politics and international behaviour. As a professor put it: 'Domestically I think Chinese politics is mad, but internationally it appears to be very rational and sensible.'

Respondents who applied this criterion were more likely to have a 'positive' orientation. Some respondents who had a very negative view of the Chinese Government turned out to hold a positive view of its international behaviour. Some respondents referred to various negative things in answering previous questions. When they came to make an overall affective judgement, however, they still applied the 'traditional' criterion and chose 'somewhat positive'.

The second criterion can be called a 'post-Cold War' perspective. The American respondents applying this criterion were not satisfied with the fact that China is no longer a military threat to the United States and the international community. Rather, their standard is to what extent China has positively contributed to the establishment of a post-Cold War international order and has met some general principles of international conduct. In the words of some respondents, 'China has stopped doing the bad things it did before, but has not done a whole lot positively beyond that.' Unlike the 'traditional' perspective, this criterion does not make a clear distinction between domestic politics and international conduct. Domestic 'wrongdoings', because of their impact on the world community, can be viewed as negative internationally.[31] Applying this criterion, China falls short of American expectations. According to a former diplomat, China failed to 'redefine its policy to accommodate new circumstances' and tended to 'backslide toward a comfortable old-fashioned policy that has no relevance to them and to the world'. Therefore some respondents described Chinese realpolitik as 'cynical', 'short-sighted', and even a 'sick game'. As mentioned earlier, this is a newly developed system of reference in the American image, and respondents with this criterion in mind tended to have a negative orientation.

The third criterion is less value-embedded and more functionally oriented. Some respondents gave a high mark to Chinese international behaviour simply because the Chinese 'play their cards remarkably well' and 'exercise their power in a very purposeful way internationally'.

A portion of respondents chose 'in the middle'. These respondents either perceived both good and bad aspects of Chinese international behaviour or considered it improper to pass 'a value judgement' because China is doing things in its own interest as do other major powers. As a senior scholar put it: 'China is not pro-Russian, not pro-American, it is pro-Chinese. Therefore I won't pass judgement on this. That does not mean I agree with everything China does. But if one asks, is this natural behaviour? Yes.'

Chinese elites also applied different systems of reference in making their affective judgement. The first one may also be called a 'traditional' criterion. This perspective originates from the Leninist framework of international relations. It sees little qualitative change in the nature of international politics in the post-Cold War era and postulates an inevitable struggle for hegemony among major powers. Although the Chinese subscribing to this framework usually did not perceive the United States as a military threat to China's security, some still believed that the United States has an ambition to establish a US-dominated unipolar world through ideological and economic means. In this respect, they viewed the United States as a political threat to China's stability. This criterion also has a nationalistic dimension that emphasizes the inviolability of national sovereignty and denies the validity of universal values and standards on issues such as human rights.

Some respondents noted that 'American interventionism has become aggravated since the collapse of the Soviet Union', and 'it [the United States] declares publicly that the goal of its foreign policy is to promote democracy all over the world'. They were convinced that 'most countries will not buy this policy, because the so-called democracy will create unrest in many countries and is not in the interest of world peace and people's will'. In addition, some Chinese did not believe that Americans were sincere in pursuing these 'universal values'. As a diplomat put it: 'The United States likes to flaunt the banner of justice, virtue, and morality. Don't believe it. That kind of stuff is only possible when its national interest coincides with its moral principles. The Gulf War is one of the few such cases. Otherwise, interests rather than morality will prevail.' As elaborated earlier, some respondents felt offended by the 'self-righteousness' and 'double standards' of American policy. On issues such as arms transfer and human rights, they asserted, the United States and other Western countries 'have always been the ones to set the concepts, criteria, and the rules of game, and it is not fair'.

For some respondents, the on-going American political and economic pressure on China was a sufficient reason to select a 'negative' choice. A young scholar was quite blunt: 'At this moment, as a Chinese I simply cannot say "positive", because the United States is exerting pressure on China.' Other respondents chose 'negative' because they perceived a sort of hypocrisy in American behaviour: Americans talk a lot about helping the Chinese people, but deliver little when real help is needed. A number of respondents cited American aid during China's serious floods in 1991 as an example. A professor said: 'You Americans just offered aid of $25,000. What the hell is this? You talk about human rights and humanity every day, where are they?' A business person described the amount as 'laughable'. He asserted: 'American foreign aid is characterized by very strong political motivations. As I understand it, the United States seldom offers aid out of pure humanitarian considerations. . . . Since the 1970s, has the United States ever been generous to China? Hardly.'

In contrast to American respondents, Chinese respondents who applied the 'traditional criterion' usually showed a negative evaluation of American international behaviour. Some respondents might have mentioned some positive features or even endorsed American policy to some extent in their general cognitions, but when they were making an overall affective judgement, they were unable to escape their pre-existing 'schema'.

Nevertheless, a considerable number of Chinese respondents were guided by a more cosmopolitan post-Cold War criterion in their affective evaluation. The starting point for this perspective is the world community as a whole rather than pure Chinese interests. Respondents embracing this criterion perceived a greater role for the United States in the post-Cold War international order as a positive sign of exerting necessary leadership rather than as a negative sign of seeking hegemony. Similarly to that of their American counterparts, this criterion also recognizes, to a certain extent, some transnational values and principles in evaluating international behaviour, and the connection between 'internal affairs' and world opinion.

Some respondents stood on the positive side because 'the US has the guts to stand up' and 'is willing to take a stand against injustice'. Even the Americans' strong reaction to the Tiananmen crackdown was not entirely regarded as an intervention in Chinese internal affairs. A former diplomat had the following comments:

> Deng Xiaoping argues that this is our internal affair. Americans say there are also international standards. Well, I agree. Just like parents beating their children, if you beat them too much, neighbours will come to say, 'don't beat too hard'. The same logic applies. You cannot regard this as an interference in your internal affairs. Of course you

can say, 'this is none of your business'. But others' concerns are out of good intentions.

In contrast to the United States sample, the Chinese respondents applying this 'post-Cold War' criterion generally had a positive affective orientation toward American international behaviour, even though they might still have some reservations about United States foreign policy. A young scholar who conveyed a 'somewhat positive' orientation remarked:

> Generally speaking, the United States can uphold justice. Of course, on some issues it sits on the unjust side because of its self-interest. For example, the United States has a strong opinion on the June 4th Incident. That immediately reminds me of the September 30th Incident in Indonesia in 1965. At that time, the military regime massacred at least several hundreds of thousands of communists and Chinese. But the United States did not say anything. Indonesia was considered a very important anti-communist ally then. Also the United States treated Iraq and Israel differently. Israel also has nuclear weapons, but the United States will never try to destroy them as it did with Iraq. So the United States has different standards, which sometimes might lead it to stand for unjust causes. But no country handles international affairs with a single standard. In most cases, the United States is responsible. Supporting the unjustified course is not the mainstream of American policy.

Compared to the US sample, a larger portion of the Chinese respondents (29%) chose 'in the middle'. On the one hand, this indicates an increased ability of the Chinese elites to make an 'inner differentiation'. Many respondents would say: 'it depends on which period', 'it depends on which administration', or 'it depends on which event'. For these respondents, they preferred to talk about concrete behaviour rather than making a sweeping judgement. On the other hand, it further confirmed the ambivalent feelings evident in their general cognitions. Many respondents were struggling to keep a balance between their internationalist propensity and nationalist syndrome. A young business person expressed a typical 'yes, but . . .' feeling: 'Of course, for some international affairs, you have to have somebody to maintain order; just like a family or a unit you have to have somebody to stand up. The problem is that when a country's internal affairs do not affect other countries, you do not let it solve its own problem first but jump into the mud instead. You make things worse rather than better. I don't appreciate that.' As also reflected in their previous comments, some Chinese respondents generally endorsed American leadership in world affairs. Nevertheless this role is only acceptable when the United States leaves China alone. The mentality is: 'It is fine for the US to take care of international affairs, but do not bother China. China is special.' However, as indicated earlier, some American respondents no longer saw the need and rationale to regard China as 'special'. This perceptual gap constitutes another potential source for Sino-American conflict. The net result of the interactions between the United States and China since the time this study was done is that the number of people holding a 'post-Cold War' standard on the American side and of people holding a 'traditional' criterion on the Chinese side has been increasing, thus leading toward a more negative evaluation of each other's international behaviour.

Patterns of Perceptual Changes

We have hypothesized that mutual images of international behaviour are more changeable in the context of ever-evolving international circumstances. They are also more vulnerable to big international events, which may well change people's reference points and consequently their image of the target nation and the relationship with that nation. The above analysis, to a degree, has revealed these features. In this section, an attempt is made to assess the intensity and direction of perceptual change in mutual images of international behaviour. Respondents were first asked to compare their current image of the target country's international behaviour with that held

Table 6.5 Percentage Distribution of Perceptual Change Regarding Chinese and American International Behaviour

Perceptual Change	Percentage (%)	
	US Respondents	Chinese Respondents
1 (changed greatly)	15.0	5.1
2	42.9	23.7
3	20.7	27.9
4	7.1	7.6
5	7.1	12.7
6	7.1	19.5
7 (no change at all)	0	3.4
Total	100.0	100.0
Sample size	140	118
Mean/SD	2.73/1.39	3.77/1.67

before 1970, and to give a score on a 7-point scale of perceptual change. Table 6.5 provides a comparison in this regard.

It is evident from the Table that American elites evinced a greater extent of perceptual change compared to Chinese elites. Close to four-fifths of the American respondents opted for the points 1–3, whereas the parallel percentage for the Chinese respondents is below 60%. At the same time, over 30% of the Chinese respondents considered continuity greater than change in their perceptions (points 5–7). The difference is quite significant when comparing the two means.[32] This pattern is consistent with the evolutionary orientation of mutual images of people and society, in which American respondents often described a greater perceptual change than Chinese respondents did.

The gap might simply result from the different American and Chinese personalities, as often reflected in their respective cognitive and affective orientations. But it also could reflect substantial differences in their perceptions. For the American respondents, their perceptions of Chinese international behaviour have undergone dramatic changes in the last two decades: from the number one threat to the anti-Soviet ally to the last communist hold-out. To some extent, the greater perceptual change mirrors the greater change in Chinese international behaviour since the early 1970s: from a very isolated and ideologically oriented power to a normal power increasingly becoming a part of the world community. It is equally true that most Chinese respondents have stopped perceiving the United States as a military threat to China. Yet many of them regard the 'hegemonic' nature of American international behaviour as unchanged, although they characterize it much less with ideological labels.

Respondents were then asked to describe their perceptual change regarding the 'nature' of the target international behaviour and the 'importance' of Sino-American relations over the last two decades. The first issue was measured along a 7-point scale, with 1 representing 'very warlike' and 7 'very peaceful'. Table 6.6 provides a comparison of American and Chinese responses.

The Table indicates that in the 1970s, a majority of the American and Chinese respondents perceived the other side as very 'warlike'. However, about four-fifths of the Chinese respondents selected points 1–3, while only about half of the American respondents made the same choice. That might reflect the reality at that time: the United States was still trapped in the Vietnam War, while China was threatened by the Soviet Union. The picture changed considerably in the 1980s. More than half of the American respondents put China on a more 'peaceful side'. Chinese respondents again turned out to be more conservative. Only fewer than four out of ten

Table 6.6　Percentage Distribution of Perceptual Change Regarding the
'Nature' of Chinese and American International Behaviour

Scale	US Sample (%)			China Sample(%)		
	1970s	1980s	1990s	1970s	1980s	1990s
1 (warlike)	6.0	0.7	0	29.1	1.7	1.7
2	22.4	4.3	1.4	39.3	7.6	7.6
3	25.3	12.9	5.8	13.7	12.7	14.4
4	24.6	23.7	22.3	13.7	43.2	36.4
5	11.9	30.3	36.7	2.6	25.4	24.5
6	7.5	24.5	30.2	1.8	9.3	15.3
7 (peaceful)	2.2	3.6	3.6	0	4.2	0
Total	100.0	100.0	100.0	100.0	100.0	100.0
Sample size	134	139	139	117	118	118
Mean	3.47	4.68	5.01	2.30	4.14	4.25

respondents chose points 5–7, while almost half of them opted for a middle stance.[33] The American perception in the 1990s continued to improve, with little evidence to suggest that the trend was reversed by the Tiananmen Incident. The trend on the Chinese side is more mixed. Some respondents advanced to the more 'peaceful' side, whereas others moved back to the more 'warlike' side. As indicated in their comments, American intervention in the Gulf War apparently reminded some Chinese respondents of American war-proneness. Over time, Chinese respondents tended to perceive American international behaviour as more 'warlike' than did American respondents regarding Chinese international behaviour. This perceptual trend is consistent with their respective affective and evaluative orientations analysed earlier. The Chinese cognition of American war-proneness is related to the observations about the 'hegemonic' nature and 'blunt' style of American international behaviour. For both samples, as a whole, a linear upward model for perceptual change holds, indicating that Americans and Chinese perceived each other as more peaceful than before. However, the upward trend for both samples flattens out during the early 1990s.

It is assumed that respondents' perceptual change regarding the target country's international behaviour can be further reflected in their evaluation of Sino-American relations, which is often a function of mutual images of international status and behaviour. Respondents were asked to describe their perceptual evolution concerning the importance of Sino-American relations along a 7-point scale, with 1 meaning 'very important' and 7 'not important at all'.

The data in Table 6.7 suggest that even in the early 1970s, a majority of the Chinese and American respondents regarded the relationship as very important. For both sides, over half of the respondents selected points 1–3. At that time, although both countries primarily continued to perceive the other side as an adversary rather than a friend, the threat of Soviet expansionism was prominent and the new relationship began to gain momentum. On the other hand, about 30% of the American and Chinese respondents put the relationship on the 'not important' side. This percentage greatly decreased in the 1980s. While 81% of the American respondents chose numbers on the more 'important' side, an even greater portion of the Chinese respondents (85%) opted for points 1–3, with more than 40% selecting 2. Of course, the normalization of the relationship at the end of the 1970s greatly enhanced the perception of importance regarding the relationship. The Soviet factor was still crucial for the cohesion of the relationship. Bilateral economic relations were rapidly expanding. All these factors contributed to the strong perception of importance. During that period, American and Chinese respondents demonstrated little disagreement on the issue.

A perceptual gap, however, emerges from their more recent perceptions. Even more Chinese respondents (close to 90%) have moved to the more

Table 6.7 Percentage Distribution of Perceptual Change Regarding the 'Importance' of Sino-American Relations

Scale	US Sample (%)			China Sample(%)		
	1970s	1980s	1990s	1970s	1980s	1990s
1 (important)	12.8	15.7	9.3	17.9	25.4	28.0
2	21.9	39.2	28.6	25.9	44.0	41.5
3	24.1	26.4	26.4	12.5	16.1	19.5
4	11.3	12.9	23.6	9.8	9.3	7.6
5	12.8	5.0	7.9	17.0	4.2	1.7
6	15.8	0.7	3.6	13.4	0.8	1.7
7 (not important)	1.5	0	0.7	3.6	0	0
Total	100.0	100.0	100.0	100.0	100.0	100.0
Sample size	133	140	140	112	118	118
Mean	3.44	2.56	3.08	3.41	2.30	2.23

'important' side, with few respondents picking up numbers 5 and above. The percentage of the American respondents opting for points 1–3, however, has dropped by nearly 20%. This perceptual gap is consistent with the early analysis of mutual images of power status. While a good portion of the American respondents no longer saw China as a major power and as critically important to American interests, a majority of the Chinese respondents were increasingly aware of American power and its crucial role in China's economic development. Therefore, starting from the 1980s, mutual perceptions regarding 'importance' go in different directions. A 'regression' phenomenon has occurred in the American perception, as reflected in comments about an 'overrated China'. At the same time, the Chinese perception in general keeps moving along the more 'important' line. This cognitive gap can be regarded as an important source for constant friction in the relationship in the years immediately after the Tiananmen Incident and the collapse of the Soviet Union. A more stable relationship only became possible after the United States attached more importance to the relationship in 1994.

Sources of Mutual Images

Regarding the sources of mutual images of international behaviour, it can be hypothesized that the variables of personal contact may not have a measurable impact, since international behaviour is more a collective output of the target nation-state. Compared to other dimensions of mutual images, it is the least directly observable through contact or visits. People can form their opinions through indirect interaction with the target country by reading newspapers, watching television, and so forth. The Tiananmen Incident should have different effects for the American and Chinese elites. As a domestic event in China, it should not overwhelmingly influence the American image of Chinese international behaviour. On the other hand, the American reaction to this event could have a greater impact on Chinese respondents. Profession and age may still account for the variation to some extent, because they could mean different historical and value orientations in judging the target country's international behaviour.

The same set of explanatory variables is crosstabulated against the data on cognitive differentiation in Table 6.3. Among the variables of interaction, contact before 1949 again stands out as a good indicator of cognitive differentiation. Those who had contact before 1949 on both sides demonstrated the lowest outer differentiation of international behaviour. It can be said that historical memories such as the American-Chinese alliance against the Japanese during World War II, which some respondents touched upon, might contribute to this greater sense of similarity. Other than that, contact during various time periods does not show a consistent association with cognitive differentiation for the two samples. The crosstabulation between the number of visits and cognitive differentiation yields an interesting pattern. While the degree of outer differentiation decreases with the increase in visits, the respondents who never visited the target country had the highest mean score, indicating lowest cognitive differentiation. That confirms the proposition that respondents' cognitive differentiation of international behaviour may not be contingent upon intensity of personal interaction, such as visiting the target country.

The Tiananmen Incident has a parallel impact on both sides. 'Greatly affected' respondents were inclined to see the target international behaviour as differing more from that of other major powers. Considering the foregoing analysis, Chinese respondents might point to the more 'interventionist' tendency on the American part, whereas American respondents might find China's ignorance of world opinion unique.

Understandably, diplomats in both samples tended to view the international behaviour of the target country as more similar to that of other countries. Business people, on the other hand, demonstrated the lowest mean score, indicating their higher outer differentiation. American business respondents usually were more aware of the 'inward-looking' nature of Chinese international behaviour, whereas their Chinese counterparts were more sensitive to the unique American power status.

The association between age and cognitive differentiation is somewhat expected on the part of the Chinese respondents. As in other dimensions of mutual images, older respondents tended to see more similarities. Unexpectedly though, American respondents younger than forty displayed the highest mean score. This suggests that while young American respondents usually are more sensitive to social and cultural differences between the two countries, they consider nation states as more similar in their external behaviour. In both samples, middle-aged respondents perceived the least similarity between the target country's international behaviour and that of other major powers.

The second variable of analysis is the affective orientation toward one another's international behaviour. The data of crosstabulation with the same set of independent variables suggest that American and Chinese respondents who visited or had contact with the other side prior to 1949 tended to have a more positive view of each other's international behaviour. However, the effect of contact during the years 1950–1970 and in the 1970s is not consistent for both samples. The frequency of contact during the 1980s tends to nurture more positive affective feelings for both sides. This finding may have something to do with the state of the Sino-US relationship at that time. The time of visits does not produce a consistent pattern for both sides. This phenomenon further strengthens the point that perceptions of the target country's international behaviour are less related to direct exposure to the target country.

The Tiananmen Incident, though somewhat differently from our prediction, has a negative impact on 'greatly affected' American and Chinese respondents alike. 'Greatly affected' Chinese respondents naturally felt angry over perceived American interference in Chinese domestic affairs. Their American counterparts, however, did not appear to regard the event as a purely domestic event, and were more sensitive to its international repercussions.

Profession, as is often the case, has a different impact in each of the United States and China samples. In the American sample, it is the business person who had the most unfavourable opinion of Chinese international behaviour. This is consistent with their outer differentiation. As reflected in their responses to previous questions, they tended to complain more about the Chinese arm sales, support of the Khmer Rouge, and hostility to Israel. On the other hand, Chinese diplomats evinced the least favourable feeling toward American international behaviour. This tendency can also be verified by their stronger resentment toward American 'arrogance', as reflected in their comments. American diplomats and intellectuals had a more favourable opinion of Chinese international behaviour, and quite a few of them were simply impressed by China's 'effective' diplomacy. Compared to diplomats, Chinese intellectuals and businessmen were inclined to have more favourable feelings about the American international role. As seen in their comments, many of them appreciated American leadership in international affairs.

Accounting for the impact of age, the data again demonstrate that a lower outer differentiation does not necessarily indicate a more favourable affective orientation. Younger American respondents who evinced a higher mean score on cognitive differentiation turned out to have the least favourable opinion of Chinese international behaviour. The same logic is pertinent to the older Chinese respondents. It can be argued that older Chinese respondents have stronger nationalist sentiments in viewing American international behaviour, whereas younger American respondents are more inclined to make value judgements about Chinese international behaviour. On the other hand, for the middle-aged American respondents, their higher cognitive differentiation could go together with a more favourable affective feeling.

The same set of explanatory variables is further applied to account for the differentials in perceptual change quantified in Table 6.5. It seems that contact as a whole does not explain the perceptual change regarding international behaviour very consistently. While the Chinese respondents who had contact before 1949 experienced less perceptual change than those who did not have contact, the same pattern does not hold for the American respondents who visited China before 1949. One might say that these respondents saw China as so weak internationally before 1949 that they have been more impressed by the change in China's international status since then. For the Chinese respondents who had contact before 1949, their cognition of either American powerfulness or American interventionism shaped then could be quite consistent, and is less prone to change.

Contact during the period 1950–1970 and in the 1970s does not appear to facilitate perceptual changes on either side. More likely, those who had contact with the other side during these time periods were less inclined to change their perceptions, either positive or negative. Both frequency of contact during the 1980s and number of visits do not yield a clear pattern for perceptual change on either side, indicating that perceptual change regarding the target country's international behaviour, as in cognitive and affective orientations, is less contingent upon the intensity of direct contact. The impact of the Tiananmen Incident does not seem to be a good indicator of perceptual change either.

Profession, as expected, exerts something like opposite influences on American and Chinese respondents. While American intellectuals indicated the least perceptual change and diplomats the most, Chinese intellectuals evinced the most perceptual change and the business people the least. American intellectuals might have perceived more continuity in Chinese international behaviour from their value and analytic frameworks. Diplomats, on the other hand, might have experienced more perceptual changes regarding China's actual power and role in international strategic configuration. Chinese intellectuals, on the other hand, were more likely to change their conceptual framework in viewing American international behaviour, while diplomats and some business people tended to stick with the traditional 'hegemonic' transcript.

Age proves to be a valid indicator accounting for perceptual change related to international behaviour. Consistent with other dimensions of mutual images, younger respondents on both sides were susceptible to more perceptual changes, while older respondents, due to their long-established preconceptions, were more resistant to accepting new information about the target country's international behaviour.

The bivariate analysis seems to indicate that respondents' cognitive, affective, and evolutionary orientations toward the target country's international behaviour are less determined by the intensity of personal contact. The frequency of contact during the 1980s and the time of visits in most cases do not yield consistent patterns for either sample. With regard to other variables of contact, both American and Chinese respondents who had contact with the other side before 1949 tended to exhibit a lower cognitive differentiation and a more positive orientation toward one another's international behaviour. Contact during the period 1950–1970 and in the 1970s did not produce a consistent pattern for American and Chinese respondents in terms of cognitive and affective orientations, but these contacts do not seem to facilitate perceptual change for either side. The Tiananmen Incident is correlated with a higher cognitive differentiation and a less favourable affective orientation, but its effect on perceptual change is not obvious. Profession often means different perceptual orientations for American and Chinese respondents. In the United States sample, American diplomats tended to have a lower outer differentiation, a more positive affective orientation, and a greater extent of perceptual change. American intellectuals showed the least perceptual change. It is the American business people who displayed the highest outer differentiation and the most negative feelings. In the China sample, Chinese diplomats also displayed a lower outer differentiation, but more negative feelings. Both Chinese intellectuals and business people had more favourable feelings toward American international behaviour. Like American business people, Chinese business people displayed the highest outer differentiation. Unlike American intellectuals, Chinese intellectuals experienced the most perceptual change. Age demonstrates both parallel and divergent influences for the two samples. The American and Chinese respondents aged sixty and older usually evinced the least perceptual change, and those younger than forty the most. In terms of affective orientation, the American respondents younger than forty had the most negative feelings, whereas their Chinese counterparts had the most favourable opinion. The American middle-aged respondents evinced the least unfavourable affective orientation, while the Chinese older respondents expressed the most unfavourable one.

Notes to Chapter 6

1   For a conceptual and psychological analysis of enemy images, see Finlay, *Enemies in Politics*.

2   Yusheng Yang had a vivid description of this arch-enemy image on the Chinese side. See *Zhongguoren de meiguoguan* (Chinese Images of the United States), pp. 234–243.

3   For instance, the American respondents who had negative views of Chinese society might have more positive opinions of Chinese international behaviour. On the other hand, the Chinese respondents who had positive views of American society might hold unfavourable feelings about American international behaviour.

4   Some respondents described China in the following phrases: 'China has been consistently overrated', 'China doesn't have a whole lot of power', 'China is a non-player in world politics', 'China as a big power is a joke', and 'China is a third-class power'.

5   A journalist commented: 'It [China] is relatively powerless. I think that is one thing Americans never understood. We have been victims of listening to *Radio Peking* during the Korean War and the Vietnam War. We listened to what they said and we got terrified. China has been so weak for so long. They couldn't even beat the Vietnamese in a border war. Come on, it's ridiculous. China has been subjected to so much internal interruption and is isolated from high technology. I don't find China will be half as threatening as some politicians would suggest.'

6   A number of respondents cited the Tiananmen Incident as an indicator of China's reduced political influence abroad. What they suggested was that with dramatic political transformations in the Soviet Union and Eastern European countries, China lost its political appeal as the most advanced reformist communist country.

7   Some respondents still felt uneasy when they talked about the potential of China and they thought it might not be a bad thing to keep the potential just a potential. As a business person said: 'China is a sleeping giant, you'd better not wake him up.'

8   This finding is consistent with the public opinion polls conducted during this time period. See Harding, *A Fragile Relationship,* p. 363, Table A.1.

9   See, for instance, Nicholas D. Kristof, 'China's Rise', *Foreign Affairs,* November/December, 1993, pp. 59–74; Richard Bernstein and Ross H. Munro, *The Coming Conflict with China,* New York: Alfred A. Knopf, 1997.

10   A researcher commented with apprehension: 'Uncertainty. China is a country with considerable potential. I am not sure whether they are going to be able to have national power. I am not sure how they are going to use it. I don't think the Chinese are sure. They don't have a very solid tradition in foreign policy. China is a country with no permanent allies. China is China, then everybody else.'

11   Quite a few respondents mentioned the Tiananmen Incident and its aftermath as indicators of China's unpredictable domestic and international behaviour.

12   Some respondents cited China's behaviour in the Gulf crisis as a good example: 'It neither had the courage to say no nor the courage to say yes. It sat on the sidelines without being serious.'

13   This new system of reference will be further elaborated later in this chapter.

14   Chinese elites described American power status in terms such as 'all-out champion', 'first-class military power', 'the sole superpower', 'a great power whose name matches the reality', and 'number one in the world'.

15   These respondents mentioned both strength and weakness of American power in their initial reaction to the question.

16   Subtle differences exist in perceptions of the comprehensiveness of American power. For instance, one view held that while the United States 'has plenty of wealth and power, it lacks cultural tradition and influence'. Another opinion argued that even in the cultural domain, 'American culture has a very strong influence and is very penetrating in the world'.

17   It is interesting to note that those who held a 'declining' image of American power also used the Gulf War to prove their argument. A senior scholar argued: 'The United States

should not be muddleheaded about its victory in the Persian Gulf. It had to initiate the war through the United Nations and that indicates that the United States could not completely control the international situation. The interesting thing about this war is that the United States sent soldiers and the other countries offered money. It is the reverse of the historical pattern that other powers sent troops and the United States provided dollars. The United States sent half of its military forces to deal with a country with a population of a mere 20 million. The American troops turned out to be a "mercenary army". That is not something very honourable.'

18   For a more detailed analysis of Chinese concepts of hegemony, see Shambaugh, *Beautiful Imperialist,* pp. 78–83.

19   There are reasons to believe that this anti-hegemony feeling has been intensified in the years after this research was conducted, due to a series of incidents in US-China relations. Yusheng Yang touched upon this trend in his book. See *Zhongguoren de meiguoguan* (Chinese Images of the United States), pp. 279–287. This sentiment burst into massive public demonstrations with the US-led NATO attack against Yugoslavia and the subsequent bombing of the Chinese embassy in 1999.

20   It should be pointed out that very few respondents with this image analysed American international behaviour in terms of ideological doctrine or Marxist theory. Almost no one applied the term *meidiguozhuyi* (American imperialism). Rather they perceived the feature as either a natural tendency of all great powers or a more salient style of American behaviour. Some even suggested that American 'intervention' in world affairs might be 'out of good intention[s]'.

21   Although in practice the Chinese have a tendency to ask about others' affairs, conceptually, those people who are perceived as *aiguan xianshi*, whether they are colleagues, friends or relatives, usually are not highly regarded, but not necessarily hated. The term *dabaobuping* does not necessarily have a negative connotation, rather it often means that a person has a tendency to stand up for something unjust.

22   A former diplomat said: 'Americans from top to bottom have a sense of mission. They want to remake the world according to their own model. They oppose the communist attempt to transform the world with Marxism-Leninism. Nevertheless they want to put their harness on the world. It doesn't make sense to me. I am not saying that American values are all wrong. But even the best food could turn sour if you stuff it into people's mouths.'

23   A business person said: 'When you talk about the American role in the world, you have to pay attention to both aspects. Gains and losses always go together. It is not easy to be a world leader.' A former government official remarked: 'Americans sometimes are a little bit too dominant. But I don't know what China would do if it were in the American position. It could be the same thing. So sometimes we cannot be overly critical of the United States'.

24   As a reflection of these mixed feelings, many respondents said both good and bad things about American international behaviour in a typical proviso of 'but'. Even so, considering the previous black and white images of American international behaviour, this pattern of 'dividing one into two' is a considerable sophistication.

25   However, the difference is insignificant in statistical terms ($t = -0.23$, the null hypothesis that there is no difference between the two means can not be rejected).

26   The data confirmed a proposition made earlier: some American respondents, even though they might not have a very high opinion of China's national power, would like to see China more involved in the world community and taking more responsibility in international affairs.

27   Indeed, some Americans considered that China 'absolutely has got no clue as to the public relations aspects of diplomatic behaviour', and suggested that China hire some public relations experts. As a business person said: 'The perception is very important. It's not only a question of what you say, what you say is only as good as how it is perceived. It's not enough to tell the truth, you have to understand what the other person thinks you are saying and how he hears you.'

28   They mentioned, among other things, the traditional US China policy, the Marshall plan, the Peace Corps, etc.

29   A significance test shows that the difference between the two means is statistically significant at an alpha level of 0.025 (t = 2.06).

30   An educator expressed the same feeling: 'Compared to many other superpowers over the years, I don't think China has been so terrible, I really don't. China has been more inward-looking and it hasn't been in my mind a sort of monster on the international scene. So I think it's mildly positive relative to the Soviet Union in Afghanistan or the United States in Vietnam.'

31   Some respondents chose 'negative' simply because of the Tiananmen Incident.

32   A t-test demonstrates that Chinese respondents on average evinced less perceptual change regarding American international behaviour (t = 5.50, p < 0.0005).

33   In their side comments, Chinese respondents often mentioned the occasional American military intervention overseas as an indicator of its willingness to use force in foreign policy.

CHAPTER 7 ·
STRUCTURE AND SOURCES OF MUTUAL IMAGES

In Chapter 2, Sino-American mutual images were defined in terms of a 3 x 4 matrix of three attitudinal dimensions (cognitive, affective, and evaluative) and four object dimensions (people, society, culture, and international behaviour). Based on theoretical assumptions about the dynamic linkage between routine interaction, 'big' events, and perceptual evolution, four heuristic models (static, linear, fluid, and curvilinear) were hypothesized to conceptualize the evolution of Sino-American mutual images in the last two decades. In the preceding four chapters, we analysed the mutual images of people, society, culture, and international behaviour respectively along the cognitive, affective, and evaluative dimensions in a comparative fashion. We preliminarily explored the evolution and differentials of mutual images manifested in the two elite samples. In this chapter, we will further investigate the structure and sources of mutual images at both macro- and micro-level.

First, the internal structure of mutual images will be analysed to delineate patterns and relationships running through different image dimensions. The focus will be shifted from horizontal and one-dimensional comparisons to vertical and multi-dimensional comparisons. While the foregoing chapters concentrated on comparing the two samples within one image dimension, here we will examine the internal consistency or inner differentiation of mutual images in terms of cognitive differentiation, affective orientation, and perceptual change.

Second, the sources of mutual images will be further explored in a more systematic and rigorous way. For this purpose, two modes of analysis, subjective and objective estimations, will be employed. The former delineates major sources of mutual images through respondents' self-assessment. The latter tests the strength of the relationship between selected independent variables and perceptual orientations, using the method of multivariate analysis.

Structure of Mutual Images

Patterns of Cognitive Differentiation
It was suggested in Chapter 2 that one indicator of cognitive complexity is low outer differentiation and high inner differentiation of a target country. A sophisticated national image tends to perceive some similarities between the subject and the target countries and to make a differentiation regarding

various dimensions within the target country. Chapters 3–6 compared American and Chinese elites' outer differentiation between the subject and target countries. We now want to compare their scores of outer differentiation across four image dimensions to see the degree of inner differentiation. This is seen in a comparison of the mean scores of differentiation at an aggregate level in Table 7.1.

Table 7.1   Mean Scores of Cognitive Differentiation Across Four Image
Dimensions

Image Dimensions	Mean Scores of Cognitive Differentiation[*]	
	US Sample	China Sample
People	3.73	3.00
Society	2.19	1.81
Culture	2.14	2.09
International behaviour	3.77	3.72
Overall mean	2.96	2.66
Sample size	141	127

* Mean scores are calculated from responses to a 7-point scale. 1 = 'very different', and 7 = 'very similar'.

The comparison indicates that, overall, the United States sample displays higher mean scores than the China sample, reflecting a lower degree of outer differentiation. It can be said that at a collective level, American elites evinced a more cosmopolitan tendency than their Chinese counterparts in mutual images. This is not surprising, given China's fairly recent entry into the world system, and the 'melting pot' nature of American society. However, for both sides, none of the mean scores pass the threshold of 4 on a 7-point scale. In general, American and Chinese elites perceived more differences than similarities between the two countries. This high degree of outer differentiation reflects the realities of the two countries in many ways. Perceptions about these differences may well set an outer limitation for the relationship. Therefore, these seemingly trivial numbers convey a basic fact of Sino-American relations: 'you and we are different'.

As analysed earlier, the difference in mean scores between the two samples is statistically significant for mutual images of people and society, but insignificant for mutual images of culture and international behaviour. Apparently, the biggest perceptual gap exists in the mutual images of people, where the mean score in the United States sample is close to 4 but in the China sample remains at 3. This phenomenon can be explained by the proposition suggested in Chapter 3. American respondents tended to see Chinese and Americans as more similar at the individual level and attribute the difference to China's socio-economic system. They were prone to underestimate the social adaptability of the Chinese under different circumstances. Chinese respondents were more aware of the distance between Chinese and Americans in terms of personality, values, and behavioural patterns. Although this perceptual gap usually manifests itself at a personal level, it may also create perceptual problems for the relationship at a macro-level. Americans often see Chinese as more similar to themselves than they really are. When Chinese eventually turn out to be rather different, Americans naturally feel frustrated. On the Chinese side, the problem is viewing Americans as more different than they actually are. As a result, they are often too conscious of the difficulties in communicating with Americans and worry that they cannot make themselves understood.

The distribution of mean scores in Table 7.1 reflects the vertical degree of consistency or inner differentiation in each sample. The inconsistency is obvious for both samples, suggesting a pluralistic feature of cognitive differentiation. The basic pattern indicates that both American and Chinese respondents perceived more similarity between the two peoples and international behaviours, and more difference between the two societies and cultures. For both sides, the highest mean score is given to the target country's international behaviour. This is a remarkable perceptual sophistication from a historical perspective. As revealed by the analysis in Chapter 6, American and Chinese respondents demonstrated a certain degree of dimensional independence in their mutual perceptions of international behaviour. That is, they tended to take the target country's international behaviour as it is. Mutual cognition of differences in other dimensions, such as social and value systems, apparently did not play a big role in their cognitive differentiation of international behaviour. With 'national interest' as a common denominator, neither side regarded the other as an international abnormality. For the American elites, the lowest mean score belongs to the difference between Chinese and American cultures. For many American respondents, Chinese culture still represents something exotic, especially when defined as a civilization spanning millenia. For the Chinese respondents, the greatest difference lies in the two social systems. It seems that at the time of this research, Chinese elites were more sensitive to the normative difference between 'socialism' and 'capitalism'. On the other hand, they saw relatively less difference between the two cultures. As illustrated in Chapter 5, Chinese respondents spontaneously mentioned more similarities than the American respondents did. Perhaps in a country where people's values and lifestyle have been changing rapidly, Chinese respondents were more aware of the convergence of the two cultures, at least on the surface. It is a considerable perceptual sophistication for the Chinese elites, as they had started to view American culture from a non-ideological perspective, thus finding more common ground between the cultures as human ways of life.

Pattern of Affective Orientation

In the previous four chapters, we also measured respondents' affective orientations, namely, their favourable or unfavourable feelings toward various aspects of the target country. According to the two standard image models suggested in Chapter 2, Image I is characterized by consistency in respondents' affective orientations, while Image II is characterized by discrepancy. We expect that the traditional all 'black and white' image of the target country has been replaced by more discriminating affective orientations. Table 7.2 provides a comparison of the mean scores of affective orientations across four image dimensions.

Table 7.2 Mean Scores of Affective Orientations Across Four Image
Dimensions

Image Dimensions	Mean Scores of Affective Orientation*	
	US Sample	China Sample
People	1.45	2.04
Government	3.88	2.78
Culture	1.93	2.45
International behaviour	2.97	3.22
Overall mean	2.56	2.62
Sample size	141	127

* Mean scores are calculated from responses to a set of 5 choices: 1 = very favourable; 2 = somewhat favourable; 3 = in the middle; 4 = somewhat unfavourable; 5 = very unfavourable.

In general, judging from the overall mean scores in the table, American respondents had more positive orientations toward China than the other way round. As illustrated in preceding chapters, Chinese respondents tended to be more conservative and level-headed in making their affective judgement. In contrast, American respondents were more inclined to go to either extremes of 'very favourable' or 'very unfavourable'. This might mirror their different national characters and ways of perceiving things. As their substantive remarks often reveal, Chinese respondents were more willing to talk about positive things concerning the United States in the context of their own problems. American respondents, on the other hand, tended to express their positive feelings in a more abstract and emotional fashion.

Comparing mean scores across the two samples, US-China mutual affective orientations manifest both convergence and discrepancy. Both sides generally held positive feelings toward the target people and culture, although the American respondents showed a greater intensity of feeling. As discussed in previous chapters, mutual attraction of personalities and cultures constitutes a natural tie connecting Americans and Chinese. Taking into consideration the parallel mean scores on cognitive differentiation, it might be said that Americans and Chinese like each other as people because they perceive some similarities in personality; and they like each other's cultures because of the intrinsic differences between these two cultures. Here the social psychology propositions of 'likeness begets liking' and 'opposites attract'[1] both apply. Cognitive discrepancies can be detected by comparing the mean scores for government and international behaviour. As discussed in Chapter 4, many American respondents, largely affected by the Tiananmen crackdown, expressed strong resentment against the Chinese Government. The same resentment does not exist proportionally among Chinese elites in their attitudes toward the American Government. Ironically, the only image domain in which Chinese respondents, on average, expressed more positive views than their American counterparts is their affective orientation toward the American Government. This does not mean that Chinese respondents did not have complaints against the United States on the Tiananmen Incident. Rather, the target for their criticism is American international behaviour rather than the American Government as a whole. As a result, Chinese respondents showed a higher mean score in their affective orientation toward American international behaviour than was the case for the American orientation toward Chinese international behaviour.

These perceptual discrepancies obviously can become real or potential sources for friction and conflict in the relationship. From the perspective of image structure, they also demonstrate a considerable degree of inner differentiation in their affective orientations. Among the four image dimensions, American respondents expressed the strongest negative affective judgement of the Chinese Government and the most positive affective orientation toward the Chinese people. For Chinese respondents, the most negative feeling was aimed at American international behaviour, while the most positive orientation was given to the American people. Looking at

Table 7.2, we find that the degree of inner differentiation is higher in the United States sample.[2] For instance, regarding affective feelings toward the target people and government, the difference between mean scores in the US sample is 2.43, but it is only 0.73 in the China sample, indicating that American respondents had a greater affective inconsistency. In other words, Americans could have greater cognitive dissonance in their attitudes toward the Chinese Government and Chinese people, while Chinese usually did not feel that way. The perceptual sophistication rests with the fact that both American and Chinese elites manifested a cognitive ability to separate domestic and international functions of the target country. Negative orientation in one domain did not prevent them from making a more positive judgement in another. In the American case, some respondents' strong negative feelings toward the Chinese Government were able to coexist with their more favourable view of Chinese international behaviour. In the Chinese case, resentment over American international behaviour did not stop some respondents from giving the American Government a high mark. These dimensional complexities provide a viable, albeit limited, cognitive 'window of opportunity' for Sino-American cooperation. American moral objections to the Chinese regime probably will not eliminate China as a possible partner in international affairs, and Chinese nationalist resentment of American 'hegemonism' may still allow the Chinese to absorb American political and cultural values on their own terms.

Patterns of Perceptual Changes

The preceding four chapters explored the evolution of Sino-American mutual images in each dimension. As discussed earlier, a scientific study of perceptual changes over the two decades of 1970–1990 requires a longitudinal data set unavailable for this study. A systematic inquiry as to respondents' own estimations of their perceptual changes, however, yields some interesting findings and provides some reference points for future studies. To compare the trends of perceptual change across the two samples and the various dimensions within a sample, we table the mean scores of perceptual change in Table 7.3.

The data show that Sino-American mutual images have experienced significant perceptual change, except the mean score for the American image of Chinese culture, which leans toward the 'no change' side of the scale. Other scores point to change rather than continuity in mutual perceptions. Again, Chinese elites were more conservative than their American counterparts in perceptual change. Apart from the mean scores for mutual images of culture, American elites expressed greater perceptual change as indicated by their lower mean scores. This perceptual gap could also be

Table 7.3 Mean Scores of Perceptual Changes Across Four Image
Dimensions

Image Dimensions	Mean Scores of Perceptual Change*	
	US Sample	China Sample
People	2.93	3.39
Society	2.64	3.61
Culture	4.21	3.52
International behavior	2.73	3.77
Overall mean	3.13	3.57
Sample size	141	127

* Mean scores are calculated from responses to a 7-point scale. 1 = 'changed greatly' and 7 = 'no change at all'.

ascribed to the difference in personality between American and Chinese respondents in our samples. More plausibly, it reflects the different situations of the two countries. In the last two decades, China has experienced greater change in all these four dimensions than the United States has, thus leading to greater perceptual change on the American part. On the other hand, it may also to some extent reveal the fragility of American perceptions of China. More American respondents described their perceptual regression as being caused by both macro and micro factors, such as the Cultural Revolution, personal business experience, and the Tiananmen Incident. Fewer Chinese respondents spontaneously mentioned similar experiences. It could be argued that the changeability of the American perception of China has both objective and subjective reasons. Objectively, China itself is more changeable. Subjectively, Americans tend to be unduly influenced by dramatic, yet often superficial, fluctuations.

The only exception is in mutual perceptions regarding culture. In this dimension, Chinese respondents on average declared greater perceptual change than their American counterparts. As argued in Chapter 5, this gap can be partially attributed to the different conceptualization of the target culture. In American eyes, Chinese culture is primarily a historical concept characterized heavily by continuity and stagnation. Most American respondents did not have much of an impression of contemporary Chinese culture. Some respondents had difficulty in finding a linkage between what they saw in today's Chinese culture and what they had learnt about the traditional culture. On the other hand, Chinese respondents were inclined to see American culture as a dynamic process, which is characterized by change rather than stability. Moreover, before the 1970s, Chinese elites had very limited access to American culture. Their recent exposure to American culture might have led to greater perceptual changes.

The inner differences in perceptual changes also reveal different patterns for the American and Chinese elites. In the United States case, apparently American elites experienced the greatest change in their perception of Chinese society and the least change in their perception of Chinese culture. As mentioned earlier, more American respondents experienced a cognitive process of 'negative–positive–negative' in their perceptions of Chinese society and Government. If a cycle has ever occurred in the American image of China, it is in this image domain. On the Chinese side, respondents declared greatest change in their perceptions of the American people and least change regarding American international behaviour. For a majority of the Chinese respondents, 'American' (*meiguoren*) was a very abstract and one-dimensional concept until the late 1970s and the early 1980s. Consequently, their images of Americans are still evolving even today. Their comments did indicate that many Chinese respondents perceived the 'hegemonic' nature of American international behaviour as unchanged, although they were much less inclined to interpret the phenomenon through Marxist ideology. An interesting feature is that Chinese respondents on average declared more change in their perception of American culture than in that of American society. One possible explanation could be that while the content of Chinese perceptions of American society had changed considerably, the conceptual 'schema' of 'socialism versus capitalism' they had in mind remained the same. Their perceptual sophistication rests with the fact that capitalism is no longer seen as inherently bad and socialism as necessarily good. The greater change in Chinese perceptions of American culture is consistent with their cognitive and affective orientations.

The above data reveal the patterns of perceptual evolution in Sino-American mutual images at an aggregate level. In previous chapters, we elicited respondents' perceptual changes on some specific attitudinal issues pertinent to mutual images of people, society, and international behaviour. The findings appear to be that, irrespective of the twists and turns in Sino-American relations following the Tiananmen Incident in 1989, an upward linear model is a more accurate approximation of perceptual change for both American and Chinese elites. On some issues, American elites displayed a stronger tendency to 'regress' in their perceptions, and as a result a curvilinear model fits. But we still do not know much about the patterns of perceptual change for individual respondents. One approach to addressing this question is to ask respondents to describe their overall trends of perceptual changes over the last two decades. Respondents on both sides were thus presented with five figures of perceptual change[3] discussed in Chapter 2 and asked to choose one that best fitted their situation. By providing respondents with this frame of reference, plausible patterns of perceptual changes at an individual level can be delineated. Table 7.4 compares the self-proclaimed patterns of perceptual change of the American and Chinese elites.

Table 7.4 Overall Patterns of Perceptual Change

Patterns of Perceptual Change	Perceptual Evolution (%)	
	US Respondents	Chinese Respondents
Static	9.4	25.6
Upward	35.3	45.3
Downward	3.6	1.7
Fluid	12.2	7.7
Curvilinear	32.4	17.9
Multiple*	7.2	1.7
Total	100.0	100.0
Sample size	139	117

* Respondents in this category declined to choose only one model to represent their perceptual changes. Instead, they preferred to apply multiple models to describe their perceptual changes regarding various dimensions of their images.

The comparison illustrates some notable differentials in the patterns of perceptual change between American and Chinese elites. The data further confirm an earlier observation that Chinese respondents, as a whole, claimed less perceptual change compared to their American counterparts. While less than one in ten American respondents opted for the static model, which emphasizes the stability of their image of China, one in four Chinese respondents chose this model. On both sides, respondents with this pattern stressed that their 'basic image' or 'core image' of the target country did not change 'fundamentally', although cognitively they did experience some minor ups and downs. Apparently, Chinese respondents were more inclined to use this model to rationalize their images prior to the 1970s. Some of them argued that even then, through limited access to information,[4] they acquired a fairly objective and realistic view of the United States. Some Chinese respondents argued that their original images of the United States, formed before the Chinese revolution, remained intact during the Mao era, although outwardly they had to pretend to have a different, officially sanctioned image. As a result, what they articulated reflected their once-suppressed images rather than new perceptions. For these Chinese respondents, while the images of the United States at the national level have changed dramatically, their individual images have remained stable.

An upward linear model indicates that a respondent's overall image of the target country has been moving in a more positive direction over the last two decades. In both samples, the respondents who opted for this pattern represent the largest sub-group. For these respondents, the Tiananmen Incident apparently did not reverse the course of their overall perceptions. As mentioned earlier, Chinese respondents were less affected by the aftermath of this event, since it was regarded largely as a matter internal to China. Few Chinese respondents subscribed to the notion that the turmoil was caused by 'external interference or influence'. Among those Chinese respondents who claimed the incident had a great impact on their image of the United States, 33% of them still chose this model, indicating that the American reaction to the event might have affected their perception of the United States in certain aspects, but did not reverse their overall perceptual trend.

The event hit American respondents harder. Yet 7% of the 'greatly affected' American respondents selected this model. Some American respondents recognized the negative impact of the event, but taking the whole period since 1970 as a frame of reference, they decided to choose the upward linear model. Some even suggested that the Tiananmen Incident was a 'passing event'. Among those American and Chinese respondents who endorsed this model, some modified it to indicate that instead of going all the way up, their cognitive curve flattened out at certain time points, mostly in the late 1980s. For them, this was a natural development of the 'maturation' of their perceptions or 'better understanding' of the target country. For others, the levelling off was partially caused by the Tiananmen Incident. Yet they emphasized that their image curve did not go down, and in the long run they still 'have great hopes'.

However, if we look at the relative weight of this model in each sample, the difference is salient. While nearly half of the Chinese respondents chose this pattern, the parallel percentage for the American respondents is just about 35%. This gap might be partially attributed to the fact that more American respondents opted for a curvilinear model to describe their perceptual changes. This model, as analysed in Chapter 2, draws people's attention to the possible regression phenomenon, and points to a mount-shaped curve in perceptual change. While only about 18% of the Chinese respondents picked this pattern, over 30% of the American respondents favoured it. For these respondents, their perceptions of the target country started climbing quickly at the initial stage of the relationship, as reflected in the episodes of 'China fever' and 'America fever'. At a certain point, due to either micro or macro stimuli, they experienced a disillusionment, and the cognitive curve regressed in a more negative direction. Most respondents who adopted this model hastened to add that the slope of their regression was not so deep as to reach their pre-1970s images of the target country. To some extent, the regression is a natural function of on-going contact and interaction. In other words, the initial idealization of the other side starts 'regressing' to a perception closer to reality through routinization of interaction, thus representing perceptual sophistication. As the bivariate analyses in previous chapters imply, more contact does not necessarily lead to more favourable views of the other side. Some respondents' regression was largely based on their personal experience.[5] However, the regression could also be touched off by non-personal macro events and developments. Clearly, the regression of a considerable portion of respondents, especially on the American side, was primarily caused by the Tiananmen Incident. For American respondents, it was an event that shattered their upward expectation of the progress of democracy in China. Among those who claimed a great effect of the Tiananmen Incident on their image, 66% chose this model. For other respondents, the process of regression started long before this incident. The revelation of the Cultural Revolution destroyed some respondents' hopes that China was developing a new society superior to the declining Western capitalist society. Suppression of the Democracy Wall Movement disillusioned the American expectation that economic modernization would move China toward Western-style democratization. For some American respondents, so to speak, the Tiananmen Incident reinforced or dramatized their on-going process of regression rather than suddenly reversing the course of their perceptual evolution.

Fewer Chinese respondents experienced perceptual disillusionment than their American counterparts. Chinese respondents tended to be more conservative and less emotional, as often manifested in their articulation of mutual images that we have seen in previous chapters. At the individual level, some of them also suffered disillusionment through experiences such as working at the United States consulate or having business negotiations. But in general, the United States was not an object for their instinctive moral or value judgement. The repercussions of the Tiananmen Incident in the United States did surprise some Chinese respondents, as they 'never expected that Americans would react so strongly to the event for such a long time'. Among the 'greatly affected' Chinese respondents, 33% selected the curvilinear model to indicate their cognitive frustration with the United States. For them, the overwhelming moral judgement of China by the American public was perceived as a reflection of the 'lack of understanding of China', as 'the self-proclaimed sense of mission', and as 'shallow emotionalization'.

On both sides, very few respondents selected a downward linear model that would indicate that their image of the target country had been deteriorating. More American respondents exhibited this cognitive inclination. Some respondents mentioned their gradual realization of the 'magnitude of problems' and 'the depth of troubles' in China, which made them more 'pessimistic' and 'depressed' about China's future.

More American respondents chose the fluid model to represent their perceptual change (12% as opposed to 8% of the Chinese respondents). This reflects, in part, China's domestic political instability. Theoretically, this model draws people's attention to the perceptual inconsistency and irregularity across situations. The assumption is that people's perceptions and behaviours are often determined by circumstances rather than deep-seated preconceptions. In the case of Sino-American mutual images, instead of seeking a consistent image of the other side, some respondents tended to let their perceptions drift in accordance with major events and policy shifts in Sino-American relations. On the one hand, this pattern may indicate the fragility of these respondents' perceptions of the target country. A signal event such as the Tiananmen Incident could topple the balance of their tension system, thus leading to perceptual change. On the other hand, this pattern could point to perceptual sophistication. In other words, people's images of the target country are less dictated by their pre-existing 'schemata'. Rather, a more ad hoc approach is applied to make observations of the target country. Some American and Chinese holders of this pattern described their perceptions as 'dispassionate', and 'judging things as they stand', and more contingent upon issues and image dimensions. A positive or negative opinion of one event or aspect pertinent to the target country did not dictate their views on other subjects.

Another group of respondents were reluctant to generalize their perceptual changes with only one pattern. Rather, they preferred to apply different models to describe their perceptual changes in various image dimensions. Table 7.4 indicates that more American respondents adopted this approach. Typically, they made a differentiation between their attitudes toward the Chinese Government and the Chinese people. They usually applied an upward linear model to describe their perceptual change regarding the Chinese people, and a downward linear, or curvilinear, model to approximate their perceptual evolution toward the Chinese Government.

This conscious separation of the Chinese Government from the Chinese people, as mentioned in Chapter 1, has its roots in the American traditional image of the PRC. Apparently, the democratic aspirations of Chinese intellectuals and constant reliance on authoritarian rule by the Chinese regime revived this 'script' among the American elites. While this approach reflects a higher inner differentiation, overemphasis on the mutual independence of the people and the government could distort reality and lead to another type of misperception. It is interesting to note that the conceptual separation of the American Government and the American people used to be a popular Chinese perception during the Mao era as well. But as reflected in the affective orientation of the Chinese respondents, this distinction has become blurred since the 1980s. Few Chinese respondents spontaneously mentioned it. The two Chinese respondents who adopted the multiple approach emphasized their different perceptions toward other dimensions, such as the differentiation between American domestic governance and international behaviour.

To further explore the relationship between image patterns and respondents' backgrounds, it might be interesting to know what types of respondents are more likely to hold what types of image patterns in terms of their professions and ages. Tables 7.5 and 7.6 crosstabulate the image patterns with these two variables.

Table 7.5 Percentage Distribution of Image Patterns by Profession

| | Profession | | | | | |
| | Intellectuals (%) | | Business people (%) | | Diplomats (%) | |
Model	US	China	US	China	US	China
Static	9.1	30.6	9.3	20.0	9.8	26.1
Upward	34.6	49.0	39.5	48.9	31.7	30.4
Downward	5.5	0	2.3	0	2.4	8.7
Fluid	12.7	4.1	18.6	13.3	4.9	4.4
Curvilinear	29.1	16.3	27.9	13.3	41.5	30.4
Multiple	9.1	0	2.3	4.4	9.8	0
Total	100.0	100.0	100.0	100.0	100.0	100.0
Cases	55	49	43	45	41	23

Table 7.6 Percentage Distribution of Image Patterns by Age

| | Age | | | | | |
| Model | < 40 (%) | | 40–59 (%) | | ≥ 60 (%) | |
	US	China	US	China	US	China
Static	7.7	0	7.3	24.5	12.5	38.3
Upward	15.4	66.7	36.2	44.9	37.5	36.2
Downward	0	0	2.9	0	5.4	4.3
Fluid	30.8	14.3	10.1	4.1	10.7	8.5
Curvilinear	38.5	19.1	33.3	22.5	30.4	12.8
Multiple	7.7	0	10.1	4.1	3.6	0
Total	100.0	100.0	100.0	100.0	100.0	100.0
Cases	13	21	69	49	56	47

From Table 7.5 we can see that the distribution of image patterns across three groups of respondents shows both similarities and differences between the two samples. In the category of 'intellectuals', the upward model has the largest percentage in the China sample. Almost half of the Chinese intellectuals endorsed this model. At the same time, far more Chinese intellectuals (31%) than American intellectuals (9%) chose a static pattern. Apparently, for a majority of the Chinese intellectuals, their images of the United States either remained the same or changed positively. On the other hand, however, more American than Chinese intellectuals selected both the curvilinear pattern (29% versus 16%) and the fluid pattern (13% versus 4%). Moreover, while a portion of the American intellectuals chose the downward and multiple modes, none of the Chinese intellectuals did so. Interestingly, in both samples, business people were more likely to select the fluid model but were less likely to choose the curvilinear model. Yet American business people had the largest percentage for the upward model compared with American intellectuals and diplomats. In both samples, diplomats had the highest percentages for the curvilinear pattern (41% in the case of Americans and 30% in the case of Chinese) and the lowest percentages for the upward model (32% and 30% respectively). The Chinese respondents who chose the downward model were all diplomats. In the United States sample, fewer American diplomats (5%) opted for the fluid model compared to American intellectuals (13%) and American business people (19%).

As for the relationship between age and model selection, older respondents, not surprisingly, were more likely to choose static patterns to describe their perceptual evolution. This is particularly the case on the Chinese side. None of the Chinese respondents younger than 40 selected this model, while the percentage of those respondents aged 60 and older that did is 38%. The distribution patterns for the upward model are quite the opposite in the two samples. In the Chinese case, the percentage for this model is largest for respondents younger than 40 (67%), while in the United States sample, the same age group had the smallest percentage (15%). On the other hand, the American age group of 60 or older had the largest percentage for this model, whereas the same age group in the China sample had the smallest percentage. In addition, all Chinese respondents who opted for the downward model are 60 or older. This interesting pattern suggests that the perceptual gaps between Americans and Chinese could be related to generational differences. Both American and Chinese respondents younger than 40 were more likely to be erratic in their perception of the target country (31% and 14% respectively). The same thing is true for the curvilinear pattern in the United States sample (39%), but it is the Chinese respondents aged 40–59 who were more likely to have regression in their perceptions of the United States (23%).

In short, the patterns of mutual images reveal in numerical terms that American elites generally demonstrated lower outer differentiation, more positive affective orientation, and more perceptual change. In cognitive differentiation, Chinese respondents showed a greater degree of inner differentiation, while in affective orientation and perceptual change, American respondents evinced higher inner differentiation, especially in their attitudes toward the Chinese Government and the Chinese people. In self-identification of the patterns for perceptual change, a larger percentage of the Chinese endorsed the upward linear model, while a larger percentage of the Americans regressed in their perceptions.

Sources of Mutual Images

The theoretical framework set forth in Chapter 2 casts the aforementioned patterns of cognitive differentiation, affective orientation, and perceptual evolution in Sino-American mutual images in the context of cross-national interactions between the two countries. We delineated two forms of interaction that are likely to have an impact on these mutual images. One is indirect interaction, in which one party learns about the other through indirect sources, such as books, newspapers, and television. The other takes the form of direct and personal contact and observations. It is the second type of interaction that has become an important source for mutual images since the 1970s. These two forms of interaction are subject to the influence of various events in bilateral and international developments. While a systematic and comprehensive image of the target country often results from an accumulation of knowledge and conceptualization over time, 'reorganizing' events, such as the Tiananmen Incident, could have a disproportional effect on people's cognition. In previous chapters, we explored the associations between respondents' perceptual orientations and a set of explanatory variables including contact, the Tiananmen Incident, profession, and age. In this section, the relationship between these source variables and mutual images will be further investigated from both subjective and objective vantage points.

Subjective Evaluation of Sources

First, it may be pertinent to see how American and Chinese elites themselves weighed the importance of various sources forming their images. As one of the main explanatory variables in this study, the impact of personal contact on image formation and evolution is difficult to measure but critical to know. To get some sense about the relationship between this variable and various dimensions of mutual images, American and Chinese respondents were asked to estimate the impact of their personal contact on shaping their image of the target people, society, culture, and international behaviour along a 7-point scale, with 1 representing 'great impact' and 7 'no impact'. Table 7.7 represents a comparison of the American and Chinese responses.

Some important patterns emerge from the Table. For both American and Chinese respondents, relatively speaking, personal contact had the strongest impact on respondents' images of the target people and the least impact on their images of the target country's international behaviour. In the United States case, if we look at the mean scores, the impact of personal contact decreases in the following order: people, society, culture, and international behaviour (from 1.83 to 4.38). Many American respondents pointed out that perception about Chinese culture and international relations can be formed primarily through reading and distant observation.

The pattern for the China sample is slightly different in an interesting way. The weight of impact follows this order: people, culture, society, and international behaviour. Chinese respondents, on average, considered that personal contact had more impact on their image of American culture than on that of American society (3.58 versus 3.88). As we may recall, Chinese respondents experienced greater perceptual change in their image of American culture. This could be the result of their personal contact with

Table 7.7 Percentage Distribution of the Impact of Personal Contact on Mutual Images

| | Impact of Personal Contact on Images | | | | | | | |
| Scale | People (%) | | Society (%) | | Culture (%) | | International Behaviour (%) | |
	US	China	US	China	US	China	US	China
1	50.3	6.8	20.0	3.4	14.1	4.2	4.4	0
2	34.8	33.1	32.6	19.4	23.7	25.4	12.6	13.6
3	5.9	33.9	20.7	28.0	23.0	29.7	20.8	14.4
4	3.0	13.5	8.9	9.3	18.5	11.8	11.1	7.6
5	3.7	7.6	6.7	19.4	7.4	12.7	14.8	19.5
6	2.2	4.2	10.4	19.5	11.1	14.4	28.9	38.9
7	0	0.8	0.7	0.8	2.2	1.7	7.4	5.9
Total	100.0	100.0	100.0	100.0	100.0	100.0	100.0	100.0
Sample size	135	118	135	118	135	118	135	118
Mean/SD	1.83/	3.05/	2.87/	3.88/	3.28/	3.58/	4.38/	4.79/
	1.17	1.24	1.58	1.54	1.61	1.51	1.72	1.56

Americans. Regarding their image of American society, Chinese respondents had a stronger 'schema' in their minds. While personal contact could change their perceptions about the function and performance of American society, it did not redefine their overall conceptualization of the 'nature' of American society. Another reason for this difference might come from the different characteristics of Chinese and American cultures. While American respondents could learn about traditional Chinese culture purely through reading literature and viewing artifacts, American culture is more of a 'live thing', which can be better grasped through personal contact.

Overall, Chinese respondents perceived their images of the United States to be less influenced by personal contact. In each of the four dimensions, the China sample has a higher mean score, indicating a weaker impact of personal contact. The difference is more salient in the image domains of people (1.83 versus 3.05) and society (2.87 versus 3.88). In terms of the impact of personal contact on mutual images of people, while half of the American respondents selected number 1, only 7% of the Chinese respondents did so. In the domain of mutual images of society, less than 20% of the American respondents opted for points 5–7, whereas the equivalent percentage for the China sample is close to 40%. The difference can again be accounted for by the more conservative and cautious Chinese character and the more exaggerated American personality. However, it could also be a function of the relatively low intensity of personal contact conducted by the Chinese elites.[6]

We further asked respondents to compare the importance of personal contact with other indirect sources of mutual images: newspapers and magazines, books, and television. By such a comparison, we may find the relative importance of direct interaction and indirect interaction in image evolution. Respondents on both sides were thus required to rank the importance to them of four image sources: newspapers and magazines, books, television, and personal contact. Table 7.8 summarizes the findings.

The Table illustrates that for the United States sample, more than half of the respondents (55%) selected personal contact as the most important source for their image. This is followed by newspapers and magazines (31%), books (14%), and television (2%). On the Chinese side, the percentages for personal contact and newspapers and magazines are very close (35% versus 34%). The image source cited by the smallest percentage of the Chinese respondents as number one is books rather than television.

A sizeable difference between the two samples exists in the relative weights given to television and to personal contact. Only 2% of the American respondents considered television the most important image source, while

Table 7.8 Percentage Distribution of Four Image Sources

| | Sources of Image | | | | | | | |
| Rank* | Newspapers and Magazines (%) | | Books (%) | | Television (%) | | Personal Contact (%) | |
	US	China	US	China	US	China	US	China
1	31.4	34.2	13.7	12.8	2.3	18.8	55.1	35.3
2	39.4	32.5	31.7	25.6	11.3	22.2	21.0	20.7
3	23.4	23.9	38.8	26.5	16.5	24.8	19.6	24.1
4	5.8	9.4	15.8	35.0	69.9	34.2	4.3	19.8
Total	100.0	100.0	100.0	100.0	100.0	100.0	100.0	100.0
Sample size	137	117	139	117	133	117	138	116

* In the American data, there are four cases of double counts, and these respondents gave more than one image source the same ranking.

70% of them regarded it as the least important. In the China sample, however, the same percentages are 19% and 34% respectively. This finding is somewhat puzzling. The United States is recognized as a country in which mass media has tremendous power over people's perceptions and images of foreign countries. The live television coverage of the Tiananmen crackdown is regarded as instrumental in the strong American reaction to China. Yet in this sample, very few American respondents selected television as their main image source. Some even denied the relevance of television at all. This might reveal a gap regarding what image sources are more important for the general public and the American elites. While the former, as some Chinese respondents pointed out, are easily carried away by media manipulation, the latter are much less so. This may also reflect the increasing awareness of the American elites of the inherent bias and hollowness of television images of a foreign country. Therefore, some respondents tried to distance themselves from the influence of television and public opinion.

Another major difference is the importance of personal contact. While more than one in two of the American respondents regarded it as the most important image source, only about one-third of the Chinese elites held the same opinion. This finding is consistent with the data in Table 7.7. It can be suggested that for the Chinese elites, direct and indirect interactions do not differ greatly in their importance for image formation.

To further relate image source to respondents' social and demographic background, we crosstabulate the percentage of respondents who chose each source as the most important with their professions and ages. Table 7.9 summarizes the results.

It seems that, compared to American intellectuals and diplomats, a greater percentage of American business people tended to regard newspapers and magazines as the most important source for their image of China (48% versus 22% for intellectuals and 24% for diplomats). Chinese business people were less likely to do so (24% versus 40% for Chinese intellectuals and 39% for Chinese diplomats). With regard to books, in the United States sample, 16% of American intellectuals and 19% of American diplomats picked them as their most important image source, whereas only 5% of American business people made the same choice. On the Chinese side, intellectuals were far more likely than business people and diplomats to select books as their major image source. Relatively speaking, a smaller percentage of American intellectuals (1.8%) considered television to be the most important source compared to American business people (2.4%) and American diplomats (2.4%). Only 8% of Chinese intellectuals regarded television as the most important image source, while the equivalent percentages for Chinese business people and diplomats are 24% and 30%

Table 7.9 Percentage Distribution of the Respondents Regarding each
Source as the Most Important by their Profession and Age

Variables	Most Important Image Source					
	Newspapers (%)	Books (%)	Television (%)	Contact (%)	Total (%)	Cases
	US Sample					
Profession						
Intellectuals	21.8*	16.4	1.8	60.0	100.0	55
Business people	47.6	4.8	2.4	45.2*	100.0	42
Diplomats	23.8	19.1	2.4	54.8	100.0	42
Age						
< 40	23.1*	15.4	0	61.5	100.0	13
40–59	27.5	13.0	4.4	55.1*	100.0	69
≥ 60	35.7	14.3	0	50.0	100.0	56
	China Sample					
Profession						
Intellectuals	40.0	20.0	8.0	32.0	100.0	50
Business people	24.4	8.9	24.4	42.2	100.0	45
Diplomats	39.1	4.4	30.4	26.1	100.0	23
Age						
< 40	14.3	19.1	47.6	19.1	100.0	21
40–59	28.6	14.3	14.3	42.9	100.0	49
≥ 60	47.9	8.3	10.4	33.3	100.0	48

* There are two American respondents who ranked both 'newspapers and magazines' and
'personal contact' as the most important image sources. I randomly selected one of them.

respectively. As expected, more American intellectuals (60%) were inclined
to select personal contact as their most important image source. For Chinese
respondents, however, it is the business people who most often selected
personal contact as their primary image source (42%), with only 26% of
Chinese diplomats choosing personal contact.

Age makes some parallel differences in both samples. Older respondents
were more likely to select newspapers and magazines as their major image
source, while younger respondents were more inclined to learn about the

target country from books. All American respondents who claimed television as their most important source fall into the age group of 40–59. Interestingly, the percentage of American respondents who claimed personal contact as their primary image source decreases correspondent with an increase in age. Among the respondents younger than forty, 62% took it as their most important source, while the equivalent percentage of the respondents aged 60 and older was only 50%. In contrast, Chinese respondents younger than 40 represent the largest percentage (48%) of those who viewed television as the most important source, and the smallest percentage (19%) of those who regarded personal contact as their primary source.

One important question this study intends to address is whether a 'reorganizing' event such as the Tiananmen Incident reversed American and Chinese elites' evolution of mutual images based on on-going personal interactions. The analysis in previous chapters suggests that while some perceptual regression did occur, especially in the United States case, the Tiananmen Incident did not cause a complete reversal in the pre-Tiananmen mutual images for the elites in our samples. The explanatory variable used in the preceding bivariate analysis is based on a question aimed at measuring the impact of the event on respondents' overall image of the target country. Table 7.10 is developed from responses to the following question: 'Some people say that Tiananmen (the American reaction to Tiananmen) changed their image of China (the United States) entirely, others say their general image was little affected by the event. What was your situation?'

The responses fell into three categories: great effect, some effect, and no effect. Contrary to what we might have expected about the impact of the event, in both samples a majority of respondents apparently did not think the event affected their overall image of the target country very much. This

Table 7.10 Percentage Distribution Regarding the Effect of the Tiananmen Incident on Mutual Images

Measurement	Impact of Tiananmen on Image	
	US Sample (%)	China Sample (%)
Great effect	21.6	8.4
Some effect	36.0	34.5
No effect	42.4	57.1
Total	100.0	100.0
Sample size	125	119

might be a function of the 'hindsight effect', by which knowledge of the result of an event tends to distort one's perception of how likely the event was to occur in the first place: 'I knew it would happen.'[7] However, it could also reflect the limited power of a single event, even one as dramatic as the Tiananmen turmoil, to affect the intellectually sophisticated elites' overall image of the target country, especially when we treat national image as a structure with partially overlapping but also mutually independent dimensions. In comparison, as expected, the incident has a greater effect on the American respondents. While one in five American respondents thought that their image of China was greatly affected by the crackdown, only 8% of the Chinese respondents was influenced significantly by the American reaction to the event. Indeed, more than half of the Chinese respondents claimed that the American reaction to the event had little impact on their overall view of the United States. The asymmetric effect partially reflects the nature of the event, since it was largely a domestic development. It also reflects blind spots in Sino-US mutual perceptions. Some Chinese respondents could not understand why what happened in China domestically should arouse such outrage among Americans. Some American respondents could not understand how a government which allegedly had used tanks to kill its own people could still govern and even be supported, albeit with some reservations, by the people.

Which groups of American and Chinese respondents, then, were more likely to be affected by the incident? We can crosstabulate this variable with respondents' professions and ages as shown in Table 7.11.

Table 7.11 indicates that among the American respondents, a larger percentage of business people (25%) were greatly affected by the Tiananmen crackdown as compared to diplomats (22%) and intellectuals (19%). On the Chinese side, however, it is the diplomats who were hit most by the American reaction to Tiananmen (13%), while business people were the least affected (4%). The table also shows that for American elites, the age group younger than 40 has the highest percentage (31%) of 'greatly affected' respondents, while the age group 40–59 has the lowest percentage (18%). The pattern for Chinese elites is just the opposite. The age group 60 and older has the highest percentage of 'great effect', whereas none of the Chinese respondents younger than 40 considered that the American reaction affected their image of the United States greatly. Again, the generational influences on American and Chinese respondents are not identical.

A more interesting question is how the two major explanatory variables for image articulation and evolution in this study, personal contact and the Tiananmen Incident, are related to each other in respondents' perceptual propensities. No question directly addressed this issue in the interviews.

Table 7.11   Percentage Distribution of the Effect of the Tiananmen
Incident by Profession and Age

| Variables | Effect of Tiananmen | | | | |
	Great (%)	Some (%)	None (%)	Total (%)	Cases
		US Sample			
Profession					
Intellectuals	19.2	44.2	36.5	100.0	52
Business people	25.0	27.8	47.2	100.0	36
Diplomats	21.6	32.4	46.0	100.0	37
Age					
< 40	30.8	30.8	38.5	100.0	13
40–59	18.2	44.0	37.9	100.0	66
≥ 60	23.9	26.1	50.0	100.0	46
		China Sample			
Profession					
Intellectuals	10.0	36.0	54.0	100.0	50
Business people	4.4	35.6	60.0	100.0	45
Diplomats	12.5	29.2	58.3	100.0	24
Age					
< 40	0	38.1	61.9	100.0	21
40–59	8.0	36.0	56.0	100.0	50
≥ 60	12.5	31.3	56.3	100.0	48

However, the relationship between these two factors might be partially revealed by connecting respondents' assessments of the effect of Tiananmen and their self-evaluation of image sources. Therefore, in Table 7.12 we crosstabulate the percentage of respondents who ranked each of the four image sources as the most important with their views on the effect of the Tiananmen Incident.

The data reveal a similar pattern for both American and Chinese elites. In both samples, the respondents who perceived personal contact as their most important image source comprise the smallest percentage being 'greatly affected' by the Tiananmen Incident (16% for the United States sample and 2% for the China sample). Chinese respondents who regarded television as their primary source comprise the highest percentage of 'greatly affected'

Table 7.12 Percentage Distribution of the Respondents Regarding each
           Image Source as the Most Important by the Effect of
           Tiananmen

	Image Sources							
	Newspapers & Magazines (%)		Books (%)		Television (%)		Personal Contact (%)	
Effect	US	China	US	China	US*	China	US	China
Great	26.2	12.5	28.6	6.7	–	13.6	16.2	2.4
Some	31.0	42.5	42.9	20.0	–	36.4	38.2	31.7
None	42.9	45.0	28.6	73.3	–	50.0	45.6	65.9
Total	100.0	100.0	100.0	100.0	100.0	100.0	100.0	100.0
Cases	42	40	14	15	3	22	68	41

* Since there are only three cases in this column, it is not meaningful to present the percentage distribution.

respondents (14%). This indirectly confirms a major hypothesis of this study: national images formed through cumulative personal contact are less susceptible to the dramatic impact of a big event such as the Tiananmen Incident.[8] It is also noticeable that on the Chinese side, respondents who regarded books as their primary source were less likely to be greatly affected by the aftermath of the incident than those who chose newspapers and magazines as their major image source. One can argue that books provide more sustainable intellectual analysis about the United States, while newspapers and magazines are more reflective of current affairs, such as American reactions to the Tiananmen crackdown.

To further verify the relationship between the impact of the Tiananmen Incident and personal interaction, we associated respondents' opinions of the Tiananmen Incident with their actual contact with the other side in terms of the frequency of contact in the 1980s and the number of visits to the target country since 1970. Table 7.13 presents the results.

The data further support the observation that respondents who had more contact with the other side were less likely to be greatly affected by the Tiananmen Incident. In the case of contact in the 1980s, a smaller percentage of the respondents who had contact with the other side every week were 'greatly affected' compared with those who had contact with the other side less frequently. Likewise, respondents who visited the target

Table 7.13 Percentage Distribution of the Effect of Tiananmen by the Frequency of Contact in the 1980s and the Number of Visits Since 1970

Variables	Effect of Tiananmen				
	Great (%)	Some (%)	None (%)	Total (%)	Cases
US Sample					
Frequency of contact (1980s)					
Every week	14.9	34.0	51.1	100.0	47
Every month	25.0	38.9	36.1	100.0	36
Every year or several years	25.0	35.0	40.0	100.0	40
Number of visits					
0	33.3	33.3	33.3	100.0	9
1	34.8	21.7	43.5	100.0	23
2–3	35.0	20.0	45.0	100.0	20
4–5	7.7	53.9	38.5	100.0	13
≥ 6	13.3	43.3	43.3	100.0	60
China Sample					
Frequency of contact (1980s)					
Every week	5.4	35.1	59.5	100.0	37
Every month	8.5	40.7	50.9	100.0	59
Every year or several years	9.1	18.2	72.7	100.0	22
Number of visits					
0	9.5	33.3	57.1	100.0	21
1	8.8	32.4	58.8	100.0	34
2–3	9.1	30.3	60.6	100.0	33
4–5	6.7	40.0	53.3	100.0	15
≥ 6	0	46.7	53.3	100.0	15

country more frequently were less likely to claim that the incident had a great impact. On the American side, the percentage representing 'great effect' is relatively higher for the respondents who did not visit China or just visited a few times (around 35%), but starts decreasing when the number of visits reaches about 4–5 times or more (8% and 13% respectively). For the China sample, the percentage of 'great effect' decreases with the increase in visits. None of the Chinese respondents who visited the United States more than five times considered that the event had a great impact on their image of the United States.

Objective Estimation of Image Sources

On the whole, the above subjective estimation of image sources suggests that American and Chinese elites in our samples tend to view on-going interaction (both direct and indirect) as more important sources forming their image of the target country, in comparison with the impact of a single event such as the Tiananmen Incident. It might be illuminating, therefore, to determine how their perceptions of the target country, expressed in this study, are related objectively to these and other image sources. In previous chapters, we tabulated bivariate relationships between a set of explanatory variables and respondents' cognitive, affective, and evolutionary orientations toward the target country along the four image dimensions. Some interesting findings were reported. However, as indicated earlier, bivariate associations do not necessarily reflect causal linkages, because the explanatory variables per se may be highly correlated. To establish the true amount of covariation between two variables, multivariate regression analysis is used to control for the confounding effects of other factors on image orientations. A caveat should be made clear here. Due to sampling problems discussed in Chapter 2, we do not attempt to estimate population parameters from data by employing multivariate regression analysis. Rather, we try to test hypotheses and gain insights about the relationships between contact, big events, and respondents' perceptual propensities. Therefore, procedures such as establishing confidence intervals for regression results will be skipped.

The set of dependent and independent variables for the multivariate analysis remains the same as those for the bivariate analysis in preceding chapters. Three dependent variables to be regressed are cognitive differentiation, affective orientation, and perceptual change. Independent variables include five variables of contact: contact before 1949, during the years 1950–70, and in the 1970s, the frequency of contact in the 1980s, and the number of visits since 1970. Also treated as independent variables are the impact of the Tiananmen Incident, profession, and age. Their coding and measurement are presented in Table 7.14.

Based on the preliminary findings in bivariate analysis, we expect that contact before 1949, in general, will decrease respondents' outer differentiation and perceptual change. In the United States sample, this variable will yield more favourable affective orientation toward the target country, although the same effect is not necessarily true for the China sample. Contact during the period 1950–1970 and during the 1970s is

Table 7.14 Variable Definition and Measurement for Multivariate
           Analysis

Dependent Variables	**Measurement**
Cognitive differentiation	A 7-point scale to measure respondents' outer differentiation between the subject country and the target country along different dimensions. 1 = very different; 7 = very similar. Treated as continuous.
Affective orientation	A range of five choices to measure respondents' affective feelings toward the target country. 1 = very favourable; 2 = somewhat favourable; 3 = in the middle; 4 = somewhat unfavourable; 5 = very unfavourable. Treated as continuous.
Perceptual change	A 7-point scale to measure respondents' perceptual change over time regarding various image dimensions. 1 = changed greatly; 7 = no change at all. Treated as continuous.

Explanatory Variables	**Measurement**
Contact before 1949 (C49)	Whether a respondent had contact with or visited the target country before 1949. Originally coded as 1 = had contact; 5 = no contact; 3 = NA (those respondents who were born after 1940 were considered too young to have meaningful contact before 1949). Recoded into two dummy variables: A49 = 1 if there was contact, 0 = otherwise; B49 = 1 if there was no contact, 0 = otherwise.
Contact during 1950–70 (C50)	Whether a respondent had contact with the other side during this time period. Coded into one dummy variable: C50 = 1 if there was contact, 0 = no contact.

Table 7.14 (*cont.*)

Explanatory Variables	Measurement
Contact in the 1970s (C70)	Whether a respondent had contact in the 1970s. Coded into one dummy variable. C70 = 1 if there was contact, 0 = no contact.
Contact in the 1980s (C80)	The frequency of personal contact with the target country in the 1980s. 1 = every week; 2 = once or twice a month; 3 = a few times a year; 4 = once or twice in several years. Treated as continuous.
Visit	How many times a respondent visited the target country since 1970. The actual number of visits reported by respondents. Treated as continuous.
Tiananmen	The impact of the Tiananmen crackdown and its aftermath on respondents' perception of the target country. Originally coded as 1 = great impact; 2 = some impact; 3 = no impact. Recoded into one dummy variable: TAM = 1 if there was great impact, 0 = some or little impact.
Profession	Respondents were grouped into three professions: 1 = intellectuals; 2 = business people; 3 = diplomats. Coded into two dummy variables: Prof1 = 1 if profession = intellectual, 0 = others; Prof2 = 1 if profession = business person, 0 = others.
Age	Actual age reported by respondents.

more or less related to less favourable affective feelings and less perceptual change, but its impact on outer differentiation is not always consistent. We do not expect that frequency of contact in the 1980s and number of visits to the target country will produce consistent patterns in people's cognitive differentiation and affective orientation across the board. Instead, their impact is more contingent upon different image dimensions. However, we do anticipate that these two variables are somehow positively related to perceptual change. We believe that the influence of the Tiananmen Incident will be more readily observed in respondents' affective orientations, but its bearing on cognitive differentiation and perceptual change will not be very significant. The variable of profession often implies different perceptual orientations for the American and Chinese elites. Finally, aging will usually contribute to lower cognitive differentiation and less perceptual change, but not necessarily cause positive affective feelings.

To further test these suggested relationships, a series of multivariate Ordinary Least Squares (OLS) regression models have been estimated. The results concerning the relationships between the set of independent variables and respondents' cognitive differentiation are reported in Table 7.15.

The Table indicates that for the American elites, the variable of age has a stronger impact on respondents' outer differentiation. This is fairly consistent with the findings of the preceding bivariate analysis. The positive direction of the regression coefficients suggests that older respondents tended to see more similarities between the two countries in terms of various image dimensions. This is particularly the case in their image of the Chinese people. A one-year increase in age is expected to bring an increase of 0.07 points on the scale of differentiation. The only exception is the domain of Chinese international behaviour. The sign of the coefficient suggests a negative relationship between age and respondents' scores on cognitive differentiation, indicating that younger American respondents had lower outer differentiation than older ones in this image dimension.[9]

In the bivariate analysis, American respondents who visited China before 1949, on average, demonstrated a lower degree of outer differentiation than those who did not have such contact. This pattern has largely been verified within the multivariate framework. In most image domains, the score for the American respondents who had been to China before 1949 (A49) is higher than for those who had not (B49). The impact of this variable is stronger in cognitive differentiation of Chinese culture and international behaviour, where the coefficient differentials are 0.36 and 0.72 respectively. Only in their differentiation of Chinese society did the 'contact' respondents have a slightly lower score. As a whole, the relationship between this variable

Table 7.15 Regression Results for Cognitive Differentiations of Four
Image Dimensions of the Target Country

Explanatory Variables	Cognitive Differentiation			
	People	Society	Culture	International Behaviour
	US Sample			
Intercept	0.0160	0.8190	0.5884	5.8666
A49	-0.9949**	-0.2182	-0.2981	1.5384***
B49	-1.0742***	-0.2168	-0.6590**	0.8152**
C50	-0.3581*	-0.2842*	0.0536	-0.0623
C70	0.4490*	0.1604	0.1560	-0.0681
C80	-0.1081	-0.0414	0.0449	-0.2462*
Visit	0.0115**	-0.0142	0.0038	-0.0080
Visit²		0.0001*		
Tiananmen	0.2642	-0.1933	0.0268	-0.2924
Intellectuals	-0.0462	0.3248*	0.1037	0.1584
Business people	0.1514	-0.0130	0.0640	-0.4255
Age	0.0737***	0.0277**	0.0282**	-0.0339*
R^2	0.1963	0.1247	0.0907	0.1048
N	134	134	134	133
	China Sample			
Intercept	1.6073	1.6426	1.7264	4.2484
A49	-0.1639	0.2832	-0.1149	0.2384
B49	0.1793	0.2007	-0.1263	0.2856
C50	-0.0586	-0.2713	0.4955**	-0.1108
C70	-0.3851*	0.1521	-0.0428	-0.5112**
C80	-0.3263**	0.1226	-0.1853	-0.0357
Visit	0.0390	0.0981**	-0.0502*	0.0136
Visit²		-0.0052**		
Tiananmen	0.8252**	0.6219**	-0.1939	-0.6156
Intellectuals	0.5230*	-0.2412	0.6458**	-0.2951
Business people	0.1654	-0.3126*	0.4390*	-0.6129*
Age	0.0338**	-0.0043	0.0089	0.0012
R^2	0.2008	0.1169	0.0803	0.0716
N	118	118	118	115

* $0.05 < p \leq 0.1$, one-tail
** $0.01 < p \leq 0.05$, one-tail
*** $p \leq 0.01$, one-tail

and American respondents' cognitive differentiation appears weaker, other things remaining constant.

Contact during the period 1950–1970 and in the 1970s apparently have different functions for American respondents' outer differentiation. The former tends to increase the outer differentiation, while the latter decreases it. As suggested earlier, this might be attributed to the different circumstances under which contact occurred. The signs of regression coefficients also indicate that more contact in the 1980s tends to be associated with higher scores on cognitive differentiation,[10] though with statistical insignificance. The only exception is in the domain of international behaviour, where the relationship between more contact and higher coefficients is modestly significant. Compatible with the function of contact in the 1980s, more visits to China since 1970 seems to lead to a lower outer differentiation in image dimensions such as people and culture. For instance, the coefficient for the dimension of people suggests that American respondents found more similarities between Americans and Chinese with more visits. However, more visits also could lead to the discovery of more difference in image domains such as society and international behaviour, as indicated by the minus signs of the coefficients.[11] The somewhat curved patterns seen in bivariate analysis concerning these two dimensions are not supported by running a quadratic model in multivariate analysis.[12]

As predicted, the association between the effect of 'Tiananmen' and cognitive differentiation is not strong in statistical terms. Nevertheless, the direction of the coefficients, as also somewhat reflected in bivariate analysis, suggests that 'greatly affected' American respondents tended to see more similarities between Chinese and American peoples and cultures but more differences between Chinese and American societies and international behaviours.

Profession usually does not make significant differences in cognitive differentiation for the United States sample. American intellectuals tended to perceive more similarities between Chinese and American society, culture, and international behaviour. For instance, their score of differentiation regarding Chinese international behaviour is 0.58 greater than that of American business people. However, regarding the Chinese people, American business people perceived the most similarities, while intellectuals saw the least. Business people, on the other hand, tended to see more differences between Chinese and American societies and international behaviours, while American diplomats were more impressed by the differences between the two cultures.

The data on the Chinese side reveal some interesting differences from the American sample. Age is not as powerful as in the United States sample in accounting for the differentials. Yet, the general trend is still that older respondents tended to have higher scores, indicating a lower cognitive differentiation. This relationship is statistically significant in the image domain of people, where a unit increase of age would usher in an increase of 0.03 in the score, implying the perception of more similarity between the two peoples. One plausible reason for a weaker association between age and cognitive differentiation is the existence of non-linearity in the data. The earlier bivariate analysis displayed curved patterns for Chinese respondents' cognitive differentiation of societies and international behaviours. That is, both younger and older respondents tended to have relatively higher mean scores, while the middle-aged respondents were prone to having lower mean scores. This non-linear pattern was verified through examining the interaction effect of 'age' and 'age²'.[13]

In previous bivariate analysis, the variable of contact before 1949 was not shown to have an impact on cognitive differentiation as strongly as it did for the American respondents. Accordingly, none of the regression coefficients on the four image dimensions is statistically significant. While in bivariate analysis the general trend was still that 'contact' Chinese respondents yielded higher mean scores than 'no-contact' respondents, the pattern disappeared in some image domains, controlling for other variables. For instance, with regard to the perception of people, the score for 'contact' respondents is 0.34 lower than for 'no-contact' respondents, reflecting higher outer differentiation.

More or less parallel to the findings in bivariate analysis, contact during the years 1950–1970 (C50) and in the 1970s (C70) tends to be associated with higher cognitive differentiation, although the relationship in general is not statistically significant. There are some exceptions. The respondents who had contact during the 1970s tended to view American international behaviour and the American people as more different, as indicated by their lower coefficients (-0.51 and -0.39 respectively). This could be a function of the initial contact after twenty years of mutual isolation, which revealed more differences than similarities for these respondents. Another exception is that the respondents who had contact with Americans during the period 1950–1970 displayed a 0.5 higher coefficient in the image domain of culture, conveying a lower outer differentiation. This might not be a direct function of the contact itself but may rather be due to the background of some 'contact' respondents who had studied English and Western culture in their education.

More contact in the 1980s (C80), as in the United States data, tends to be associated with a decrease in outer differentiation, particularly in terms of respondents' images of the American people. The coefficient significantly decreases with a reduction in the frequency of contact by a margin of 0.33. The only exception is in the domain of societal difference, where the coefficient is positive rather than negative, indicating that respondents with less contact could have higher scores, other things being equal.[14] Apparently the number of visits to the United States also facilitates a reduction in cognitive differentiation, but the effect is more complicated. More visits, when researching a certain point, could lead to higher outer differentiation. While more visits do relate to a higher coefficient (0.04) in perceptions of the American people, the same thing can not be said about differentiation of American culture. A unit increase in 'visit' leads to a 0.05 point decrease in the regression coefficient, reflecting a higher outer differentiation. In regard to the differentiation of the two societies, an inverse U-shaped curve emerges, reflected in the signs of the coefficients for 'visit' and 'visit[2]'. Initially, the score of outer differentiation decreases with an increase in visits. After reaching a threshold, more visits could lead to the perception of more differences between the two societies.[15]

Another notable though puzzling difference between the China sample and the US sample is reflected in the stronger association between 'Tiananmen' and Chinese respondents' cognitive differentiation. The 'greatly affected' Chinese respondents perceived more similarities between the two peoples and societies by a margin of 0.83 and 0.62 in coefficients. On the other hand, they perceived less similarity between the two countries' cultures and international behaviours. It is more understandable that the Chinese respondents greatly affected by America's reaction to the event would perceive its international behaviour and culture as very different. Their lower outer differentiation of peoples and societies, as speculated in previous chapters, should come from other sources. 'Tiananmen' did not change their cognition in this regard.

As already illustrated in bivariate analysis, the influence of profession on cognitive differentiation is distinct in the two samples. Profession seems to have a stronger impact on the Chinese respondents. Chinese intellectuals were inclined to perceive more similarities between the two peoples and cultures, as reflected in their coefficients, which are greater than those for Chinese diplomats by a margin of 0.52 and 0.65 respectively. Chinese diplomats expressed the lowest outer differentiation regarding American society and international behaviour, while Chinese business people, like their American counterparts, saw more differences in these two image domains.[16]

Another important dependent variable is respondents' affective orientation toward the target country. We regressed it on the same set of independent variables. Table 7.16 summarizes the regression coefficients.

Looking at the American part of the table we find that, in contrast to the data on cognitive differentiation, age no longer serves as a strong predictor for variations. Instead, other variables such as contact before 1949 and 'Tiananmen' stand out as more powerful explanatory variables. Across the board, the American respondents who visited China before 1949 evinced more favourable feelings toward China than those who had not had that experience. For example, their coefficients regarding Chinese people and international behaviour are 0.34 and 0.27 lower than 'no-contact' respondents, reflecting more favourable affective feelings. If we compare their scores with 'not applicable' respondents, the gap is even bigger in terms of affective orientations toward the Chinese government and culture (0.74 and 0.71 lower respectively). As expressed in these respondents' comments, the sharp contrast between 'old China' and 'new China' regarding economic development, basic welfare, and national coherence was instrumental in their more benign image of the communist rule in China.

Contacts during the period 1950–1970 and in the 1970s do not show strong associations with American respondents' affective orientations toward China. In general, these contacts did not bring more favourable feelings toward China[17]. For instance, the respondents who had contact with Chinese during the period 1950–1970 have a coefficient 0.22 higher than those who did not in their attitudes toward the Chinese people, indicating a less favourable orientation.

The influence of the frequency of contact in the 1980s seems to suggest a different direction: more contact with Chinese could induce more positive feelings, although only the coefficient for the attitude toward the Chinese government withstands a statistical test.[18] As the data in Chapter 4 showed, respondents who did not have much contact with Chinese during this period had a higher mean score than those who had contact with Chinese every week or every month, indicating their more unfavourable feelings toward the Chinese government. The number of visits, as is often the case, has a more complicated function regarding affective orientations. An increase in visits tends to bring the score on the affective scale down, indicating a movement toward the more favourable side. However, in the case of attitudes toward the Chinese Government and culture, creating a quadratic term for 'visit' by taking its square produced an inverse U-shaped curve. The opposite signs of 'visit' and 'visit^2' suggest that affective coefficients initially go up with the first couple of visits, and then decline with more visits.[19]

Consistent with the previous bivariate analysis, the Tiananmen Incident has a negative impact on American respondents' attitudes toward China. In all four image dimensions, 'greatly affected' respondents had higher coefficients than 'somewhat affected' or 'not affected' respondents.

Table 7.16 Regression Results for Affective Orientations Toward Four
Image Dimensions of the Target Country

Explanatory Variables	Affective Orientations			
	People	Government	Culture	International Behaviour
		US Sample		
Intercept	1.2519	0.1489	0.8455	2.8615
A49	-0.3442*	-0.7412**	-0.7073**	-0.2392
B49	-0.0086	-0.6963**	-0.5806**	0.0354
C50	0.2207**	0.0371	0.1213	0.1570
C70	0.0433	0.2599	0.2626	-0.0546
C80	-0.0508	0.3025***	0.0869	0.0683
Visit	-0.0023	0.0406***	0.0216**	-0.0054
Visit^2		-0.0002***	-0.0001**	
Tiananmen	0.0393	0.7503***	0.2559	0.5817***
Intellectuals	0.1557	0.0192	0.1383	0.0858
Business people	0.1720	0.0038	0.1975	0.8727***
Age	0.0029	0.1029*	0.0120	-0.0065
Age^2		-0.0009*		
R^2	0.0728	0.2057	0.0814	0.2360
N	133	133	133	134
		China Sample		
Intercept	2.1009	1.9352	3.2192	2.7998
A49	-0.0569	-0.2372	0.6493**	0.0537
B49	0.0867	-0.1517	0.3617*	0.3439
C50	-0.0711	0.0824	0.4395***	-0.0273
C70	0.0380	-0.0729	-0.2375*	0.0630
C80	-0.0428	-0.2060*	-0.0778	0.2768**
Visit	-0.0053	-0.0295	0.0157	0.0261
Tiananmen	0.2655*	0.7250***	0.1287	0.6464**
Intellectuals	-0.1583	-0.2684	-0.5662**	-0.7299***
Business people	0.0693	-0.1085	-0.2649*	-0.5127**
Age	0.0009	0.0292**	-0.0113	0.0027
R^2	0.0883	0.1968	0.2331	0.1727
N	117	112	115	115

* $0.05 < p \leq 0.1$, one-tail
** $0.01 < p \leq 0.05$, one-tail
*** $p \leq 0.01$, one-tail

Understandably, adverse influences are more strongly seen in American attitudes toward the Chinese Government and international behaviour, as indicated by the statistically significant coefficients (0.75 and 0.58 respectively).

So far as the impact of profession is concerned, overall, American diplomats had the most favourable affective feelings toward China, since their coefficients are lower than those of intellectuals and business people in all four dimensions. On the other hand, American business people, in most cases, exhibited the most unfavourable orientations toward China. This negative feeling is particularly strong in their opinion of Chinese international behaviour, as the coefficient is higher than those for diplomats and intellectuals by margins of 0.87 and 0.79 respectively. Intellectuals had the highest coefficient in the affective orientation toward the Chinese Government, indicating more negative attitudes.

Age is not related strongly with American respondents' affective orientations, although the regression coefficient tends to go up with an increase in age, indicating more negative feelings. However, age can show a non-linear function when we add a quadratic term to 'age' by taking its squared values. Regarding attitudes toward the Chinese Government, the signs of the coefficients reflect an inverse U-shaped pattern, suggesting that middle-aged American respondents tended to have more negative feelings compared with their younger and older counterparts.[20]

The multiple regression analysis again yields some different patterns for the China sample. Contact before 1949 does not have such a strong effect on Chinese respondents' affective orientations as that manifested in the United States sample. In terms of the attitudes toward the American people, government, and international behaviour, 'contact' respondents tended to hold a more positive opinion than 'no-contact' ones, though with statistical insignificance. The coefficient for attitudes toward the American Government is at odds with the bivariate analysis in which 'contact' respondents expressed the least favourable opinion of the American Government. It is interesting to note that this pattern reversed itself when controlling for other variables. However, their attitudes toward American culture turned out to be significantly more unfavourable than those of the rest of the respondents, as indicated by the highest score (0.65).

Although some patterns observed in bivariate analysis reversed themselves under statistical control, contacts with Americans during the period 1950–1970 and during the 1970s, as in the case of American respondents, generally do not make a big difference for Chinese respondents' affective orientations, and there is no universal pattern. The only area in which these two variables have brought out a significant difference is the affective orientation toward American culture. The coefficients suggest that the Chinese respondents who had contact with Americans during the years 1950–1970 tended to have a more negative feeling toward American culture, while those who had contact during the 1970s demonstrated a more favourable opinion. This might again have something to do with the contrasting settings in which these contacts occurred.

As manifested in the previous bivariate analysis, for Chinese respondents more contact in the 1980s does not necessarily lead to more favourable affective feelings. The signs of coefficients seem to suggest that more contact is related to less favourable feelings toward Americans, the American government, and American culture. The only exception is the Chinese attitude toward American international behaviour, in which less contact is associated with higher scores by a margin of 0.28, indicating a positive association between contact and affective feelings. The effect of number of visits on affective orientation is neither unitary nor strong. While the direction of the coefficients for orientations toward the American people and Government points to a positive association between visits and favourableness, the coefficients for attitudes toward American culture and international behaviour suggest a different direction.[21]

As in the United States sample, a more powerful variable to explain Chinese respondents' affective orientation is the impact of the Tiananmen Incident. In the Chinese case, this variable implies respondents' feeling about the American reaction to the event. The multivariate analysis verifies the results of the bivariate analysis: the 'greatly affected' Chinese respondents tended to have a more negative feeling toward the United States across all four dimensions. This impact is more significant in their attitudes toward the American Government and international behaviour. The coefficients for the 'greatly affected' respondents are 0.73 and 0.65 greater, respectively, than those for 'somewhat affected' or 'not affected' respondents, reflecting strong unfavourable attitudes. The implication is that although fewer Chinese respondents were greatly affected in terms of their perceptions of the United States, for those who were, their resentment could be as strong as that of their American counterparts.

Professional differentials apparently explain more variation in the Chinese affective orientations than in the United States case. In contrast to their American counterparts, in general Chinese intellectuals held the most favourable feelings toward the United States, as they had the lowest coefficients in all four image dimensions. On the other hand, Chinese diplomats demonstrated the least favourable attitudes toward the United States. In the image domains of culture and international behaviour, the coefficient differences between these two groups are 0.57 and 0.73

respectively. Chinese business people usually took a position closer to that of intellectuals. However, they did have the least favourable view of the American people.

As in the case of cognitive differentiation, age is not shown to be a strong predictor of Chinese respondents' affective orientations. However, the directions of coefficients suggest that older Chinese respondents tended to hold a less favourable view toward the American Government and international behaviour. That difference is statistically significant in their attitudes toward the American Government. A one-year increase in age is expected to bring a 0.03 increase in the affective coefficients. But in terms of attitudes toward American culture, older respondents, as indicated by the sign of coefficients, could have more favourable views. This pattern contradicts the bivariate relationship in which an increase in age was related to less favourable attitudes toward American culture. A test of curvilinearity by adding a quadratic term shows an inverse U-shaped curve, suggesting that much older Chinese respondents (say, older than 70) could have more favourable views of American culture. A similar phenomenon can be observed in the case of the Chinese attitude toward the American people. As the earlier bivariate analysis showed, while the mean score on affective orientation moved up with the respondents aged 40–59, it declined with the respondents who were 60 or older. Their comments reflected that although older respondents tended to hold more conservative views on the American Government and international behaviour, some of them still held favourable impressions of Americans and American culture as they knew them before 'liberation'.

The final dependent variable to be regressed on the independent variables is respondents' intensity of perceptual change regarding the target country in the last two decades. Table 7.17 presents regression coefficients for the covariation between perceptual change and explanatory variables.

Apparently, contact before 1949 has some impact on perceptual changes of American elites. In terms of perceptual change regarding the Chinese people, the coefficient for those who had visited China is greater than for those who had not by a margin of 0.83, indicating significantly less perceptual change. This pattern also holds for the perceptual change regarding Chinese society. However, regarding Chinese culture and international behaviour, 'visited' respondents had lower coefficients related to greater perceptual changes. Regarding Chinese international behaviour, the coefficient for 'visited' respondents is 0.78 smaller than that for 'not-visited' respondents, reflecting more perceptual change.

In the preceding bivariate analysis, contact during the period 1950–1970 and during the 1970s was often related to less perceptual change for

American respondents. This pattern still holds while controlling for other variables. In image dimensions of people and society, the coefficients for the respondents who had contact with Chinese during the years 1950–1970 are 0.95 and 0.72 higher than for those who did not, pointing to less perceptual change. For contact during the 1970s, the coefficient difference in perceptual change regarding Chinese culture is also statistically significant. Apparently, images formed through these contacts are more stable and less subject to change. The frequency of contact in the 1980s suggests an opposite impact for perceptual change. The regression coefficients largely indicate a positive relationship between contact and perceptual change. This trend is statistically sustained in perceptual change regarding the Chinese people and Chinese society. The function of this variable for perceptual change regarding Chinese culture and Chinese international behaviour is less straightforward. The emergence of opposite signs for coefficients by creating an offsetting quadratic factor of C80 indicates the existence of curvilinearity. The implication is that perceptual evolution in these image dimensions is not always contingent upon the intensity of personal contact.

Parallel to the function of the contact in the 1980s, the number of visits since 1970 in general also facilitates perceptual change, as indicated by the negative sign of the coefficients, although the differences in most cases are not statistically significant. The relationship could also be characterized by nonlinearity, as reflected in the case of perceptual change regarding Chinese society. The bivariate analysis showed that the American respondents who never visited China and those who visited many times both declared greater change in their perception of Chinese society.[22]

The impact of the Tiananmen Incident on American respondents' perceptual change is not statistically significant, although the 'greatly affected' respondents tended to declare less perceptual change in most areas. This confirms an earlier observation that the event has not fundamentally changed American elites' image of China. On the other hand, we can also say that the event has verified rather than disproved some of these respondents' preconceptions about China.

Profession can account for the differentials in perceptual change fairly well. Regarding the images of Chinese society and international behaviour, the coefficients suggest that American intellectuals demonstrated the least perceptual change. For instance, in the case of international behaviour, the coefficients for intellectuals are 0.70 and 0.54 respectively, higher than for business people and diplomats. Interestingly, American intellectuals displayed greater perceptual change regarding Chinese culture than the other two groups. American diplomats experienced the most change in

Table 7.17   Regression Results for Perceptual Changes Regarding Four Image Dimensions of the Target Country

Explanatory Variables	Perceptual Change			
	People	Society	Culture	International Behaviour
US Sample				
Intercept	0.5789	-0.4036	3.6558	-0.2670
A49	1.4080**	-0.1850	0.4237	-0.9966**
B49	0.5731	-0.3200	0.8736*	-0.2204
C50	0.9491***	0.7201***	0.3245	0.2136
C70	0.4307	0.2884	0.8731**	-0.1165
C80	0.3310**	0.2734**	-1.3449*	0.9515*
C80^2			0.3733**	-0.1965*
Visit	-0.0112	0.0150	-0.0088	-0.0041
Visit^2		-0.0001*		
Tiananmen	0.1037	0.3163	0.1790	-0.2718
Intellectuals	0.1067	0.5608**	-0.7161**	0.6973***
Business people	0.2932	0.2736	-0.4396	0.1609
Age	0.0108	0.0311**	0.0109	0.0373**
R^2	0.2380	0.2346	0.2180	0.1838
N	135	135	135	135
China Sample				
Intercept	2.1811	0.0504	1.7498	1.7646
A49	1.1279*	0.7510	0.9491*	0.3391
B49	0.8128*	0.3310	0.8237*	0.5005
C50	0.4884	0.1224	0.2458	-0.4988
C70	-0.2414	0.0965	-0.0706	0.0870
C80	-1.4559**	0.0409	0.1327	0.0332
C80^2	0.3438**			
Visit	0.0018	-0.0640*	-0.1260*	0.0154
Visit^2			0.0065*	
Tiananmen	-0.1987	-0.7027*	-0.2813	-0.0295
Intellectuals	-0.6963*	-0.1206	-0.9524**	-0.3165
Business people	-0.4688	0.5987*	0.3263	0.2753
Age	0.0457**	0.0581***	0.0277	0.0324
R^2	0.3878	0.3246	0.2646	0.1143
N	118	118	118	118

* $0.05 < p \le 0.1$, one-tail
** $0.01 < p \le 0.05$, one-tail
*** $p \le 0.01$, one-tail

their images of the Chinese people, society, and international behaviour, but their image of Chinese culture remained the most stable, as indicated by a coefficient difference of 0.72 between diplomats and intellectuals. American business people declared more perceptual continuity in their images of the Chinese people.

Consistent with the results of bivariate analysis, increased age is negatively associated with perceptual change for American respondents in all four image dimensions. This retarding effect of age on perceptual change was particularly strong with regard to Chinese society and international behaviour.

Regression results for the China sample illustrate both parallel and divergent patterns in comparison with the United States sample. The Chinese respondents who had contact with Americans before 1949 also declared less perceptual change than those who had no contact in most cases. For instance, in terms of perceptual changes regarding American people and society, the coefficient differences between 'contact' and 'no-contact' respondents are 0.32 and 0.42 respectively. Interestingly enough, it is also in the image domain of international behaviour where 'contact' respondents had a lower coefficient than 'no-contact' respondents, suggesting more perceptual change.

The bivariate crosstabulation suggested a trend that contact during the period 1950–1970, as in the case of the United States sample, usually was associated with less perceptual change. This pattern remains, though it is statistically insignificant. The only exception is perceptual change regarding American international behaviour. 'Contact' respondents showed greater perceptual change by a margin of 0.5. Contact during the 1970s is also related to less perceptual change in the previous bivariate analysis. This pattern changes in the domains of people and culture under statistical control, suggesting that contact during this period could be associated with more perceptual change. However, none of the coefficients is statistically significant.

In line with the pattern in the United States sample, the frequency of contact in the 1980s and the number of visits since 1970 tend to facilitate perceptual changes, though inconsistently. The relationship is, however, not always linear. For instance, the association between the frequency of contact in the 1980s and perceptual changes regarding the American people, and that between the number of visits and perceptual changes regarding American culture, exhibit U-shaped curves when quadratic terms, taking the form of 'C80^2' and 'visit^2', are added. For the former, the pattern implies that respondents who had contact with Americans both very often and rarely could have experienced less perceptual change regarding the American people. For the latter, the pattern suggests that some respondents who visited the United States many times could still sustain quite stable views of American culture.[23]

For Chinese respondents, in contrast to the United States sample, the effect of 'Tiananmen' is apparently associated with more perceptual change in their images of the United States.[24] In all dimensions, the coefficients for the 'greatly affected' respondents are lower than those for other respondents. The difference is moderately significant in the case of the perceptual change regarding American society. One might assume that the 'greatly affected' Chinese respondents have a less complex cognitive structure, so that perceptual change in one dimension might spill over to other dimensions.

The impact of profession also diverges from the United States sample. While American intellectuals generally evinced the least perceptual change, Chinese intellectuals demonstrated the most perceptual change in their image of the United States. This feature is more noticeable in their attitudes toward the American people and culture, as indicated by their significantly lower coefficients. On the other hand, Chinese business people exhibited the highest coefficients in image domains of American society, culture, and international behaviour, indicating the least perceptual change. With regard to American society, culture, and international behaviour, the coefficient differentials between intellectuals and business people are 0.72, 1.28, and 0.59 respectively. Chinese diplomats usually had a degree of perceptual change in between, although they held a more stable image of the American people.[25]

Similar to the United States sample, older Chinese respondents declared less perceptual change than their younger counterparts in all four image dimensions. This trend is more salient in terms of perceptual changes regarding the American people and American society, as the coefficients are significant at different alpha levels. The results of multivariate analysis have confirmed previous observations in bivariate analysis.

Within the multivariate framework, we can describe the relationships between explanatory variables and the American and Chinese elites' perceptual orientations with more confidence. Most of the findings from the multivariate analysis are reasonably consistent with those from the bivariate analysis, but some patterns do change or disappear when controlling for the confounding effects of other factors.

In estimating the function of personal contact regarding mutual images, we have found that contact during different time periods can have different impacts. In general, the respondents who visited or had contact with the other side before 1949, especially on the American side, were inclined to have lower outer differentiation, more positive affective orientation, and less perceptual change in their images of the target country. The perceptions of the target country formed through these experiences, even though occurring a long time ago, provide stable points of reference for their current mutual images. For some respondents, historical comparisons and memories help them adopt more tolerant affective attitudes toward the other side.

Contacts during the period 1950–1970 and during the 1970s were also more likely to be associated with more stable perceptions, but their function regarding respondents' cognitive and affective orientations often differs from that of contact before 1949, namely higher outer differentiation and less favourable feelings. This pattern, of course, is attributable to the circumstances under which these contacts took place: mutual isolation, ideological hostility, and restrictive access to the reality of the target country. The frequency of contact in the 1980s and the number of visits to the target country since 1970, on the other hand, tend to facilitate perceptual changes on both sides. Nevertheless, the direction of those changes is by no means fixed. While more contact and visits might reduce alienation and hostility, they also could have opposite effects. The relationship between the intensity of contact and respondents' cognitive and affective orientations is not necessarily linear. Rather, curvilinear patterns frequently occur, indicating the existence of a threshold at which perceptions could go either way. Moreover, people's perceptual orientation toward some more macro and abstract subjects, such as the subject country's government, culture, and international behaviour, could be less determined by direct personal contact.

The Tiananmen Incident exerts the most visible impact on the respondents' affective feelings toward the subject country. The 'greatly affected' respondents were inclined to exhibit more negative attitudes in viewing the various dimensions of the subject country. For these respondents, this event had a cross-dimensional negative influence; but for both sides, it is more likely to affect their attitudes toward the subject government and international behaviour rather than the subject people and culture. Its impact on people's cognitive differentiation and perceptual change is neither strong nor unitary. It could either confirm some respondents' predispositions about the subject country or disprove some former perceptions.

Profession often yields divergent functions for American and Chinese respondents. American intellectuals tended to evince the lowest outer differentiation and the least perceptual change in most dimensions, but their opinion about Chinese culture changed the most. They also expressed the most negative feelings toward the Chinese Government. American business people were inclined to perceive the least similarity between the two societies and the two countries' international behaviours. For them, this high cognitive differentiation was related to the least favourable attitudes toward China in most domains. American diplomats displayed the least unfavourable affective orientations toward China in all image dimensions and, in general, experienced the greatest perceptual change. However, their view of Chinese culture remained the most stable. In this domain, their high cognitive differentiation and positive affective orientation go together. In the China sample, Chinese intellectuals saw more similarities between the two peoples and cultures. Like American diplomats, as a whole they had experienced the most perceptual change and evinced the most favourable feelings toward the United States. On the other hand, Chinese diplomats perceived more similarities between the two countries' societies and international behaviours and more differences between the two peoples and cultures. They also exhibited the most negative affective orientations in most image dimensions. Similar to American business people, Chinese business people showed a higher outer differentiation between the two societies and two countries' international behaviours, but their affective orientations were closer to those of Chinese intellectuals. In most domains, they declared the least perceptual change.

Increased age on both sides is more likely to be associated with lower outer differentiation, more negative affective orientation, and less perceptual change, although curved patterns exist. For instance, both younger and older American respondents tended to have less unfavourable views of the Chinese Government than the middle-aged respondents. Both younger and older Chinese respondents saw more similarities between the two societies and between American international behaviour and that of other major powers than did the middle-aged. Comparatively speaking, the impact of age on respondents' affective orientation is weaker and inconsistent.

Notes to Chapter 7

1   Myers, *Social Psychology* (1990), pp. 425–429.
2   While the range (the difference between the highest and lowest mean scores) in the United States sample is 2.43, the same range in the China sample is only 1.18.
3   These five models are static model, upward linear model, downward linear model, fluid model, and curvilinear model, which designate different inclinations of perceptual change. For a detailed description of these models, see Chapter 2.
4   They mentioned some sources of information, including reading *Reference News* and other internally circulated materials and books.
5   Some American and Chinese respondents mentioned similar experiences in which they usually had very good impressions of the target country during their first visit, especially when the visit was short. With subsequent substantial visits and contacts, they started to see darker aspects of the other side, and therefore had a more balanced view.

6   In our samples, excluding missing data, only 7% of the American respondents had not visited the target country, while the equivalent figure for the Chinese respondents is 18%. Of the American respondents, 48% visited China more than five times and only 12.7% of the Chinese respondents had the same opportunity. The maximum number of visits for the Chinese respondents is 25, while some American respondents visited China more than 100 times. Regarding the intensity of contact in the 1980s, 38% of the American respondents had contact with Chinese every week, whereas the parallel percentage for the Chinese elites is 31%.

7   See Elliot Aronson, *The Social Animal,* New York: W. H. Freeman and Company, 1988, p. 240.

8   Americans who have had first hand experience working or living in China tend to be less susceptible to the influence of the American media. An American business manager who worked in China for four years observed: 'The reality of the China I see every day couldn't be more different from what I have seen in movies and heard on the news here in the United States.' Michael Wenderoth, 'Seeing the real China', *Newsweek,* October 27, 1997, p. 14.

9   However, a closer look at the bivariate crosstabulation of mean scores finds a curved pattern characterizing the relationship. The American respondents younger than 40 displayed the highest mean score on cognitive differentiation of Chinese international behaviour. The mean score goes down for the respondents aged 40–59. For people aged 60 and older, the score goes up again. This trend can be seen by adding a quadratic term (a new variable with squared values of age). The coefficients for 'age' and 'age^2' are -0.1201 and 0.0008 respectively, indicating a U-shaped curve, albeit not a statistically significant one. A similar trend can be seen in the image domain of culture.

10   This direction of association in the image domain of society is inconsistent with the result of bivariate analysis, which in certain image dimensions also displayed some curvilinearity. None of them proved to be statistically significant in the multivariate analysis.

11   The data in bivariate crosstabulation indicate that in cognitive differentiation of Chinese society, the mean score drops for those American respondents who visited China more than five times. In the case of international behaviour, it is the respondents who never visited China that evinced the highest mean score.

12   Although the coefficient of 'visit^2' is modestly significant in the case of society, the face value is almost negligible.

13   The coefficients of 'age' and 'age^2' are -0.0288 and 0.0002 for the dimension of society, and -0.0154 and 0.0001 for the dimension of international behaviour, indicating a U-shaped curve.

14   In some dimensions, the data of bivariate crosstabulation displayed a curvilinear trend. In domains such as society and international behaviour, respondents with most and least contact could both have higher mean scores, but none of the curvilinear patterns proved to be statistically significant in multivariate analysis.

15   This pattern, however, is somewhat different from the bivariate data that, in general, indicated a positive association between the number of visits and the decrease in outer differentiation. On the other hand, the relationship between the number of visits and the degree of cognitive differentiation could be U-shaped. For instance, as reflected in the data of bivariate analysis, in viewing American international behaviour, as in the United States sample, respondents who did not visit the United States at all could have quite low outer differentiation. The degree of differentiation increased with more visits.

However, when respondents visited the United States five times or more, they again perceived American international behaviour as being more similar to that of other powers. This pattern can be illustrated by adding a quadratic term to 'visit'. The coefficients are -0.0580 and 0.0042 respectively.

16   The differences between their coefficients are 0.31 in the domain of society and 0.61 in the domain of international behaviour.

17   In some image dimensions, the directions of coefficients are not consistent with the data of bivariate crosstabulation.

18   The curvilinearity often shown in bivariate crosstabulations has not been ascertained within the multivariate framework.

19   The regression coefficients apparently do not reflect the possible 'regression' phenomenon displayed in the previous bivariate analysis. That is, American respondents who visited China more than five times again evinced more negative feelings toward the Chinese Government and Chinese culture.

20   The non-linearities shown in the bivariate analysis regarding affective orientations toward Chinese culture and international behaviour are not statistically confirmed in the multivariate analysis.

21   In bivariate analysis, the relationship between the number of visits and Chinese respondents' affective orientation was not always clear. One thing quite common for various dimensions was that the mean score tended to 'regress' when the number of visits reached a threshold of more than five times. As mentioned earlier, this phenomenon can also be seen in the American data.

22   This mount-shaped pattern in a measure also applies to the perceptual change regarding Chinese international behaviour, although the coefficients are not statistically significant. Apparently, for some respondents, their perceptual evolution for more macro and abstract dimensions were not directly related to contact and visits. This was also true in the China data. Mean scores in bivariate crosstabulations in the domain of international behaviour, for instance, showed no clear patterns for respondents on either side.

23   The data on bivariate crosstabulation demonstrated that Chinese respondents' perceptual changes regarding more macro dimensions such as culture and international behaviour were less contingent upon the intensity of the visits.

24   This trend was not observed in the domain of people in the previous bivariate analysis.

25   These findings differ somewhat from those in the previous bivariate analysis. For instance, Chinese diplomats previously had the highest mean scores of perceptual change regarding American society and culture, but when all other factors were equal, the pattern changed.

CHAPTER 8 · CONCLUSION

In preceding chapters, a systematic effort has been made to present a comparative and in-depth profile of Sino-American mutual images along the dimensions of people, society, culture, and international behaviour. The evolution and sources of mutual images have also been explored with available data. It is now time to summarize our main findings and to discuss their implications for Sino-American relations in particular and for national image studies in the post-Cold War context in general.

A Précis of the Findings

As indicated in the first two chapters, this study is motivated by a profound theoretical and empirical concern about the importance of national images in the study of post-Cold War international relations. With this in mind, the immediate goal of this volume has been to establish a rich and valid system of reference for understanding mutual perceptions in Sino-American relations. The significance of this research has been reinforced by the difficult, sometimes painful process of mutual adjustment in the relationship to the post-Cold War international dynamics, as dramatized by the animosity over the Tiananmen Incident in 1989. Undertaken in the shadow of this critical event, this study empirically investigated mutual images held by selected American and Chinese elites in three aspects: (1) the cognitive structure and components of their mutual images; (2) the pattern of image evolution; and (3) the sources for image differentials.

The bulk of mutual images of Sino-American elites was articulated in terms of respondents' cognitive, affective, and evaluative orientations toward the target country's people, society, culture, and international behaviour. In terms of mutual images of people, as a function of 'reference power', American and Chinese elites exhibited a relatively low outer differentiation. Both sides tended to attribute the resemblance between the two peoples to their compatible personalities. American elites were more inclined to attribute differences between Americans and Chinese to social background, while Chinese elites were more aware of the potential conflict in personalities. This perceptual gap could be a source of frustration for the Americans, since their exaggerated perception of similar personality might lead to disappointment when profound differences are eventually discovered.

Affectively, the Americans and Chinese elites held quite positive attitudes toward each other as individuals, although the American respondents often evinced a stronger intensity in their feelings. By comparing the target people with other peoples in the same category, both sides found a 'special' affinity between the two peoples. The 'mirror' images of each side perceiving the other as 'open', 'friendly', and 'working hard', and the 'contrasting' images of Americans perceiving the Chinese as 'humorous', 'resourceful', and 'intelligent', and Chinese seeing Americans as 'enterprising', 'honest', and 'pragmatic' constitute intrinsic sources of mutual attraction, which are lacking in their respective relations with many other peoples.

On the other hand, negative evaluations of the target people are also deep-seated. Cognitive dissonance and ambivalence are pervasive. The Chinese were perceived as both open and reserved; culturally rich and materially poor; individually resourceful and politically impotent. The Americans were seen in part as both candid and shallow; civilized in manner and dissipated in life style; internationally arrogant and domestically egalitarian; and so forth. I found that within the mutual images of people are embedded many important cognitive threads, running through other more macro and abstract image dimensions. In a sense, mutual perceptions at the individual level may point to potentials and limitations inherent in the Sino-American relationship. For instance, both Americans and Chinese described the other side as 'open' and 'frank' in initial contact but 'reserved' or 'easy come, easy go' in more substantial relations. These cognitions may partially explain why US-China relations were easy to resume initially, but have failed to take deep root up to the present.

In terms of mutual images of society, cognitively both sides perceived a higher incompatibility level between the two societies. The overarching framework applied by the American and Chinese elites in observing the target society is value-ridden: 'totalitarian versus democratic' or 'socialist versus capitalist', although the substance of their mutual images could be quite factual and functionally based. Unlike the mutual images of people that converge in many aspects, the American and Chinese respondents possessed more contrasting images of the target society characterized by dichotomies such as 'developed versus undeveloped', 'individual-oriented versus group-oriented', 'politically stable versus politically unstable', 'polarized versus egalitarian', and 'centralized versus decentralized'.

Affectively, American and Chinese elites exhibited quite asymmetric feelings toward the target government. Affected by the Tiananmen crackdown and its aftermath, a majority of the American respondents held a negative opinion of the Chinese Government. The Tiananmen Incident inevitably aroused American respondents' natural disgust with and fear of a 'totalitarian' regime. On the other hand, the incident also brought 'the difficulty of governance' to their attention. While many American respondents tended to attribute the problem to the 'evil nature' of the communist regime, some respondents evinced more 'situational' explanations, attributing the difficulties to objective constraints under which the Chinese Government operates. Moreover, the normative value judgement did not prevent American elites from demonstrating their inner differentiation of Chinese society, such as the distinction between the Chinese 'state' and 'society', between government as a whole and individual officials, between personal experience and larger observations, or between short-term negative feelings and long-term evaluations.

Chinese respondents, in contrast, as a whole held a more positive view of the American Government. There is little indication that this trend was reversed by the Tiananmen Incident or affected by the end of the Cold War. In a sign of perceptual sophistication, many Chinese respondents evaluated the American Government in a functional rather than value-oriented manner. Chinese elites displayed a perceptual consensus on the 'good governance' of American society in political and administrative terms, as manifested in its political stability, decentralized management, and high efficiency, though they still held different views on the representativeness of this system and its applicability elsewhere. Chinese respondents also perceived a discrepancy between the American polity and American society. They were skeptical about the system's ability to maintain social justice and tranquillity, and had philosophical reservations about its laissez-faire approach to handling social problems.

In brief, the perceptual gap in mutual images of society rests with the fact that American elites exhibited an 'inherent' negative orientation toward the Chinese state but a more benign view of Chinese society. In contrast, Chinese elites held a positive image of the American polity, but were suspicious and uneasy about American society. This perceptual gap is a manifestation of the increased inner differentiation as well as a potential source for perceptual dissonance and, hence, conflicting expectations and misperceptions.

In terms of mutual images of culture, incompatibility of mutual images results from different conceptualizations of the target culture. For the American respondents, Chinese culture is largely a historical concept, and its content and form are attached to the past rather than the present. What the American elites appreciated was the 'vertical' dimension of Chinese culture, namely its longevity and its accumulated wisdom and sophistication in intellectual and artistic heritage. They were also very conscious of a perceived discrepancy between 'traditional' and 'modern' Chinese cultures, the latter being, in many respondents' eyes, equivalent to 'party culture' or 'communist culture'. Admiration of the former and contempt for the latter are sharply contrasted in the American image.

Chinese respondents primarily perceived American culture as a dynamic and ever-changing entity associated with modernization. They were more impressed by the 'horizontal' characteristics of American culture, namely its diversity and inclusiveness, which mean that it better 'reflects human nature and aspirations' and is 'the most rational culture' in the world. On the other hand, Chinese elites were aware of the 'lack of tradition' and 'crudeness' in American culture. As reflected in the metaphor of 'a sword in hand' (American culture) and 'a cloud in the sky' (Chinese culture), Chinese elites regarded American culture more as a manifestation of its advanced economy and science and technology rather than being based on an intellectual tradition.

The high degree of outer differentiation in the area of culture leads to a favourable affective orientation, a reversal of the pattern seen in mutual images of society. In other words, the perception of cultural difference becomes a source of mutual attraction rather than of mutual alienation. Whereas the American elites tended to like the 'intellectual' and 'artistic' aspects of traditional Chinese high culture (art, philosophy, literature), the Chinese respondents were inclined to appreciate the 'material' and 'popular' components of American culture (science and technology, movies, music). However, the perceived gap between the 'traditional' and 'modern' manifestations of the target culture nurtured a combination of admiration and contempt on both sides. The American elites saw Chinese culture as having a brilliant 'past' but lacking a viable 'present', namely a dynamic and functional modern culture. The Chinese elites perceived American culture as lacking an adequate historical and intellectual foundation necessary to be the leading culture in the world. Therefore, the so-called American 'cultural egotism' was perceived as self-serving and ungrounded.

In terms of mutual images of international behaviour, American and Chinese elites both perceived the lowest outer differentiation in comparison with mutual images in other dimensions, indicating that they saw each other basically as normal powers in world politics. Some new perceptions have arisen in evaluating the target country's power status and international behaviour, reflecting changing world circumstances. In the realm of power status, the perceptual gap is self-evident in this data set. In the American estimation of Chinese power status, apparently the trend in the early 1990s was to downplay China's power and role in the aftermath of Tiananmen and the demise of the Soviet Union. In the Chinese assessment of American power status, an almost unanimous 'powerful' image emerged, emphasizing the unique American position of power in the post-Cold War international order.

Regarding affective and evaluative orientations toward the target country's international behaviour, Chinese elites evinced stronger negative feelings toward American international behaviour, reflecting their resentment and apprehension at the American 'interventionist' tendency in post-Cold War international affairs. In their evaluation of the target country's international behaviour, American and Chinese elites applied both 'traditional' and 'post-Cold War' criteria. The 'traditional' perspective on the American side emphasizes that considering its past behaviour, China in general has become a non-threatening normal power in world affairs and has been gradually joining the international mainstream. Applying this standard, a large portion of the American respondents expressed a somewhat positive opinion of China's international performance in recent decades. The 'post-Cold War' perspective, however, asserts that the standard for evaluating China's international behaviour should no longer be guided by pure geopolitical considerations. Rather, it should be based upon the extent to which China positively contributes to world stability and meets some universal principles of international and domestic conduct. In this regard, China falls short of American expectations, since the PRC handles its domestic affairs inhumanely and often proves disruptive in international affairs on issues such as weapons proliferation. Applying these criteria, China's international behaviour was viewed quite negatively.

Application of 'traditional' and 'post-Cold War' criteria has a different function for the Chinese elites. The Chinese 'traditional' perspective perceives a 'hegemonic' motive in American international behaviour, which has the goal of establishing a US-dominated, unipolar world. Indeed, American 'hegemonism' has become aggravated due to the collapse of the balance of power resulting from Soviet disintegration. This trend is exemplified by the strong United States reaction to Tiananmen and its leading role in the Gulf War. Chinese respondents applying this system of reference often took a negative tone in their affective orientation. On the other hand, more cosmopolitan Chinese respondents developed a 'post-Cold War' criterion in judging American international behaviour. This perspective argues that in a world of transition and economic interdependence, American leadership is both necessary and desirable. Objectively, the United States is the only country that has 'comprehensive power' and can thus exert world leadership. Subjectively, if there has to be a leader, the United States is the best candidate for the position given its historical and political heritage. Chinese respondents having this 'leadership' image were more likely to take a positive attitude toward American international behaviour.

The 'traditional' and 'post-Cold War' criteria on both sides are underlined by quite different assumptions about the nature of international relations.

The coexistence of these two systems of reference underscores the transitional nature of the Sino-American relationship, which provides opportunities for both perceptual convergence and perceptual collision.

In light of the two standard models suggested in Chapter 2, the contents of the above-summarized mutual images display a considerable degree of inner differentiation and dimensional complexity. Both American and Chinese elites demonstrated an ability to distinguish various dimensions of the target country in cognitive, affective, and evaluative terms. In regard to cognitive differentiation, as a whole the degree of outer differentiation is still high in numerical terms, reflecting the real 'distance' between the two countries. However, the degree of outer differentiation attributed to each image dimension varies, indicating the respondents' inner differentiation. In both samples, American and Chinese elites displayed a lower degree of outer differentiation between the two peoples and between the target country's international behaviour and that of other major powers, while they evinced a higher degree of outer differentiation between the two societies and cultures. Few respondents still regarded the target country as a unitary actor and consequently numerous inner differentiations were found in their articulated images of the target country.

In the domain of affective orientation, an inconsistency in respondents' attitudes toward various image dimensions prevailed. This also reflects high inner differentiations. Both American and Chinese elites tended to have positive feelings about the target people and culture. However, their attitudes toward the target country's government and international behaviour displayed different patterns. The American respondents evinced the most negative feeling toward the Chinese Government but a more benign view of Chinese international behaviour. In contrast, the Chinese respondents demonstrated the least favourable attitudes toward American international behaviour but held more positive opinions of the American Government.

Finally, in terms of evaluative orientation, cognitive dissonance and tensions between contrasting image elements were pervasive. As a trend, the traditional 'black and white' images had been replaced by more balanced views that took into account the 'two sides of one coin'. Both 'dispositional' and 'situational' attributions were present in respondents' evaluations of the target country. In making these attributions, they often used 'horizontal' and 'vertical' comparisons as a way of cognitive reasoning. The 'dispositional' image of the target people, once prevalent in the traditional American image of the Chinese, had been largely replaced by a 'situational' approach. The ideological approach traditionally seen in evaluation of the target society had been challenged by a more 'functionalist' perspective, especially in the

Chinese case. The conceptual differentiation between socialism and capitalism no longer served as a deterministic yardstick for the Chinese evaluation of American society. While 'dispositional' attribution regarding the target government remained valid for both sides, a more 'situational' approach also emerged. In their evaluation of the target culture, many American and Chinese interviewees were inclined to separate culture as a way of life or as artistic and intellectual expressions from ideology and politics. For most Chinese respondents, ideology had lost its power to interpret American culture, and consequently American culture was no longer perceived as synonymous with a 'corrupt American life style'. In the domain of international behaviour, both sides had ceased to perceive the other party as an irrational 'monster' and started to recognize each other's legitimate interests and concerns. Their evaluation of the other side was less sweeping than before, and more discriminating and issue-oriented.

These perceptual orientations indicate a remarkable departure from the Sino-US mutual images prior to the 1970s. The quantitative data on perceptual evolution revealed both change and continuity in mutual images. In general, both American and Chinese respondents claimed significant perceptual changes in various image dimensions. American elites, on average, experienced the most change in their image of Chinese society and the least change in their image of Chinese culture. On the Chinese side, the most change occurred in their perceptions of the American people and the least change in their image of American international behaviour. Measurements of respondents' attitudinal change on some specific issues concerning the target people, society, and international behaviour show that for the Chinese respondents, the predominant pattern of perceptual evolution is what we termed an upward linear model that indicates a change in perception in a more positive direction. The Tiananmen Incident generally did not reverse this course. While an upward linear model also holds for the American respondents, a 'regression' phenomenon occurred in their perceptions of the Chinese Government and Sino-US relations, largely as a function of the Tiananmen Incident and the post-Cold War structural change in international relations. However, the degree of regression is limited and these new developments did not totally reverse the course of their perceptual evolution since the 1970s. The limited impact of the Tiananmen Incident on the overall image held by the American and Chinese elites is further reflected in respondents' self-identification of patterns in perceptual change. On both sides, the largest percentage of respondents chose the upward linear model to approximate their perceptual change, although more American respondents selected a curvilinear model to represent their perceptual regression. For some respondents on both sides, a 'regression' is not a simple negation of their previous image. Rather, the curve is an indication of perceptual sophistication and maturity.

With the Tiananmen Incident as the most recent and dramatic stimulation to Sino-American mutual images, this study investigated the relative impact of personal contact, of other indirect means of interaction, and of big events on mutual images of the American and Chinese elites using multiple methods.

One method involves subjective estimation by the respondents of the importance of various image sources. The data indicate that a majority of the American and Chinese elites in our samples regarded personal contact as the most important source for their image of the target country. At the same time, only a small portion of the respondents on each side acknowledged the great impact of the Tiananmen Incident on their overall image of the target country. Even for the American respondents, the percentage of the 'greatly affected' is not very high. Moreover, those respondents who had more contact with the other side were usually less vulnerable to the influence of the event. On the other hand, the impact of personal contact on various dimensions of mutual images is asymmetric. It has the greatest influence on mutual images of people and the smallest influence on mutual images of international behaviour.

Other methods involve objective estimation of perceptual differentials by bivariate and multivariate analysis. Although the findings are far from conclusive due to the limitations of the data, some interesting associations have been discovered. We find that personal contact at different times can have different influences on mutual images. For instance, respondents who visited or had contact with the other side before 1949 often demonstrated lower outer differentiation, more positive feelings, and less perceptual change in their images of the target country. The contacts during the period 1950–1970 and in the 1970s are more likely to be associated with higher cognitive differentiation, more negative feelings, and less perceptual change. Frequency of contact in the 1980s and number of visits to the target country since 1970 tend to be positively associated with perceptual change. However, the direction of these changes can go either way. After reaching a certain threshold (e.g. five visits to the target country), more contact and visits can lead to either higher or lower outer differentiation, to more favourable or less favourable feelings toward the target country. A curvilinear function frequently occurs. Moreover, mutual images of more macro-subjects such as culture and international behaviour are less strongly associated with direct contact. Big events such as the Tiananmen Incident exert a major effect on respondents' affective orientations. 'Greatly affected' respondents tended to have more negative feelings toward the target country. Finally, respondents' professions and ages often meant different perceptual orientations for the American and Chinese elites.

In short, based on the above findings about the structure, evolution, and sources of Sino-American mutual images, we can conclude with some confidence that, at least in this sample, the Tiananmen Incident did not fundamentally negate the positive perceptual changes that had taken place over the two decades of dynamic interactions between the American and Chinese elites. To be sure, the event hit some respondents harder than others. Respondents who did not have intensive contact with the other side tended to be more psychologically vulnerable to such a dramatic episode. Respondents who had stronger ideological and value orientations in their images were also more inclined to take the event as a sweeping confirmation of their deep-seated 'schemata' regarding the target country. For the majority of the respondents, though Tiananmen might have affected one or more dimensions of their mutual images, such as the target government or international behaviour, their overall image of the target country shaped during the 1970s and 1980s survived. In significant measure, their reaction to the event reflected their short-term affective feelings rather than their long-held images.

Image Sophistication and 'Fundamental Attribution Error'

The findings summarized above conform to one of the key assumptions of this study: compared to the pre-1970s configuration, Sino-American mutual images have become significantly more sophisticated in the 1970s and 1980s, through dynamic contact and interaction. This increased sophistication was not totally nullified by the Tiananmen Incident. In the American case, as Harold Isaacs and others repeatedly point out, historically the American image of China has been characterized by a cyclical love–hate syndrome. Such a cyclical perspective implies little image sophistication: what occurs is a simple cycle that polarizes the 'bad' and 'good' traits of the Chinese and China in turn. Apparently, the American public's reaction to Tiananmen can be regarded as another downturn in this cycle, moving once again toward the 'hate' pole. Yet the images of China held by the American elites in our sample show signs of a cognitive spiral representing a growing image sophistication. In other words, while perceptual regression did occur, it was not simply a cycle eventually returning to the original point. Rather the Tiananmen Incident, as a 'reorganizing' event, regressed their image to a point closer to reality rather than to the cognitions held before 1970, which were even further from reality. As a result, although the perceptual swing is still observable, its range and duration are smaller and shorter.[1]

In the Chinese case, the Tiananmen Incident did not cause a large-scale perceptual 'regression'. One could argue that the event was a domestic development and thus should not greatly affect the Chinese perception of the United States in the first place. However, the strong American reaction to the crackdown ever since 1989 has been by no means uneventful to the Chinese. For the first time since the normalization of relations the United States imposed sanctions against China, and for the first time since 1970 the United States supported, at least morally, the political forces inside and outside China endeavouring to overthrow the Chinese communist Government. This 'interference', nevertheless, did not rekindle in the memory of many Chinese respondents the spectre of 'evil American imperialism'. Rather, they thought that the initial American response was understandable, even acceptable, although they did not consider that imposing pressure on China is necessarily a proper way to make changes occur.

Of course, perceptual sophistication does not necessarily mean more positive opinions of the target country. Rather, it is synonymous with 'dimensional complexity' in mutual perceptions, which forestalls all-black-and-white images. The key expression of this complexity is the relative independence of various image dimensions.[2] That is, the perceptual orientation of one image dimension will not dictate the orientation of another image dimension. Both sides see the other side as a multifaceted society in which there are many different 'Americas' and 'Chinas'.[3] As already described in the previous analysis, while the Tiananmen Incident considerably negated the American elites' view of the Chinese Government, it did not prevent them from viewing Chinese international behaviour more positively. By the same token, the American reaction to Tiananmen aroused negative feelings in Chinese respondents toward American international behaviour, but these negative feelings did not automatically transfer to their evaluation of the American Government. This dimensional complexity provides a cognitive foundation for the continuation of the relationship.

Given the sampling problem, we are in no position to use the findings from this study to infer population parameters of American and Chinese elites, let alone the general public in both countries. By including three different groups of respondents in our study and by introducing randomness into the samples whenever possible, however, we can at least claim that the mutual images elaborated here represent a considerable portion of American and Chinese elites. It is my sense that these views are not well reflected and are underrepresented in the public opinion of the respective countries. In

China, as is well known, mass media are tightly controlled by the government, and only sanctioned messages get across to the public. Perceptions articulated by the Chinese elites, such as the 'good governance' of the American Government and the 'leadership' role of American international behaviour, thus do not have much chance to appear publicly.

In the United States, while government agencies do not have direct control over public opinion, prevailing social norms often have sufficient power to deter dissenting voices.[4] As some American and Chinese respondents pointed out, after the Tiananmen Incident the American public media had been full of value judgements of China, and 'China bashing' became a political fashion.[5] Under such circumstances, it would be very unpopular to say good things about the communist government publicly. Comments about 'the remarkable accomplishments of the CCP' or about 'American self-righteousness' in dealing with China could hardly be heard from the media in the last few years.[6] But more balanced and less value-laden views on China did exist even when the memory of the Tiananmen crackdown was still fresh in the Americans' minds. It is therefore important to make these perceptions known to the public in both countries and to provide another system of reference for the understanding of mutual images.

While the perceptual sophistication of mutual images manifested in this study is real, my findings also indicate numerous perceptual gaps and biases in the mutual images of the American and Chinese elites. These gaps and biases can be attributed to various sources. Some of them reflect real differences between the two countries. For instance, the perceptual gap on the importance of the relationship is a function of asymmetric national power and international position. The divergent working mechanisms in the two systems lead to the perceptual gap regarding the target 'polity' and 'society'. Other gaps arise from a lack of knowledge. Even the image of the target country held by the relatively well-informed elites could be handicapped, either seeing the forest while overlooking the trees or the other way round. For example, some Chinese respondents did not have a good understanding of the pluralistic nature of American society, so they tended to simplify the input and output of the American political system. Some American respondents did not know much about modern Chinese culture, so they tended to exaggerate the gap between the 'traditional' and 'modern' culture.[7] Still other gaps are manifestations of deep-rooted ideological convictions. For instance, some Chinese respondents held that 'capitalism must be ruled by monopolies', and some American respondents believed that 'everyone is an informer under communism'.

What will be discussed in more detail here are some cognitive or psychological sources for misperceptions revealed in this study. One such source are the so-called 'mirror images'. As discussed in Chapter 1, a 'mirror image' in the study of Cold War national perceptions is regarded as a typical configuration of distorted perceptions that aggravate hostilities between nations. In this study, we found that this is not necessarily the case. Positive 'mirror images' of perceiving each other as 'open', 'enterprising', and 'warm' can be valuable sources of mutual attraction. The experimental findings of social psychology do suggest that people tend to like those who have dispositions similar to their own.[8] Perceived similarities between the Chinese and Americans often arouse 'sympathy' for each other. However, overestimation of the similarities could also lead to cognitive frustration when these similarities turn out to be illusory. As noted in Chapter 3, American respondents tended to emphasize that the Chinese are 'like us'. They often neglected to take into account the adaptability of the Chinese under different social conditions. The perception of individual similarity between the Americans and Chinese often creates cognitive dissonance for the American respondents. Some respondents could not figure out why, though individually quite 'similar', the Chinese could have a political and social structure so different from that of the United States. Therefore cognitive disillusionment is more likely to occur.

Negative 'mirror images' of course tend to intensify one another's existing stereotypes or even turn a perception into reality. For example, both the American and Chinese elites were inclined to describe the other side as 'arrogant' or 'ethnocentric', although for different reasons. In American eyes, the Chinese are 'ethnocentric' due to their unique cultural heritage. Some American respondents were convinced that 'Chinese always think of themselves as the best in the world' and that 'they don't have to learn anything from others'. The Chinese perceived Americans as 'arrogant' because of America's economic and military power. They asserted that Americans 'do not know how high is the sky and how thick is the ground' and 'lack self-knowledge'. The problem with such kinds of 'mirror images' is that they are convictions that do not need the support of empirical evidence and therefore are almost incapable of being disproved. Some Chinese respondents confessed that they personally had not been treated 'arrogantly' by Americans, but they still believed that Americans have the 'smell of arrogance in their bones'. Some American respondents evinced a similar mentality and asserted that 'fundamentally, most Chinese instinctively are a little arrogant about their own culture'. As social psychological studies on prejudice suggest, such preconceptions function to influence people's dealing with people from the target country in such a way as to 'elicit from them the very characteristics and behaviours we expected in the first place'.[9] This phenomenon of self-fulfilling prophecy reveals the psychological roots of many 'mirror' or 'contrasting' images discussed in preceding chapters.

The 'mirror images', as well as other misperceptions, are often based on judgements and convictions about the 'disposition' or 'nature' of the other side in either individual or collective terms. Here another source for misperceptions—fundamental attribution error (FAE)[10]—creeps in. This theory points to the psychological tendency that 'people often fail to recognize the extent to which observed actions and outcomes, especially surprising or atypical ones, may prove to be diagnostic not of the actor's unique personal disposition but rather of the objective situational factors facing the actor and the actor's subjective construal of those factors'.[11] Simply stated, 'In general, we tend to attribute our own blunders to the situation in which we find ourselves; conversely, we attribute other people's blunders to some personality defect or lack of ability in that person.'[12] Although this theory has been developed to describe the cognitive process regarding individual behaviour, it also can be used to approximate people's attribution process regarding national behaviour. In other words, FAE can occur at both individual and national levels of mutual images.

I found that FAE is not a serious problem in mutual images of people. Conceptually, both American and Chinese respondents can make a distinction between the target people and the target social system. When they made evaluations of the target people, they did not just offer a 'dispositional' explanation, but also took into consideration their socio-economic background. This 'situational' attribution is more popular on the American side. American respondents tended to attribute some distasteful qualities of the Chinese to their social systems. From the social psychological perspective, this is an indication of perceptual sophistication. Compared to the traditional American image of the Chinese, this is also progress, as some dispositions traditionally attributed to the Chinese, such as being devious, calculating, or passive, now were attributed to their social circumstances.

However, in evaluating impersonal aspects of the other side, 'dispositional' rather than 'situational' attribution still is the norm in Sino-American mutual images. In other words, in perceiving some phenomena or problems of the target country, some American and Chinese respondents tended to attribute them to the 'disposition' or 'nature' of the target government or social system, and often neglected the 'situational' factors. As mentioned earlier, American respondents were inclined to attribute China's problems, such as economic backwardness, cultural stagnation, and international irresponsibility, solely to the 'evil nature' of the communist government, as if everything would be fine once the communist system were gone. The attribution of the Tiananmen crackdown is a typical example. In many American respondents' eyes, the crackdown was simply a manifestation of the brutality of the Chinese communist regime, and few questions were asked about the contingent situation under which the incident happened. This 'dispositional' tendency in attribution can partially explain why the American public reacted so emotionally to the incident and was so disgusted by the Chinese regime.[13]

Chinese respondents were also vulnerable to FAE. Again taking the Tiananmen Incident as an example, some Chinese respondents simply could not understand why the United States reacted so strongly to this event. They attributed it simply to the 'hegemonic' characteristics of the United States government and failed to understand the 'situational factors' shaping the American policy: the importance of public opinion in American foreign policy and the pluralistic institutional structure under which the American Government operates. Similarly, some Chinese respondents largely attributed American foreign policy to its 'interventionist' disposition and failed to take into consideration the systematic constraints under which the United States acts as the sole superpower.

If the United States and China were the two 'most similar' countries, like the United States and Canada, FAE might be a less serious problem in mutual perceptions. In reality, the United States and China are two of the 'most different' systems in both political and cultural terms. 'Cultural differences accentuate the likelihood for misperception and miscommunication.'[14] FAE is then more likely to occur and with far more serious consequences, as it will inevitably create distrust, frustration, or even resentment in the relationship. From a social psychological viewpoint, the challenge is how to build 'empathy' between the nations, namely 'the ability to put oneself in another's position (sheshen chudi)'. It is difficult to establish empathy between two persons, let alone between two countries. People usually do not think of others with the same generosity they extend to themselves. Empathy is even harder to establish between two unequal partners such as the United States and China. In talking about social prejudice in the United States, Elliot Aronson points out, 'It is not always easy for people who have never experienced prejudice to fully understand what it is like to be a target of prejudice. For relatively secure members of the dominant majority, empathy does not come easily. They may sympathize and wish that it were not so, but frequently a hint of self-righteousness may nevertheless creep into their attitudes, producing a tendency to lay the blame on the victim.'[15] While the Sino-American relationship is different from racial relations within a country, a similar cognitive mechanism may be applicable. Undoubtedly, the Sino-US relationship is asymmetrical in the sense that the United States is in a more powerful and secure position. 'It goes without saying that the smaller partner in asymmetrical relationships will have to conform to the assumptions and practices of the larger, and not vice versa.'[16] As a result, both a superiority complex and an inferiority complex can be readily discovered in mutual images, which can easily lead to mutual frustration and alienation.[17]

One way to increase mutual empathy is to adopt a more 'situational' approach in perceiving the target country. Especially in perceiving the target country's government and international behaviour, dehumanizing the other side or easily excluding the other side from the rest of 'us nice people' can only reinforce mutual hostility rather than empathy. In fact, a number of American and Chinese respondents in our samples exhibited this 'situational' tendency. Some American respondents expressed 'sympathy' for the Chinese Government in ruling a 1.2 billion population. Although they disliked what this regime did in Tiananmen, they 'understood' why it did so. After all, 'every government makes mistakes' and 'our government shot its own people too'. Some Chinese respondents recognized the complexity in governing a society as diverse and pluralistic as the United States. They also thought that to be a world leader 'is not an easy job'. American 'interventionism' sometimes was dictated by circumstances rather than being a manifestation of a 'hegemonic' disposition.

The tendency of 'dispositional' attribution in mutual images may also cause people to overestimate their ability to predict and infer the behaviour of the target country from those perceived 'dispositions'. Social psychology finds that people staunchly believe that individual dispositions can be used to predict how people will behave in new situations. In reality, people's behavioural inconsistency across situations is very high, and therefore the 'predictability ceiling' for human behaviour is very low.[18] On the other hand, the I-knew-it-all-along phenomenon indicates that once people know the result of an event, it appears to be far more predictable and less surprising. Consequently, people overestimate their ability to have foreseen the events.[19] These cognitive propensities can also be found in Sino-American mutual images. A 'dispositional' attribution of an event associated with the target country often leads to ungrounded predictions. In some American respondents' eyes, since the Tiananmen crackdown proved the totalitarian and brutal 'disposition' of the Chinese regime, its other policies will be equally reactionary and inhumane. For many Americans, Tiananmen became a schema or short cut to observe and judge everything in China.[20] In some Chinese respondents' eyes, since the Gulf War proved the interventionist 'disposition' of the United States, it will be equally hegemonic and aggressive in other international crises. Again, a more 'situational' approach will reduce the likelihood of making erroneous predictions and deductions regarding the target country since 'situations' are much more changeable than 'dispositions'.

'Structural Uncertainty' and 'Limited Adversaries'

This study represents a novel application of the perceptual-psychological approach of international relations studies to an important bilateral relationship—Sino-American relations. It is a 'macro'- rather than a 'micro'-study of the cognitive aspect of international relations. In other words, the unit of analysis is aggregate images at the level of 'states' and 'state interaction' rather than at the level of individual foreign policy-makers.[21] Although it does not directly address the issue of foreign policy-making as 'micro'-studies often do, its findings sketch out a 'psychological environment' for 'micro'-policy-making. The importance of this study, therefore, does not lie in the short-term, direct, and causal relationship of national images to specific foreign policy or behaviour. Its significance rests with the revelation of some broad psychological assumptions regarding the target country on which foreign policies might have been based, and of the possible congruence or discrepancy between public images and government policies. In turn, the findings on the national mentality toward the target country can provide useful references for the general public as well as for policy-makers of both countries to understand each other.

One important assumption of this book is that in the present transition from a post-World War II bipolar structure to a post-Cold War new world order, misperceptions among major international actors could more easily arise due to the 'structural uncertainty' and 'perceptual lag' resulting from a rapidly changing international situation and, hence, countries' rapidly changing foreign policy goals and strategies.[22] This 'structural uncertainty', applicable to other nations in different ways, is reflected in several dimensions in the light of Sino-American relations. First, the status quo of the balance of power in world politics has collapsed due to the disappearance of the Soviet Union as a superpower on the world stage. Countries like the United States and China lost a 'common enemy', which they used to define their mutual relations and to project their political, sociological, and psychological needs. Consequently, they both have to re-identify their roles in international affairs as well as their relative positions toward each other. The process of this adjustment is full of dangerous pitfalls, and both countries tend to suffer from the 'syndrome of enemy deprivation'. Second, related to this structural change, the end of the Cold War deprived countries of a clear priority in their foreign policies and further blurred the division between high politics and low politics. Moreover, due to the increase in functional interdependence, world affairs in various issue areas and a nation's external and internal affairs have become so intertwined that they can no longer be treated separately. In Sino-American relations, the geopolitical strategic consideration, which once served as the foundation for the relationship, has to compete with other priorities such as human rights, trade, and weapons proliferation. The strategic factor is not necessarily the most important. These diversified priorities often pull the relationship in different directions at the same time, leading to diffusion of common interests. Moreover, they are all related, and an accident in one domain could trigger a chain reaction in other domains. Third, because of the diversification of the foreign policy agenda and the de-emphasizing of traditional national security issues, foreign policy-making in a broad sense is no longer the exclusive concern of a small group of top national leaders. As H. Saunders notes: 'Relations between nations today are increasingly a continuous political process of complex interaction among policy-making and policy-influence communities on both sides of a relationship.'[23] This phenomenon is typically reflected in the policy-making process in Sino-US relations. Human rights activists, Chinese dissidents, the business community, and other interest groups exert a much greater influence on both countries' policies toward each other, adding unpredictable variables to the relationship. In sum, in the post-Cold War circumstances, world structure, issue structure, and domestic structure all became less certain compared to the Cold War period.

Under such 'structural uncertainty', I would argue, studies of national perceptions become even more important and misperceptions could cause consequences equally as devastating those as a generation of scholars tried hard to tell people of during the Cold War period. Of course, the traditional theories about 'enemy image' have increasingly lost their validity. It is time to establish a new typology of national images to incorporate relationships beyond pure enemies or allies.[24] This book is an effort in that direction. To take the risk of being simplistic, the findings suggest that Sino-American mutual images can be better characterized as those of 'limited adversaries' or 'cooperating adversaries'.[25] These images are different from both those of 'pure enemies' before the 1970s and those of 'quasi-allies' during the 1970s and 1980s. While more systematic and rigorous studies are needed to further explore this subject, several salient features can be generalized.

First, both sides largely perceive the target country as a normal power rather than an international outlaw. One party usually does not see the other side as an 'active threat' to its own security and interest in military terms. However, the target country is still considered a political 'annoyance or nuisance'. Borrowing a term from David Finlay, the United States and China are 'ego-relevant' to one another, in the sense that one party's social and value systems are affected and influenced by the very existence of the other.[26] Second, ideology has lost much of its weight in evaluating the target country's international behaviour. Consequently the two parties perceive each other's actions from a zero-sum perspective to a much lesser extent. In other words, they are aware of the interdependence of their respective national interests. They also recognize the legitimate interests and rights of the other side in international affairs. Nevertheless, they may still perceive incompatibilities between their foreign policy priorities owing to their different stages of nation-building, power status, ideological residues, and strategic concerns (the United States as a status quo capitalist power and China as a rising socialist power) in world politics. These 'incompatibilities' could reflect a real clash of national interests as well as 'illusory' cognition 'simply as a result of the reactions of the parties to each other, not as a result of any basic differences of interest'.[27] Third, in contrast to the all black-and-white 'enemy' image, the 'limited adversary' image exhibits a greater 'structural complexity', whereby various image dimensions can take divergent directions simultaneously. To put it another way, a negative or positive cognitive orientation in one domain does not necessarily 'spill over' into other areas. Therefore, the image cannot be simply labelled as 'positive' or 'negative'. Even within one image dimension, contradictory elements can coexist. In the meantime, uncomfortable ambivalence also creeps into such an image. Each side is less certain about the other party's goals, motivations, capabilities, and strategies in international relations.[28] Consequently, a long-term policy consensus regarding the other side no longer exists and any short-term or contingent development or event could upset the balance of people's tension system, leading to perceptual shift and change. In short, this image of 'limited adversary' sets an outer boundary for both cooperation and conflict in bilateral relations.

The development of Sino-American relations in recent years is to a significant extent a function of the 'limited adversaries' mentality. It also reflects the degree and limit of perceptual sophistication described in the previous sections. In the early years of the Clinton administration, due to the 'structural uncertainty' analysed above, both sides had difficulty defining the other side in their overall foreign policy strategy, particularly the United States. Because of the lack of an overarching strategic rationale for the relationship, each side was extremely sensitive and suspicious about the other side's international behaviour and had a hard time putting things into a broad perspective. As a result, during the years 1989–1996, friction was rampant in the relationship and several times brought things to the verge of rupture. The normative differences on human rights and governance, the perceptual gap on the utility of the relationship, the conflicting national priorities, and the uncertainties concerning the target country's foreign policy goals and means all contributed to the deterioration of the relationship. The perceptual ambiguity and vicious interaction between the two countries provided fertile ground for heated policy debates such as 'engagement' versus 'containment' on the American side and 'confrontation' or 'compromise' on the Chinese side. It also opened the door for the emergence of radical trends of thought in both countries, which attempted to depict the other side as an 'evil empire' and irreversible adversary. Various political forces, such as the right-wing anti-communist Cold War warriors and left-wing moralistic liberals in the United States, and die-hard communist ideologues and 'neo-conservatives' in China, joined clouts to advocate a more ideological and confrontational approach to dealing with the other side. Periodic 'China bashing' or 'America bashing' from both sides often unduly poisoned the atmosphere for the relationship, making the formation of a perceptual consensus hard to come by. This was particularly true in the United States.

However, while the relationship has been turbulent, the mutual images of 'evil empire' and 'all-out adversary' have seldom become the mainstream in either country. Even immediately after the Tiananmen crackdown, the perceptual 'regression' was limited, as seen in this study, and neither side desired to return to the old 'enemy image' and the state of confrontation. A Gallup poll conducted in June 1989 shows that although Americans held a quite unfavourable opinion of China, a solid majority of the respondents opposed breaking off diplomatic relations (72% versus 27% in favour) and more opposed than supported recalling the United States ambassador from Beijing (49% versus 42%). Indeed, Bush's handling of events in China was supported by the majority of Americans.[29] By 1990, 60% of the Americans interviewed already thought the time had come to resume normal economic and trade relations with China.[30]

In the early post-Tiananmen years, as reflected in this study, one important factor responsible for the instability in the relationship was Americans' low estimation of China's power status and the significance of the relationship resulting from their pessimistic views about China's domestic politics. Immediately after Tiananmen, many Americans believed that China would reverse its course of economic reform and that a popular uprising or civil war was likely to erupt.[31] These apprehensions, however, have proved erroneous. Instead of systemic collapse, continuing reform brought about a dynamic economic boom. This unexpected development, coupled with new security concerns in the post-Cold War world, exemplified by the North Korean nuclear crisis, soon modified the American perception of China's weight in international relations. By 1992–1993, American opinion leaders started talking about China as a 'coming' and 'emerging' power, and they advocated remedying some 'inaccurate and harmful' perceptions downplaying China's strategic importance.[32] This perceptual change was also reflected in American public opinion. While in 1990 only 47% of respondents believed that the United States had a 'vital interest' in China, this figure rose to 74% by 1994.[33] In a December 1993 survey, the US-China relationship was seen as one of the most important in the next five years, tailed by US-Russian and US-Japanese relations.[34] By 1996–1997, many Americans concluded that 'China is the only country on the horizon that could threaten United States pre-eminence'.[35] The public opinion surveys conducted by the Chicago Council on Foreign Relations show that during 1990–1998, the percentage of the American general public and leaders to see a United States vital interest in China has increased from 47% to 74% and from 73% to 95% respectively, the highest since 1978.[36]

The narrowing perceptual gap on the intrinsic value of Sino-American relations as well as the new recognition of security and economic interdependence between the two countries have gradually moved United States China policy away from the normative- and value-oriented to the strategic- and economic-oriented, climaxing in President Clinton's delinking of China's Most Favoured Nation status from human rights issues in May 1994. Ironically, the Taiwan Strait crisis in 1996 reminded the decision-makers on both sides that the United States and China could not afford to turn the relationship of 'limited adversary' into that of 'full-fledged adversary'. The stakes are simply too high.[37] The pledge to establish a 'constructive strategic partnership' from both sides during Chinese President Jiang Zemin's visit to the United States in 1997 reflected this common interest in avoiding confrontation and essentially confirmed the nature of the relationship of 'limited adversaries' in which conflict and cooperation will coexist for a long time to come without direct and all-round antagonism. Along these lines, President Clinton's visit to China in June 1998 further 'normalized' the relationship in the post-Cold War period. Public opinion polls conducted in both countries indicated that the policies pursued by both governments were in concert with mutual images. In a survey of 2,000 American respondents conducted by the Pew Research Center in September 1997, while respondents were pretty certain that China would become an assertive world power, most regarded China as a serious problem rather than as an adversary. Only one in seven saw China as an adversary and most 'are not alarmed about China'.[38] Public opinion polls conducted in China in October

1997 also found that most Chinese consider the relationship between the United States and China that of neither friends nor enemies, but 'partners in competition on an equal footing'. While 27.1% of the respondents described the United States as China's friend, 47.2% defined the United States as China's competitive partner, and only 13% considered the two countries to be in a state of hostility.[39]

Needless to say, some profound perceptual gaps in mutual images remain unfilled, and the psychological foundation of the relationship is still 'fragile'.[40] For instance, the value conflicts on human rights remain salient nine years after the Tiananmen Incident. Americans are still very concerned about China's human rights situation. Should large-scale and severe human rights abuse or political repression reoccur in China, Americans are willing, at least conceptually, to bear economic costs to support a punitive American policy toward China.[41] This value conflict is also reflected in one of the most sensitive issue in Sino-US relations—Taiwan. Not an insignificant proportion of American politicians and public are willing to defend Taiwan in cross-strait conflicts simply because Taiwan is a democracy, while the Mainland remains an authoritarian regime. On the other hand, while the increasing Chinese economic and military might raised Americans' awareness of China's importance, it also created apprehension or even fear about China as a potential competitor to the United States. As reflected in this study, Americans always have an ambivalent feeling toward the emergence of China as a real world power. To many of them, the gap between China's potential and reality as a power, often cited in their comments, is a comfort more than a pity. In the 1940s and 1970s, the Americans attempted to 'make China a great power' for geopolitical purposes. Now that they are facing the real prospect of a powerful China, however, they are not so sure how to deal with it. The episode of the alleged Chinese espionage and a 'Red China scare' aroused by the Cox Report in 1999 once again revealed the American public's genuine, although not always warranted, fear of a rising China.

On the Chinese side, the Chinese believe that human rights issues essentially fall into the category of 'internal affairs'. As this study shows, for many Chinese, human rights by the Western definition are still 'luxuries' that are either too 'fussy' or dispensable for other purposes. Because of their unique historical experience, the Chinese can hardly escape the mentality of viewing the American policy, no matter how well-disposed it is, as a part of the Western conspiracy to keep China poor and backward. China is still very suspicious of the 'new international order', allegedly under American leadership, and so far remains half in and half out of it. On many controversial issues, such as weapons proliferation, the Chinese consider themselves merely doing what the United States is doing or has already done. Why can you steal a horse while we can not even look over the hedge? For many Chinese, the elite and general public alike, the answer lies in a simple fact: because 'you are strong, we are weak'. The seemingly endless frictions in Sino-American relations since 1989 left a lot of Chinese with the strong feeling that the United States, as the sole superpower in the world, treated China unequally and unfairly. This 'inferiority complex', as vividly seen in this study, was further reinforced by the unfortunate United States bombing of the Chinese embassy in Yugoslavia in May 1999.

For both American and Chinese policy-makers, therefore, handling a relationship of 'limited adversaries' within the overall context of value and cognitive dissonance is an extremely complicated and delicate business. Under certain conditions, the limited adversaries can turn into either 'all-out adversaries' or 'cooperative partners'. Political and social elements that tend to move this relationship in the direction of doomed adversaries will never disappear in both countries.[42] Misperceptions, rather than conflict of real interest, could well push US-China relations to the edge.[43] If a confrontation does occur, it will be the biggest diplomatic tragedy of the 21st Century, because neither country is expansionist in nature and they do not have fundamentally incompatible strategic interests.[44] They had a confrontation in the Cold War and do not need and cannot afford another one in the new millennium.

In this regard, decision-makers and the general public in both countries can draw ample policy and cognitive implications from the findings in this book to improve their mutual understanding and to modify some of the fallacious assumptions they may hold about one another. Among other things, Americans may not overemphasize the likeness between the Americans and Chinese as people and the chasm between the Chinese people and Government. It is unrealistic to assume that indiscriminately imposing pressure on the Chinese Government about issues such as human rights will necessarily benefit or be supported by the Chinese people. To be sure, many among the Chinese elite appreciate and even admire American political systems and values. Yet that kind of pro-American feeling may not automatically translate into an unconditional support for American attempts to influence Chinese domestic politics. Americans' 'missionary complex' regarding transforming China according to their own image[45] may make them feel good, but will not be well received by the Chinese. Many among the Chinese elite doubt the replicability of American political institutions, mechanisms, and values in China; they have ambivalent feelings, even fear, about some American values such as 'excessive individualism'. Moreover, for some of the Chinese elite, their personal value preferences do not dictate their attitude toward American policy at a national level. In their eyes, a voluntary absorption of Western values and a 'manifest' imposition of these values are very different things. The Chinese saying, 'Even the best food can turn sour if you stuff it into people's mouths', typically reflects this mentality.[46] Many among the Chinese elite firmly believe that, as powerful as the United States is, it will never have the ability to control the development of Chinese politics according to the American image.[47] The Chinese might be at odds with their government on many issues, but they nevertheless share with their government a strong national self-esteem. In other words, pro- and anti-American perceptual trends among Chinese could well converge under certain external stimuli. The change of mood among the younger Chinese generation from being pro-American to anti-American in recent years is a typical example. Excessive American pressure on the Chinese Government, therefore, is more likely to foster solidarity and cohesion between the Chinese people and government, rather than drive a wedge between them.[48] If the Chinese perceive that Americans want to turn their concerns about human rights and democracy into an ideological crusade to transform China according to their own image, with disregard for the practical interests of the majority of the Chinese, such an attempt is bound to be rejected not just by the Government but also by the people, as manifested in the 1950s and 1960s.[49]

The key challenge for Americans, therefore, is how to perceive the domestic developments in China in a balanced fashion. Events in China (either good or bad) tend to be magnified under American lenses, leading to unnecessary perceptual swings. The cognitive change overnight from 'a liberalizing Chinese regime' to 'an atavistic Communist dictatorship imprisoning the Chinese people';[50] that within a few years from a 'collapsing China' to a 'rising China'; and that from 'China as a paper tiger' to 'China as a threat' reflects the typical volatility of the American image of China. On the other hand, many Americans still hold a deterministic view about the linkage between China's domestic system and its international behaviour. For them, a domestically authoritarian regime is bound to be expansionist and aggressive externally. What they need is the sort of cognitive complexity demonstrated by some American respondents in this study. Today's authoritarianism in China is very different from the Maoist authoritarianism characterized by a revolutionary ideology, and its impact on China's foreign policy has been diminished. Even a domestic crisis such as the Tiananmen Incident did not radicalize China's foreign policy orientation. In no small measure, how China behaves internationally is not determined by its domestic political system but rather by the American response to its rise as a major power.

The Chinese should not assume that there is a clear-cut boundary between a country's 'internal' and 'external' affairs in the post-Cold War era. The American concerns regarding human rights and democracy are more than just a 'fig leaf' or 'smokescreen' for its selfish national interest, and these concerns can not be easily neutralized by some *realpolitik* deals, as used to be the case during the Cold War period. Given their historical experience and cultural legacy, Americans, including policy-makers, are sincerely concerned with the human rights of the Chinese, albeit applying their own standards. Without a dramatic change in the world balance of power and in the domestic political system, Chinese policy-makers have to learn to live with this thorny issue in the relationship. If China wants to benefit fully from the world community in economic terms, it has to be prepared to bear some political costs. The mentality of 'leaving China alone' is equally as unrealistic as the mentality of 'America can transform China'.[51]

Furthermore, the Chinese should not continue to take for granted the assumptions held dear in the 1970s and 1980s. For example, Chinese policy-makers should not expect that the United States will give Sino-US relations as high a priority as the former would like to see. As the findings of this study suggest, many Americans perceive China's role in the 'new world order' as marginal. Although this perception has been modified recently by China's rapid economic growth, the consensus on China's strategic importance such as the one that existed in the 1970s and 1980s is definitely gone. The traditional Chinese mentality of 'you need us', therefore, has lost much of its validity to Americans. Indeed, for many Americans it is now China that needs America much more than the other way round. Due to the asymmetry of national power,[52] absolute equality between the two countries is difficult, if not impossible. The Tiananmen 'regression' also tells Chinese that they should not assume that American goodwill toward China, manifested in the late phase of the Cold War, can survive under any circumstances. In reality, what Americans admire is the 'traditional' rather than the 'modern' Chinese civilization. What they like is Chinese as individuals rather than China as a country. The chronic and cyclical political turmoil in China has diminished Americans' confidence in China as a viable social system, no matter how they individually love the Chinese and their culture. China has yet to prove its worthiness as a viable and humane political entity to Americans.

With these thoughts, I conclude this book as a first step in the long journey of mutual understanding between Americans and Chinese in the post-Cold War circumstances, and as a system of reference for more issue-oriented, behaviour-related, and theory-guided research in the field of comparative national images.

Notes to Chapter 8

1   Comparing the historical manifestation of the love–hate cycle and the impact of Tiananmen, an American professor said: 'I would say, maybe now Americans are less extreme on one side or another . . . I don't think in general there has been a swing back, although it [Tiananmen] had a great impact. I think there was a great swing in 1949–1950. There was a great swing in 1970–1971. There has been some swing this time. But I have a feeling that they are getting smaller. There is more a base of continuity perhaps.'

2   Scott, 'Psychological and Social Correlates of International Images', p. 80.

3   Michael Wenderoth, 'Seeing the real China', *Newsweek,* 27 October 1997, p. 14.

4   As an American diplomat said, 'You have to say something critical of the Chinese first before saying something positive, in order to appear credible.' Frank Ching, 'Needed: informed China debate', *Far Eastern Economic Review,* 19 June 1997, p. 38.

5   The impact of American media coverage of China on US policy and public opinion was the subject of a conference at an American University in May 1998. For the Chinese participants, the American media coverage of China is unbalanced, excessively negative, and often follows an ideological agenda. See Teresa J. Lawson, *US Media Coverage of China,* a report on the 6–8 May 1998 Conference on US Media Coverage of China, New York: National Committee on United States-China Relations, 1998.

6   A conformist tendency to the prevailing public opinion can be found in both samples. Some American and Chinese respondents mentioned the impact of public opinion on their cognitive orientations.

7   For example, many Americans believe that Chinese literature came to a halt after the founding of the PRC. They are prejudiced against modern Chinese literature. They think it is just political propaganda rather than 'true literature'. Zhuoye Liu, 'Americans view Chinese literature: perceptions begin to change', *Beijing Review,* 25–32 January 1988, p. 28.

8   Aronson, *The Social Animal,* pp. 306–307.

9   Aronson, *The Social Animal,* p. 243.

10   This attribution theory is largely defined by Lee Ross. See 'The Intuitive Psychologist and His Shortcomings', in L. Berkowitz (ed.), *Advances in Experimental Social Psychology,* Vol. 10, New York: Academic Press, 1977, pp. 174–220; Nisbett and Ross, *Human Inference.*

11   Ross and Nisbett, *The Person and the Situation,* p. 13.

12   Aronson, *The Social Animal,* p. 236.

13   Indeed, as Ross and Nisbett pointed out, 'dispositionalism' is widespread in American culture. A comparative study on attribution difference between Hindus and Americans shows that American subjects were much more likely to offer 'dispositional' explanations. See *The Person and the Situation,* pp. 185–186.

14   Jerel A. Rosati, 'The power of human images and cognition in foreign policy and world politics', paper delivered at the Annual Meeting of International Studies Association, Minneapolis, 17–21 March 1998, p. 47.

15   Aronson, *The Social Animal,* p. 239.

16   J. K. Holsti, *Change in the International System,* p. 10.

17   As an American professor remarked: 'I think we are constantly passing value judgements on China. You can see that the papers are full of it now. This is one of the things that are going on in American culture now. It's an incredible self-righteousness, self-righteousness

of the kind Mao used to have. We are correct. We stand for good things. We are judging China. It's going to get worse, worse and worse. The Chinese are going to be more and more French. They are not going to go along with us on military sales, not going to go along with respect to human rights. We will get angrier and angrier because we feel we are really right, they are wrong. But I think it's stupid. There is a way to deal with this as there is a way to deal with France. But Americans want people to be like us, to follow us, then they are OK. Now since the Japanese are not doing that, my God, we are going to get those guys, which is stupid. The only way we can get the Japanese is to screw ourselves. So I try to stay away from these kinds of judgements.'

18   Ross and Nisbett, *The Person and the Situation*, pp. 2–3.

19   Myers, *Social Psychology* (1990), p. 18.

20   As one China scholar observed, for a lot of Americans, 'nothing has happened since Tiananmen and we should treat China as if Tiananmen had just occurred'. Jonathan Peterson, 'China's president will tour US as pop culture villainizes his nation', *Los Angeles Times*, 26 October 1997.

21   Christer Jonsson categorized studies of cognitive aspects of international relations into three units of analysis: individuals, states, and state interaction. See *Cognitive Dynamics and International Relations*, p. 10.

22   Ibid., pp. 2–6.

23   Harold H. Saunders, 'An Historic Challenge to Rethink How Nations Relate', in Vamik Volkan, Demetrios Julius, and Joseph Montville (eds.), *Psychodynamics of International Relations*, Vol. I, *Concepts and Theories*, Lexington: Lexington Books, 1990, p. 9.

24   As Herrmann and Fischerkeller pointed out: 'We need more than the enemy image'. They articulated five ideal types of images of target actors: enemy, ally, degenerate, imperialist, and colony, and used these images to conduct a case study of the Gulf War. Richard K. Herrmann and Michael P. Fischerkeller, 'Beyond the enemy image and spiral model: cognitive-strategic research after the cold war', *International Organization 49*, No. 3 (1995): 415–50.

25   In his refinement of the OC system, Alexander George mentioned the concept of 'limited adversary'. But he did not elaborate on it. See 'The "Operational Code": A Neglected Approach', p. 221.

26   David Finlay, *Enemies in Politics*, pp. 1–2.

27   Boulding, 'National Images and International System,' p. 130.

28   As Kenneth Lieberthal put it, 'Where leaders are insecure in their knowledge and grasp of crucial factors in other political systems, they tend to let broad images and untested assumptions relieve their uncertainty, enabling them to act with confidence.' See Kenneth Lieberthal, 'Domestic forces and Sino-US Relations', in Ezra E. Vogel (ed.), *Living with China, US-China Relations in the Twenty-First Century*, New York: W. W. Norton & Company, 1997, p. 255.

29   *The Gallup Report*, August 1989, p. 14.

30   Karlyn H. Bowman, 'Public Attitudes toward the People's Republic of China,' in Lilley and Willkie, *Beyond MFN*, p. 149.

31   *The Gallup Poll, 1989*, p. 140.

32   For fine analyses of this 'rising China' theme, see Barber B. Conable, Jr. and David M. Lampton, 'China: the Coming Power,' *Foreign Affairs*, Vol. 72, No. 5, Winter 1992–93: 133–149; William H. Overholt, *The Rise of China, How Economic Reform Is Creating a New Superpower*, New York: W. W. Norton & Company, 1993; and Yoichi Funabashi, Michel Oksenberg, and Heinrich Weiss, *An Emerging China in a World of Interdependence*, New York: The Trilateral Commission, 1994.

33 See Willam Watts, 'American Attitudes toward China and Asia: New Findings', Potomac Associates, 1994, p. 13.

34 Karlyn H. Bowman, 'Public Attitudes toward the People's Republic of China', p. 151.

35 'James Schlesinger addresses annual meeting', 17 November 1997, *United States-China Relations, Notes from the National Committee,* Summer/Fall 1998, p. 8.

36 Chicago Council on Foreign Relations, 'American Public Opinion and U.S. Foreign Policy 1999', p. 30.

37 As David Lampton pointed out, both Beijing and Washington learned through the crisis that 'their bilateral relationship was not simply about trade, technology, or promoting individual rights. Rather, the relationship was about war and peace'. David Lampton, 'China and Clinton's America', *Asian Survey,* December 1997, p. 1103.

38 The Pew Research Center for the People & The Press, 'America's place in the world II'; Lena H. Sun, 'Broad coalition in US closes ranks for human rights protests', *Washington Post,* 29 October 1997; Jonathan Paterson, 'China's president will tour US as pop culture villainises his nation', *Los Angeles Times,* 26 October 1997.

39 *The China Press,* 6 October 1997; Fong Tak-ho, 'Survey show Chinese view the United States in a new light', *Hong Kong Standard,* 5 October 1997.

40 See the title of Harry Harding's book on Sino-American relations: *A Fragile Relationship.*

41 A survey taken 17–18 February 1994 by Opinion Dynamics Corporation indicates that a majority of the respondents (60%) were supportive of restricting economic relations with China for human rights purposes even if doing so will hurt American business interests, limit choice of goods in the marketplace, and cost many American jobs. See William Watts, *American Attitudes Toward China and Asia,* pp. 28–29

42 Books like *The Coming Conflict with China* (Richard Bernstein and Ross H. Munro, New York: Alfred A. Knopf, 1997) and *Zhongguo keyishuo bu* (*China That Can Say No,* Qiang Song, Zangzang Zhang, and Brian Qiao, Beijing: Chinese Industrial and Commercial Joint Press, 1996) reflect such a psychological tendency.

43 More and more scholars have realized the detrimental effect of misperceptions in the relationship and feel compelled to present the truth rather than misconceptions about China, e.g. David Lampton, 'China', *Foreign Policy,* Spring 1998: 13–27.

44 As Andrew Nathan and Robert Ross pointed out, 'If the US-China Cold War of the 1950s and 1960s was a tragedy, painful but unavoidable, a new Cold War would be simply a needless and wasteful mistake.' Andrew Nathan and Robert Ross, *The Great Wall and the Empty Fortress, China's Search for Security,* New York: W. W. Norton & Company, 1997, p. 81.

45 David Shambaugh, 'The United States and China: cooperation or confrontation?' *Current History,* September 1997, p. 242. In Zhongyun Zi's words, 'One of the basic urges of Americans of all sorts in dealing with China throughout the years was to influence, educate, and change China to its like.' Zhongyun Zi, 'The Impact and Clash of Ideologies: Sino-US Relations from A Historical Perspective', *Journal of Contemporary China 16,* No. 6 (1997), p. 531.

46 Ji Liu, the Vice-President of the Chinese Academy of Social Sciences in Beijing, put it bluntly: 'The attempt to export one's own culture and ideology by revolutionary, military, coercive, or administrative means will necessarily end in failure, even if the culture and ideology is advanced.' Ji Liu, 'Making the Right Choices in Twenty-first Century Sino-American Relations', *Journal of Contemporary China 17,* No. 7 (1998), p. 100.

47 As an American reporter put it: 'The frustrating truth is that the US simply can't change China as much as it would like.' Ronald Brownstein, 'Summit was sometimes blunt, but China kept its edge on key point', *Los Angeles Times,* 3 November 1997.

48 Zhongyun Zi argued that the United States policy of high pressure in the post-Tiananmen era significantly changed the general attitude of Chinese intellectuals and young students towards the United States. The admiration and favourable views of the United States have faded considerably. People no longer turn to American examples and support when they are dissatisfied with the domestic situation. Chinese identify themselves more with the Chinese Government versus the United States as compared with the pre-1989 years. Zhongyun Zi, 'The Impact and Clash of Ideologies: Sino-US Relations from a Historical Perspective', pp. 549–550. Qiang Song, one of the authors of the book *China That Can Say No,* most typically expressed this mentality: 'Don't think that the Chinese youth appreciate the sanctions by the United States against China. You cannot divorce the individual from the state and when you hurt the Chinese Government, you hurt the Chinese people.' Patrick Tyler, 'Take that, Yankee! It's Chinese rebel's new cause', *New York Times,* 4 September 1996.

49 As Michel Oksenberg pointed out, 'China won't behave constructively in world affairs if it's just handed a list of demands.' Michel Oksenberg, 'What kind of China do we want?' *Newsweek,* April 1996, p. 53.

50 Nathan and Ross. *The Great Wall and the Empty Fortress,* p. 70.

51 In the words of Andrew Nathan and Robert Ross, 'China can no longer protect itself behind a Great Wall that deters foreign invasion and fends off foreign influence.' Nathan and Ross. *The Great Wall and the Empty Fortress,* p. 231.

52 Ibid., pp. 78–79.

APPENDIX A ·
SAMPLING AND FIELDWORK

Sampling Procedure

As mentioned in Chapter 2, due to technical infeasibility and limited sources and time, 'softer' sampling methods had to be applied for this research. The target sample size was set at about 100 Americans and 100 Chinese distributed among three categories: intellectuals, business people and diplomats. Due to different situations in the United States and China, sampling methods had to accommodate local conditions. On the American side, the method used to draw the sample was a combination of quasi-random and purposive sampling, which represents some compromise between ideal and reality. The study used the membership directory of the National Committee on US–China Relations as the primary population universe. A few words about the nature of this list are in order. There were two concerns about possible biases built into this list. One was that the majority of people on the list was involved in Sino-American relations or at least interested in China. The other was that the organization might be weighted toward pro-PRC people and might not represent a full spectrum of opinions. The first concern was not a problem, since the target group for this study was the 'China elite' of the United States. The second concern could be a source seriously contaminating the external validity of the data. With this issue in mind, I contacted one of the senior staff of the National Committee. He described the list in the following words:

> All the people on the National Committee list are interested in China. Therefore, it is not a representative list because most Americans are not particularly interested in China. But I do not believe it is a biased list in terms of those people being pro-China. Politically, I would say it's a very centrist, mainstream list. We try to recruit responsible people with all sorts of different political views. So conservative people can be interested in China; liberal people can be interested in China. We try to be politically representative. . . . The other thing is when you say pro-China, that has a political connotation. It means pro-Communist China. It means, therefore, left politically and so on. There are many people on our membership who would rather describe it as they have a deep feeling for the Chinese people, China's culture, China's history. They may not particularly like the current government on the Mainland. There are other people who may well be sympathetic to Taiwan. Others who primarily care about Hong Kong, and still others who are Chinese Americans who feel a loyalty to China in the abstract.

So I would be very unhappy if it was true that this is a pro-China organization. . . . If you look at those people, they frequently are in charge of major organizations or they have major positions of responsibility, either in their universities or in their cities or as editors of newspapers.[1]

This characterization of the population fits my sampling goals well. My late fieldwork largely confirmed his observations. Since it was not practical to conduct interviews nationwide, I first stratified the list according to geographic locations. Four cities with the largest pools of members were selected for fieldwork: Washington DC, New York City, San Francisco, and Los Angeles. Next, I listed and numbered all members located in these four cities under the headings of intellectuals, business people, and diplomats.[2] Finally, using a list of random numbers, I drew a sample from each city proportionately to fulfil the target sample size. Allowing for possible interview refusals, the sample drawn for each city was larger than its actual proportion of the target sample. In doing so, at least a certain degree of randomness was introduced to the sample.

However, the sample thus selected was heavily weighted toward intellectuals and business people. Diplomats were underrepresented because the Committee has a policy not to recruit active government officials unless they have left the government. To make up for this shortfall, I tracked down the inactive diplomats listed and located in the four selected cities. I managed to get an additional list of active and inactive diplomats who are serving or have served in China-related fields and who are living in Washington DC. This pool formed my diplomat sample. Since the sample was not large enough to permit a random drawing, I tried to interview everyone who was accessible on the list. Finally, to overcome a possible pro-China bias in the directory of the Committee, individuals whose views could be located at the other end of the opinion spectrum, such as scholars in several conservative think-tanks, were intentionally included.

The situation on the Chinese side was more complicated. Obtaining an equivalent list from which to draw a sample proved impractical. Access to membership lists or directories is more limited in China. No counterpart of NCUSCR exists in China and parallel organizations usually do not accept individual members. As a result, the study had to rely more heavily on the methods of purposive and snow-ball sampling. Beijing, Shanghai, and Guangzhou were the three geographic locations selected for fieldwork. In each city, whenever possible, I tried to compile lists of the three groups of people who were involved in Sino-American affairs.[3] For intellectuals and business people, some random selection of the respondents was possible.

For diplomats, again, I did not have the luxury of selecting respondents but used whoever was available. During the interview process, I also asked respondents to refer other potential interviewees.

In sum, the selection of respondents in both countries was not based on the procedures of scientific probability sampling. However, efforts were made to introduce randomness to the samples whenever possible. When using the method of purposive or snow-ball sampling, some control was exercised to ensure that the sample comprised an array of respondents reflecting the general characteristics of the targeted population, including such variables as age, occupation, contact experience, and geographic distribution. Overall, given the sampling procedures employed, the likelihood of having covered the range of influential views on mutual images is reasonably high.

Fieldwork

The initial version of the questionnaire was drafted in English and pretested during July and August of 1990 when I was a research fellow at Stanford University. I interviewed approximately 30 people at Stanford, in Los Angeles, Berkeley, and San Francisco. My respondents included professors, professionals, and business people. The questionnaire was also circulated to experts for comments and suggestions. The instrument then was substantially revised and the subsequent version was pretested among the faculty at the University of Michigan during September and October of the same year. Further improvement was made on the basis of this second pretest. The Chinese version of the questionnaire was first pretested on some Chinese scholars in the United States and then on the faculty of a university in Shanghai.

Fieldwork on the American side was conducted from November 1990 to May 1991. In all I formally interviewed 141 respondents located in Washington DC, New York City, San Francisco, and Los Angeles. The standard procedure involved several steps. I first sent potential respondents a letter of introduction in which I briefly described myself and the nature of this research. In about a week, I tried to call my respondents to make appointments and an interview would follow. Afterwards I sent out another short letter to interviewees expressing my appreciation.

Most of those contacted were quite cooperative. Of course, there were always exceptions. Some respondents showed little interest in academic research, skipped appointments, or were even suspicious and rude. These minor frustrations, however, did not seriously impede the research.

There were several problems that might have affected the quality of the data. First, as a Chinese person asking Americans about their perceptions of China and the Chinese, I was concerned that respondents might shy away from saying bad things about my fellow country people. To minimize this interviewer's effect, I often precautioned my respondents at the outset about this potential bias, and asked them not to be too polite in answering questions. More often, as the interview unfolded, respondents appeared to forget my nationality and just treated me as a neutral interviewer.

Another concern was that some respondents refused to answer closed-ended questions or to provide the numbers associated with responses. They argued that their thoughts were too complicated to be generalized into numbers or that they hated to be forced to make choices. In these circumstances, I acknowledged that numbers might not be a perfect reflection of their perceptions and opinions, but that they might reflect a general tendency at aggregate levels. Some respondents were eventually persuaded to cooperate.

There was also the problem of incomplete interviews. The length of each interview varied from about 30 minutes to more than 2 hours, and some respondents were unable to answer all the questions. Additional interviews with such respondents were not always possible. Consequently, some data are missing. Given the nature of the study, which does not rely heavily on powerful statistical tests, this shortcoming might not pose a great problem.

Similar problems affected fieldwork in China. From June 1991 to March 1992, I formally interviewed 127 Chinese respondents in Shanghai, Beijing, and Guangzhou (including Shenzhen). In spite of low expectations because of the unfavourable political climate in the aftermath of the Tiananmen Incident, interviews were more fruitful than expected. The major challenge, of course, was to make respondents give their own opinions rather than just the official lines. To do this, I had to neutralize interviewees' possible fear of repercussions for being frank. Accordingly, I seldom contacted people through formal channels. Instead, private connections were used to arrange interviews. In each case, I underlined the anonymity of the interview and assured the respondent that the research was purely for academic research purposes and had nothing to do with any 'unit'. In other words, I tried hard to create a friendly atmosphere in which respondents would take me as a trustworthy 'insider' rather than a suspicious 'outsider'. On the whole, respondents displayed remarkable candour. While some respondents were more cautious than others and reluctant to answer political questions, few appeared to deliberately conceal their real thoughts.

Compared with the American respondents, the Chinese respondents were less accustomed to structured interviews. Many of them never before had been interviewed in this fashion. Often I had to explain the choices and scales to them. They proved to be fast learners. As in the United States sample, some intellectually sophisticated people refused to answer closed-ended questions and appeared to be offended by simple yes/no choices. However, there were fewer incomplete interviews on the Chinese side than in the United States sample. In spite of a growing consciousness that 'time is money', Chinese respondents appeared to feel guilty about stopping in the middle of their interviews. Compared with their American counterparts, active Chinese diplomats were less accessible. Consequently, the sample size of Chinese diplomats fell short of the target. The results of the fieldwork are summarized in Table AA.1.

Table AA.1 A Summary of Fieldwork

Interview	US Sample		China Sample	
	Cases	%	Cases	%
Complete	117	68	119	81
Incomplete	24	14	8	5
No response	32	18	20	14
Total	173	100	147	100

Notes to Appendix A

1   Personal interview, New York City, December 27, 1990.
2   I excluded Chinese Americans and people not belonging to the three groups I identified.
3   For instance, I used the membership directory of the Center for American Studies at Fudan University, a directory of Shanghai joint ventures, and a directory of the Chinese Association for American Studies in Beijing.

APPENDIX B ·
SAMPLE PROFILES

In both samples, respondents were broadly grouped into three major professions: intellectuals, business people, and diplomats. On the American side, the category of intellectuals included professors, researchers, artists, educators, academic administrators, and journalists. The category of business people comprised corporation executives, bankers, and lawyers. The category of diplomats consisted of active and retired foreign service officers and government officials. On the Chinese side, the category of intellectuals was roughly the same in composition as the American category. The group of business people included government trade officials, managers and executives of state enterprises, and joint venture and private sector entrepreneurs. In the category of diplomats, besides active and retired diplomats in the Ministry of Foreign Affairs, some local foreign affairs officials were also included. Table AB.1 provides a comparison of the two samples.

For both samples, most respondents were male. This feature is reflected in Table AB.2. With regard to age, the distribution is quite similar for both samples. The mean scores in table AB.3 indicate that, on average, respondents were middle-aged.

The majority of respondents in both samples had a college or graduate education. More American respondents had a graduate education than Chinese respondents, as seen in table AB.4. Most American and Chinese respondents in this study had an academic background in the social sciences and humanities. As Tabel AB.5 shows, within the category of business people, more Chinese managers and executives were engineers and scientists by training than their American counterparts.

Due to limited resources and time, the fieldwork was conducted in several major cities in both countries. Table AB.6 provides a summary of the respondents' geographic locations.

Table AB.1   A Comparison of Profession

Profession	US Sample		China Sample	
	N	%	N	%
Intellectuals	56	39.7	55	43.3
Business people	43	30.5	46	36.2
Diplomats	42	29.8	26	20.5
Total	141	100.0	127	100.0

Table AB.2   A Comparison of Gender

Sex	US Sample		China Sample	
	N	%	N	%
Male	115	81.6	112	88.2
Female	26	18.4	15	11.8
Total	141	100.0	127	100.0

Table AB.3   A Comparison of Age

Age	US Sample		China Sample	
	N	%	N	%
< 40	13	9.2	22	17.3
40-49	44	31.2	27	21.3
50-59	26	18.4	25	19.7
60-69	34	24.1	38	30.0
≥ 70	22	15.6	14	11.0
Missing	2	1.4	1	0.8
Mean	55		54	
Total	141	100.0	127	100.0

Table AB.4　A Comparison of Education

Education	US Sample		China Sample	
	N	%	N	%
High school	1	0.7	6	4.7
Undergraduate	31	22.0	81	63.8
Graduate	108	76.6	39	30.7
Missing	1	0.7	1	0.8
Total	141	100.0	127	100.0

Table AB.5　A Comparison of Academic Training

Training	US Sample		China Sample	
	N	%	N	%
Social science	90	63.8	37	29.1
Humanities	34	24.1	44	34.6
Natural science	2	1.4	8	6.3
Business	12	8.5	16	12.6
Applied science	1	0.7	18	14.2
NA	0	0	3	2.4
Missing	2	1.4	1	0.8
Total	141	100.0	127	100.0

Table AB.6　A Comparison of Location

Location	US Sample			China Sample	
	N	%		N	%
Washington DC	65	46.1	Shanghai	66	52.0
New York City	48	34.0	Beijing	45	35.4
San Francisco	18	12.8	Guangzhou	16	12.6
Los Angeles	10	7.1			
Total	141	100.0	**Total**	127	100.0

APPENDIX C •
INTERVIEW SCHEDULE

SECTION I

First of all, I would like to get some sense of your images of China (the United States).

1. When you think about the Chinese/American people, what comes to your mind first?

2. Considering Chinese/Americans as individuals, would you say that Chinese/Americans are very different from or very similar to Americans/Chinese? Here is a 7-point scale, 1 means 'very different', 7 means 'very similar', which number you would like to choose on this scale?

   (Very different) 1 — 2 — 3 — 4 — 5 — 6 — 7 (Very similar)

2 a. What are the most important differences and similarities?

3. I would like your overall opinion of the Chinese/American people. Would you say that your overall opinion of the Chinese/American people is very favourable, somewhat favourable, somewhat unfavourable, or very unfavourable?

   Very favourable   Somewhat favourable
   Somewhat unfavourable   Very unfavourable

4. How do you feel in dealing with the Chinese/Americans? Based on your personal experience, what are the qualities you like most and least about the Chinese/American people?

5. When you think about China/the United States as a society, what comes to your mind first?

6. Considering Chinese/American society as a whole, would you say that Chinese/American society is very different from or very similar to American/Chinese society?

   (Very different) 1 — 2 — 3 — 4 — 5 — 6 — 7 (Very similar)

6 a. What are the most important differences and similarities?

7. I would like your overall opinion of the Chinese/American Government. Would you say that your overall opinion of the Chinese/American Government is very favourable, somewhat favourable, somewhat unfavourable, or very unfavourable?

   Very favourable   Somewhat favourable
   Somewhat unfavourable   Very unfavourable

8. When you were in China/the United States, how comfortable did you feel? Based on your personal experience, what aspects of the Chinese/American system impress or irritate you most?

9. When you think about China/the United States as a cultural identity, what comes to your mind first?

10. Would you say that Chinese/American culture is very different from or very similar to American/Chinese culture?

(Very different) 1 — 2 — 3 — 4 — 5 — 6 — 7 (Very similar)

10 a. What are the most noticeable differences and similarities?

11. I would like your overall opinion of Chinese/American culture. Would you say that your overall opinion of Chinese/American culture is very favourable, somewhat favourable, somewhat unfavourable, or very unfavourable?

Very favourable   Somewhat favourable
Somewhat unfavourable   Very favourable

12. How do you like Chinese/American culture? What are the things that you feel are most fascinating or distasteful?

13. When you think about China/the United States as a power in world politics, what comes to your mind first?

14. Would you say that China's/America's international behaviour is very similar to or very different from that of other major powers?

(Very different) 1 — 2 — 3 — 4 — 5 — 6 — 7 (Very similar)

14 a. What are the most important differences and similarities?

15. I would like your overall opinion of China's/America's international behaviour. Would you say that your overall opinion of China's/America's international behaviour is very favourable, somewhat favourable, somewhat unfavourable, or very unfavourable?

Very favourable   Somewhat favourable
Somewhat unfavourable   Very unfavourable

SECTION II

Now I would like to ask you some questions about possible changes in your images of China/the United States since the 1970s.

1. With regard to your current image of the Chinese/American people, how does it differ from that you held before 1970? Here is a 7-point scale, 1 means 'changed greatly', 7 means 'no change at all', what is your situation?

   (Changed greatly) 1 — 2 — 3 — 4 — 5 — 6 — 7 (No change at all)

1 a. How about your image of China/the United States as a society?

   (Changed greatly) 1 — 2 — 3 — 4 — 5 — 6 — 7 (No change at all)

1 b. How about your image of Chinese/American culture?

   (Changed greatly) 1 — 2 — 3 — 4 — 5 — 6 — 7 (No change at all)

1 c. How about your image of China/the United States as an international actor?

   (Changed greatly) 1 — 2 — 3 — 4 — 5 — 6 — 7 (No change at all)

2. Think back to around the 1970s, how would you have described the attitude of Chinese/Americans toward foreigners? Here is a 7-point scale, 1 means 'very xenophobic' ('very discriminatory'), 7 means 'very cosmopolitan' ('very egalitarian'), where was your position on the scale?

   (Very xenophobic) 1 — 2 — 3 — 4 — 5 — 6 — 7 (Very cosmopolitan)
   (Very discriminatory)   (Very egalitarian)

2 a. How about around the 1980s?

   (Very xenophobic) 1 — 2 — 3 — 4 — 5 — 6 — 7 (Very cosmopolitan)
   (Very discriminatory)   (Very egalitarian)

2 b. How about presently?

   (Very xenophobic) 1 — 2 — 3 — 4 — 5 — 6 — 7 (Very cosmopolitan)
   (Very discriminatory)   (Very egalitarian)

3. Think back to around the 1970s, how would you have described the nature of Chinese/American society? Here is a 7-point scale, 1 means 'very totalitarian' ('very monopolistic'), 7 means 'very democratic', where was your position on the scale?

   (Very totalitarian) 1 — 2 — 3 — 4 — 5 — 6 — 7 (Very democratic)
   (Very monopolistic)

3 a. How about around the 1980s ?

(Very totalitarian)   1 — 2 — 3 — 4 — 5 — 6 — 7   (Very democratic)
(Very monopolistic)

3 b. How about presently?

(Very totalitarian)   1 — 2 — 3 — 4 — 5 — 6 — 7   (Very democratic)
(Very monopolistic)

4. Think back to around the 1970s, how would you have appraised the communist/capitalist rule in China/the United States since 1949? Here is a 7-point scale, 1 means 'a complete failure', 7 means 'a complete success', where was your position on the scale?

(A complete failure) 1 — 2 — 3 — 4 — 5 — 6 — 7   (A complete success)

4 a. How about around the 1980s?

(A complete failure) 1 — 2 — 3 — 4 — 5 — 6 — 7   (A complete success)

4 b. How about presently?

(A complete failure) 1 — 2 — 3 — 4 — 5 — 6 — 7   (A complete success)

5. Think back to around the 1970s, how would you have evaluated the nature of Chinese/American external behaviour? Here is a 7-point scale, 1 means 'very warlike', 7 means 'very peaceful', where was your position on the scale?

(Very warlike)   1 — 2 — 3 — 4 — 5 — 6 — 7 (Very peaceful)

5 a. How about around the 1980s?

(Very warlike)   1 — 2 — 3 — 4 — 5 — 6 — 7 (Very peaceful)

5 b. How about presently?

(Very warlike)   1 — 2 — 3 — 4 — 5 — 6 — 7 (Very peaceful)

6. Think back to around the 1970s, how would you have evaluated the importance of Sino-American relations to the US/China? Here is a 7-point scale, 1 means 'very important', 7 means 'not important at all', where was your position on the scale?

(Very important)   1 — 2 — 3 — 4 — 5 — 6 — 7   (Not important at all)

6 a. How about around the 1980s?

(Very important)   1 — 2 — 3 — 4 — 5 — 6 — 7   (Not important at all)

6 b. How about presently ?

    (Very important) 1 — 2 — 3 — 4 — 5 — 6 — 7   (Not important at all)

SECTION III

I am also interested in your contact and interaction with China/the United States and the resulting impact on your image of China/the United States.

1.   Before 1949, had you ever visited or lived in Mainland China (had contact with Americans)?

        Yes   No

1 a. Could you tell me something about your contact with China/the United States before 1949? How did it influence your images of China/the United States?

2.   During 1950–1970, did you ever have any personal contact with people from the People's Republic of China/the United States?

        Yes   No

2 a. Could you tell me something about your contact with the PRC/the United States during 1950–1970? How did it influence your images of China (the United States)?

3.   Since 1970, have you had any personal contact with people from the People's Republic of China/the United States?

        Yes   No

4.   During the 1970s, on average how often did you have contact with Chinese/Americans?

    Every week   Once or twice a month
    A few times a year   Once or twice in several years

5.   During the 1980s, on average how often did you have contact with Chinese/Americans?

    Every week   Once or twice a month
    A few times a year   Once or twice in several years

6.   From 1970 to 1990, approximately how many times have you visited China/the United States?

7.   Starting from 1970, what is the longest consecutive period you have lived in China/the United States?

8. When did you visit China/the United States for the first time after 1970?

9. To what extent did your image of China/the United States change through your first visit after 1970? Here is a 7-point scale, 1 means 'changed greatly', 7 means 'no change at all', what was your situation?

(Changed greatly) 1 — 2 — 3 — 4 — 5 — 6 — 7 (No change at all)

9 a. Why do you say so? To what extent was your original image of China/ the United States shown to be false or verified by the trip?

10. Based on your personal experience, how great an impact have your personal contacts had on shaping your image of Chinese/Americans as individuals? Here is a 7-point scale, 1 means 'great impact', 7 means 'no impact', where is your position on the scale?

(Great impact) 1 — 2 — 3 — 4 — 5 — 6 — 7 (No impact)

10 a. Why do you say so?

11. How great an impact have your personal contacts had on shaping your image of China/the United States as a society?

(Great impact) 1 — 2 — 3 — 4 — 5 — 6 — 7 (No impact)

11 a. Why do you say so?

12. How great an impact have your personal contacts had on shaping your image of Chinese/American culture?

(Great impact) 1 — 2 — 3 — 4 — 5 — 6 — 7 (No impact)

12 a. Why do you say so?

13. How great an impact have your personal contacts had on shaping your image of China/the United States as an international actor?

(Great impact) 1 — 2 — 3 — 4 — 5 — 6 — 7 (No impact)

13 a. Why do you say so?

14. Here are some sources for possible perceptual changes regarding your images of China/the United States. Please rank them in their importance to you.

Ranking

Newspapers and magazines
Books
Television
Personal contact

15. Some people say that the Tiananmen Incident/the American reaction to Tiananmen entirely changed their image of China/the United States; others say that their general image was affected little by the event, what was your situation?

    Great effect
    Some effect
    No effect

16. Here are some figures that illustrate possible perceptual changes regarding China/the United States. Which one do you think best describes your situation since 1970?

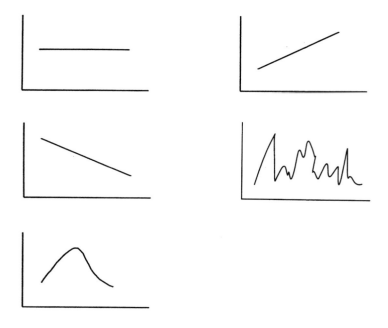

SECTION IV

Finally, I would like to get a little bit of background information about you.

1. What is your employment?
2. What was the year of your birth?
3. When did you start your higher education?
4. What is the highest grade you completed in school?
5. In which field or discipline is your academic training?

BIBLIOGRAPHY

Adler, Emanuel, 'Cognitive Evolution: A Dynamic Approach for the Study of International Relations and Their Progress'. *Working Paper*, Center for Science and International Affairs, Harvard University, No. 89–4.

Alger, Chadwick, 'Personal Contact in Intergovernmental Organizations', in Herbert Kelman, (ed.), *International Behavior,* pp. 523–547.

Allport, Gordon W. *The Nature of Prejudice*, Cambridge: Addison-Wesley, 1954.

Almond, Gabriel and Verba, Sidney, *The Civic Culture: Political Attitudes and Democracy in Five Nations*, Princeton: Princeton University Press, 1963.

Amir, Yehuda, and Ben-Ari, Rachel, 'International Tourism, Ethnic Contact, and Attitude Change', *Journal of Social Issues 41*, No. 3 (1985): 105–115.

Arkush, David R. and Lee, Leo O. (eds.), *Land Without Ghosts: Chinese Impressions of America From the Mid-Nineteenth Century to the Present*, Berkeley: University of California Press, 1989.

Aronson, Elliot, *The Social Animal*, New York: W. H. Freeman and Company, 1988.

—— and Osherow, Neal, 'Cooperation, Prosocial Behavior, and Academic Performance: Experiments in the Desegregated Classroom', in L. Bickman (ed.), *Applied Social Psychology Annual*, Vol. 1, Beverly Hill: Sage, 1988, pp. 163–196.

—— and Bridgema, D., 'Jigsaw Groups and the Desegregated Classroom: in Pursuit of Common Goals', *Personality and Social Psychology Bulletin 5*, No. 4 (1979): 438–446.

Austin, William G. and Worchel, Stephen, (eds.), *The Social Psychology of Intergroup Relations*, Monterey: Brooks/Cole, 1979.

Axelrod, Robert, *Structure of Decision: The Cognitive Maps of Political Elites*, Princeton: Princeton University Press, 1976.

——, *The Evolution of Cooperation*, New York: Basic Books, 1984.

Barnds, William J., (eds.), *China and America: The Search for a New Relationship*, New York: New York University Press, 1977.

Barry, Carol Barner and Rosenwein, Robert, *Psychological Perspectives on Politics*, Englewood Cliffs: Prentice Hall, 1985.

Bauer, Raymond A., 'Problems of Perception and the Relations Between the United States and the Soviet Union', *The Journal of Conflict Resolution 5*, No. 3 (1961): 224–229.

Bem, Daniel J. 'Self-Perception: An Alternative Interpretation of Cognitive Phenomena', *Psychological Review 74*, No. 3 (1967): 183–200.

Bernstein, Richard and Munro, Ross H., *The Coming Conflict with China,* New York: Alfred A. Knopf, 1997.

Boardman, Robert, 'Perception Theory and the Study of Chinese Foreign Policy', in Roger Dial (ed.), *Advancing and Contending Approaches to the Study of Chinese Foreign Policy,* Halifax: Center for Foreign Policy Studies, Department of Political Science, Dalhousie University, 1974, pp. 321–352.

——, 'Self-Perception Theory', in L. Berkowitz (ed.), *Advances in Experimental Social Psychology* Vol. 6, New York: Academic Press, 1972, pp. 2–62.

Boulding, Kenneth, *The Image Knowledge in Life and Society,* New York: Vail-Ballou Press, 1956.

——, 'National Images and International Systems', *Journal of Conflict Resolution 3*, No. 2 (1959): 120–131.

Bowman, Karlyn, 'Public Attitudes Toward the People's Republic of China', in Lilley and Willkie (eds.), *Beyond MFN*, pp. 145–151.

Brecher, Michael, Steinberg, Blema, and Stein, Janice, 'A Framework for Research on Foreign Policy Behavior', *Journal of Conflict Resolution 13*, No. 1 (1969): 75–101.

Brehm, Sharon S. and Kassin, Saul M., *Social Psychology*, Boston: Houghton Mifflin, 1989.

Brinberg, David and Castell, Pat, 'A Resource Exchange Theory Approach to Interpersonal Interactions: A Test of Foa's Theory', *Journal of Personality and Social Psychology 43*, No. 2 (1982): 260–269.

Brody, Richard A., 'Cognition and Behavior: A Model of International Relations', in O. G. Harvey (ed.), *Experience, Structure, and Adaptability,* New York: Springer, 1966, pp. 321–348.

Bronfenbrenner, Uri, 'The Mirror Image in Soviet-American Relations: A Social Psychologist's Report', *Journal of Social Issues 17*, No. 3 (1961): 45–56.

Burstein, Daniel and Keijzer, Arne de, *Big Dragon: China's Future: What it Means for Business, the Economy, and the Global Order,* New York: Simon & Schuster, 1998.

Chicago Council on Foreign Relations, 'American Public Opinion and U.S. Foreign Policy', Chicago: Chicago Council on Foreign Relations, 1974, 1978, 1982, 1987, 1991, 1995, 1999.

Cairns, Robert B., (ed.), *The Analysis of Social Interactions: Methods, Issues, and Illustrations,* Hillsdale: Lawrence Erlbaum Associate, 1979.

Cialdini, Robert B., (ed.), Petty, Richard E., and Cacioppo, John T., 'Attitude and Attitude Change', *Annual Review of Psychology 32* (1981): 357–404.

Cohen, Warren, *America's Response to China: An Interpretative History of Sino-American Relations,* New York: John Wiley & Sons, 1971.

——, 'American Perceptions of China', in Michel Oksenberg and Robert Oxnam, (eds.), *Dragon and Eagle,* pp. 54–86.

Cooper, Joel, and Croyle, Robert T., 'Attitude and Attitude Change', *Annual Review of Psychology 35* (1984): 395–426.

Cottam, Martha L., *Images and Intervention: U.S. Policies in Latin America,* Pittsburgh: University of Pittsburgh Press, 1994.

Davies, James Chowning, 'Where from and Where to?', in Jeanne N. Knustion, (ed.), *Handbook of Political Psychology,* pp. 1–27.

Dennis, Everette E., Gerbner, George, and Zassoursky, Yassen N., *Beyond the Cold War: Soviet and American Media Images,* Newbury Park: Sage Publications, 1991.

Eagly, Alice H. and Himmelferb, Samuel, 'Attitudes and Opinions', *Annual Review of Psychology 29* (1978): 517–54.

Eckhardt, William, 'A Test of the Mirror-Image Hypothesis: Kennedy and Khrushchev', *The Journal of Conflict Resolution 11*, No. 3 (1967): 325–332.

Eiser, J. Richard, *Social Psychology: Attitudes, Cognition and Social Behavior*, London: Cambridge University Press, 1986.

Elkins, David and Simeon, Richard, 'A Cause in Search of its Effect, or What Does Political Culture Explain?' *Comparative Politics 11*, No. 2 (1979): 127–144.

Fairbank, John K., *China Perceived: Images and Policies in Chinese-American Relations,* New York: Alfred A. Knopf, 1974.

——, *Chinese-American Interactions: A Historical Summary,* New Brunswick: Rutgers University Press, 1975.

——, *The United States and China,* Cambridge: Harvard University Press, 1983.

Falkowski, Lawrence S., (ed.), *Psychological Models in International Politics,* Boulder: Westview Press, 1979.

Festinger, L. A., *Theory of Cognitive Dissonance,* Stanford: Stanford University Press, 1957.

Finlay, David J., Holsti, Ole R., and Fagen, Richard R., *Enemies in Politics,* Chicago: Rand McNally, 1967.

Frank, Jerome D., *Sanity and Survival: Psychological Aspects of War and Peace*, New York: Random House, 1967.

——, 'Nuclear Arms and Prenuclear Leaders: Sociopsychological Aspects of the Nuclear Arms Race', *Political Psychology 4*, No. 2 (1983): 393–407.

Frei, Daniel, *Perceived Images: U.S. and Soviet Assumptions and Perceptions in Disarmament*, Totowa: Rowman and Allanheld, 1986.

Funabashi, Yoichi, Oksenberg, Michel, and Weiss, Henrich, *An Emerging China in a World of Interdependence*, New York: The Trilateral Commission, 1994.

Gallup, George, *The Gallup Poll, Public Opinion 1935–1971*, New York: Random House, 1972.

——, *The Gallup Poll, Public Opinion 1972–1977*, Wilmington: Scholarly Resources Inc., 1978.

Garrett, Banning and Glaser, Bonnie, 'Chinese Estimates of the U.S.-Soviet Balance of Power'. Washington, DC: *Occasional Paper*, No. 33, The Woodrow Wilson International Center for Scholars, 1988.

George, Alexander, 'Quantitative and Qualitative Approaches to Content Analysis', in I. S. Pool (ed.), *Trends in Content Analysis*, Urbana: University of Illinois Press, 1959, pp. 7–32.

——, 'The "Operational Code": A Neglected Approach to the Study of Political Leaders and Decision-Making', *International Studies Quarterly XIII*, No. 2 (1969): 190–222.

—— and Smoke, Richard, *Deterrence in American Foreign Policy: Theory and Practice*, New York: Columbia University Press, 1974.

——, 'The Causal Nexus between Cognitive Beliefs and Decision-Making Behavior: The "Operational Code" Belief System', in L. Falkowski, (ed.), *Psychological Models in International Politics*, pp. 95–124.

——, *Presidential Decisionmaking in Foreign Policy: On the Effective Use of Information and Advice*, Boulder: Westview Press, 1980.

Gladstone, Arthur, 'The Conception of Enemy', *Journal of Conflict Resolution 3*, No. 2 (1959): 132–137.

Gladue, E. Ted, Jr., *China's Perception of Global Politics*, Washington DC: University Press of America, 1982.

Goldstein, Jonathan, Israel, Jerry, and Conroy, Hilary, (eds.), *America Views China: American Images of China Then and Now*, Bethlehem: Lehigh University Press, 1991.

Gorlitz, Dietmar, (ed.), *Perspectives on Attribution Research and Theory, The Bielefeld Symposium*, Cambridge: Ballinger, 1980.

Gralnick, Alexander, 'Trust, Deterrence, Realism, and Nuclear Omnicide', *Political Psychology 9*, No. 1 (1988): 175–188.

Grayson, Benson Lee, *The American Image of China*, New York: Frederick Ungar, 1979.

Hall, Edward Payson, Jr., 'A Methodological Approach to the Study of National Images: Perceptions of Modern and Traditional China and Japan', Ph.D. dissertation, University of Washington, 1980.

Harding, Harry, 'From China with Disdain: New Trends in the Study of China', *Asian Survey 22*, No. 10 (1982): 934–958.

——, 'The Study of Chinese Politics: Toward a Third Generation of Scholarship', *World Politics XXXVI*, No. 2 (1984): 284–307.

——, *A Fragile Relationship, The United States and China since 1972*, Washington DC: The Brookings Institution, 1992.

Hart, Thomas G., 'The Cognitive Dynamics of Swedish Security Elites: Beliefs About Swedish National Security and How They Change', *Cooperation and Conflict 11*, No. 4 (1976): 201–219.

Harvey, John H. and Weary, Gifford, 'Current Issues in Attribution Theory and Research', *Annual Review of Psychology*, Vol. 35 (1984): 427–459.

Heradsveit, Daniel, *Arab and Israeli Elite Perceptions*, Oslo: Universitetsforlaget, 1974.

——, 'Decision-Making in the Middle East: Testing the Operational Code Approach', Norwegian Institute of International Affairs, 1977.

——, *The Arab-Israeli Conflict: Psychological Obstacles to Peace*, Oslo: Universitetsforlaget, 1979.

—— and Bonham, G. Matthew, 'Attribution Theory and Arab Images of the Gulf War', *Political Psychology 17*, No. 21 (1996): 271–292.

Hermann, Margaret, (ed.), *A Psychological Examination of Political Leaders*, New York: Free Press, 1977.

——, 'Indicators of Stress in Policymakers During Foreign Policy Crises', *Political Psychology 1*, No. 1 (1979): 27–46.

Herrmann, Richard K., *Perceptions and Behavior in Soviet Foreign Policy*, Pittsburgh: University of Pittsburgh Press, 1985.

—— and Fischerkeller, Michael P., 'Beyond the Enemy Image and Spiral Model: Cognitive-Strategic Research after the Cold War', *International Organization 49*, No. 3 (1995): 415–450.

——, 'American Perceptions of Soviet Foreign Policy: Reconsidering Three Competing Perspectives', *Political Psychology 6*, No. 3 (1985): 375–411.

Holmes, Kim R. and Przystup, James J., *Between Diplomacy and Deterrence, Strategies for U.S. Relations with China*, Washington, DC: The Heritage Foundation, 1997.

Holsti, K. J., *Change in the International System, Essays on the Theory and Practice of International Relations*, Aldershot: Edward Elgar, 1991.

Holsti, Ole R., 'The Belief System and National Images: A Case Study', in James Rosenau, (ed.), *International Politics and Foreign Policy: A Reader in Research and Theory*, pp. 543–550.

——, 'The Operational Code Approach to the Study of Political Leaders: John Foster Dulles' Philosophical and Instrumental Beliefs', *Canadian Journal of Political Science 3*, No. 1 (1970): 123–157.

——, 'Foreign Policy Formation Viewed Cognitively', in Robert Axelord (ed.), *Structure of Decision*, pp. 18–54.

——, 'The "Operational Code" As an Approach to the Analysis of Belief Systems: Final Report to the National Science Foundation Grant, No. SOC75-15368', December, 1977.

——, 'The Operational Code Approach: Problems and Some Solutions', in Christer Jonsson, (ed.), *Cognitive Dynamics and International Politics*, pp. 75–90.

—— and Rosenau, James N., *American Leadership in World Affairs: Vietnam and the Breakdown of Consensus*, Winchester: Allen & Unwin, 1984.

—— and Rosenau, James N., 'The Domestic and Foreign Policy Beliefs of American Leaders', *Journal of Conflict Resolution 32*, No. 2 (1988): 248–294.

——, 'What Are the Russians Up to Now: The Beliefs of American Leaders About the Soviet Union and Soviet-American Relations, 1976–1984', in Michael Intriligator and Hansa-Adolf, Jacobson, (ed.), *East-West Conflict: Elite Perceptions and Political Options*, pp. 45–105.

Holt, Robert R. and Silverstein, Brett, 'On the Psychology of Enemy Images: Introduction and Overview', *Journal of Social Issues 45*, No. 2 (1989): 1–11.

Hopple, Gerald, *Political Psychology and Biopolitics: Assessing and Predicting Elite Behavior in Foreign Policy Crises*, Boulder: Westview Press, 1980.

——, *Biopolitics, Political Psychology and International Politics*, New York: St. Martin's Press, 1982.

Horner, Charles, 'Sinology in Crisis', *Commentary 91*, No. 2 (1991): 45–48.

Horowitz, Irving Louis, 'Paradigms of Political Psychology', *Political Psychology 1*, No. 2 (1979): 99–103.

Hovland, Carl I., Janis, Irving L. and Kelley, Harold H., *Communication and Persuasion*, New Haven: Yale University Press, 1953.

Huber, Robert T., *Soviet Perceptions of the US Congress: The Impact on Superpower Relations*, Boulder: Westview Press, 1989.

Hunt, Michael, Shambaugh, David, Cohen, Warren, and Iriy, Akira, 'Mutual Images in U.S.-China Relations', Washington, DC: *Occasional Paper*, No. 32, The Woodrow Wilson International Center for Scholars, 1988.

Intriligator, Michael D. and Jacobson, Hans-Adolf (eds.), *East-West Conflict: Elite Perceptions and Political Options*, Boulder: Westview Press, 1988.

Isaacs, Harold R., *Scratches on Our Minds: American Images of China and India*, New York: John Day, 1958.

——, Schell, Orville, Tu Wei-ming, and Chen, Jack, 'China and America: Looking at Us Looking at Them', Boulder: The China Council of the Asia Society, 7 September 1978.

Jacobson, Eugene H., 'Sojourn Research: A Definition of the Field', *Journal of Social Issues 19*, No. 3 (1963): 123–129.

Janis, Irving Lester, *Victims of Groupthink; A Psychological Study of Foreign-Policy Decision and Fiascoes*, Boston: Houghton Mifflin, 1982.

Jervis, Robert, *The Logic of Images in International Relations*, Princeton: Princeton University Press, 1970.

——, *Perception and Misperception in International Politics*, Princeton: Princeton University Press, 1976.

——, 'Political Decision Making: Recent Contributions', *Political Psychology 2*, No. 2 (1980): 86–101.

——, 'Representativeness in Foreign Policy Judgements', *Political Psychology 7*, No. 3 (1986): 483–503.

——, Lebow, Richard Ned, and Stein, Janice Gross, *Psychology and Deterrence*. Baltimore: the Johns Hopkins University Press, 1986.

Jerspersen, Christopher, *American Image of China 1931–1949*, Stanford: Stanford University Press, 1996.

Johnson, Loch K., 'Operational Codes and the Prediction of Leadership Behavior: Senator Frank Church at Midcareer', in Margaret Hermann (ed.), *A Psychological Examination of Political Leaders*, pp. 80–119.

Johnson, Sheila K., *The Japanese Through American Eyes*, Stanford: Stanford University Press, 1988.

Jonsson, Christer, (ed.), *Cognitive Dynamics and International Politics*, London: Frances Pinter, 1982.

——, 'Introduction: Cognitive Approaches to International Politics', in *Cognitive Dynamics and International Politics*, pp. 1–17.

—— and Westerlund, Ulf, 'Role Theory in Foreign Policy Analysis', in *Cognitive Dynamics and International Politics*, pp. 122–157.

Karnow, Stanley, 'Changing (Mis)Conceptions of China', in Benson Grayson (ed.), *The Image of China*, pp. 284–304.

Kaplowitz, Noel, 'National Self-Images, Perception of Enemies, and Conflict Strategies: Psychopolitical Dimensions of International Relations', *Political Psychology*, No. 11 (1990): 39–82.

Kapur, Harish (ed.), *As China Sees the World: Perceptions of Chinese Scholars*, London: Frances Pinter, 1987.

Kelley, Harold H. and Michela, John L., 'Attribution Theory and Research', *Annual Review of Psychology*, Vol. 31 (1980): 457–501.

Kelman, Herbert, 'The Reactions of Participants in a Foreign Specialists Seminar to Their American Experience', *Journal of Social Issues 19*, No. 3 (1963): 61–114.

—— (ed.), *International Behavior: A Social-Psychological Analysis*, New York: Holt, Rinehart and Winston, 1965.

——, 'Social-psychological Approaches to the Study of International Relations: Definition of Scope', in *International Behavior*, pp. 3–39.

——, 'Israelis and Palestinians: Psychological Prerequisites for Mutual Acceptance', *International Security 3*, No. 1 (1978): 162–186.

Keohane, Robert O. and Nye, Joseph S. (eds.), *Transnational Relations and World Politics*, Cambridge: Harvard University Press, 1971.

——, *Power and Interdependence: World Politics in Transition*, Boston: Little, Brown and Company, 1977.

Knutson, Jeanne N., *Handbook of Political Psychology*, San Francisco: Jossey-Bass, 1973.

Koopman, Cheryl, Snyder, Jack, and Jervis, Robert, 'American Elite Views of Relations with the Soviet Union', *Journal of Social Issues 45*, No. 2 (1989): 119–138.

Kristof, Nicholas D. and WuDann, Sheryl, *China Wakes: the Struggle for the Soul of a Rising Power*, New York; Vintage Books, 1995.

Kuo Tai-chun and Myer, Ramon H., *Understanding Communist China: Studies in the United States and the Republic of China 1949–1978*, Stanford: Hoover Institute Press, 1986.

Kusnitz, Leonard A., *Public Opinion and Foreign Policy: America's China Policy, 1949–1979*, Westport: Greenwood Press, 1984.

Lampton, David M., 'The U.S. Image of Peking in Three International Crises', *The Western Political Quarterly 26*, No. 1 (1973): 28–50.

——, and Wilhelm, Alfred D. (eds.), *United States and China Relations At A Crossroads*, Lanham: University Press of America, 1995.

Larson, Deborah Welch, *Origins of Containment: A Psychological Explanation*, Princeton: Princeton University Press, 1985.

——, *Anatomy of Mistrust: US-Soviet Relations During the Cold War*, Ithaca: Cornell University Press, 1997.

Lebow, Richard Ned., 'The Deterrence Deadlock: Is There a Way Out?' *Political Psychology 4*, No. 2 (1983): 333–354.

Leites, Nathan Constantin, *The Operational Code of the Politburo*, New York: McGraw-Hill, 1951.

——, *A Study of Bolshevism*, New York: Free Press, 1953.

Lenczowski, John, *Soviet Perceptions of U.S. Foreign Policy: A Study of Ideology, Power and Consensus*, Ithaca: Cornell University Press, 1982.

Liao Kuang-sheng and Whiting, Allen S., 'Chinese Press Perceptions of Threat: the U.S. and India, 1962', *The China Quarterly*, No. 53 (Jan–March, 1973): 80–97.

Lilley, James R. and Willkie II, Wendell L. (eds.), *Beyond MFN, Trade with China and American Interests*, Washington, DC: AEI Press, 1994.

Lindbeck, John M. H., *Understanding China: An Assessment of American Scholarly Resource*, New York: Praeger, 1971.

Lindgren, Henry Clay, 'Friends and Enemies' Enemies: Heider's Balance Theory and Middle East Relations', *Political Psychology 1*, No. 2 (1979): 104–105.

Little, Richard and Smith, Steve (eds.), *Belief Systems and International Relations*, Oxford: Basil Blackwell, 1988.

Liu Ji, 'Making the Right Choices in Twenty-first Century Sino-American Relations', *Journal of Contemporary China* 17, No. 7 (1998): 89–112.

Liu Kwang-ching, *Americans and Chinese*, Cambridge: Harvard University Press, 1963.

Liu Liqun, 'The Image of the United States in Present-Day China', in Everette E. Dennis, George Gerbner, and Yassen N. Zassoursky (eds.), *Beyond the Cold War: Soviet and American Media Images*, pp. 116–125.

Malcolm, Neil, *Soviet Political Scientists and American Politics*, London: MacMillan Press, 1984.

Mandel, Robert, 'The Desirability of Irrationality in Foreign Policy Making: A Preliminary Theoretical Analysis', *Political Psychology* 5, No. 4 (1984): 643–660.

Mann, Jim, *Beijing Jeep: the Short, Unhappy Romance of American Business in China*, New York: Simon and Schuster, 1989.

McLellan, D., 'The "Operational Code" Approach to the Study of Political Leaders: Dean Acheson's Philosophical and Instrumental Beliefs', *Canadian Journal of Political Science* 4, No. 1 (1971): 52–75.

Miller, Norman and Brewer, Marilynn B. (eds.), *Groups in Contact: The Psychology of Desegregation*, Orlando: Academic Press, Inc., 1984.

Mishler, Anita, 'Personal Contact in International Exchange', in Herbert Kelman (ed.), *International Behavior*, pp. 550–561.

Mosher, Steven W., *China Misperceived: American Illusions and Chinese Reality*, New York: Basic Books, 1990.

Myers, David G., *Social Psychology*, New York: McGraw-Hill, 1983, 1990.

Nathan, Andrew J. and Ross, Robert S., *The Great Wall and the Empty Fortress*, New York: W. W. Norton & Company, 1997.

Neils, Patricia, *China Images in the Life and Times of Henry Luce*, Savege: Rowman & Littlefield, 1990.

Newcomb, Theodore M., Koeing, Kathryn E., Flacks, Richard, and Warwick, Donald P., *Persistence and Change: Bennington College and its Students After 25 Years*, New York: Wiley, 1967.

Niemi, Richard G., Mueller. John. and Smith. Tom W., *Trends in Public Opinion, A Compendium of Survey Data*, New York: Greenwood Press, 1989.

Nisbett, Richard and Ross, Lee, *Human Inference: Strategies and Shortcomings*, Englewood Cliffs: Prentice-Hall, 1980.

Oksenberg, Michel and Oxnam, Robert B. (eds.), *China and America: Past and Future*, New York: Foreign Policy Association, 1977.

——, *Dragon and Eagle: United States-China Relations: Past and Future*, New York: Basic Books, 1978.

Overholt, William H., *The Rise of China, How Economic Reform is Creating a New Superpower*, New York: W. W. Norton & Company, 1993.

Oxnam, Robert B., 'Surveys of American Opinion on China'. Background paper prepared for Wingspread Conference: Chinese and Americans: Mutual Perceptions, September, 1977.

Pollack, Jonathan D., 'Chinese Attitudes Towards Nuclear Weapons, 1964–9', *The China Quarterly*, No. 50 (April–June, 1972): 244–245.

Plous, Scott, 'Psychological and Strategic Barriers in Present Attempts at Nuclear Disarmament: A New Proposal', *Political Psychology* 6, No.1 (1985): 109–133.

——, 'Perceptual Illusions and Military Realities: the Nuclear Arms Race', *Journal of Conflict Resolution* 29, No. 3 (1985): 363–389.

——, 'Perceptual Illusions and Military Realities: Results from a Computer-Simulated Arms Race', *Journal of Conflict Resolution 31*, No. 1 (1987): 5–33.

Pool, Ithiel de Sola, 'Effects of Cross-National Contact on National and International Images' in Herbert Kelman (ed.), *International Behavior,* pp. 106–129.

Purkitt, Helen E. and Dyson, James W., 'The Role of Cognition in U.S. Foreign Policy Toward Southern Africa', *Political Psychology 7*, No. 3 (1986): 507–532.

Putman, Robert, *The Comparative Study of Political Elites,* Englewood Cliffs: Prentice Hall, 1976.

Rae, A. E. I., 'Talking Business in China', *The China Quarterly*, No. 90 (June 1982): 271–280.

Rapoport, Anatal, *The Big Two: Soviet-American Perceptions of Foreign Policy,* Indianapolis: Pegasus, 1971.

Richardson, Lewis A., *Statistics of Deadly Quarrels,* Pittsburgh: Boxwood Press, 1960.

Rivera, Joseph H. de (ed.), *The Psychological Dimension of Foreign Policy,* Columbus: Charles E. Merrill, 1968.

Rokeach, Milton, *The Open and Closed Mind,* New York: Basic Books, 1960.

——, *Beliefs, Attitudes and Values,* San Francisco: Jossey-Bass, 1968.

——, *The Nature of Human Values,* New York: Free Press, 1973.

Rosati, Jerel A., 'The Power of Humans and Cognition in Foreign Policy (and World Politics)', paper delivered at International Studies Association Annual Meeting, Minneapolis, 17–21 March 1998.

——, *Carter Administration's Quest for Global Community: Beliefs and Their Impact on Behavior,* Columbia: University of South Carolina, 1987.

——, 'Continuity and Change in the Foreign Policy Beliefs of Political Leaders: Addressing the Controversy Over the Carter Administration', *Political Psychology 9*, No. 3 (1988): 471–505.

Rosenberg, J. Philipp, 'Presidential Beliefs and Foreign Policy Decision-Making: Continuity during the Cold War Era', *Political Psychology 7*, No. 4 (1986): 733–751.

Rosenau, James N., *Public Opinion and Foreign Policy,* New York: Random House, 1961.

——, *National Leadership and Foreign Policy: A Case Study in the Mobilization of Public Support,* Princeton: Princeton University Press, 1963.

—— (ed.), *International Politics and Foreign Policy: A Reader in Research and Theory,* New York: Free Press, 1969.

——, 'Learning in East-West Relations: The Superpowers as Habit-Driven Actors', in Michael Intriligator and Hans-Adolf Jacobsen (eds.), *East-West Conflict: Elite Perceptions and Political Options,* pp. 19–44.

Ross, Lee, 'The Intuitive Psychologist and His Shortcomings', in L. Berkowitz (ed.), *Advances in Experimental Social Psychology,* Vol. 10, New York: Academic Press, 1977, pp. 174–220.

—— and Nisbett, Richard, *The Person and the Situation: Perspectives of Social Psychology,* Philadelphia: Temple University Press, 1991.

Rozman, Gilbert, *The Chinese Debate about Soviet Socialism: 1978–1985,* Princeton: Princeton University Press, 1987.

Sande, Gerald N., Goethals, George R., Ferrari, Lisa, and Worth, Leila T., 'Value-Guided Attributions: Maintaining the Moral Self-Image and the Diabolical Enemy-Image', *Journal of Social Issues 45*, No. 2 (1989): 91–118.

Schaller, Michael, *The United States and China in the Twentieth Century,* Oxford: Oxford University Press, 1979.

Schwartz, Morton, *Soviet Perceptions of the United States,* Los Angeles: University of California Press, 1978.

Scott, William, 'Psychological and Social Correlates of International Images', in Herbert Kelman (ed.), *International Behavior*, pp. 71–103.

Shambaugh, David, *Beautiful Imperialist: China Perceives America, 1972–1990*, Princeton: Princeton University Press, 1991.

Sherif, Carolyn W, Sherif, Muzafer, and Nebergall, Roger E., *Attitude and Attitude Change: The Social Judgement-Involvement Approach*, Philadelphia: W. B. Saunders Company, 1965.

Sherif, Muzafer and Sherif, Carolyn W., *Groups in Harmony and Tension; An Integration of Studies on Intergroup Relations*, New York: Harper Brothers, 1953.

——, White, B. Jack and Harvey, O. J., 'Status in Experimentally Produced Groups', *American Journal of Sociology 60*, No. 4 (1955): 370–379.

——, et al., *Intergroup Cooperation and Competition: The Robbers Cave Experiment*, Norman: University Book Exchange, 1961.

Shih Chih-yu, 'National Role Conception as Foreign Policy Motivation: The Psychocultural Bases of Chinese Diplomacy', *Political Psychology 9*, No. 4 (1988): 599–631.

Shimko, Keith L., *Images and Arms Control: Perceptions of the Soviet Union in the Reagan Administration*, Ann Arbor: University of Michigan Press, 1991.

Shinn, James (ed.), *Weaving the Net, Conditional Engagement with China*, New York City: Council on Foreign Relations Press, 1996.

Silverstein, Brett and Holt, Robert R., 'Research on Enemy Images: Present Status and Future Research', *Journal of Social Issues 45*, No. 2 (1989): 159–175.

Singer, David J., 'The Level-of-Analysis Problem in International Relations', in James Rosenau (ed.), *International Politics and Foreign Policy*, pp. 20–29.

Singer, Eric and Hudson, Valerie (eds.), *Political Psychology and Foreign Policy*, Boulder: Westview Press, 1992.

Sjoblom, Gunnar, 'Some Problems of the Operational Code Approach', in Christer Jonsson (ed.), *Cognitive Dynamics and International Politics*, pp. 37–74.

Slavin, Robert, 'Cooperative Learning: Applying Contact Theory in Desegregated Schools', *Journal of Social Issues 41*, No. 3 (1985): 45–62.

Smith, Steve, 'Belief System and the Study of International Relations', in Richard Little and Steve Smith (eds.), *Belief System and International Relations*, pp. 11–82.

Snyder, Glenn and Diesing, Paul, *Conflict Among Nations: Bargaining, Decision-making and System Structure in International Crisis*, Princeton: Princeton University Press, 1977.

Snyder, Richard C., Bruck, H. W., and Sapin, Burton (eds.), *Foreign Policy Decision-Making: An Approach to the Study of International Politics*, New York: Free Press, 1962.

Song Qiang, Zhang Zangzang, and Qiao Bian, *Zhongguo keyishuo bu—lenzhanhou shidai de zhengzhi yu qinggang jueze* (China That Can Say No—the Political and Emotional Choice in the Post-Cold War Era), Beijing: Chinese Industrial and Commercial Joint Press, 1996.

Sprout, Harold and Sprout, Margaret, *Man-Milieu Relationship: Hypotheses in the Context of International Politics*, Princeton: Center of International Studies, Princeton University, 1956.

——, 'Environmental Factors in the Study of International Politics', in James Rosenau (ed.), *International Politics and Foreign Policy*, pp. 41–56.

Steele, A. T., *The American People and China*, New York: McGraw-Hill, 1966.

Stein, Janice Gross, 'Building Politics into Psychology: The Misperception of Threat', *Political Psychology 9*, No. 2 (1988): 245–271.

Stoessinger, John G., *Nations in Darkness: China, Russia, America*, New York: Random House, 1971.

Stross, Randall, *Bulls in the China Shop and Other Sino-American Business Encounters*, New York: Pantheon Books, 1990.

Stuart, Douglas and Starr, Harvey, 'The "Inherent Bad Faith Model" Reconsidered: Dulles, Kennedy, and Kissinger', *Political Psychology 3*, No. 3/4 (1981–1982): 1–33.

Stupak, R. J., *Dean Rusk on International Relations: Theories and Evidence,* Englewood Cliffs: Prentice-Hall, 1976.

Tajfei, Henri, 'Social Psychology of Intergroup Relations', *Annual Review of Psychology,* No. 33 (1982): 1–39.

Tetlock, Philip E., 'Policy-Makers' Images of International Conflict', *Journal of Social Issues 39*, No. 1 (1983): 67–86.

Tu Wei-ming, 'Chinese Perception of America', in Michel Oksenberg and Robert Oxnam (eds.), *Dragon and Eagle,* pp. 87–106.

Tweraser, Kurt K., 'Changing Patterns of Political Beliefs: The Foreign Policy Operational Codes of J. William Fulbright 1943–1967', Sage Professional Papers in American Politics 2, Series/No. 04–016, Beverly Hills: Sage, 1974.

Twing, Stephen, *Myths, Models, and US Foreign Policy: The Cultural Shaping of Three Cold Warriors,* Bounder: Lynne Rienner Publishers, 1998.

Vallone, Rober P., Ross, Lee, and Lepper, Mark R., 'The Hostile Media Phenomenon: Biased Perception and Perception of Media Bias in Coverage of the Beirut Massacre', *Journal of Personality and Social Psychology 49*, No. 3 (1985): 577–585.

Vertzberger, Yaacov Y. I., *Misperceptions in Foreign Policymaking: The Sino-Indian Conflict, 1959–1962,* Boulder: Westview Press, 1984.

——, *The World in Their Minds: Information Processing, Cognition, and Perception in Foreign Policy Decisionmaking,* Stanford: Stanford University Press, 1990.

Vogel, Ezra F. (ed.), *Living with China, US-China Relations in the Twenty-first Century,* New York: W. W. Norton & Company, 1997.

Volgy, Thomas, 'Learning About the Value of Global Cooperation', *Journal of Conflict Resolution 19*, No. 2 (1975): 349–374.

Volkan, Vamik D., Juliu, Demetrios A., and Montville, Joseph V. (eds.), *The Psychodynamics of International Relationships, Vol. I, Concepts and Theories,* Lexington: Lexington Books, 1990.

Walker, Stephen G., 'The Interface Between Beliefs and Behavior: Henry Kissinger's Operational Code and the Vietnam War', *Journal of Conflict Resolution 21*, No. 1 (1977): 129–168.

——, 'National Role Conceptions and Systemic Outcomes', in Lawrence Falkowski (ed.), *Psychological Models in International Politics,* pp. 169–210.

——, 'The Utility of the Operational Code in Political Forecasting', *Political Psychology 3*, No. 1/2 (1981–1982): 24–60.

——, and Falkowski, Lawrence S., 'The Operational Codes of U.S. Presidents and Secretaries of State: Motivational Foundations and Behavioral Consequences', *Political Psychology 5*, No. 2 (1984): 237–266.

Watts, William, Clough, Ralph N., and Oxnam, Robert B., *The United States and China: American Perceptions and Future Alternatives,* Washington, DC: Potomac Associates, 1977.

——, 'American Attitudes toward China and Asia: New Findings', Potomac Associates, 1994.

White, Gordon D., 'A Comparison of the Operational Codes of Mao Tse-Tung and Liu Shao-Chi', Mimeographed, Stanford University, 1969.

White, Ralph K., 'Misperception in the Arab-Israeli Conflict', *Journal of Social Issues 33*, No. 1 (1977): 190–221.

——, 'Empathizing with the Rulers of the USSR', *Political Psychology 4*, No. 1 (1983): 121–137.

——, *Fearful Warriors: A Psychological Profile of US-Soviet Relations,* New York: Free Press, 1984.

Whiting, Allen S., *China Crosses the Yalu*, New York: Macmillan, 1960.

——, *The Chinese Calculus of Deterrence*, Ann Arbor: University of Michigan Press, 1975.

——, 'New Light on Mao: Quemoy 1958: Mao's Miscalculations', *The China Quarterly*, No. 62 (June, 1975): 263–270.

——, *China Eyes Japan*, Berkeley: University of California Press, 1989.

Yang Yusheng, *Zhongguoren de meiguoguan, yige lishi de kaocha* (Chinese Images of the United States, A Historical Survey), Shanghai: Fudan University Press, 1996.

Yatani, Choichiro and Bramel, Dana, 'Trends and Patterns in Americans' Attitudes Toward the Soviet Union', *Journal of Social Issues 45*, No. 2 (1989): 13–32.

Zhang Jishun, *Zhongguo Zhishifenzi de Meiguoguan, 1943–1953* (Chinese Intellectuals: Impressions and Views of the United States, 1943–1953), Shanghai: Fudan University Press, 1999.

Zi Zhongyun, 'The Impact and Clash of Ideologies: Sino-US Relations from A Historical Perspective', *Journal of Contemporary China 16*, No. 6 (1997): 531–50.

Zimbardo, Philip and Ebbesen, Ebbe, *Influencing Attitudes and Changing Behavior*, Menlo Park: Addison-Wesley, 1969.

Zimmerman, William, *Soviet Perspectives on International Relations, 1965–1967*, Princeton: Princeton University Press, 1969.

INDEX

Note for users:
- The arrangement of entries is word-by-word. Sub-headings are arranged alphabetically.
- Endnotes are referred to by page number and note number which is prefixed with the letter 'n'.
- References to figures and tables comprise the page number followed by the figure or table number with the prefix 'fig.' or 'tab.' in brackets.

Index compiled by Don Brech